**Stephanie Cronin** is Lecturer in Iranian History at the Faculty of Oriental Studies, University of Oxford. She is the author of *Shahs, Soldiers and Subalterns: Opposition, Protest and Rebellion in Modern Iran* (2010); *Tribal Politics in Iran: Rural Conflict and the New State, 1921–1941* (2006) and *The Army and the Creation of the Pahlavi State in Iran, 1910–1926* (I.B.Tauris, 1997); and editor of *Anti-Veiling Campaigns in the Muslim World: Gender, Modernism and the Politics of Dress* (forthcoming, 2014); *Iranian–Russian Encounters: Empires and Revolutions since 1800* (2012); *Subalterns and Social Protest: History from Below in the Middle East and North Africa* (2007); *Reformers and Revolutionaries in Modern Iran: New Perspectives on the Iranian Left* (2004) and *The Making of Modern Iran: State and Society under Riza Shah, 1921–1941* (2003).

# ARMIES AND STATE-BUILDING IN THE MODERN MIDDLE EAST

## POLITICS, NATIONALISM AND MILITARY REFORM

STEPHANIE CRONIN

I.B. TAURIS

LONDON · NEW YORK

Published in 2014 by I.B.Tauris & Co. Ltd
6 Salem Road, London W2 4BU
175 Fifth Avenue, New York NY 10010
www.ibtauris.com

Distributed in the United States and Canada Exclusively by Palgrave Macmillan
175 Fifth Avenue, New York NY 10010

Library of Modern Middle East Studies: 149

ISBN:    978 1 78076 739 0 (HB)
         978 1 78076 740 6 (PB)

A full CIP record for this book is available from the British Library
A full CIP record is available from the Library of Congress

Library of Congress Catalog Card Number: available

Designed and typeset by 4word Ltd, Bristol
Printed and bound in Great Britain by T.J. International, Padstow, Cornwall

# Contents

# Acknowledgements

I would like to thank the Smith Richardson Foundation for the funding which enabled me to work on the research and writing of this book, and Al Song of the Foundation for his help in fine tuning the project. I would also like to thank Cheryl L. Ramp and Paula Landesberg of the Henry L. Stimson Center for their assistance in managing the funding. I am especially grateful to Mark Gasiorowski who was most generous in sharing with me material from the US archives. Bruce Vandervort of the Virginia Military Institute made a valuable contribution to shaping the Afghan narrative and Fakhreddin Azimi helped with Iran. Rowena Abdul Razak was especially helpful in providing me with certain documents from the National Archives. I also owe a debt of gratitude to Maria Marsh, for guiding the manuscript through the production process and to the insights of the anonymous reviewers who read the text for I.B.Tauris. Errors of fact and interpretation naturally remain my own.

Chapters and parts of chapters have appeared in earlier publications and are reproduced here with permission. Earlier versions of Chapter 2 appeared as 'Building a modern army in Iran: Qajar reform reassessed' in *War and Peace in Qajar Persia*, edited by Roxane Farmanfarmaian (Routledge, 2007), and 'Importing modernity: European military missions to Qajar Iran', *Comparative Studies in Society and History* 50/1 (2008), pp. 197–226. Chapter 3, 'Building and rebuilding Afghanistan's army', was originally published by *The Journal of Military History* 75/1 (2011), pp. 45–91. A summary appeared as 'Afghanistan's armies, past and present', *History and Policy* 105 (2010) (www.historyandpolicy.org/papers/

policy-paper-105.html). Chapter 5 originally appeared as 'Tribes, coups and princes: building a modern army in Saudi Arabia', *Middle Eastern Studies* 49/1 (2013), pp. 2–28. I am grateful to the editors and publishers for permission to republish here.

INTRODUCTION

# Armies, State-Building and Politics in the Middle East

The 'Arab Spring', which erupted so spectacularly and so unexpectedly in early 2011, has once again propelled Middle Eastern armies to the centre of the political stage. In Egypt and Tunisia, the military high commands moved adroitly to eliminate hated figureheads of army and state, Presidents Husni Mubarak in Egypt and Zine al-Abidine Ben Ali in Tunisia. In July 2013, the Egyptian army again intervened to immense popular acclaim, removing the democratically elected president, Muhammad Morsi of the Muslim Brotherhood. Elsewhere, national armies reacted differently to outbreaks of popular anger and dissent. In Libya a weak and disorganized military almost immediately split into two, an eastern faction based on Benghazi supporting the opposition, a western army based on Tripoli remaining loyal to Ghadafi. In Syria, after some early defections and despite almost universal Western predictions that the army would collapse, the bulk of military personnel at all levels stubbornly refused to disintegrate or to launch a coup against Bashar al-Assad, but continued to back his regime, month after long and weary month. In Bahrain the army, its rank and file largely composed of Sunni Pakistanis, quickly abandoned any pretence that it could meet the challenge from the streets and surrendered its role to the Saudi National Guard invited in by a panicking al-Khalifa ruling family.

The experience of the first decade of the twenty-first century provides ample reason to re-examine Middle Eastern armies and the historical context which produced them. Post-invasion Iraq and Afghanistan still struggle to create coherent national military forces. Although the Tunisian army, after its decision not to back the regime of Ben Ali, has receded into the political background, in Egypt the struggle between the military, the Muslim Brothers and the wider civil society remains in full swing, while the Syrian army is locked in a bitter endgame with the opposition. Meanwhile, the Syrian quagmire has increasingly drawn in its neighbour, Turkey, focusing attention on the Turkish army, its newly invigorated capacity to play a regional role, its domestic tensions with its own Islamist AKP government, and perhaps even its latent coup-making propensities. The Middle East continues to constitute a market of massive dimensions for Western defence industries, while the survival of individual regimes, and regional security in general, remains an obsession with Western and especially American policy-makers. The presence of Western, again especially American, military and defence personnel across the region is greater than ever, while Iran's alleged nuclear ambitions have provided a renewed opportunity for other states to lavish ever-larger sums on their conventional military and security apparatuses.

Any analysis of the reasons for the specific behaviour of the military in each national context must take account of a complex web of factors relating to both the immediate political conjuncture, including the character of the opposition and the options which the military perceive to be open to them, and also the historical context which had moulded both regime and armed forces. In Egypt, for example, the Supreme Council of the Armed Forces (SCAF) moved against Mubarak in order to preserve the essential features of the existing political and economic systems and their own privileged position within these structures. Certainly their first inclination was to suppress the opposition as it gathered in Tahrir Square. Such efforts, however, clearly signalled the risk of an escalating, polarizing and radicalizing dynamic. As a consequence, they attempted compromise, this too failing to mollify a mass movement conscious of its new power as it established an extraordinary hegemony over the Egyptian population, especially in Cairo but also in many other towns and cities across the country. Finally, calculating the danger to the entire edifice of state and army represented by the popular clamour against Mubarak and aware of the loss of US support which had begun to waver under the impact of global public opinion and the weight of its own contradictions, the generals acted. In a covert coup, the Supreme Council ruthlessly sacrificed their leader and the clique around him. Taking interim power themselves, they inaugurated a long struggle with civil society over the constitutional future of the country. A new watershed was reached in July 2013 when, following a disastrous year in office of the Muslim Brotherhood president, Muhammad Morsi, the army took the opportunity provided by mass popular mobilizations to strike against their old adversaries and remove him from office.

The response of the Egyptian army to the political crisis of January/ February 2011 must first be placed within the context of the immediate political conjuncture, especially the nature of the opposition which had emerged to confront it. Yet beyond this, the behaviour of the army can further be explained by the formulation of an understanding of its historical position and of its relations to the society in which it is embedded. Indeed, the greater the historical depth, the greater the clarity. Certainly the SCAF officers were prompted to act by the uprising, and would never have acted without it, their move an attempt to manage and limit, as far as possible, any more far-reaching change. A particular spur to action was provided by the fear of growing fraternization between the conscript troops and the opposition, a fear which prevented the full deployment of the army against Tahrir Square.[1] But the addition of an account of developments over the previous decade sheds a brighter light on their actions.[2] The last years of Mubarak's rule had incubated dissatisfaction among the high command who feared that their position was deteriorating. They in particular resented the growing power of Mubarak's son, Gamal, and the immensely rich and corrupt clique around him.[3] This growing unease helps explain their ready and unsentimental abandonment of their leader of 30 years. Looking further back, the economic empire built up by the senior offices, which has been called 'Military, Inc.,'[4] may be traced back to Sadat's *infitah* policies, and the origins of the army's dominance over civilian political life found in the Free Officers coup of 1952. The army's residual ideological strength, its pose as defender of the people and nationalist icon, which it exploited during the 2011 and 2013 crises and which exercised a powerful pull on the demonstrators in Tahrir Square, has an even older pedigree, dating back through the Free Officers to the revolt of Urabi Pasha against European colonial control. Furthermore, the extent to which the Sadat and Mubarak years had eroded and tarnished the army's self-image and mythology may be seen in the speed with which a pervasive fear and suspicion of the generals resurfaced immediately after Mubarak's departure and was again anticipated after Morsi's removal.

Immediately prior to the uprising in Cairo, the military high command in Tunisia had also taken drastic action against one of their own, the career army officer and president since 1987, Zine al-Abidine Ben Ali, but they operated within a very different political and historical context to that of the Egyptian army.[5] The 'Arab Spring' had indeed begun in Tunisia in January 2011, announced by the outpouring of popular anger which followed the suicide of a street vendor, Muhammad Bouazizi. But the Tunisian army reacted differently from the SCAF to the regime's implosion. The senior officers, unlike their Egyptian counterparts, singularly refused, from the beginning, to back Ben Ali in his suppression of the protests and demonstrations which filled the streets of Tunis, the president being forced to rely on police and security units. Indeed, Ben Ali's flight to refuge in Saudi Arabia was apparently finally provoked by the point blank refusal by the army chief, General Rachid Ammar, of his request to fire on the protesters and use force.[6] As in Egypt, the army became heroes to the demonstrators on the streets. Unlike Egypt, however, the army in Tunisia had no significant corporate military and economic interests of its own to defend, and it made no bid for a political role after Ben Ali's departure. General Ammar made it clear that the army would return to its barracks and would continue to safeguard the constitution.[7] In Tunisia, unlike Egypt, the unfolding of a post-dictatorship political process has not been marred by an ongoing struggle with the military.

As in Egypt, the precise character of the Tunisian army's response to the January uprising may be elucidated by reference to both its recent and its older history. The Tunisian army was initially a product of the French colonial environment. After independence, the new Tunisian government under President Habib Bourguiba built the army using former colonial troops and with extensive French assistance, the former colonial power hoping thus to consolidate the post-independence state around factions it considered moderate. Under the influence of the former colonial power, an apolitical attitude was instilled in the Tunisian army. President Bourguiba, determined to avoid the military interventions which had become so routine in the eastern Arab countries, made every effort to keep the army from any political involvement during his long period of power. The elite that ruled Tunisia under Bourguiba between 1957 and 1987, in stark contrast to Egypt, contained no generals, the army high command being invisible in public life. The military were not brought into the ruling party, the neo-Destour, nor did they develop economic empires as in Egypt. In order to forestall a growth in the military's power, Bourguiba, in contrast to many other countries in the region, even put limits on the army's size and its budget, preferring to build up a security apparatus under the Ministry of the Interior including the National Guard and the Gendarmerie.

Nonetheless, the growing social and political unrest of the region from the late 1970s began to raise the army's profile while the aging and sick Bourguiba placed increasing trust in the career military officer, Brigadier Zine al-Abidine Ben Ali. Although Ben Ali took control from Bourguiba in a bloodless coup in 1987, the military did not seize and retain power; the new regime which resulted was again a highly personalized and civilian one, built around Ben Ali and his clique. The army once again became an object of suspicion to the regime, and, although its budget grew, that of the police grew much faster. Officers were closely watched and a series of purges at junior as well as senior levels were carried out. When the crunch came in 2011, a resentful officer corps, with little stake in a regime which excluded it in favour of family connections and cronies, seemed content to return to its role as guardian of the constitution.[8]

Although their immediate objectives and wider agendas, as illuminated by their historical contexts, were very different, both the Egyptian and the Tunisian armies were able to act with a remarkable degree of organizational and political cohesion and decisiveness. Thus they furnished a stark contrast to the Libyan army. A small, weak and politically marginal force, its senior officers reacted to the burgeoning conflict in the country, rapidly involving a Western air campaign, in a chaotic, unpredictable and opportunistic way, reflecting the organizational and political incoherence of the regime.[9] As the Ghadafi regime fell, the conflict in Syria worsened. In the Western euphoria over Ghadafi's demise, the European and American press was full of speculation that the Ba'th regime in Syria would go the same way as the Libyan. Western hopes were especially focused on the army which, it was believed, would crumble under the impact of prolonged civil war, possibly prompting a coup against Bashar al-Assad, these hopes arising from a view of the Syrian army which emphasized its historical disassociation from the majority Sunni Arab population of Syria.

The modern Syrian army was the creation of France during its period as mandatory power. In their approach to army-building, both major imperial powers in the Middle East and North Africa, Britain and France, favoured the recruitment of minorities. Such minorities often found themselves accepting the imperial embrace as a means of improving their historically subordinate position, while their new dependence on foreign patronage meant they were deemed more reliable than former majority ruling communities. This minority identification with empire, and the consequent alteration in their power relations with the majority community, had the inevitable corollary of worsening ethnic and sectarian tensions across the region. In early twentieth-century Morocco the force raised by the French was largely Berber rather than Arab. The first preference of the British in Iraq was for Assyrian Levies. In 1930s Transjordan, Glubb Pasha relied on beduin for the Desert Mobile Force, part of the Arab Legion, an element which was to prove crucial to the survival of the Hashemite monarchy in the post-independence decades. In mandatory Syria, the vast majority of recruits to the French-officered Troupes Spéciales du Levant were from minorities, Christians and Circassians, but also Alawis, Kurds and Druze. The French expected that their patronage would buy the loyalty of minorities, to whom the army offered economic opportunities and educational and social advancement. For the majority Sunni Arabs, however, this new force was a despised tool of empire, and service in it only for those at the lower end of the social scale.[10]

Accordingly, by the end of World War II and as Syria gained its independence, the officer corps of the new army was dominated by minorities, Alawis being especially prevalent in the lower echelons, among the non-commissioned officers (NCOs) and the rank and file. Indeed, several infantry battalions were composed entirely of Alawis. Much of the officer corps was therefore drawn from outside the old Sunni Arab notable elite which had prospered under the Ottomans, differing from this elite not only in ethnic and religious but also in class terms, the Alawis in particular coming from impoverished rural areas. The Troupes Speciales had acted for the French against the notables during the mandatory period and they continued a tradition of hostility to the 'old social classes'[11] after independence. In 1949 the army took matters into its own hands and three military coups followed in quick succession. Although the Syrian army's seizure of power coincided with the Free Officers in Egypt, the historical evolution of the two armies was different in certain crucial respects. In particular, the

Egyptian army was able to present itself, in the tradition of Urabi Pasha, as nationalist, patriotic and anti-imperialist and, in its Arab and Muslim character, possessed a homogeneity which reflected the general homogeneity of Egyptian society. The Syrian army, on the contrary, still laboured under its old reputation, at least for Sunni Muslims, as a French creation, while its composition emphasized rather than transcended the ethnic and sectarian divisions in Syrian society.

This first period of military rule, which lasted until 1954, severely damaged but did not destroy the political power of the notable class. However, after the fall of the army from power in 1954, the officers' attempts at reassertion were again frustrated, but now by the rise of new ideological parties, including the Syrian Communist Party and, perhaps most significantly, the Ba'th Party. The secular nationalism of the Ba'th, which would mitigate the disadvantages of minority status, and its progressive social and economic programme was appealing to the Alawis, and they flocked to it in large numbers. In 1963 Hafiz al-Assad, from an impoverished Alawite family, who had risen through the military academy to become an air force officer, and a group of Ba'thist fellow officers, carried out a coup which installed the Ba'th Party in government but also signalled the rise of a coterie of Alawite Ba'thist officers who retained the levers of power in their own hands. In 1966 a further internal coup produced a regime which, although it was apparently led by Ba'thist civilians, was in reality controlled by army officers around Assad, fellow Alawites and even relatives occupying key positions.[12]

Thus Alawi networks became entrenched in the armed forces and security services and also in the Ba'th Party and the civilian structures of government. These networks naturally stiffened the backbone of regime and military when the challenge of 2011 began. However, although many career soldiers and officers, perhaps as many as 60 per cent of the upper echelons, were Alawis, the vast rank and file was preponderantly, reflecting the wider society, Sunni Arab. Although there were some significant defections, from all levels of the officer corps and from the rank and file in general, the army has held together. This may partly be explained by turning attention away from the army itself and the regime it maintained towards the opposition. In contrast to Egypt, the Syrian opposition was far from hegemonic, itself fragmented, based largely on a single community, the Sunni Arabs, with an

Islamist agenda and tarnished by Turkish, US and Saudi patronage and the arrival of foreign 'jihadis'. It has been unable to offer a plausible option to Syria's minorities or to its secular urban elites. In this situation, therefore, its magnetic pull on the army, whether officer corps or rank and file, remained limited while the regime's propaganda and its systems of Ba'thist indoctrination retained much of their power. As the struggle between regime and opposition became prolonged and increasingly violent, a deadlock ensued.

A decade before the 'Arab Spring', another series of events had drawn attention to the condition and role of Middle Eastern armies. The al-Qaida attacks on the World Trade Centre and the Pentagon on 11 September 2001, and the subsequent US-led invasions of Afghanistan and Iraq, raised fundamental issues regarding the existing and future role of the army in those countries. Afghanistan had in effect possessed no national army and only the shadow of a central state since the overthrow of the People's Democratic Party in 1994. With the dispersal of the Taliban after the US–NATO invasion in late 2001, Western countries became reluctantly but unavoidably drawn into the task of state-building, the formation of an effective army an important, perhaps indeed pre-eminent, prerequisite to an exit strategy. In Iraq the Coalition Provisional Authority, on 23 May 2003, took the extraordinary decision to disband the Iraqi army, which it identified not with the Iraqi state but with the rule of Saddam Hussein. This was the most widely criticized of all the policies which the coalition attempted to impose on a chaotic postwar Iraq, and was identified as a key factor in opening the way to further looting, political violence and organized crime while furnishing the infant insurgency with waves of recruits possessing military training and access to weapons.[13] In making this decision, the coalition either ignored or had no knowledge of an earlier Iraqi experience. In 1941 Britain had invaded Iraq in order to overthrow a nationalist and pro-Axis regime based on the army. After a month-long conflict Britain succeeded in installing a government more to its liking but, rather than disbanding the army, only purged it of its nationalist officers. Britain thus preserved a military force which the new government could use to preserve internal security, but denuded it of any oppositional potential.[14] In Iraq after 2003, as in Afghanistan after 2001, the US and its allies were obliged to expend much blood and treasure in reconstructing what they had just destroyed.

The extraordinary events of 2011, therefore, following the wars in Afghanistan and Iraq, focused a level of attention on armies not seen since the heyday of the Middle Eastern coup and the elaboration of modernization theory in the 1950s and 1960s. Following their disastrous performance against Israel in 1948, a series of military coups took place in the Arab world aimed at overthrowing the old order considered responsible for the humiliation of defeat in 1948. The Iraqi army had in fact pioneered the technique a little earlier, first intervening in 1936 and, from the early 1950s, coups proliferated, in Syria, Egypt, and again in Iraq, and in North Africa. Beyond the Arab world, in Turkey and Iran, the army acted as the spearheads and guardians of Kemalist and Pahlavi modernity. The regimes which these coups brought to power or backed, whether overtly military, as in Egypt, quasi-civilian, as in Syria, Iraq and Turkey, even monarchist in Iran, were generally secular and assumed to be progressive, albeit highly authoritarian. The army was seen as a modernizing institution, its officers 'high modernists, par excellence',[15] indeed the main tool of a rising middle class.[16] However, during the late 1960s and 1970s this image of modernizing, nationalist, often left-leaning officer-rulers began to change. Military defeats continued, land reforms and industrialization programmes faltered, wider social change appeared exhausted, while the brutally repressive dimension of these regimes, enforcing their rule through the army and especially the security apparatus, became more difficult to ignore. In countries such as Egypt, Syria and Iraq the army was transformed into a conservative institution, its main purpose to eradicate political dissent, its only remaining goal to preserve the status quo in the establishment of which it had once been a revolutionary instrument. In Turkey the army intervened repeatedly in the political system in defence of the Kemalist status quo while in Iran the army was advertised as the key protection of an increasingly discredited monarchy until these pretensions were laid bare by the revolution of 1979.

Although Middle Eastern militaries had, after the high nationalist and coup-making period of the 1950s–60s, somewhat receded into the background, they remained of immense importance in political, economic and social terms. In size alone, many of the armies of the region grew immensely in the decades since independence, becoming massive institutions. This was especially true of the armies of countries such as Egypt, Syria and Iraq, where senior military officers occupied the commanding heights of economy and politics and where conscription was an important element of national development. The Egyptian armed forces, for example, mushroomed from 180,000 in 1966 to 460,000 in 1984, although the population grew by only just over 10 per cent. In Iraq, which had a population of around 15 million, the armed forces, by the end of the war with Iran in 1987, reached 850,000.[17] Even Syria's population of 7.1 million supported armed forces of 362,000 in the same year.[18] On the other hand, the relatively weak political position of the Tunisian army was also reflected in its size. With a population similar to Syria's, its armed forces only numbered 35,000 in 1984.[19]

Inevitably, large armies were expensive to equip, train and maintain and constituted a drain on sometimes scarce national resources. The defence ministries of the oil-rich Gulf countries naturally became the target of the international arms industry and an efficient mechanism for the recycling of petrodollars to the benefit of the industrialized world. The lure of the 'arms bazaar' even began to capture Western diplomatic policy, British attitudes to the Shah in the late 1970s, for example, being crucially determined by the opportunities offered by Iran to British arms industries.[20] Poorer countries, especially those of strategic significance such as Egypt, became locked into dependence on the US for military aid, Egypt receiving as much as 1.3 billion dollars per year at the time of the Arab Spring. The corruption associated with the procurement of weapons grew phenomenally, while the scale and nature of the purchases often distorted national military priorities and led to the arrival of foreign advisors and experts who, in turn, became a focus for popular hostility.

As the examples of Saudi Arabia and Pahlavi Iran show, the acquisition of ever more complex and sophisticated equipment led, in the post-World War II world, to the increasing presence of American military personnel, a presence which contributed materially to undermining the legitimacy of the regimes and their veneer of independence and sovereignty. From a broader historical perspective, it may be seen in general that the adoption of a strategy of military 'modernization' or 'Westernization' very frequently opened the way to the deeper penetration of the state by one or other imperial power. The very beginning of this process in the nineteenth century brought European military missions to North Africa, the Ottoman Empire and Iran, first British and French, then later in the century German. Although the watershed of World War I destroyed the old order across the

Middle East, many of the newborn states in the region found themselves, as a result of the mandate system, with British or French officers installed at the heart of their state-building projects, in actual command of their fledgling armies. Certainly the resolutely nationalist regimes of Mustafa Kemal in Turkey and Riza Shah in Iran rejected any such arrangement. But as Iran, unlike Turkey, became embroiled in World War II, the weakened regime of Muhammad Riza Shah, beleaguered by domestic opposition and in the forefront of the Cold War, succumbed to the lure of US missions and the weaponry they promised.

The number of European and American military missions which have been active in various countries of the Middle East in the twentieth century is extraordinary. In the nineteenth century a dazzling array of foreign missions had advised on military reform in various parts of the region, their arrival often synchronized with a partial or sometimes total loss of sovereignty. While Iran clung to a semblance of independence as British, French, Austrian, Italian, Russian and Swedish officers came and went in quick succession, Egypt, Tunis and Morocco saw their *nizam* (new order) troops taken over by Europeans as part and parcel of the establishment of full colonial control. The relatively resilient Ottoman Empire, on the other hand, resisted the siren call of foreign officers until the late nineteenth century, and even then managed to sustain the subordination of the German missions of von der Golz Pasha and Liman von Sanders to its own authority until the end. Indeed the Ottoman Empire attempted with some success to project itself not as a recipient but as a supplier of military assistance, its officers assisting the Sultan of Morocco and the Amir of Afghanistan in the early twentieth century.

As World War I and the defeat of the Ottoman Empire left Britain and France in control of the new countries of Iraq, Palestine, Transjordan, Syria and Lebanon, as well as the older possessions of Egypt and North Africa, the presence of European military missions increased across the region, symbolizing new, and now formally enshrined, relations of dependence. Britain, devastated by the human and financial costs of the World War and under domestic pressure, focused on building local security forces as a prelude to the withdrawal of its own troops. In the British mandate of Iraq, a British military mission first created the Iraqi army, and then retained command until formal Iraqi independence in 1932, Britain maintaining considerable influence even after that. In Transjordan, the British, led by Frederick Peake and then John Glubb, officered new military forces, the Transjordan Frontier Force and the Arab Legion. Glubb in fact survived as commander of the Arab Legion until as late as 1956 when he was dismissed by King Husayn in deference to the rising tide of Arab nationalism and the ambitions of Jordanian officers resentful of their British superiors. In Egypt, Britain had officered the army, which was kept small lest there be a repetition of the Urabi episode, since the beginning of its occupation in 1882. Although Egypt gained a conditional independence in 1922, British officers remained in command of its army until finally evicted in 1946. Of its Middle Eastern dependencies, only Palestine, its destiny already divorced from that of its Arab neighbours, was excluded from the British obsession with building local armies quickly and cheaply. In the Syrian and Lebanese mandates, and in the colonial possessions of Tunisia, Algeria and Morocco, French officers remained in command in the interwar decades, their grip only prised loose in Syria and Lebanon as a result of the hostility of the local populations and the British during World War II, and in North Africa as a result of the global decolonization of the 1950s.

The circumstances of their departure were profound in their longer-term impact. Whereas in Morocco and Tunisia the departing French had been able to shape the armies, as well as the regimes they supported, in their own interests, the Algerian army finally emerged, by contrast, out of the long and brutal struggle against French rule and continued to offer succour and support to other anti-colonial movements throughout the 1960s and 1970s. Libya, on the contrary, saw not the departure but the arrival of foreign advisors in the World War II years. The Libyan army, in contrast to the typical Middle Eastern and North African experience, did not owe its existence to the policies of the colonial power, Italy. The intense hostility and resistance shown by the population of Libya to colonial rule had discouraged any attempt by the Italians to raise local forces after their conquest in 1912. During World War II, Britain, fighting the Axis Powers in North Africa, organized a few battalions of beduin which eventually became the Royal Libyan Army of an independent Libya, British and US bases secure in the country till after the coup of Colonel Ghadafi in 1969.

Just as World War I had heralded a new phase in the narrative of Western military missions to the Middle East, so too did World War II represent a turning point. Before this date, neither the USA nor the USSR had involved themselves in military modernization in the region. After 1945, however, both the new superpowers, but especially the US, came to see military missions as a key method for expanding their spheres of influence in the context of a global Cold War rivalry. In a change perfectly symptomatic of shifting postwar dominance, Britain was, in the 1940s, displaced by the US as military mentor to the armies of both Iran and Saudi Arabia. By the 1960s, countries suspicious of the new US dominance in the Middle East were increasingly turning to the Eastern Bloc, Soviet missions arriving most notably in Egypt and Afghanistan. The regional conflicts which broke out in the Gulf from the 1980s led to ever-greater Western involvement, the sophistication of the weaponry requiring increasing numbers of foreign technicians and exacerbating the degree of dependence. By the twenty-first century, Western, especially American, military missions could be found in almost every corner of the region. The US and other NATO countries were bogged down in 'security sector reform' in Iraq and Afghanistan. In the Gulf, the US was entrenched in the Saudi Arabian military and the security forces of other Gulf monarchies, in fact offering a security umbrella to clients who possessed oil, but not the manpower or political space to build indigenous militaries, the British still actually providing officers for the Omani army. The US had also moved quickly to fill the void created by the flight of Yemeni President Salih in 2011, American military planners immediately beginning discussions with the new president. In the Gulf region, only Iran maintained its splendid isolation. Not only were twenty-first century Middle Eastern armies seething with American and British military personnel, but the broad phenomenon of military assistance had reinvented itself and was rapidly proliferating in areas of crisis. Most notably in Iraq and Afghanistan, defence contracting and security had become a major growth area, merging official military advice and assistance with profit-making private enterprise, with personnel even circulating between the two spheres.[21]

The five chapters which follow attempt to offer some explanation of the historical context which has produced these outcomes. In its methodological approach, it interprets the term 'Middle East' in the widest possible sense, as an area stretching from Morocco in the west to Afghanistan in the east. This area is deemed to possess certain unifying historical contexts, provided by the broad Arab, Turkish and Iranian worlds. Afghanistan, for example, is here included as a Middle Eastern country, although on the fringes of the region as conventionally conceptualized, owing to the similarity of its state-building processes to those of other Middle Eastern states in general, and to Iran in particular, and to Afghanistan's adoption of models, programmes and even personnel drawn from the Middle East, especially from the Ottoman Empire.

This is a book about armies, not wars; indeed, it deals with military conflicts only insofar as they impinged on the army in terms of its political and social roles, development and interventions. Using the existing literature, with some archival materials for the case-studies of individual countries, the chapters attempt to reinterpret scholarly understanding of the character of military reform in the Middle East. Chapter 1 looks at the arrival of the 'military revolution' in the Middle East, at the desperate and ultimately futile struggle of local rulers to follow the path taken in an earlier historical period by the dynastic monarchies of early modern Europe, and at the catastrophic consequences, bankruptcy and the imposition of formal or informal colonial control, which followed. Chapter 2 examines the impact of the arrival of European military advisors and missions to the Middle East through the prism of the experience of one country, Iran, an experience so disastrous that after 1921 opposition to foreign military assistance became a cardinal principle of the new Pahlavi state. Chapters 3, 4 and 5 furnish three case-studies of the building of modern regular armies, in Afghanistan, Iran and Saudi Arabia, while the conclusion assesses the successes and failures of each in the light of the precepts of the military revolution thesis and reasseses the general applicability of this thesis to the wider region.

The book's underlying argument suggests that, by adding an historical understanding to a contemporary political analysis, the behaviour of Middle Eastern armies may become more comprehensible and even perhaps a little more predictable. Their particular and specific place in the history, culture, politics and economy of each individual country may furnish a guide firstly to the actions and reactions of senior officers, junior officers and rank and file, and secondly to the dynamic and reciprocal character of army–society relations, as events unfold across a region in crisis.

# CHAPTER 1

# The Military Revolution in the Middle East

## The *Nizam-i Jadid* in the Nineteenth Century

In the late eighteenth and early nineteenth century, when the Middle East and North Africa first began to attract the sustained attention of modern European imperialism and colonialism, Arab, Ottoman, Iranian and Afghan polities began what was to be a protracted experiment with army reform. These decades saw the birth of a mania in the Middle East for the import of European methods of military organization and techniques of warfare. Everywhere, in Tunis and Morocco, the Ottoman Empire, Egypt, Iran and Afghanistan, *nizam-i jadid* (new order) regiments sprang up, sometimes on the ruins of older military formations, sometimes alongside them, unleashing a process of military-led modernization which was to characterize state-building projects throughout the region until well into the twentieth century. The ruling dynasties in these regions embarked on army reform in an effort to meet a number of separate objectives. Certainly they wished to strengthen their defensive capacity and resist growing European hegemony and direct or indirect control by imitating European methods of military organization and warfare. Every indigenous ruler who confronted direct or indirect European control, from the sultans of pre-Protectorate Morocco in the west to the amirs of Afghanistan in the east, followed this path, although with varying degrees of success and often radically different outcomes. But such rulers also adopted novel models of military organization for other purposes: in order to gain an advantage against rival states and enemies in the immediate region and, most importantly, to strengthen their personal position inside their own territories at the expense of competing domestic social, political and military forces. By creating a modern army loyal exclusively to themselves, the Ottoman and Moroccan sultans, the beys of Tunis, the khedives of Egypt, the shahs of Iran and the amirs of Afghanistan hoped to equip their dynasties with a coercive weapon capable of quelling internal autonomous and centrifugal challenges and buttressing their own power as expressed in the form of a modern autocratic state.[1]

Early attempts by Middle Eastern rulers to modernize their military forces have usually been understood as driven by shock at successive defeats by European powers, especially by the relentless Russian conquests of Ottoman and Iranian territory and the consequent extension of infidel control over Muslim populations. Napoleon's occupation of Egypt in 1798, although temporary, provided both a reminder of local military weakness and an impressive display of the power of a modern army. Yet in fact dynastic rulers such as the Qajar shahs of Iran and, most notably of all, Muhammad Ali Pasha of Egypt, desired a large modern army not only for defensive but also for offensive warfare. They wished not only to defend themselves against the relentless pressure from an expanding Europe but also, at least at first, to reconquer territories lost to European control, and to establish and often also to consolidate imperial possessions of their own. One of the very earliest attempts at modern military reform, the request from the Moroccan Sultan in 1767 for Ottoman assistance to organize a unit of artillerymen, was made in preparation for the attempt to recover coastal cities lost to Spanish and Portuguese occupation.[2] In the late eighteenth and early nineteenth centuries, the Qajar shahs of Iran struggled for decades to reassert their hegemony against Russian challenges in the eastern Caucasus, especially over Georgia, and creating reformed regiments was a key element in their strategy. Egypt under Muhammad Ali Pasha and Khedive Ismail provides perhaps the most spectacular example of military reform and expansion in the pursuit of empire-building. Muhammad Ali used his *nizam* to establish Egyptian power in the Arabian peninsula, in the Sudan, and especially in Syria, while Ismail deployed his numerically inflated and unsustainably expensive regiments in imperial adventures in the Horn of Africa, Sudan and Abyssinia.[3]

Yet undoubtedly military defeats at the hands of European armies, as they came to be generalized across the Muslim world in the late eighteenth and early nineteenth centuries, did gradually transform the local elites' perception of their relationship to the West. At the beginning of the nineteenth century, for example, the newly consolidated Qajar state had sufficient self-confidence to envisage the reclamation of Safavid supremacy against the Russian Empire in Transcaucasia. Yet defeat in two disastrous wars with Russia (1804–13, 1826–8) ended such hopes while compensatory attempts to enforce Iranian claims to Herat (1837–8, 1856–7) also ended after two brief but humiliating military conflicts with Britain. As the century wore on, Iranian self-confidence turned to doubt, and the objectives of reform turned inwards to become defensive, focusing on the survival of the state. Muhammad Ali Pasha and the Khedive Ismail might continue to dream of an empire in the Horn of Africa, but no Middle East state could now conceive of offering a military challenge to a European army.

As well as stimulating elite programmes of reform, military defeat was central to Middle Eastern political development in another, more radical, sense. Egypt in both the nineteenth and twentieth centuries illustrates perfectly the linkage between military defeat and the emergence from within the officer corps of a radical political challenge. The multiple failures of the Egyptian army during Khedive Ismail's empire-building in Abyssinia discredited the old Turco-Circassian command, paving the way for the Urabi Revolt, and the linkage continued in the twentieth century, defeat in Palestine in 1948 galvanizing the Free Officers and leading directly to the 1952 coup.

During the nineteenth century, ruling dynasties across the Middle East and beyond learned a harsh lesson concerning the expense of modern armies. Standing armies were inherently massively more costly than older types of military forces. Based on conscription, they required bureaucratic and administrative expansion and rationalization. They also depended on the ability of the state to organize the receipt and disbursal of regular supplies of cash, all ranks having to be paid whether on active service or not. They required uniforms and especially the kind of weapons, usually only available from abroad, appropriate to modern warfare. Both men and officers required modern education and training. Older military forces made none of these demands. Irregular tribal forces might be raised for specific campaigns and then disbanded and, in any case, were often paid in kind or by means of revenue remission to tribal khans and aghas. In this way, the state had to find no extra cash, but only lost potential revenue which was often in reality only theoretically due. The institution of the *timar*, the grant of land in return for military service, also freed the state from the necessity of raising additional cash. Officers of such irregular or semi-feudal formations, whether khans or *sipahis*, were responsible for raising and paying men from among their own peasantry or tribes, and used the tactics, especially that of tribal raiding, with which they were familiar, neither they nor their men requiring formal training or the literacy necessary to modern troops. Although, as rulers introduced the *nizam-i jadid*, their need for more regular and larger fiscal sources for the new regiments led to the successful abolition of older forms of taxation, notably the *timar*, yet newer revenue streams were much more difficult to produce and manage efficiently in the absence of administrative and economic development. The inevitable result was a turn to borrowing from those very European countries from whom the *nizam* regiments were supposedly a defence.

With the partial exception of the Ottoman Empire, the protracted struggles of these states in the nineteenth century to build up modern military forces capable of securing the independence of their realms from European control and achieving the autonomy of their own rule from local intermediary social layers, tribal groups, provincial notables and so on, largely failed. In fact such struggles more often led, through the ruinous debts incurred, to an actual and complete loss of sovereignty and direct European control. By 1869, 1875 and 1876, Tunisia, Egypt and the Ottoman Empire respectively had each been bankrupted by the crippling expense of their modernization programmes, at the heart of which were the *nizam* regiments. In the Middle East, unlike Europe, the military revolution had been supported neither by any substantive fiscal revolution nor by the agricultural and industrial revolutions which were powering European military development.

Nonetheless, whatever the degree of success or failure experienced by various countries with the ostensible objective of military modernization, the creation of a modern army, the attempt itself wrought profound change on a number of levels, administrative, social, political and intellectual. Educational institutions developed, at least at first, largely in response to the needs of the new armies for officers. Expanding educational opportunities and increased contact with the wider world, not only with Europe but across the Middle East, led to the growing salience of a discourse of reform. Conscription, based on a census, began administrative centralization, and the need for modern weapons led to experiments with industry. As these processes began to gather pace, wider changes in society and its relationship to the state became evident. In the Ottoman Empire, the new army became a route for the social advancement of officers from modest provincial backgrounds, while in Egypt it also provided the mechanism for the articulation of a new Egyptian national consciousness, such developments imparting a revolutionary dimension to the modern army's burgeoning sense of its own national mission. Everywhere, the ability of the state to extend its reach, and therefore its sovereignty, across the entire national territory and over the lives of the national population increased exponentially.[4]

Although the late eighteenth century marked the beginning of *nizam* mania in the Middle East, military reform, reorganization and modernization was itself nothing new. In the sixteenth century the threat from Portugal had led the Saʿdi dynasty in Morocco to introduce sophisticated military reforms, integrating arquebusiers and artillery into their forces and developing combined infantry–cavalry tactics for their battles. In 1578 the Moroccans, with these forces, inflicted a crushing defeat on the Portuguese, leaving Morocco safe from European invasion until 1844.[5] In late sixteenth- and seventeenth-century Iran, the Safavids had organized corps of musketeers and artillery while the eighteenth century saw a consistent determination by the Ottomans to overcome the deficiencies of their reliance on Janissaries and *timariots*. By the time of the Russo–Ottoman war of 1768–74, the Ottomans were already relying to a great extent on an increased enrolment of infantry and cavalry regiments from indigenous, Muslim, landless peasants and their payment from the central treasury.[6] Nor were specific developments, such as the presence of European advisors in the Middle East, novel innovations in the late eighteenth and early nineteenth centuries. Hungarian and German gunners had assisted Mehmed II at Constantinople in 1453 and in the early sixteenth century the Portuguese provided Iran with cannon for use against the Uzbeks.[7] Throughout the eighteenth century, European adventurers, the Hungarian and French converts, Ibrahim Muteferrika and the Comte de Bonneval, and later the French officer Baron de Tott, had provided a conduit through which the Ottoman elite might gain access to European ideas of military organization.

These dynamics of military change, evident at various times and in various locations across the Middle East, arose from the competitive emulation between warring polities which had also driven the evolution of armies in Europe where states were locked in prolonged dynastic conflict.[8] They were generated from within the societies concerned, were prompted by the logic of conflict with near neighbours, and do not appear to have produced any marked cultural or religious opposition. By the eighteenth century, however, an awareness was spreading across the Middle East of a fundamental reversal of its relationship with Europe, perhaps best exemplified by the treaty of Küçük-Kaynarca in 1774, when for the first time the defeated Ottomans were forced to cede sovereignty over a Muslim population, the Crimean Tartars, to a Christian power, Russia. The resulting consciousness of a new and inexplicable vulnerability produced both a determination to unlock the secrets of an apparently novel European military pre-eminence, but also a crisis of confidence and legitimacy for the Muslim rulers initiating this project. From now on, experiments in military modernization were to become a lightning rod for wider resentments, elite but also popular, against foreign infidel encroachments.

The renewal projects of the dynastic rulers of the late eighteenth- and early nineteenth-century Middle East were informed by a range of different influences. Direct emulation of the armies of western Europe, especially Britain and France, often with the assistance of European renegades, was one model for change. The efficacy of French armies was, for example, vividly illustrated at close quarters by Napoleon's crushing defeat of the Mamluks[9] at the Battle of the Pyramids in 1798. Across North Africa and the Middle East in the early decades of the nineteenth century, considerable numbers of veterans, deserters, converts to Islam, and unemployed officers demobilized after the Napoleonic wars, offered their knowledge of European armies and their experience of modern warfare to sultan, bey and pasha.

For the shahs of Iran and perhaps too the Ottoman sultans, the Russian example was most present and visible. Here Russia's Petrine Revolution appeared to offer a template of especial relevance. By the 1820s, Iran had fought and lost two wars against the encroaching Russian Empire. The shah, Fath Ali Shah, and especially his son, Abbas Mirza, responded to this newly apparent vulnerability by concluding that Iran's military weakness vis-à-vis imperial Russia was a result of its failure to adopt European military organization and disciplined tactics.[10] Abbas arrived at this conclusion not only on the basis of direct experience of Russian military prowess but also because of an emerging ideological predisposition to adopt Russian autocratic reform as an appropriate model for Qajar political objectives. For the early Qajar elite in general, the arrival of Russian armies within Iranian territories in the Caucasus and their menacing of Tabriz appeared to be the culmination of a process of reform and state-building which had begun in Russia a century earlier with Peter the Great. According to this Enlightenment interpretation, transmitted to Abbas Mirza through the medium of Voltaire, Peter's success was due to his introduction of military and administrative reforms based on a western European model and his suppression of opposition from military and clerical representatives of the old order. This was the model for military reform, albeit highly partisan and even mythical, which the early Qajar shahs were determined to import into Iran.[11]

Yet the rapid diffusion of notions of military reorganization was not due to a simple process of borrowing from Europe. As noted above, Middle Eastern armies had shown considerable organizational dynamism at earlier periods, sharing in the competitive emulation which was driving military change both in Europe and beyond. The routes by which concepts of military organization and innovations in military technology were transmitted throughout the Middle East and North Africa were complex. Nineteenth-century Europe itself offered no single model of military development, and Middle Eastern countries in general appear to have been influenced at least as much by each local effort at reform as by the unmediated European example. In the early nineteenth century, it was not the European example, but those of the Ottoman Empire and of Muhammad Ali in Egypt which were of key significance in spreading ideas of military reform throughout the Middle East and North Africa. The adoption of a template of the standing army, recruited from conscripts, led by professional officers, paid regularly in cash from a central treasury, and armed with modern weapons, by rulers possessing the military prowess of Muhammad Ali or the prestige of the Ottoman sultan-caliph, made these patterns to some extent palatable to wider elite Muslim opinion.

The existence of local models, the Ottoman Empire, Egypt under Muhammad Ali Pasha, was of some utility in rendering palatable in the wider region innovations in military practice which, in an era of an unprecedented European menace, aroused widespread distrust. Earlier emulation had been untarnished by the political and civilizational risks which were becoming ever more apparent as the nineteenth century wore on. Now, fears of European cultural and intellectual, as well as political and military domination, made the introduction of practices originating in Europe deeply problematic. Everywhere, the *nizam* regiments faced growing opposition and hostility. Such hostility was further aggravated by the harsh burdens which military reform, and the wider centralization of government in general, imposed on the population at large.

One response to the opposition evoked by the *nizam* regiments was to attempt to indigenize the proposed reforms. This attempt, its changing impact in the context of an apparently irresistible European colonial drive, and the ultimate revelation of its hollowness is best demonstrated by the Moroccan experience. In the first reform period in Morocco, between 1845 and 1873, the Sultan introduced typical New Order forces, following the example of Tunisia, Egypt and the Ottoman Empire, as well as the model of the French Armée d'Afrique. Criticism of the apparent mimicking of infidel methods was nonetheless strong, and intensified after the defeat of the Moroccans by the French at the Battle of Isly in 1844. The response of the court was to sponsor a literature which located the *nizam* troops within the local political and religious culture, arguing that the Sultan's formation of these regiments was a requirement of his duty to wage jihad, and that the regiments themselves were an historical type, rather than a European invention, for which precedents could be found in Islamic history and military traditions.[12] In the second reform period, the *nizam* continued to consolidate itself as a real coercive force as well as a symbol of state power.[13] But this period also saw the relentless growth of the French determination to incorporate Morocco into its empire, and the increasing subordination of the court to French influence. Popular hostility, never entirely banished by the literature extolling the religious benefit of the New Order, re-emerged accordingly, aggravated by the new burdens of conscription and higher taxation. The first decade of the twentieth century finally saw the new army split between those who supported a sultan who was legitimate yet who was apparently ready to abandon them to French control, and his brother who advocated a jihad against the infidels. When the French invaded, the army was unable to lead the resistance, which fell to popular urban and rural leaders.[14] In a final abandonment of the original ostensible purpose of the military reforms, the remnants of the *nizam* were taken over by the French, incorporated into the colonial army, and used to suppress opposition throughout the country.[15]

Another method used to obviate opposition was to turn to another Muslim state for advice and assistance. The Ottoman Empire was itself, in fact, a particularly important practical as well as an ideological conduit for military reform. Although the Ottoman Empire is usually integrated within the discourse of military modernization as a recipient of military assistance, it was also an important provider. In earlier periods the Empire had been a key route for the diffusion of firearms. In the sixteenth century, for example, the Ottomans gave light cannon and firearms to the ruler of the Crimea. By the eighteenth century the pace of Ottoman military reform, and the admiration which it excited elsewhere in the Islamic world, may be seen in the Sultan of Morocco's request for Ottoman assistance in the organization of a unit of artillerymen. Despite the reputation acquired by the later Empire in European eyes as militarily backward and incompetent, as the nineteenth century advanced and the menace of European control grew, the Ottomans became increasingly valued by Muslim states as a culturally and politically compatible model for military development and a source of practical advice. In the 1870s the Amir of Kashgar in Central Asia requested military assistance, via a delegation to the Ottoman Sultan, the Sultan immediately responding with a five-man military mission and supplies of weapons.[16]

In countries such as Morocco and Afghanistan, the Ottoman role as military advisors was particularly politically driven. Afghan amirs had consistently rejected British, or any other European, military missions which might compensate for Afghanistan's own lack of professional officers out of a fear of a consequential political subservience. In the early twentieth century, following the foundation of the Royal Military College, the new Afghan amir, Habibullah, asked the Ottoman Empire to provide officer-instructors and in 1907 an Ottoman military mission arrived in Kabul.[17] In the 1840s the Ottomans had offered Morocco munitions, skilled workers and military instructors and in 1909 Sultan Mawlay Abd al-Hafiz, as part of his struggle to reassert central authority and resist growing French colonial power, invited the Young Turk government in Istanbul to provide him with military advisors to replace an existing French mission. Turkish officers arrived in Morocco in November of that year and began to serve with the Moroccan army against rebellious tribes. By November the following year, however, France had forced the Turkish mission's withdrawal and re-imposed its own monopoly of military assistance.[18] Even in Iran, which had a long experience of military conflict and rivalry with the Ottomans, education in Ottoman military institutions was highly sought after by aspiring officers and seen as a route to professional advancement.[19] By the early twentieth century, modern Turkish military influence was widespread across the Middle Eastern and Muslim world.

It was not only the adoption of European methods of military organization but also the actual arrival of European officers to take charge of the projects which aroused hostility. In building *nizam* forces, all the reforming rulers of the early nineteenth-century Middle East faced the same difficulty of accumulating a cadre for a professional officer corps.[20] Since the region then possessed no modern educational institutions, let alone military colleges, nor had there yet been any significant effort by local elites to acquire training abroad, Middle Eastern rulers turned directly to European officers. This was quickly recognized as an enterprise fraught with danger. The initial employment of renegades, deserters and converts quickly turned into requests for official missions, such missions then acting as new mechanisms for the assertion of European political influence, and only secondarily as conduits for the transfer of military knowledge.

The number of European adventurers occupying advisory positions in the new *nizam* forces, for various lengths of time and under a variety of conditions, was quite astonishing. The demobilizations following the end of the Napoleonic wars in particular provided large numbers of officers without prospects in Europe. In 1820, for example, Muhammad Ali Pasha recruited the French ex-officer, 'Colonel' Sèves, later known as Sulayman Pasha, who eventually became second-in-command of the army ranking below only Muhammad Ali's son, Ibrahim Pasha, as well as a number of obscure French officers. Khedive Ismail later expanded this practice, hiring several hundred European and American soldiers of fortune.[21] Although reaching high and sometimes honorary rank in their new posts, most of these advisors had only ever occupied modest, if indeed any, rank in their original units; 'Colonel' Sèves, for instance, had probably never risen higher than captain in the French army. Other states, such as Iran and Morocco, took the employment of renegades a step further. Iran possessed an entire regiment of Russian deserters throughout the first half of the nineteenth century, mostly ex-serf Russian conscripts commanded by a former non-comissioned officer, while reports credited the Moroccan Sultan with a corps of deserters and ex-prisoners of war amounting to 6,000 men.[22]

The employment of officers of this type was of only very limited use and was eventually superseded by the arrival of official military missions provided by various European governments. States which wished to preserve their political independence and autonomy in military reorganization resorted to a variety of expedients to obtain Western advice without inviting further Western influence. Iran, for example, experimented with a succession of military missions from different European countries; Morocco and Afghanistan turned to the Ottoman Empire for assistance and advice, the Ottoman Empire itself enlisting help from Germany, a supposedly disinterested European power. States which fell under indirect or direct European control, however, had military missions from the principal imperial power imposed upon them. The presence of military missions may indeed be interpreted as a barometer of foreign influence. In Morocco, for example, the fortunes of the French military mission in the early twentieth century mirrored the success of the French colonial project in general. France first insisted upon a monopoly of military assistance, to the exclusion of all other military advisors, British but also Ottoman, then demanding that the scope of the French mission should be expanded from an advisory role to include command and management responsibilities.[23]

The religious, cultural, political and ideological resentments aroused by the *nizam-i jadid* were evident among sections of the elites of various Middle Eastern states, but the burdens imposed by the New Order weighed most heavily on the lower and poorer classes. Everywhere conscription, a pillar of the *nizam*, was viewed with horror, and evaded and resisted, sometimes by desperate expedients.[24] Given the inadequacies of existing administrative systems, and the opportunities to avoid service provided by a variety of expedients possessed by those with wealth and influence, conscription, although supposedly universal, in fact fell almost exclusively on the urban and rural poor. Nationalist historiography has tended to applaud the state-building dimension of conscription, and certainly the incorporation into a national institution of large numbers of people who had hitherto had little direct contact with the state did contribute to the eventual emergence of a national consciousness. Yet, as state after state introduced the measure, the poorer classes manifested a supreme indifference to the national or dynastic interests articulated by their rulers, and greeted the recruiting sergeant almost invariably with individual or collective avoidance or resistance, with flight and rebellion.

It is perhaps the class dimension, revealed by, for example, opposing attitudes of elite and subaltern to conscription, which has received least attention in the study of *nizam* projects in the Middle East. The implications of these projects were indeed entirely different for rulers and the elites around them than for the mass of the population. In fact, the *nizam* projects may ultimately be best understood as a means by which elites and dynasties attempted to defend themselves not against European control but against the clamour and the claims of their own populations.

For all the rulers of the nineteenth-century Middle East, to reform meant to Europeanize.[25] The reforming elite's preference for regular disciplined forces on the European model never seems to have been questioned. Yet, in terms of defence against foreign attack, other modes of military organization appear to have been much more successful while *nizam* armies experienced defeat after defeat at the hands of European troops. At the beginning of the nineteenth century, Iran's traditional forces were able to stalemate Russia in the eastern Caucasus for many years, yet by the beginning of the twentieth century Russian armies could march through northern Iran unopposed by the *nizam* regiments. In Morocco, the *nizam* troops were not only incapable of offering resistance to French control but actually became a mechanism for the fuller imposition of that control. Throughout the nineteenth century, across the Middle East, the most powerful and successful opposition to European expansion was offered not by the *nizam* forces of the established dynasties but by well-organized, disciplined and militant sufi brotherhoods led by charismatic figures whose legitimacy was derived from religious origins. Shaikh Shamyl of the Naqshbandi sufi order in the Caucasus, Abd al-Qadir of the Qadiriyyah in Algeria, and Shaikh Muhammad Ahmad (the Mahdi) of the Samaniyyah in the Sudan put up fierce resistance for years and sometimes decades.[26]

Such movements, however, with their subaltern and radical dimensions, were as much a menace to the established local rulers as they were to the European empires. Such paradoxes continued into the twentieth century. National armies, preserved in practice, if not in theory, by regimes for internal security, repeatedly proved unable to offer any significant defence against imperial power, resistance falling to non-state military forces with politically dissident leaderships. In 1967, for example, the comprehensive defeat of the Arab armies was followed by the rise of the Palestinian guerrilla movement, while the resistance offered by Hizbullah during the 2006 Israeli invasion was more effective militarily than had been any operations by regular Arab armies in the previous 50 years.[27]

From the perspective of nineteenth-century rulers, military reform was intimately linked not only to external defence but also to state-building in an entirely novel sense. The establishment of reformed regiments enabled the ruler to embark on a project in which the existing balance between the state, embodied in his own person, and the rest of society would be fundamentally altered, and his own position, expressed as a form of political authoritarianism, permanently consolidated. It was the centrality of this function to programmes of military reform and, indeed, its eventual overriding importance, which determined the choice of model to be adopted. There was no evidence that *nizam* troops were superior in warfare to the forces which they were intended to replace. Their great advantage was that they were entirely dependent on and, formally at least, loyal to the ruler, possessing no other allegiance than to the state. They were intended as much to shore up the power of rulers as to defend the national territory against Europe, yet the role played by the *nizam* regiments, and especially their officer corps, was complex. By the latter part of the nineteenth century, they were already beginning to turn against their creators, by the twentieth century becoming a revolutionary force across the region.

The new armies therefore both provided rulers with a mechanism of coercion and confronted them with an instrument of their own potential overthrow. The process of building the new armies also had a profound effect not only on the polity but also on the society from which they sprang. In each country where military reform was initiated, the logic of the process resulted in the 'nationalization' of the new armies. Through conscription, each local army ceased to rely on older forces drawn either from outside the emerging national territory, such as Ottoman garrisons and Mamluks in North Africa and Egypt, or from domestic but largely autonomous tribal groups, as in Iran and Afghanistan, and came instead to be composed of indigenous conscripts recruited directly by the state. After World War I, as wave after wave of modern nationalism broke across the Middle East, the nascent leaderships of countries such as Turkey and Iran, sometimes themselves military, found themselves in possession of a ready-made core of a renewed state-building project. Where such a core institution did not exist, as in the Arab successor states to the Ottoman Empire, the first task identified by the new regimes was to facilitate its construction. In a more specific sense too, the *nizam* projects of the nineteenth-century Middle East nurtured a development of crucial significance for the future: the production of an officer corps with political ambitions. Army officers, often drawn from provincial or non-elite environments, possessing a corporate identity, a modern technical education, and a sense of their own national mission, were, by the 1870s, already a potent political force. In the twentieth century they were to play a role and occupy a position of central strategic significance in the national narratives of their respective countries.

The earliest and arguably the most classically successful case of nineteenth-century military modernization was undertaken by the Ottoman Empire. The Ottoman example illustrates both the general relevance of the military revolution thesis, and also the specific results of military reform in producing an army national in its social composition, and a politicized officer corps. During the nineteenth century the Ottoman army developed an ever-increasing reliance on Turkish-speaking Muslims for both officer corps and rank and file, laying the basis for the army of the Turkish republic. The century also saw the transformation of the Ottoman military, especially its officer corps, into an institution with its own corporate consciousness and belief in itself as the central element of the Ottoman state, with a concomitant responsibility to safeguard the state through periodic political interventions, as well as through the purely military duties of defence. Surviving World War I intact, the army, led by nationalist officers, was able to resist occupation by the Allies, defeat the Greeks and ensure the survival of the infant Turkish state, becoming the guardian of Kemalist values throughout the twentieth century. No other military revolution in the Middle East was as successful in building an effective army. Egypt, Tunis and

Morocco, although their rulers embarked on the same path had, by the late nineteenth and early twentieth century, fallen under full European control, the *nizam* forces incorporated into the colonial armies. The Egyptian army, led by Colonel Urabi, had tried in 1881–2 to assert its leadership over the country but it had not prevailed. Nonetheless, military reform in Egypt, as in the Ottoman Empire, had succeeded in 'Egyptianizing' the army, transforming the relationship between the state and the Egyptian population and also in creating an instrument, the Egyptian officer corps, which was, after the caesura of British rule, to resurrect in the twentieth century its traditions of nationalist and anti-khedivial activity. Elsewhere the results of reform were more flimsy. Neither Iran nor Afghanistan were able to create modern national armies, nor an officer corps to lead them. Iran's experiments led to military disintegration and an increased Russian presence in the country and influence over the court, while Afghanistan's *nizam* had singularly failed to play an effective role during the first and second Afghan wars, leading to the discrediting of the entire reform process and the enhancement of the tribal and religious forces which had led resistance to invasion.

*Nizam* mania had begun in earnest in the Middle East in 1797 when Sultan Selim III had announced the establishment of a corps of regular infantry equipped with modern weapons and uniform, to be known as the *nizam-i cedid* (*jadid*). Although both Selim and his *nizam* were destroyed by the Janissaries and their allies among the ulama in 1826, his successor, Sultan Mahmud II, resumed the effort. The following decades saw the model adopted everywhere. In the 1810s Abbas Mirza in Iran, and in 1815 Muhammad Ali Pasha in Egypt, formed *nizam* regiments. A little later, in the late 1820s, the bey of Tunis, Ahmad al-Husayni, and in the 1830s, Amir Dust Muhammad in Afghanistan, joined them as did Sultan Sidi Muhammad bin Abd al-Rahman of Morocco in the 1840s.

In the Ottoman Empire, the logic of sustaining the *nizam* committed the Empire to a wider reform agenda. Traces of a military revolution may be found both in the military-driven administrative and educational changes of Mahmud's reign, and in the *Tanzimat* reforms which followed it. Under Mahmud, embryonic ministries emerged, beginning with the ministry of war, while the army treasury developed into the finance ministry. In 1831 a cadastral survey and census was carried out to facilitate conscription and taxation, in simple terms men and money for the army.[28] The *Tanzimat* reforms of Mahmud's successor, Abdulmecid, involved further administrative, bureaucratic and fiscal centralization, of which the army was a key beneficiary. Education reforms were also galvanized by the need for trained officers. A military medical school was opened, followed in 1834 by the Military Academy and in 1849 a staff college was established. Indeed, for most of the nineteenth century higher education was essentially a branch of the army.[29]

But the military project immediately showed itself to be enormously expensive. By the end of his reign Mahmud was devoting some 70 per cent of his revenues to its needs.[30] By the 1870s, the reforms undertaken by the Ottoman elite in the hope of strengthening both empire and dynasty were reaching a crisis. This crisis manifested itself in financial terms, but this only masked an even deeper crisis of legitimacy and political direction. The efforts to rationalize and make more effective the system of taxation had largely failed, and there had been little or no capitalist economic development and industrialization of the kind that was supporting the armies of western Europe. On the other hand, the costs of the reforms of Mahmud and the *Tanzimat*, and most particularly of the new army and navy, the latter equipped with powerful ironclad warships, had proved to be astronomical. In 1854 the Empire began to borrow from Europe and by 1875 could no longer pay the interest on the debt, becoming effectively bankrupt, and was forced to accept European financial supervision in the form of the Ottoman Public Debt Administration.

In Egypt too, the *nizam* dragged a range of reforms in its wake. Muhammad Ali Pasha took steps to rationalize the bureaucracy, introduced embryonic ministries beginning with the war ministry, and centralized the provincial administration, making it responsible for a wide range of measures controlling and mobilizing the rural population. To staff the civil and military bureaucracies, Muhammad Ali turned his attention to education. Students were trained abroad and, as in the Ottoman Empire, educational provision was, in its initial stages, the responsibility of the war ministry. In order to provide more revenue, Muhammad Ali also intervened extensively in the structure of land ownership, taking control of much of the land in the name of the state. In order to mobilize the Egyptian peasantry for his economic and military projects, Muhammad

Ali massively expanded the state apparatus and the degree and nature of its control over the population.[31] But Muhammad Ali and his successors, the khedives, soon found, as had the Ottoman Empire, that their efforts to finance these changes by raising internal resources of revenue were inadequate. Egypt began with short-term borrowing and contracted its first loan in 1860. In 1876 Egypt too went bankrupt, owing 100 million pounds. Like the Ottoman Empire, Egypt too found itself unable to resist European supervision exercised through the Caisse de la Dette.

In Tunisia the reforming al-Husayni beys had also led the country into bankruptcy by 1869, paving the way for full colonial control. During the 1840s the enthusiastic Ahmad Bey had raised *nizam* regiments of 16,000 men in uniform, with the accompanying military school and arms factories. He sought to support his centralized administration and the *nizam* by the introduction of monopolies and a host of new taxes levied on the rural areas, and by substituting olives for grain as the principal export. By the late 1840s the state was already on the point of financial collapse and the reform project disintegrated. A later bey, Muhammad Sadiq, revived the effort but with the same result, his taxation and conscription policies additionally provoking a revolt which spread throughout the Tunisian countryside. In 1869 Tunisian finances were placed under an International Financial Commission.

In Iran and Afghanistan, the contours of a military revolution were barely perceptible in the nineteenth century. The early Qajar rulers, especially the crown prince, Abbas Mirza, launched what was perhaps the most ambitious programme, including the introduction of conscription, but this effort was dissipated as the century wore on, leaving little trace apart from an institution of higher education, the *Dar al-Funun,* and an ossified system of recruitment which served mainly to channel cash to members of the elite masquerading as officers. On the other hand, the Qajars avoided the indebtedness which ruined other states in the Middle East. By the end of the nineteenth century, as a result of the frailty of state-building in general, Iran's public debt was still tiny, although state revenues were correspondingly small. As Iran entered the twentieth century, neither the country nor the Qajar dynasty possessed any effective military force, relying on imperial rivalry to permit its continuing independence and on Russian-officered Iranian cossacks to protect the court. It was, paradoxically, this very absence of a reformed army which permitted the revolutionaries of the constitutional period, 1905–11, to succeed in obliging the Shah to accede to their demands for political reform. On the other hand, the Shah had no need to fear that such a reformed army might turn against him, as it had turned against the Ottoman Sultan and the Egyptian Khedive. Similarly in Afghanistan, the projects launched by successive amirs to introduce a standing army had come to nothing as a result of the failure of flimsy administrative and financial reforms to challenge and overcome strong centrifugal tribal, religious and ethnic forces, and the periodic internal crises caused by foreign invasion. But so hegemonic was the modernist discourse that even Afghanistan, reliant on British subsidies for its minimal state-building programme and thus avoiding the accumulation of debt, had by the early 1900s managed to introduce a form of conscription which, though not very widely applied, signalled the arrival of a state claiming modern prerogatives, and establish a military college, a pioneering educational initiative. Nonetheless, by imposing only a shadow of conscription, and confining military education to a single unsupported institution, the ruling dynasties of both Iran and Afghanistan, flimsy as was their social base, avoided both mass popular resistance and the threat of the military coup. In Iran and Afghanistan the balance between state and society remained fundamentally unaltered by a failed military revolution.

Everywhere it was introduced, the *nizam* project had, as a central element, the introduction of conscription as a method of enlisting recruits. In the Ottoman Empire, the existing haphazard and ad hoc method of relying on provincial authorities, governors and notables to provide recruits was finally superseded in 1843 by the introduction of a fully worked-out system of universal military service based on the Prussian model. This had been prefigured in the reform charter, the Rescript of Gülhane, promulgated in 1839 and, together with further reforms introduced after the Crimean War, was intended both to regularize the supply of recruits and to open up military service to non-Muslims, who might not only serve in the army but also rise to the rank of colonel.[32] This was proposed in the name of an ideology of Ottomanism, embodying civic equality and imperial patriotism, which would, it was hoped, help to bind the empire together, as well as promising the practical benefit of a substantial increase in the pool of manpower. Yet the key objective of cementing Ottoman solidarity was, paradoxically, completely undermined by the inclusion of a provision which allowed non-Muslims, horrified at the prospect of serving in the army, to buy exemption through the payment of a special tax. This tax, the *bedel-i askari*, thus in practice confirmed the Muslim character of the Ottoman army and led to its increasing homogeneity.[33]

In Egypt the introduction of conscription, although framed by a different historical context, resulted in a similar homogenization and nationalization of the army. Muhammad Ali had himself arrived in Egypt as part of a contingent of Ottoman troops, whose mission was to re-establish Ottoman control after Napoleon's invasion. His rise was rapid and in 1805 he was named governor of Egypt by the Ottoman Sultan. In 1811 he ruthlessly suppressed the existing Mamluk military forces before they could mount opposition of the kind that had destroyed the Ottoman Selim III and his *nizam*, and in 1815 he issued a proclamation calling for establishment of a *nizam-i jadid* in Egypt. After finding unsuitable for disciplined regular units both the Ottoman Albanian troops, of which he had once been one, and recruits enslaved in the Sudan, in 1822 he turned, of necessity, to the idea of recruiting Egyptian *fallahin*. In less than a year, 30,000 troops were undergoing training.[34] At first, recruiting officers simply seized peasants from Egyptian villages as and where they could find them. Gradually, more regular methods were adopted, a census was conducted, registers of absconders and lists of deserters drawn up, and the relationship of the state to the peasantry transformed.[35] From now on, in an entirely novel development, the Egyptian peasantry was forced to provide, through an increasingly sophisticated system of conscription, the manpower for the lower ranks of the army. This new development was part of no conscious nationalist plan but resulted from the logic of Muhammad Ali's determination to build a power base for himself within Egypt. This logic, however, did not extend to the officer corps, which Muhammad Ali Pasha was determined to maintain as the preserve of the old Turco-Circassian elite. He thus created an almost unbridgeable gulf between officers and men in the new army, a gulf which was to contribute to the army turning against his own dynasty, first in 1881 and secondly, and finally, in 1952.

Muhammad Ali Pasha and later khedives only succeeded in imposing conscription on the Egyptians, unaccustomed to military service, in the teeth of popular opposition, peasants resorting to self-maiming, individual or collective flight, and even occasionally open rebellion. But, notwithstanding the depth of discontent aroused, the state was strong enough to insist on its will prevailing. In Tunisia, however, the balance between state and population was less favourable to the *nizam* project of the beys.

In early nineteenth-century Tunisia, as in Egypt, the only effective military force at the disposal of the beys comprised the Ottoman garrison, supplemented by Berber infantry and some local tribal irregulars. As the beys began to build up their new *nizam* regiments, they, in a development as novel in Tunisia as it was in Egypt, turned to the Tunisian peasantry.[36] Recruitment was initially haphazard, even chaotic, but eventually Muhammad Sadiq Bey had French conscription regulations translated into Arabic and adapted by his French military advisors for a Tunisian law promulgated in 1860.[37] By 1864 the entire countryside had risen in revolt, led by the village leaders and tribal shaikhs who had been made responsible for enforcing the law. Weakened by mass desertion, and demoralized by a lack of cash, the *nizam* began to disintegrate altogether. When the Bey surrendered to the French invasion in 1881, the remnants of his *nizam* capitulated with him. From 1883 onwards French recruiting officers, using the 1860 law backed by the power of the colonial administration, began the systematic recruitment of the Tunisian peasantry and the organization of the Tunisian army along French lines.[38]

In Iran and Afghanistan, conscription was a much paler phenomenon, adopted as a signifier of modernity by rulers conscious of the wider environment, but to little practical effect. In neither country did conscription extend its reach very far into the population and both governments remained heavily dependent on irregular tribal forces, such forces, especially when victorious, as in the Anglo–Afghan wars, aggravating centrifugal tendencies rather than unifying the population under the rubric of the state. By the beginning of the twentieth century neither state possessed anything resembling an army national in its composition or loyalties.

Wherever the nineteenth-century military revolution in the Middle East reached the point of take-off, the new army, or more accurately its officer corps, began to develop political ambitions. This is most evident in the cases of the Ottoman Empire and Egypt. By the 1870s, both Ottoman and Egyptian officers were poised to inaugurate a tradition of political intervention which was to endure until the present. Although the precise dynamics of each political intervention differed, Ottoman military figures insisting on the promulgation of a constitution in 1876 as the best hope for safe-guarding the Empire, Egyptian officers leading a revolution in 1881–2 in pursuit of corporate goals as well as against European influence and khedivial authority, the contexts and motivation possessed many similarities.

In both states, the driver of the crisis which developed in the 1870s was financial, the inability of sultan and khedive to service the debts they had incurred in the pursuit of their state-building agendas and the consequent growth of direct European influence over economy and state. In the case of the Ottoman Empire, borrowing to finance an expanded army and administration had let to bankruptcy and the establishment of the Ottoman Public Debt under French and British supervision. The domestic crisis caused by this new humiliation, coupled with the outbreak of uprisings and war in the Balkans, the successful suppression of which by the Ottoman army only further raised the risk of European intervention, was resolved in 1876 by a palace revolution cum coup d'état. The high-ranking bureaucrat, Midhat Pasha, and two military figures, the *Serasker*, the highest-ranking military official, and the Head of the Military Academy, supported by his men, acted to secure the deposition of one sultan, Abdulaziz, the succession of another, Abdulhamid, and the promulgation of a constitution. The constitution, and the parliament which was assembled under its authority, survived little more than a year. But this episode, a proto-military coup, marked the open entry of the Ottoman army into politics and heralded a new era in the political consciousness and activism of the officer corps.

In Egypt, the profligate borrowing of Khedive Ismail also produced a financial and therefore a political crisis in the 1870s. In 1879, when he tried to resist new mechanisms of British and French financial supervision, he was deposed by the Ottoman Sultan, acting under European pressure, and succeeded by his son, Tawfiq. This inaugurated the crisis which became known as the Urabi Revolt and which introduced the army as an active player in Egyptian politics. The unsustainable costs incurred by Khedive Ismail's inflation of the army to 80,000 men provided the spark which lit the tinder of the Urabi Revolt. The financial retrenchment in military spending demanded by the Caisse de la Dette led to mass retirements and officers being put on half-pay, measures which produced the first army demonstrations in 1879. These economies were imposed mostly at regimental level and therefore affected Egyptians much more than the Turco-Circassian high command, spurring the already disaffected Egyptian officer corps into action under the leadership of Colonel Ahmad Urabi, the son of a village headman. Urabi had been commissioned in 1858, rising quickly, by 1862, to the rank of colonel, but had been unable to rise any higher.

Although Muhammad Ali Pasha had perforce turned to the Egyptian peasantry in the search for conscripts for his *nizam*, he had been determined to preserve the Turco-Circassian character of his officer corps. Only towards the end of Muhammad Ali's reign were native-born Egyptians permitted to enter military schools, perhaps as a result of the losses resulting from the Pasha's many wars. By 1846 there were 517 Egyptian officers, but none had been promoted beyond captain.[39] Khedive Said, who ruled between 1854 and 1863, accelerated the opening of the officer corps to Egyptians, making a concerted effort to have the sons of village shaikhs and other local notables serve in the army, commissioning them as junior officers on completion of their training. Under the next Khedive, Ismail (1863–79), as the army grew to over 80,000 men, the officer corps expanded proportionately, with an inevitable influx of native Egyptians. By the end of Ismail's reign they in fact constituted an absolute majority of the officer corps.[40] Nonetheless, promotion beyond regimental command, the rank of colonel, remained beyond their reach. The resulting sense of injustice, professional frustration and hostility towards the Turkish-speaking military command which grew among the Arabic-speaking junior officers produced a combustible resentment against which the crisis of 1879–82 was to play itself out. This sense of exclusion, furthermore, generated a strong sense of solidarity between the Egyptian officers and their men, and between them and the village notables, which promoted the popularization of the slogan 'Egypt for the Egyptians' during the Urabi Revolt, Urabi himself moving from defender of the Egyptian army officers to defender of the Egyptian nation.

Determined to protect the army and to stem the growing European intervention in Egypt's financial and political systems, Colonel Ahmad Urabi, supported by his fellow Egyptian officers and his men, put himself at the head of a burgeoning nationalist movement. Contesting not only British and French power, but also the authority of the Khedive, his government and the Turco-Circassian elite which headed the civilian bureaucracy and monopolized command within the army, Urabi and his supporters eventually assumed practical control of the government, with Urabi himself taking over the ministry of war. In September 1882, Urabi's struggle with the Khedive and with Europe was ended by the defeat of the Egyptian army by British forces at the Battle of Tel al-Kabir. To this extent, Colonel Urabi appears as a harbinger of a new sense of Egyptian identity and as a radical critic of the Khedive's inability to defend the country's interests. However, he must also be seen as a representative of a rising social group, the rural notables, and particularly as an officer insistent upon defending the interests of his own institution, the modern army. In this combination of motives, Urabi anticipated the twentieth century, when the desire to defend corporate army interests and to challenge existing indigenous elites joined simple nationalism across the Middle East as drivers of military intervention.

When the British began their occupation of Egypt, one of their first steps was to disband the army which had proved so lacking in the malleability which they found in the khedives. They then formed a new corps from its remnants but were determined to neutralize any further potential threat from this direction by imposing severe restrictions on strength. Although numbers gradually rose again as the Sudan was reconquered and garrisoned, British officers now occupied the positions formerly held by the Turco-Circassians and the small numbers of Egyptian officers sank into political passivity. Many of the *nizam* officers in Morocco were absorbed, with varying degrees of reluctance, into the French colonial army and in Tunisia into an army which was effectively at the disposal of the French Empire. Iran and Afghanistan had still, by the end of the century, failed to produce anything truly resembling a modern officer corps. In the Ottoman Empire, however, which survived the crisis of 1876–8 without succumbing to occupation, the officer corps too survived intact and continued uninterrupted its progress into a fully fledged modern military and political institution, retaining a strong sense of its own prestige and of its role as the foremost protector of *din u devlet* (religion and state).[41]

In the final decades of the nineteenth century, ideas of reform, of nationalism and constitutionalism, penetrated the Ottoman officer corps more generally and more deeply, while the corps also began to experience an accelerated change in its social composition. The younger school-educated officers, coming increasingly from the provincial lower middle classes, proved highly receptive to ideological innovation, constituting an important segment of the embryonic modern intelligentsia.[42] As in pre-1881 Egypt, the military schools and the army constituted one of the main avenues for social mobility and advancement, bringing into high rank individuals with a profoundly different outlook to that of the court and the old Ottoman elite. In 1908, in the context of the multiple crises threatening the Empire, the tensions which had been building up within the army for decades erupted.

By the early twentieth century, the provincial garrisons had become hotbeds of discontent and frustration, the junior, college-educated officers stationed there possessing, unlike the exile groups in Europe, bodies of armed men with which to carry out their programme. From 1906, mutinies grew in number and severity until, by July 1908, the army stationed in European Turkey was in effective revolt. On 23 July Sultan Abdulhamid accepted the army's demand and restored the constitution, with elections to follow. Although the army abjured any further role at this stage, its political presence was steadily to increase over the next few years. In 1909, following a rebellion against European-educated officers led by rank-and-file soldiers and theological students in Istanbul, the Third Army, stationed in Salonika, styling itself 'the army of deliverance', marched on Istanbul and put down the disturbances, the deposition of Abdulhamid following shortly after. Thus the coalition of army officers and bureaucrats, known as the Committee of Union and Progress (CUP), or Young Turks, seized effective power in the Empire. By 1913 the CUP was able to consolidate its rule as a military dictatorship under the triumvirate of Enver, Jamal and Talat Pashas. Although Talat was a civilian bureaucrat, both Enver and Jamal were typical representatives of the new breed of Ottoman army officer. Both were from modest origins, both had attended the War College in Istanbul, and both had become staff officers in the Third Army. For the first time, a modern officer corps, with a reforming agenda, had seized power in a Middle Eastern state, in defiance both of the old local elites and of Europe, thus tracing out a pattern which was to be repeated over and again in the twentieth century.

# CHAPTER 2

# Importing Modernity
## European Military Missions to Qajar Iran

In the early years of the twenty-first century the US and Britain found themselves – as a consequence of their resort to war, the resulting collapse of indigenous state structures, and their own postwar policies – once again directly involved in military reform and state-building in the Middle East. In Iraq and Afghanistan, US and British missions undertook the reconstruction of military and police forces, defining their projects in terms of building up local military forces to the point at which these forces would be politically reliable and capable of guaranteeing domestic peace and security. In this, they placed themselves within a tradition of Western-sponsored military reform in the Middle East which has a long and problematic pedigree. The nineteenth century saw a plethora of European military missions arrive in the Middle East and North Africa, from all the major powers, Britain, France, Germany, Italy and Russia, as well as from minor and supposedly neutral countries such as Sweden. The twentieth century saw a renewed eruption of military missions, notably to Iraq and Transjordan, under the aegis of the mandatory system, while after World War II the US became the principal supplier of military advisors, especially to Iran and other Gulf monarchies.

In the nineteenth century, almost every ruler across the region stretching from the Atlantic to the Hindu Kush invited European officers, sometimes as individuals, sometimes as formal missions, to assist with building a modern army. With the help of these officers, local dynasties thus sought to appropriate the secrets of European power. The narrative below looks at the history of one Middle Eastern country's experience with

Western military missions, an experience which extended over a protracted period, and which was to have a profound impact on the configuration of Iranian nationalism.

The protracted struggles of these rulers to build up military forces capable of defending their realms from external attack largely failed. Yet the Ottoman example, and the more temporary achievements of Muhammad Ali in Egypt in the 1820s and 1830s, were of immense importance in spreading ideas of military reform throughout the Middle East and North Africa. Iran in particular seems to have been fascinated by the Ottoman experience. In its military reforms, Iran shared many of the Ottoman Empire's goals. Iran, like the Ottoman Empire, conceptualized its military needs in terms of a large multi-functional army, based on mass conscription. Although the later triumphs of European imperialism, in which Iran has been cast as passive victim, have tended to obscure this motive, the Qajar shahs wanted a large modern army not only for defensive but also for offensive warfare. They wished not only to defend themselves against the inexorable pressure from Russia but also to regain lost territory in the Caucasus and to the west in Afghanistan which had been under the rule of their Safavid predecessors in the sixteenth and seventeenth centuries, in this way appropriating some of the religious charisma of the Safavids and legitimizing their own rule.[1] The first and second Qajar shahs, Aqa Muhammad Shah and Fath Ali Shah, struggled for decades to reassert their hegemony against Russian challenges in the eastern Caucasus, especially over Georgia, and creating reformed regiments was a key element in their strategy. Later shahs continued to harbour hopes of using military power to advance their dynastic claims. Muhammad Shah in 1837 and Nasir al-Din Shah in 1856 launched wars to take possession of Herat in western Afghanistan, both attacks frustrated by British diplomatic, military and naval power, and in 1860 Nasir al-Din Shah made an ill-fated attempt to assert his sovereignty over the oasis-town of Merv in Central Asia. It was only towards the end of the century that Nasir al-Din Shah finally abandoned these increasingly unrealistic objectives and Iranian opinion began to reconcile itself, in practice if not always in theory, to the country's existing borders.[2]

For the shahs of Iran in the nineteenth century, the recovery of lost territories through military means was of great significance in terms of ideological legitimization and the consolidation of the dynasty. But military reform was intimately linked to state-building in another, novel sense. The establishment of reformed regiments would enable the shahs to embark on a project in which the existing balance between the state, as expressed in the person of the Shah, and the rest of the political system, as expressed in layers of princes, courtiers, notables, tribal khans and ulama, would be fundamentally altered. It was the centrality of this function to programmes of military reform and, in the Iranian case, its eventual overriding importance, which determined the choice of model to be adopted. There was no evidence that *nizam* troops were superior in warfare to the forces which they were intended to replace. Their great advantage was that they were entirely dependent on and, formally at least, loyal to the Shah, possessing no other allegiance than to the state.

In their efforts to build disciplined regular forces, all the reforming rulers of the early nineteenth-century Middle East faced the same problem: a lack of a professional officer corps.[3] Since the region then possessed no modern educational institutions, let alone military colleges, nor had there yet been any significant effort by local elites to acquire training abroad, Middle Eastern rulers turned directly to European officers, whom they employed for varying lengths of time, under a variety of conditions. The use of such officers, however, whether renegades and adventurers engaged as individuals, or formal missions possessing the sanction of their own governments, was fraught with difficulties. For the ruler and the high officials appointed to oversee reform, European officers were useful both for their professional expertise and, perhaps more importantly, for the prestige and imperial backing which their involvement seemed to lend to programmes of modernization. Any advantage so derived was, however, invariably offset by the resentments which their presence generated among both the elite and the population at large, resentments which arose from the humiliation of seeming to mimic the ways of an enemy deemed culturally and religiously inferior, from anxiety at the loss of sovereignty implied by the presence of foreigners in command of the army, and from the specific hostility of those whose personal positions were directly undermined or threatened. In addition, the ascendancy of foreign officers from any individual country often aggravated opposition from one or all of that country's European rivals as much as it provided diplomatic cover and imperial support.

The account which follows looks at Iran's experience with building a regular army under the leadership of European military missions during the rule of the Qajar dynasty (1797–1925). The Qajar shahs and their ministers and, by the end of the nineteenth century, wider layers of reforming opinion were obsessed with the need to establish regular disciplined military forces and the nineteenth and early twentieth centuries were peppered with attempts to set up a standing army on the European model with the help of foreign officers. In all, Qajar Iran saw three formal French military missions, three British, two Austrian, one 'unofficial' Italian mission, and one Russian, this with the Cossack Brigade, and one Swedish, with the Government Gendarmerie, as well as a miscellany of foreign adventurers and mercenaries employed on an individual basis. Yet the cumulative result of this obsession was to leave Iran in the first decades of the twentieth century burdened by an immense expenditure on the army but militarily greatly weakened, its forces surviving within a maelstrom of political controversy, in conflict with each other and reflecting and exacerbating the struggles taking place within the Iranian political system. It was, paradoxically, only with the advent to power in 1921 of Riza Khan, later the first Pahlavi shah, Riza Shah (1925–41), and his dismissal of all the foreign officers commanding the remaining fragmented military forces, that Iran was finally able to build a national army on the European model.

The narrative below is divided into two parts. The first part examines the efforts made by successive Qajar shahs and their reforming ministers to establish regular *nizam-i jadid* forces and the role played in these efforts by European military missions. It argues that these efforts were not only futile but, in a period when European influence was at its zenith and Middle Eastern countries experiencing unprecedented political, diplomatic and financial aggression, were actually dangerous to Iranian independence and solvency. This part of the account highlights both the self-serving motives of the European powers, always focused on the advancement of their own strategic and diplomatic interests, and Iran's fitful attitude to the missions and their task, an attitude where admiration for Europe was tempered, and sometimes overwhelmed, by mistrust and suspicion, and where reform was essentially configured by the whims of a despotic shah.[4] It charts the process by which the shahs, always eager for new missions, finally lost control of the foreign officers, a process symbolized by the establishment of the Russian military mission with the Cossack Brigade, a unit which functioned practically as a foreign force. It concludes by showing how, partly as a result of the Russian mission's role in defending Tsarist imperial interests, bolstering a weak and reactionary shah and starkly illustrating his dependence on foreign support, the presence and role of foreign military missions became a key signifier for reforming opinion of the actual and potential loss of Iranian sovereignty.

The second part of the account discusses the new context for the politics of military reform under European leadership provided by the constitutional and post-constitutional years. It discusses how the project of army reform, and the wider state-building agenda in which it was embedded, was taken up in the early twentieth century by a new generation of constitutionalist and nationalist reformers. For these circles, the Shah was no longer, if he ever had been, capable of acting as an agent of reform, but was now rather a major impediment to Iran's regeneration. This section describes the struggle by the constitutional authorities and later Iranian governments to rid Iran of the Russian mission and resist the imposition of a British mission, and their parallel struggle to establish a military force, under European officers from a neutral country, which would be loyal to themselves and would enable them to resist the demands of the imperial powers and a puppet shah. It places this struggle within a rapidly changing diplomatic nexus, in which first Britain and Russia together, and after 1917 Britain alone, made unprecedentedly aggressive bids to take control of Iran's armed forces as part of a broader effort to establish an unchallengeable hegemony.

## Part One: The Qajar Shahs and Military Reform

### *The Military Forces of the Early Qajar Shahs*

At the end of the eighteenth century, the military forces of the Qajar rulers resembled those of preceding dynasties, bore strong traces of the Turco–Mongol military tradition which dominated the Middle East, and owed practically nothing to European military science.[5] In peacetime there was no standing army other than the Shah's household establishment.[6] James Morier described Fath Ali Shah in 1809 as having a bodyguard of 12,000 *janbaz*, mainly drawn from Mazandaran and the Qajar tribes, and 3,000 *ghulams*, or slave horsemen.[7] Similar establishments on a smaller scale were maintained by the provincial prince-governors. On the outbreak of war the Shah would assemble his forces by issuing a *farman* (edict) calling on the tribal khans and provincial governors to collect recruits. Such an army would be assembled in the spring and would generally be disbanded on the approach of winter, men joining the colours for one campaign only and then returning to their homes and families. It was largely made up of irregular cavalry, drawn from the nomadic tribes, who constituted the prestigious and effective fighting element, and whose loyalty was guaranteed by the expedient of keeping the chief or his son at court as a hostage. Footsoldiers were taken indiscriminately from the peasantry, the inhabitants of the towns never taking up arms unless in imminent danger. Enlisted men usually reached the place of assembly, designated by royal *farman*, within a relatively short space of time while those who failed to answer the call quickly were severely punished. In 1796, for example, 40 men who had refused to join the army had their eyes put out.

The early Qajar shahs appointed senior military commanders for specific campaigns. Those so appointed were either tribal khans, who officered their own irregular cavalry, or princes of the Qajar tribe, court favourites or provincial governors. These commanders then engaged their own relatives, clients and dependants as subordinate officers. The commander-in-chief of an army was known as the *sardar*, the khans or chiefs of tribal contingents as *sultans*, while chiefs of tribes or governors of provinces might act, when appointed by the Shah, as generals of divisions. Other officers were commanders of 1,000, 500, 100, 50 and 10 men, called *min-bashi*, *pansad-bashi*, *yuz-bashi*, *panjah-bashi* and *dah-bashi*, the nomenclature and organization being of Turco–Mongol origin although now with the occasional use of Persian words. There were no fixed pay-scales or hierarchical command structure, each man negotiating his terms of service individually. The troops carried firearms and also bows, lances, swords and daggers. The only artillery possessed by the early Qajar army was a corps of *zanburaks*, camels with small cannons mounted on a swivel on their pack-saddles.[8] Pay was very low and the troops fought out of the fear of the harsh consequences of disobedience and, as far as the tribal forces were concerned, loyalty to their chiefs and especially the hope of plunder. An ideological dimension was often given to major military campaigns by the declaration of a jihad.

As campaigns were undertaken only during the summer, the troops mostly marched at night, with torches and music. Early Qajar armies were capable, on occasion, of covering large distances quickly. In 1795 Agha Muhammad Khan marched with his cavalry from Tehran to Tbilisi (Tiflis) in 15 days. But the passage of an army was a catastrophe for the local populations. When on the march, the troops lived almost entirely at the expense of the inhabitants of the districts through which they travelled. The army intendants gave receipts for the supplies which the troops took and the value of the supplies was supposed to be deducted from the revenues due from the local population, but the reduction was rarely made, and the districts suffered almost as if they had been occupied by an enemy force. The sudden demands of a large number of troops for food, forage and transport threatened a rural population surviving on subsistence agriculture with a scarcity which might reach famine levels.

In its struggle with Russia in the late eighteenth and early nineteenth centuries, Iran was able to campaign with a considerable degree of effectiveness.[9] The early Qajar shahs were able to assemble large armies. During the first Russo–Iranian war (1804–13) the Iranian forces were several times larger than their Russian enemy in the eastern Caucasus, and European observers commented on the skills of marksmanship and horsemanship displayed by the cavalry. Their approach to fighting was, to European eyes, undisciplined and disorganized, resembling a tribal raid, and success was often dissipated due to the troops abandoning the battle in order to loot. But, by using the tactics of tribal raiding, the Iranians avoided the formal battles which would have favoured disciplined forces, relying primarily on guerrilla raids, picking off small, isolated detachments, harrying enemy communications and so on. With these methods the Iranian forces were able to deny victory to Russia for nine years, despite the latter's immense superiority in resources.[10]

## Early Qajar Military Reform: French and British Missions

The first attempts to introduce European concepts of military organization to Iran took place at the beginning of the seventeenth century when Shah Abbas, taking advice from the Sherley brothers, raised a large force of infantry on the European model armed with muskets. Yet, under Shah Abbas, battles continued to be little other than large-scale cavalry engagements. In the eighteenth century Nadir Shah, having concluded that the Europeans' victories over the Ottomans were due to the discipline and order with which they fought, studied foreign methods, began to organize an artillery, and entrusted the direction and command of newly raised infantry to European, mostly French, officers. Nonetheless, he too continued to depend principally on his cavalry, the new infantry regiments playing little part in fighting his wars. Nadir Shah's army collapsed after his death and by the late eighteenth century none of the several Iranian experiments with European methods had achieved any enduring effect.

The first Qajar ruler, Agha Muhammad Khan, with the military forces he was able to muster, successfully established Qajar power throughout Iran and temporarily drove the forces of the advancing Russian Empire back beyond Tbilisi, reasserting Iranian supremacy over the kingdom of Georgia. On his accession Fath Ali Shah (1797–1834) was also able to command sufficient military strength to defeat his internal rivals and secure his position as shah. However, in 1803 Russia invaded and annexed Georgia, considered by Iran as a vassal state, and continued to push southwards. Russia's inexorable pressure forced Fath Ali Shah and especially his son, the crown prince and governor of Azerbaijan, Abbas Mirza, to embark on a major military reorganization in the hope of increasing Iran's defensive capacity.[11] Abbas Mirza's initiative was the first in a long series of attempts by Qajar rulers to set up a standing army on the European model with the help of missions of foreign officers.[12]

Fath Ali Shah and Abbas Mirza made the first systematic attempt in Iran at military reform along modern European lines, the political context being provided by the first Russo–Iranian war.[13] Both the Shah and his son were convinced that the introduction of regiments of European-style troops would enable them to break the deadlock in the war with Russia and win victory, regaining lost territory in the Caucasus and thus helping to legitimize their dynasty. In the early nineteenth century the province of Azerbaijan with its capital, Tabriz, constituted the front line against Russian expansion, and was the focus of Iran's military efforts. Its military condition was also important for another reason. Tabriz was, by tradition, the seat of the crown prince, and it was essential that the heir apparent possess sufficient armed strength to impose acceptance of his claim to the throne against the inevitable challenges on the death of the shah.

Abbas Mirza, like his contemporaries in the Middle East and North Africa, had come to the conclusion that the survival of both his dynasty and his country depended on matching European military strength by imitating European military organization.[14] Abbas Mirza seems to have been fascinated by European military science and James Morier quoted him as saying that he believed it was in vain to fight the Russians without soldiers like theirs, and that their artillery could only be opposed by artillery.[15] Deeply impressed by the steps already taken on this path by the Ottoman Empire under Sultan Selim III, Abbas Mirza began the construction in Azerbaijan of his own version of the disciplined infantry and artillery regiments known in the Ottoman Empire as the *nizam-i jadid*. Like Sultan Selim and his successors, Abbas Mirza also intended that a Europeanized army would reduce and finally eliminate his dependence on tribal and provincial chiefs and notables for the raising of military forces.

Abbas Mirza faced two major problems of personnel and manpower. He lacked officers with any knowledge of European methods and he had no regularized method of enlisting recruits. The solutions he found to these problems, the employment of foreign officers and the introduction of a rudimentary form of conscription, determined the character of the Iranian reform effort for the rest of the century.[16]

At first Abbas Mirza, like the Ottomans before him, employed renegade Christian officers to raise and drill troops, drawing on the large number of Russian deserters in Tabriz.[17] Even before Abbas Mirza's arrival in Tabriz, a number of Russian deserters who had taken refuge there had brought with them ideas of European tactics. The then governor had made them officers and with his encouragement they had formed and drilled a few battalions. Abbas Mirza also initially made use of a renegade Russian to teach drilling but these initial efforts encountered great hostility from both the troops and the general population who disliked any imitation of European, and particularly Russian, methods. He was, for example, obliged to arrange for the troops and their Russian instructor to use a private courtyard so they would not be exposed to public ridicule. In order to overcome opposition to European methods, the Prince himself adopted military uniform and took instruction in drilling from a Russian, ordering his nobles to follow his example and learn to handle a musket. Abbas Mirza succeeded in teaching a few of his men to march and drill but it was the arrival of the first French military mission which provided him with the professional officers and NCOs he believed necessary for the further development of his plans.[18]

Fath Ali Shah, impressed, as he wrote to Napoleon, by French victories in the East, had begun to seek Western assistance in his war against Russia.[19] In 1807 the first French mission to Iran under General Gardane arrived in Tehran. Gardane and his staff came under the terms of the Treaty of Finkenstein by which Iran had entered into an alliance with Napoleonic France against Britain and Russia.[20] An offshoot of the struggle then taking place in Europe, Gardane's mission was to organize the Shah's forces along European lines as part of a comprehensive diplomatic and military agreement between Iran and France. By the terms of the treaty France guaranteed Iran's territorial integrity, provided for the Iranian recovery of Georgia and promised to supply Iran with arms, officers and artificers, while Iran committed itself to severing relations with and declaring war on Britain, and promising free passage to a French expedition to India. On their arrival at Tehran General Gardane and several other officers were made khans and received Iranian military decorations. Two officers, Captains Fabvier and Reboul, were sent to Isfahan to build a cannon foundry, and two, Captains Verdier and Lamy, with three NCOs and an interpreter, went to Abbas Mirza in Tabriz as military instructors. Other officers began travelling through the country with the object of gathering intelligence and surveying the districts and routes for a French march on India.

The French officers were in Tabriz for about 14 months. Captain Verdier began raising and training three regiments of infantry, between 4,000 and 6,000 men. These troops, known as *sarbaz*, were armed with muskets made in Tabriz on the French model, and clothed in uniforms also notionally on the French model but with a typical Iranian black sheepskin hat. Captain Lamy directed the construction of barracks, an arsenal, a powder mill, cannon foundry and fortifications, and also formed a kind of polytechnic school in the camp for training officer-engineers, Abbas Mirza himself being one of the students. Work was begun on organizing the artillery, which was commanded by Tahmuras Khan, a Christian nobleman of the family of the last Prince of Georgia. Abbas Mirza also still had in his camp many Russian deserters, now formed into a unit of their own, and they were also put under the orders of Captain Verdier.[21] Alongside these modern units, it was estimated that the Prince also possessed 22,000 cavalry and 12,000 unreformed footsoldiers.

The French mission, however, soon fell victim to the changing European context. Little more than two months after the conclusion of the Treaty of Finkenstein, European alignments were reversed when Napoleon and the Tsar signed the Treaty of Tilsit and French influence in Iran began to collapse. Fath Ali Shah agreed to receive a British mission and summarily expelled the French, Gardane's mission having already been severely undermined by a degree of opposition from Iranian officials in Tabriz and Tehran and by the hostility of the British at the Shah's court.

Although the British had originally rebuffed Fath Ali Shah's overtures, Gardane's arrival in Iran had galvanized them into sending missions of their own, and their efforts to displace the French were successful. The Preliminary Treaty of Friendship and Alliance, concluded in 1809, provided for a British subsidy to pay for British military stores, equipment and officers and men, in exchange for the Shah's breaking with the French. Between 1810 and 1813 members of a British military mission, officers, NCOs and men, arrived in Iran from both India and Britain. By 1813 the mission numbered over 50. In addition to the British officers and men, the mission also included a number of Indian sepoys, who were to assist with the training of the Iranian troops.[22] In Tabriz the British mission continued the work begun by the French of raising and drilling troops, beginning with an artillery unit. British muskets and sabres replaced equipment supplied earlier by the French, and an attempt was made to modify uniforms to resemble a nominally British style. In reality, however, the only European element of the uniform was the jacket introduced by the French. Other than this, uniform remained essentially similar to local Iranian costume, including wide trousers or pantaloons and the sheepskin hat. Officers apparently continued to regard their uniform as simply another version of formal dress. The British did oblige the *sarbaz* to shave, the right to wear beards being confined to officers, although the ordinary soldiers preserved their customary way of wearing their hair, a shaved head with a top-knot and side-curls.[23]

In addition to the convulsions of European diplomacy, Abbas Mirza faced other problems. Iran's revenues were insufficient for its expensive wars, and the revenues of Azerbaijan in particular were quite unequal to the demands of Abbas Mirza's agenda. In 1810 the British began paying a subsidy to Abbas Mirza, which went primarily to defray the cost of the new regiments, but training, equipping and paying these *sarbaz* was so expensive that overall, even with the British subsidy, his financial problems worsened. The reforms also encountered opposition on their own account. The population in general and occasionally the *sarbaz* themselves disliked the European appearance of the new regiments, while some of the ulama declared that the presence of infidels was harmful and the adoption of their methods betrayed the example of the Prophet. These doubts were quickly exploited by Abbas Mirza's political enemies but his supporters also mobilized religious support where they could, obtaining opinions that the reforms were in fact a return to early Islamic practice.

By 1812 Abbas Mirza possessed a European-trained army of about 13,000 infantry, cavalry and artillery, and he and the Shah believed that victory in the war with Russia was within reach. Although the fledgling regiments had achieved some minor victories in 1810, Abbas Mirza's hope of exploiting Russian weakness during Napoleon's invasion of 1812 was disappointed and the war finally ended after the Iranian *nizam* regiments suffered a series of military disasters. Four British officers and 12 NCOs actually accompanied the Iranian troops into battle and, although the Iranians snatched one victory when they routed a Russian force at Sultanabad near the river Aras in February 1812, the campaign ended in complete defeat at the battle of Aslanduz in October during which one British officer, Charles Christie, was killed.

Abbas Mirza now also faced the loss of the British mission. The alliance formed between Britain and Russia in 1812–13 caused the British government's commitment to Iran to weaken and the defeat of Napoleon at Waterloo in 1815 led to a further British loss of interest in Iran. By the end of 1815 the British mission had been withdrawn, although a small group of officers and NCOs had been allowed to stay on condition that they took no part in operations against countries (meaning Russia) with whom Britain was at peace. The remaining British officers gradually left the Iranian service after 1819, only Captain Isaac Hart continuing as commander of Abbas Mirza's bodyguard.

Both the Gardane mission and the British mission had come to Iran as a result of European conflicts and rivalries and in order to further their own political, diplomatic and military objectives. As their needs and requirements and the European context changed, so their interest in Iran waxed and waned, their military missions being merely tools of political expedience and easily dispensed with. Naturally both Britain and France did everything possible to undermine the work of the other's mission. Abbas Mirza and the Shah had done their best to manoeuvre within, and to exploit, the shifting European alignments. Although Iran was powerless over the wider context which determined the level and duration of European interest, the initiative for both the French and the British missions had clearly come from the Shah and Abbas Mirza, for whom foreign assistance with military reform was one of the major benefits of Iran's international alliances. The missions were not forced on a reluctant or conservative Iran by a forward-looking Europe. On the contrary, it was the Shah who insisted on the military missions in the face of a European consensus that, in Iran's existing circumstances, such reforms were unlikely to be beneficial, even the officers of the military missions themselves expressing scepticism regarding the extent to which Iran was really benefiting from these experiments with European models and the employment of European officers.

To European observers, Iran's military strength had always resided in its irregular cavalry, furnished by the tribal khans, which had proved itself so effective in lightning raids and defensive skirmishing, while the new *nizam* troops inspired little confidence. The remarks of a Russian staff officer, Captain N. N. Muraviev, are typical. In 1817 he is reported to have declared, 'This unfortunate infantry, of which they speak in Europe with respect, was invented to our own benefit. After losing their Asian agility and quickness, the sarbaz have not however acquired European characteristics and are a base and dirty force, badly dressed and created as victims for our grenadiers. They cannot even handle the English muskets which they have been given.'[24] Echoes of Muraviev's conclusions were to be heard throughout the century. Henry Rawlinson, for example, a member of the 1833 British military mission and later British minister at Tehran, was candid about British motives, writing in 1875 that Britain had assisted Abbas Mirza to build 'a so-called regular army' solely in order to prise Iran away from the French alliance. He frankly admitted that the *nizam* forces of Iran had been 'from the epoch of their first creation contemptible', and that all they ever had in common with the regular armies of Europe was drill and exercise while their expense was rapidly impoverishing the country. Rawlinson acutely concluded that although Iran's defensive military capacity had been progressively weakened by the introduction of European-style regiments, the Shah's power had been significantly augmented.[25]

During the 1820s, after the departure of the British, no new official military missions arrived in Iran, but Abbas Mirza continued to engage European officers on an individual basis. The end of the Napoleonic wars had left many ex-officers in Europe without employment or career prospects, and many travelled far afield in search of positions. A number of such officers, of various nationalities, French, Italian, and Spanish, eventually arrived in Iran and found employment both with Abbas Mirza and with Muhammad Ali Mirza, the prince-governor of Kirmanshah. Although these foreign officers were responsible for drilling troops, they apparently spent much of their time in quarrelling among themselves and duelling with each other, and European observers were scathing about their military capabilities and their low social class.

Many soldiers of fortune were to continue to find employment in Iran throughout the nineteenth century, their numbers diminishing only towards the end of the century with the stabilization of the Russian mission with the Cossack Brigade. Most had little impact on Iran's military development, but a few played significant roles. Among these were Isidore Borowsky, a Polish officer who became a general in Iranian service, took part in several campaigns, and finally met his death during the Iranian assault on Herat in 1837–8; a French officer named Semino who had been an NCO under Napoleon and had fought under Ypsilantis in Greece before coming to Iran where he served for 27 years, reaching the rank of lieutenant-general, and taking part in the campaigns of Abbas Mirza in 1830–3 and in the siege of Herat in 1837–8; and, towards the latter part of the century, an Italian, Major Maletta, formerly of the Egyptian Gendarmerie, who became an infantry instructor in Iran.

As well as searching for foreign officers, Abbas Mirza also tried to introduce changes in methods by which the *nizam* regiments were recruited, both to provide himself with a more predictable supply of manpower and to make himself independent of the local elite, devising the *bunichah* system, a primitive form of conscription whereby liability for military service was tied to revenue assessments in the countryside. Some sort of conscription system may have been suggested to him by his French officers, as it seems to have been suggested to Muhammad Ali in Egypt, but Abbas Mirza's system, indirect and collective, and with an implicit reliance on landowners, bears stronger traces of Russian influence and the model of Peter the Great, and may have owed something to the Russian deserters still present in Abbas Mirza's regiments.[26]

Nonetheless, when war with Russia again flared up in 1826, it again ended in a disastrous defeat, with the Russians actually entering Tabriz in November 1827, and concluding with the Treaty of Turkomanchay in 1828.

Undeterred by yet another military failure, Abbas Mirza continued to maintain the *nizam* forces of Azerbaijan which, by 1831, consisted of about 12,000 infantry, 1,200 horse artillery, and one regiment of lancers, recruited under the *bunichah* system. They were divided into ten regiments of Iranian troops and two of Russians. The Russian regiments were composed of deserters, mainly from the Russian army in Georgia. They were commanded by a former NCO from Nizhni-Novgorod, now promoted to *sartip* (general), Samson Yakovlevich Makintsev, known as Samson Khan. The deserter units, known as the *bahaduran*, were, in contrast to other troops, well and regularly paid and were apparently good soldiers, fighting well for their new masters, the authorities placing particular trust in them when facing internal rebellion or religious tumult. These *nizam* forces were sufficient to enable Abbas Mirza to suppress several revolts in the early 1830s, in central Iran and among Kurdish and Turkoman khans in the north-east.

Meanwhile, Abbas Mirza continued his search for foreign officers, making renewed appeals to Britain. The British reaction was again determined entirely by its own strategic needs. London and especially Calcutta now harboured growing concern over a possible Russian threat to India and its own loss of influence at Tehran and accordingly in 1833 sent a second

British military mission, recruited in India. This mission consisted of eight officers, 14 sergeants and an assistant apothecary under the command of Colonel Passmore of the East India Company Bengal Native Infantry, and counted among its number several officers who were later to play important roles in Anglo–Iranian diplomacy, Justin Sheil, later British minister in Tehran 1844–51, Francis Farrant, chargé d'affaires in 1848, and Henry Rawlinson, British minister 1859–60.

However, before the mission could begin its work, the domestic Iranian political context was suddenly changed by the deaths of both Abbas Mirza and the monarch, Fath Ali Shah. The mission thus found itself faced with the immediate task of ensuring the smooth succession of a new shah, Muhammad Shah (1834–48), and averting any potential crisis by suppressing rival claimants. British officers then began raising and drilling troops.

Despite their role in installing the new Shah, the British officers immediately began to encounter difficulties. The political context was becoming less and less favourable, Russian influence at Tehran was growing and the new Shah was determined to renew his claim to Herat against inevitable British opposition. The British officers received little support from either the new Shah or the Iranian government. They were also deeply resented by the Iranian *nizam* officers and constant friction arose from the struggle, sometimes subterranean, sometimes overt, over the extent and scope of British functions and responsibilities. The Iranian authorities insisted on regarding the British officers purely as instructors and refused them the control they desired over pay, rations and promotions while the *nizam* officers hated their interference and frequently disregarded their recommendations altogether.[27] The British found their work obstructed at every level as a result of the combination of political opposition to British strategy, wounded national pride and professional jealousy which their presence engendered. The British mission suffered further from intrigues both by the military officers of other nationalities in the Shah's service and by the diplomatic representatives of rival powers.[28] This second British experiment finally broke down completely after the political and diplomatic rupture occasioned by Muhammad Shah's attack on Herat in 1837. In 1838 Britain, breaking off relations with Iran, ordered all its officers in the Shah's service to quit the country.

Despite his experience with the British mission, Muhammad Shah continued to seek foreign assistance with his desultory efforts at military reform. Since relations with Britain were strained and Russia was too distrusted to be allowed the education and command of the army, the Shah turned to France. The French agreed to supply weapons and army instructors to replace the British and in September 1839 a mission led by Edouard Comte de Sercey left Paris, reaching Tabriz in January 1840.[29] However, the treasury was empty and the Shah demoralized by the Herat failure. After its arrival the French mission was treated mostly with indifference by the Iranian government. It was opposed by both Britain and Russia while the Shah made no effort of any sort on the officers' behalf. The officers were all subalterns or NCOs, some of them old enough to have served with Napoleon, and they were all much mocked by their fellow Europeans for giving themselves senior ranks and fancy uniforms. The mission remained in Iran less than four years, the officers apparently spending most of their time trying unsuccessfully to extract their pay from the authorities.[30] By the time of Muhammad Shah's death, the blue tunic of the French had again replaced the English red-coat, but little else had changed.

## Military Reform under Nasir al-Din Shah

A new phase in efforts to reform the army opened with the accession of Nasir al-Din Shah (1848–96).[31] His able prime minister, Mirza Taqi Khan Amir Kabir, impressed by the progress of the Ottoman reform movement of the *tanzimat*, immediately launched a comprehensive programme of reform, including a series of measures aimed at modernizing the army. He established the *Dar al-Funun*, an elite military and technical college, and developed the *bunichah* system of conscription devised by Abbas Mirza and originally intended only for Azerbaijan into a relatively complex measure, theoretically applicable across the country and to the entire population. He reorganized the existing *nizam* units and ordered the formation of 16 new regiments, including one of local Christians to which were added some officers and men of the old regiments of Russian deserters.

To assist him in these efforts, especially in providing tuition at the *Dar al-Funun*, Amir Kabir again turned to Europe and political considerations again determined the choice of the nation. Placing little trust in either the

British, the French or the Russians, Amir Kabir cast his net wider and, impressed by the Austrian victories over Sardinia in 1848–9, approached that country for help.[32] An Austrian mission was recruited but before it reached Tehran the political context had turned against it with Amir Kabir's fall from power.[33] The new prime minister, Aqa Khan Nuri, was unsympathetic to the reforms of his predecessor, especially the college, and to the engagement of Europeans. Despite their weakened position, the Austrians began work at the beginning of 1852, exercising recruits in the parade ground and instructing officers at the *Dar al-Funun*.

In addition to its difficulties with the Iranian government, the Austrian mission was further compromised by the arrival in Tehran of a group of Italian officers, refugees from various Italian states, who had taken an active part in the revolutionary movements of 1848–9, and who were now appointed instructors of the infantry. Relations between the Austrian and Italian officers in Iran were from the beginning extremely bad as the Italian revolutions of 1848 had been suppressed by the Austrian army. The Austrian officers, frustrated and demoralized, began to leave. By 1853 the Italians had acquired sole charge of the infantry, leaving the Austrians the artillery and the cavalry. The Austrian mission, hampered at every turn, made almost no progress while the impact of the Italians, who themselves had very little military experience, only short periods of service in revolutionary corps of volunteers, was equally small.[34]

In 1856 Nasir al-Din Shah launched another disastrous attack on Herat. After the collapse of the Herat expedition under British military and diplomatic pressure, the Shah again began to toy with the idea of Western-style reforms and again sought military advisors from Europe. Neither the Italians nor the Austrians had been a success, relations with Britain had been soured by the Herat war, and Russia was still considered more a source of danger than assistance, so the Shah again turned to France. He sought advice from Napoleon III who encouraged him in both his military reforms and his regional ambitions, Iran being useful to France as an obstacle to Ottoman influence and British ambitions, and a third French mission arrived in October 1858.[35] The mission was led by Commandant Brongniart, all its members were professional soldiers and all had served in the French colonial army in Algiers, Napoleon III having specifically recommended the combination of regular and irregular forces raised by the

French in Algeria as a model for Iran. The mission was to raise and train troops and to teach at the *Dar al-Funun*. It survived until 1867 but finally quit the country without any real achievements except at the arsenal where some progress was made under the French superintendent. Control of the infantry had remained with the Italians, with whom the French officers had clashed repeatedly, and in any case the treasury was empty after the Herat war. The Shah then again turned to Britain for assistance. Britain, however, in the grip of the policy of 'masterly inactivity', declined the Shah's request.[36] In 1870 the request was renewed but again declined.

After the departure of the third French mission, three Italians remained the principal European military advisors to the Shah. All three rose to the rank of general, and one, Enrico Andreini, who had been a lieutenant of the Tuscan volunteers in 1848, became Instructor-in-Chief and remained in service until his death in 1894.[37] During these years a miscellany of foreign adventurers and mercenaries was also to be found occupying military appointments at various ranks in Iran.

In the 1870s the reforming prime minister and minister of war, Mirza Husayn Khan, Mushir al-Dawlah launched another major effort at military reorganization, again, as in Amir Kabir's time, in deliberate imitation of the Ottoman *tanzimat* and again with the help of foreign military missions. As part of a comprehensive programme of modernization, Mushir al-Dawlah drew up extensive plans for the reorganization of the army, including measures to regulate the army budget, enforce conscription and improve military education.[38]

Like his predecessors, Mushir al-Dawlah turned to Europe for military assistance and, in 1878, the Shah, while travelling in Europe, asked both the Austrian Emperor and the Russian Tsar for the loan of instructors. In January 1879 the second Austrian mission duly arrived in Tehran. Very soon after the arrival of the Austrians, the first Russian mission came to Iran under Colonel Domantovich and began the organization of a regular cavalry in the form of the Iranian Cossack Brigade.[39]

Although the Austrian officers had been unpleasantly surprised, on their arrival in Tehran, to find the charge of the cavalry had been given to Russians, nonetheless the mission began its work.[40] It recruited about 5,000 men in western Iran, formed them into seven regiments and one battery of field artillery, and armed them with Austrian Werndl rifles, this force becoming known as the Austrian corps. But before long the Austrian mission began to attract hostility from the pro-Russian faction at court which was eager to promote the Russian military mission, funds began to be irregularly supplied or not paid at all, and the corps began to disintegrate. As well as being extremely expensive, the Austrian corps attracted much jealousy from officers in older military units, and there was also friction among the Austrian officers themselves. Although 1,200 men with a battery of six Euchatius guns did see service in Azerbaijan, where they were sent together with other troops to quell the Kurdish revolts of 1880–1, the Austrian officers were not retained after the end of their contracts and all, with the exception of the band master, left Iran at the end of 1881. The Austrian corps fell to pieces, its men being drafted into other regiments while many of its officers figured for years on the Army List without actually being in service.

### The Qajar Shahs and the European Missions: A Balance-Sheet

By the end of the century Iran's 'reformed' military forces, with the partial exception of the Cossack Brigade, still adhered essentially to the conceptions introduced in 1812 by Abbas Mirza and the first French and British missions. Throughout the century, under the combined impetus of internal reform efforts and the succession of European missions, infantry and artillery regiments had been raised which theoretically conformed to European models in terms of appearance, internal organization, methods of recruitment and training, and structures of command. In reality, however, despite repeated efforts, under a wide variety of European instruction, these efforts had not succeeded in providing Iran with a Europeanized army but the entire project had rather experienced a slow, inexorable collapse. Abbas Mirza's plan to raise regiments capable of recovering lost territories and defending the country against attack had become a simple desire to have troops suitably modern in appearance with which to provide the Shah with the trappings and accoutrements of power and statehood. Nasir al-Din Shah's army, although occasionally used against refractory tribes, was essentially a mirage.

The role of the *nizam* troops as essentially for show, to furnish a 'modern' backdrop for the Shah's power, was most clearly illustrated by the

Tehran garrison. Here the troops' only training, under the supervision of Iranian officers themselves trained by the Austrian mission, was in simple parade-ground manoeuvres to enable them to take part in a march-past before the Shah. Before a review officers would provide specially selected infantry regiments with good rifles and new uniforms. After their performance, the men marched straight back to barracks and returned the rifles and uniforms to store. For most of the time, the good Austrian Werndl rifles were stored in the magazines, where they were 'stacked up like firewood', and the troops were armed, if armed at all, with ancient percussion guns.[41] It was the same with uniform. Great attention had been paid over the previous decades to elaborating an appropriate uniform for officers and men of the *nizam* regiments. Different colours had been allotted to different branches of the Qajar army, often depending on the tradition of the particular foreign officers then employed. By 1900 the infantry wore red, the artillery blue and the cavalry green. The official uniform consisted of, in the appropriate colour: the Iranian lambskin hat known as a *kulah*, tunic, pantaloons, boots or shoes and sometimes a greatcoat. However, in practice most of the money supplied for uniforms was pocketed by senior officers and officials, and clothing was very irregularly supplied and usually made of poor-quality material. Typically, within a month of his arrival in garrison, the recruit's uniform was in rags. However, whenever the Shah was due to review the army, the troops were issued with a new set of uniform for the occasion.

On paper, the numbers of *nizam* troops had risen inexorably throughout the century, each reform wave leading to the raising of more regiments. While the French mission was at Tabriz in 1808 Abbas Mirza possessed between 4,000 and 6,000 *nizam* troops. By the late 1830s the infantry alone had risen to 50 regiments containing 54,850 officers and men. By 1900 the *nizam* infantry officially numbered 78,500 men, divided into 80 regiments. The regulation strength of a regiment, in theory, ranged from 800 to 1,000 men, with 38 officers. In reality, however, most of these troops were either absent from their regiments or entirely fictitious, the muster rolls having been falsified so that the pay of the imaginary soldiers might be retained by senior officers. Although 'given time and a fairly liberal expenditure of money', commanding officers seemed able, by rough and ready methods, to raise regiments to something approaching full strength, yet money was in ever shorter supply, Iran was falling into indebtedness, and in any case troops so raised were completely lacking in training and discipline.[42]

This relentless rise in paper regiments constituted an enormous drain on Iran's resources. Whatever the situation on the ground, the authorities invariably met in full the cost of pay for the complement of officers and men stipulated on the muster rolls, for their uniforms, weapons, and so on. This merely served to introduce a new method of redistributing resources among the elite. In fact, the possibility of acquiring an appointment in one of the *nizam* regiments, with their fixed and unfailingly honoured budgets, had opened up a novel and extremely profitable avenue of investment. Commands were bought and sold at high prices, frequently purely as an investment by civilians. Indeed so lucrative was command of a *nizam* regiment that tribal chiefs often tried to acquire such a position rather than retaining their irregular cavalry. Having bought his regiment, the colonel was then able to recoup his investment and make a profit in a number of ways, by retaining the wages of soldiers who were on the official strength but not actually maintained, by selling commissions to his subordinate officers and exemptions from service and discharges to the private soldier, and by profiteering out of rations and pay.[43]

Prior to Abbas Mirza's reforms, men were enlisted for specific military campaigns and paid only as long as they were with the colours. The introduction of a standing army based on Abbas Mirza's *bunichah* system represented an enormous increase in state expenditure and this rudimentary form of conscription became a cross which the Iranian treasury was forced to bear. Yet, although its financial impact was considerable, in practice the new method of recruitment differed little from the old. The *bunichah* system clearly defined liability for military service on the basis of a calculation of the number of ploughs required to keep village land under cultivation, one man per plough deemed liable. The authorities, however, totally lacking in modern administrative and bureaucratic resources, especially a census, fixed the responsibility for enforcing the system onto the village, not the individual. Thus the selection of recruits was actually made by the village elders and local landowners as the need arose and as they saw fit, much as it had been done prior to the reform.[44] The *bunichah* system was never enforced systematically and soldiers continued to be taken from traditional recruiting grounds, especially Azerbaijan. Even in Azerbaijan the application of the system became increasingly haphazard as the century progressed, the original tax assessment according to which liability was assessed remaining unrevised and becoming increasingly anomalous. The *bunichah* system never succeeded in overcoming tribal and clan-based recruiting, some *nizam* regiments being composed entirely of recruits from the same tribe, or the preponderance of the Turkish-speaking element. It failed to provide the authorities with a predictable supply of trained manpower and did nothing to inculcate a spirit of patriotism and loyalty to the state, an objective which it did not, in any case, espouse. Offering recruits nothing in the way of education or possibilities of advancement, or even regular pay, service in the army remained intensely unpopular with the peasantry.

The introduction by Abbas Mirza of a system of fixed rates of pay had also led to a catastrophic deterioration in the conditions endured by the *nizam* troops. Prior to this reform, terms of service had been negotiated individually and on an *ad hoc* basis, and therefore roughly reflected the cost of living and the market value of labour. In 1810, Abbas Mirza laid down fixed rates of pay for officers and men, these rates remaining more or less unchanged throughout the century. But in 1810 a private soldier's pay, in silver coin (*tuman*), was sufficient for buying food to keep a family for a month. During the course of the century the *tuman* consistently depreciated until its purchasing power had decreased by about 80 per cent.[45] By 1900 both officers and men were actually receiving only one-fifth of the pay which Abbas Mirza's original scheme intended they should have. Not only was pay worth in real terms about one-fifth of its original value, but even this pittance often remained unpaid for months or even years. With much of their pay withheld, and with daily food alone costing more than their ration allowances, soldiers were allowed, encouraged and even obliged to find other work as labourers, small shopkeepers and also often as money-lenders, in this way providing for themselves and, owing to a system of percentages, also for their officers.

The deterioration in the conditions under which the *nizam* troops lived led not only to garrisons becoming shells, empty while the troops earned their bread in the bazaars, but also to more serious breaches of discipline. Although during the nineteenth century Iran had acquired various formal codes of military discipline, in practice commanders punished their men entirely at their own discretion and soldiers guilty of individual transgressions might expect brutal treatment. However, collective disobedience, even mutiny, might occasionally be met with negotiation and concessions from the authorities, who lacked the means to suppress bodies of armed men. Soldiers, their arrears of pay becoming intolerable and finding themselves unable to make ends meet, often resorted to mass protests, taking *bast* in mosques and elsewhere, sacking food shops, refusing to attend parades and intimidating senior officers. The outcome of each protest varied according to circumstance but, although ringleaders were often victimized, the troops were often successful in obtaining at least a portion of what they were due.[46]

By the end of the century neither Iranian reformers nor the European military missions had succeeded in creating a professional officer corps for the *nizam* regiments.[47] Although Amir Kabir had founded the *Dar al-Funun* with the intention of educating a professional officer corps, its graduates were largely prevented from finding employment in the army owing to the persistent opposition of those who had bought their appointments. The authorities observed no formal regulations for the appointment and promotion of officers. These were made rather on the basis of favouritism and purchase.

Nor had Abbas Mirza's creation of a European-style graded hierarchy produced an effective command structure. Before Abbas Mirza's reforms, officers had been known simply by appellations which indicated the number of men under their command, as chiefs of 10, 50, 100, 1,000 and 10,000 men, and modern ranks with their hierarchical significance were unknown. For his *nizam* regiments, Abbas Mirza abolished the old nomenclature and introduced new ranks with titles which were the exact equivalents of European usage, *na'ib* (lieutenant), *sultan* (captain), *yavar* (major), *sarhang* (colonel) and *sartip* (general). During the course of the century, however, this system degenerated. Regulations governing hierarchy disintegrated and the designations of rank ceased to imply any fixed military responsibility or even any connection with the army. The number of officers proliferated, and the army budget paid salaries and pensions to many people who had acquired military rank by patronage or purchase simply in order to benefit financially. The confusion was aggravated by a new habit among the civilian elite, fostered by Nasir al-Din Shah, of wearing military uniform and sporting elaborate military decorations.

In operational terms, the irregular cavalry was still the most effective fighting element in Iran's military forces and it had remained untouched by the European military missions and government efforts at reform. It continued to be organized exclusively on a tribal basis, the men serving under their own chiefs and supplying their own horses and weapons. In return for keeping available for service a specified complement of men, the khans received payment in the form of a tax deduction, a dispensation which was of great financial value and which also symbolically diminished their acknowledgement of the central government's authority. The khans' military role significantly enhanced not only their own financial resources but also their personal authority within the tribal structures. In general terms, the state's continued reliance on such forces buttressed the power of the khans and negated efforts by the reforming officials to reduce their autonomy and make them more dependent upon and responsive to the central government, frustrating and even reversing a wider agenda of centralization.

The irregular cavalry was divided into 69 regiments or squadrons of varying strength, which were known by their places of recruitment or by that of their tribe. The internal organization of the regiments was based upon the old Turco–Mongol system of divisions of tens, fifties and hundreds. On mobilization, the cavalry possessed an estimated potential strength of 37,591.[48] Although of some effectiveness in campaigns against their tribal enemies and as a threat to subdue urban populations, the use of the irregular cavalry was fraught with difficulties. They were usually mobilized only for specific operations and rarely agreed to serve outside their own districts. They were motivated entirely by the prospect of plunder and when on campaign were often themselves the cause of serious disorder.

## Nasir al-Din Shah and the Russian Military Mission

By the late nineteenth century little had been achieved in creating a Europeanized army, either in appearance or reality. The reformed regiments' main significance was in providing a conduit through which state money might be channelled into the pockets of elite families and in indulging the Shah's fondness for what amounted to military fancy-dress. Nonetheless, in the 1870s, one step had been taken which was to have permanent and momentous consequences for the country, when the Shah asked the Russian Tsar for officers to help with the organization of a regular cavalry.

The Russian military mission with the Iranian Cossack Brigade was a new departure in Iran's experiments with foreign officers. It was to be the longest-lasting of all the foreign military missions to Qajar Iran, remaining until removed by the British just prior to the coup of 1921, a total of 41 years. It was also to prove itself to be of a different type to previous missions. It was openly an instrument of Russian foreign policy and was completely beyond Iranian control. By giving Iran the Cossack Brigade, Russia only partially succeeded in tying the Shah to itself but was completely successful in establishing a visible and apparently permanent affront to Iranian sovereignty.

Russia attached great importance to its mission in Iran, having been systematically excluded from providing military assistance by British opposition and Iranian suspicion since the beginning of the century. From the beginning of its life the Russian mission was able to rely on the energetic support of the Russian authorities, including the Viceroy of the Caucasus, the General Staff at Tiflis, the Russian foreign ministry and the Tsar himself.

The Russian officers encountered many of the problems familiar from the experience of previous missions, including opposition from resentful officials and courtiers, hostility from the diplomatic representatives of other Powers, social and professional tensions within the new corps, and the Iranian government's perpetual failure to provide sufficient funds. Nonetheless, the Brigade was able to sustain itself and grow, mainly as a result of unrelenting Russian pressure on the Iranian government. Russia supplied most of the arms and munitions for the Brigade free, often in the form of a present from the Tsar to the Shah. When recruiting, the Russian officers relied on volunteers and were able to offer financial incentives (the pay of a private Cossack soldier was more than double that of the *nizam* troops) and the benefits of Russian diplomatic immunity. Russia provided cash for the Brigade if the Iranian government found itself without funds, and in fact assumed directly the full cost of the force after the outbreak of war in 1914. Russia also consistently attempted to use favourable political circumstances to press for an increase in the strength of the Brigade, both its Iranian element and the Russian officers, and for an extension of their influence, especially within the 'Russian zone' established under the Anglo–Russian Convention of 1907.[49]

Perhaps the most novel aspect of the Russian military mission, in comparison with previous foreign missions, was its relationship to the Iranian government. The Russian Commandant abandoned any pretence of subordination to Iranian authorities, whether the Shah or the government, and operated more or less independently according to his interpretation of Russian interests. For the Russian officers of the Brigade, furthermore, the advance of Russian interests was indissolubly linked to the defence of Qajar absolutism. By the late nineteenth century the monarchy had become dependent on the Brigade. In 1896, after the assassination of Nasir al-Din Shah, it was the Russian Cossack officers and their men who ensured the accession of the new shah, Muzaffar al-Din (1896–1907).

The novel position of the Brigade and its commandant was reflected in a new degree of hostility from Iranian opinion and from the very beginning of its life the Russian military mission and the Brigade itself aroused great resentment both within official circles and among a broader nationalist and constitutionalist milieu which felt the Russian mission had been imposed on Iran as a result of pressure on a weak and despotic ruler.[50] After the Constitutional Revolution, the Brigade was drawn ever deeper into domestic political conflicts, not as an arm of the state but rather as a partisan of the Shah in his struggle with the constitutionalists.

## Part Two: The Constitutional Revolution and Military Reform

### Constitutional Government and the Cossack Brigade

In 1905–6 the Constitutional Revolution transformed the political and ideological contexts within which debates about military reform and foreign assistance took place. For constitutionalist opinion and the new National Assembly (Majlis), the key issue was no longer how to strengthen the monarchy but, on the contrary, how to limit the absolutism of the Shah. How were the new authorities to enforce their own power, defend themselves against their internal and external enemies, assert state power over all the national territory, and halt the disintegration that threatened Iran's existence as an independent state? The solution they found to this question was to reactivate the efforts towards state-building and specifically the construction of a modern army which had dominated nineteenth-century efforts at reform. But now these efforts had to take place against the backdrop of opposition from the Shah and the military forces on which he now depended, the Russian officers with the Cossack Brigade.

The constitutional movement developed two strategies. Firstly, the new authorities tried to establish their own effective control over the existing military forces, most significantly the Russian-officered Cossack Brigade. In this they failed. Their second strategy succeeded when in 1910 they established the first modern, national military force, the Government Gendarmerie.

In 1905–6 the Cossack Brigade was weak and demoralized. Popular hostility was intense and many of the Iranian officers and men sympathetic to the Revolution. The Russian mission was in disarray, and the military authorities in Russia preoccupied with defeat at the hands of Japan and the suppression of the 1905 revolution. Indeed, despite the Brigade's royalist and pro-Russian traditions, in 1905–6 the Commandant had been unable to provide the Shah with a coercive instrument to use against the revolutionaries. Its paralysis and the absence of other effective army units meant that the Revolution was able to achieve its objectives largely peacefully. After the Revolution, the Russians lost control completely and the Iranian officers formed a military council to take control of the Brigade.

Nonetheless, the constitutional regime was unable to grasp this opportunity to rid itself of the hated Russian military mission. The Russian authorities regained the initiative and, at what was a critical moment for the Brigade, both internally and vis-à-vis the wider political situation, a new commandant arrived. In September 1906, one month after Muzaffar al-Din Shah signed the proclamation convening a Constituent National Assembly, Colonel Vladimir Platonovich Liakhov took over the Brigade. He was determined to reassert Russian control and succeeded in abolishing the military council and in weeding out Iranian officers opposed to Russian influence. In this he encountered considerable difficulty as, besides resistance within the Brigade itself, the leading ulama, government ministers and the Majlis all continued to make efforts to curb his power.

The constitutional regime soon paid the price for allowing Russian officers to remain in control of the Brigade. In June 1908 Liakhov and the Cossacks under his command made a decisive intervention into the domestic political conflict, bombarded and suppressed the Majlis, and overthrew the constitutional government on the orders of the new shah, Muhammad Ali (1907–9), and his royalist and Russian supporters. Liakhov himself became military governor of Tehran but his ascendancy was brief. After the recapture of the capital by constitutionalist armies in 1909, the Russian officers and the Brigade were again eclipsed, to re-emerge again only after the Russian government in 1911 forced a second closure of the Majlis. In the context of the general defeat suffered by Iranian constitutionalism in 1911, the Brigade was once more consolidated into an instrument of royalism and foreign control.

## The Swedish Military Mission and the Government Gendarmerie

By the beginning of the twentieth century all the broad schemes of military modernization under missions of foreign officers had ended in failure while the establishment of the Cossack Brigade under the Russian military mission had created a new problem of loss of authority without solving the old problem of a lack of effective military strength. By the constitutional period, the issue of sovereignty had become paramount and the state-building agenda had passed from the Shah and his high ministers to a new generation representing new social forces. Iranian constitutionalists argued strongly in favour of the creation of a force which could defend Iran's borders and independence, maintain internal security, collect taxes, and uphold the authority of the constitutional authorities. In government pronouncements, Majlis debates, programmes of political parties and the press, the need for a strong national army was constantly reiterated.

Much of the hatred for the Cossack Brigade stemmed from its role as an arm of the powerful imperial presence on Iran's northern border. Yet, although horrified at the effect of the presence of Russian Cossack officers at the heart of the Iranian state, the constitutionalists could not slough off the old fascination with foreign military missions. Now, however, it was argued that officers should come from neutral countries who had no imperial ambitions in the region and be firmly under the control not of a shah compromised by his dependence on foreign support, but of the institutions of constitutional government, the Majlis and the ministries of war and the interior. In 1910 the government embarked on yet another experiment with foreign officers. As part of a general programme of reform, the Majlis voted for the establishment of the Government Gendarmerie and the following May approved a Swedish military mission to lead the force, Sweden being an acceptable source of foreign officers as it had a tradition of neutrality and was considered a minor power.[51] A mission of three Swedish officers, led by Colonel H. O. Hjalmarson, began its work at the end of 1911.[52] By 1914 seven regiments, all volunteers, had been established, in Tehran and throughout southern, south-eastern and south-western Iran.[53]

Just as the Cossack Brigade survived as a result of persistent Russian backing, so the Government Gendarmerie in its early years benefited enormously from British financial and diplomatic support. Although still reluctant to become directly involved in officering an Iranian military force, Britain hoped that, by offering its patronage to the Swedish officers, it might use the Gendarmerie to protect its growing interests in southern Iran and to counter-balance the Russian Cossack Brigade in the capital.[54] However, the danger for Iran inherent in the existence of military forces sponsored by essentially rival powers soon became apparent. The Gendarmerie was prevented from establishing itself throughout the country as Russia opposed its presence in its zone of influence, wishing to make that area the exclusive preserve of the Cossack Brigade.

Nonetheless, by 1914 the Gendarmerie represented the first real success in Iranian efforts to build a regular military force and had come to embody the state-building trend which had begun with Abbas Mirza and was now represented by the constitutional movement. The Swedish mission had been engaged by the Majlis, it offered no challenge to Iranian sovereignty, but on the contrary drew its legitimacy from its identification with the constitutional authorities. The Gendarmerie possessed a novel ideological coherence and dynamism and, unlike previous Iranian military formations, including the Cossack Brigade, was able to employ the motifs of nationalism to attract recruits and ensure their loyalty. It was, in particular, able to assemble a professional officer cadre. By the second decade of the twentieth century, the Swedish mission was able to draw on a new type of officer, with ideological commitment and occasionally with professional military training obtained abroad, often in Ottoman military institutions.[55]

## New British Missions and a Bid for Supremacy

The years of World War I saw a further transformation in the domestic and the international contexts within which the foreign missions in Iran operated.[56] The Constitutional Revolution had failed to provide Iran with the means to escape from the coils of an exhausted Qajar political order and the war brought increased imperialist intervention, both political and military, with Iran's continued independent existence threatened by national disintegration, partition, or the imposition of direct European control.

The Gendarmerie had derived significant impetus in its early years from the political and financial support of Britain but, with the outbreak of war and the concomitant political polarization, the force rejected its imperial patron and identified itself unequivocally with Iranian nationalism. The Swedish command was effectively eclipsed, freeing the Iranian officer corps to assume a leading role in the military and political conflicts of the war and postwar years.[57] Iranian Gendarmes turned their guns on their British patrons, arresting the entire British colony in Shiraz and driving Allied nationals out of much of southern and western Iran. Between 1915 and 1917 Gendarme officers offered military leadership to nationalist forces battling against foreign intervention and control and a docile and collaborating shah.

In the first years of the war the Cossack Brigade became more than ever a Russian tool while Britain, shaken by its treatment at the hands of Gendarme officers whom it had armed and financed, itself began planning to raise and officer a force directly, over which its control would be certain. Iran's strategic significance and the helplessness of its government proved an irresistible temptation to Russia and Britain. Allies in war, at first Britain and Russia acted together. In 1915 the two powers settled their differences over western Asia with the Constantinople Agreement which, although primarily concerned with Russian demands for control over the Straits into the Black Sea, also gave Britain the 'neutral zone' in Iran, and recognized a free hand for both powers in their respective zones. In 1916, with Russian armies in occupation of northern Iran and within striking distance of Tehran, they used their control of elements within the Iranian government to draw up the Sipahsalar Agreement which provided for the expansion of the Cossack Brigade to a Division and the establishment of a British-officered force, the South Persia Rifles (SPR).[58] Through the expanded Cossack Division and the SPR, Russia and Britain each intended to consolidate its power in its respective zone of influence, Russia in the north and Britain in the south.

The Agreement provoked profound opposition in Iran, where it was widely perceived as accelerating the partition of the country, and the government, while too weak and dependent on Allied support to repudiate it outright, refused any formal acceptance. Although the Agreement thus possessed no legal standing, the Russians proceeded immediately to expand Cossack numbers while Britain raised the SPR, a force whose legitimacy was always contested and which was to be a thorn in the side of Iranian nationalists throughout its existence.

In 1917 the October Revolution held out hope to the Iranian government that it could simultaneously rid itself of both the old Russian and the new British military missions. Popular hatred of the Cossack Brigade, now a Division, had reached a crescendo since the outbreak of the war and the new Soviet government's official recall of the Russian officers was greeted with widespread enthusiasm. The government was, however, too weak to take advantage of the moment and insist that the Russian officers themselves and the remaining imperial power accept the new situation and hand over control to Iranian officers.[59] On the contrary, the British seized the chance to adopt the Cossacks and refashion them into a device for advancing not Russian but British interests. In early 1918 Britain assumed political and financial sponsorship of the Division, and welcomed the seizure of command by a White Russian officer, Colonel Vsevelod Dimitrievich Starroselsky. Starroselsky's coup against the existing Cossack command, which was in fact preparing to hand over the Division to Iranian control, enraged the Iranian government, highlighting the independence of the Division and the practical irrelevance to it of any legal authority.

Britain had initially hoped to use the Division in support of its own strategic political and military plans in Iran and the Caucasus, but the fierce White Russian nationalism of Starroselsky and his efforts to carve out an independent political role for himself, and the burgeoning anti-British nationalism of the Iranian Cossacks, soon clashed with the new plans formulated by Lord Curzon for the establishment of unimpeded British control over Iran through the Anglo–Iranian Agreement of 1919. Britain began to see the Russian officers as an obstacle and even a menace to its policy, especially to its intention to create a unified army under British officers, and in October 1920 the Cossack camp at Qazvin was placed under British guns and the Russian officers summarily removed from their commands by General Sir Edmund Ironside, ending four decades of the Russian military mission in Iran.[60] Ironside placed a few British officers in temporary command and, in 1921, used the Brigade in an intervention in domestic politics more dramatic even than the coup of 1908.

## The South Persia Rifles

Meanwhile, the last episode in Qajar Iran's long experiment with foreign military missions was taking place with the establishment in 1916 of the British-officered South Persia Rifles. The SPR was intended to replace the Gendarmerie, which the British now regarded as incorrigibly hostile, and to restore and maintain order in southern Iran for the remainder of the war, but also to be available as a political instrument to secure British interests in postwar Iran.[61]

The SPR was established by Colonel Sir Percy Sykes under the Sipahsalar Agreement of 1916 as a *quid pro quo* for Russia's expansion of the Cossack Brigade to a Division.[62] The odium which the SPR attracted was a mirror-image for the British of the resentment engendered by the Russian military mission, and the linking of the two forces in the Sipahsalar Agreement gave the Iranian government the opportunity to oppose and demand the removal of both contingents of foreign officers.

The Iranian government was still wedded to the idea of a single national army under Iranian control. They wanted Allied help to finance it, and were prepared to accept that it be officered by neutrals, as long as such officers recognized Iranian sovereignty, but were resolutely opposed to another force along the lines of the Cossack Brigade. For Iranian opinion, the establishment of yet another such corps rendered the eventual creation of a national army even more remote and was one more confirmation of the *de facto* partition of the country into a Russian-dominated north and a British south. The government, although without the strength to reject outright the British mission to the SPR, yet temporized and procrastinated, refusing and resisting acceptance of the Sipahsalar Agreement.

Iranian reluctance to endorse Sykes's mission turned the SPR into the hub of a wider conflict between Iran and Britain in the years after World War I. The force took on a symbolic importance for both countries. For Iran the SPR was a visible reminder of a loss of sovereignty and the creeping dismemberment of the country, while the British saw the success of Sykes and his officers as vital to imperial prestige and as a way of cutting through the chaos resulting from war, new and growing nationalist opposition, and dangerous experiments with neutral officers.

In the early stages of the SPR's life, most of its commissioned ranks and many of its men were former Gendarmes and Sykes and his British officers were unable to eradicate their deeply ingrained nationalist and anti-British sentiments.[63] However, it seems that the main difficulty facing the British in their task of constructing the SPR resulted from the vacillating attitude of the central government and its underlying hostility. Ultimately Sykes found it impossible to create a coherent corps and to ensure the loyalty of officers and men in the face of the passive, and sometimes active, opposition of the government, and the bitter enmity of nationalist opinion.[64] After the Iranian government in March 1918 publicly declared its non-recognition of the SPR and denounced it as a foreign force, Sykes' work began rapidly to unravel. Within a few months the SPR was fighting for its survival against enemies from both within its own ranks and without. Two serious mutinies shook the Fars regiment while the force found itself overwhelmed by a tribal insurgency led by the anti-British Qashqai tribal confederation.

The SPR survived its political, military and organizational difficulties solely as a result of immense British pressure on both the central government and the provincial authorities in the south. During these years the numerical strength of the force varied considerably. Between 1916 and 1921 the Iranian element averaged around 6,000. By 1920 the two brigades, in Fars and Kirman, broke down into 47 British officers, 256 British and Indian NCOs, 190 Iranian officers and 5,400 Iranian ranks. The cost of the force was borne entirely by the British and Indian governments. Envisaged as a crucial component of the national army proposed by the Anglo–Iranian Military Commission, created under the terms of the Anglo–Iranian Agreement of 1919, the SPR never shook off its reputation as a tool of foreign influence. British determination to impose acceptance of the SPR on Iran poisoned relations with a succession of Iranian cabinets down to and even beyond the coup of 1921 and although officers and men of the force were accepted into Riza Khan's new army, they remained the object of suspicion and none achieved high rank.

## The Anglo–Iranian Military Commission

Despite the chequered history of the SPR, in 1919 Britain put forward a much more grandiose scheme for the modernization of the army under British officers. After the war, the foreign secretary Lord Curzon prevailed in his view, against the opposition of the government of India, that Britain should consolidate its new predominance in Iran, resulting from the withdrawal of Russia after the Bolshevik Revolution, through a long-term agreement with pro-British elements in the country. The mechanism adopted for this consolidation was the Anglo–Iranian Agreement of 1919. Under the terms of this Agreement, an Anglo–Iranian military commission was set up to devise plans for a complete overhaul and reorganization of Iran's military forces.[65] The mixed commission of British and Iranian officers assembled in January 1920 and at the beginning of April presented a report recommending the merging of Iran's existing forces and the construction of a uniform national force under British officers.[66] In practical terms, the commission envisaged rebuilding the Iranian army around a core constituted by the SPR.

The scheme devised by the commission bore a strong similarity to earlier plans for military modernization within a framework of comprehensive administrative reform but the role it prescribed for British officers was now, in the new political and ideological climate, an intolerable affront to national dignity. In the rapidly changing circumstances of postwar Iran, both the Agreement itself and the proposals of the military commission caused outrage among nationalist opinion and specifically among the Iranian officers and men of both the Gendarmerie and the Cossack Division.[67]

During the constitutional period the Iranian government had continued to advance schemes for creating a national army while the Sipahsalar Agreement had provided nationalist opinion with the opportunity to link the fate of the Russian mission to the Cossack Division with the British officers of the SPR and to demand the substitution of both with officers of a third and neutral power.[68] The Allies and, after 1917, the British alone had repeatedly discouraged the idea. With the Anglo–Iranian military commission, it seemed that Iran was at last to obtain a uniform national army, but without the sovereignty which had been at the heart of the state-building agenda.

By 1919 it was impossible for any Iranian government to accept the Anglo–Iranian Agreement which in any case required a now politically impossible Majlis ratification. The British refusal to relinquish the Agreement produced a protracted political crisis in Tehran and eventually led to their abandonment of any strategy of working through the existing authorities and their resort to the desperate expedient of the sponsorship of a coup.[69] The coup was carried out by the Cossacks in Qazvin led by Riza Khan in partnership with the civilian politician, Sayyid Ziya al-Din Tabatabai, and was facilitated by the British officers then in nominal command of the Cossack camp, including those of the Anglo–Iranian military commission who were intended to comprise the leadership of the proposed new army.

In 1921 the Cossack Brigade, still under foreign control, was the instrument of a decisive political intervention which would later overthrow the Qajar dynasty, which it had been established to protect, and establish another, the Pahlavi, which would shape modern Iran and endure till 1979. The British had intended the coup to install in power their protégé, Sayyid Ziya, who was committed to introducing British financial and military advisors. For the British involved in its planning, the coup was envisaged as an alternative route to the achievement of the main objectives of the 1919 Agreement. In reality, however, the coup marked a turning point in British power in Iran. Its capacity to intervene directly in the Iranian political system collapsed, the confidence and assertiveness of the new regime being symbolized by its determination to refuse foreign officers any role in the building of a national army.

In the months after the coup, a struggle for power rapidly developed between Sayyid Ziya and Riza Khan. This burgeoning political and personal conflict came to a head over Sayyid Ziya's determination to give operational command to the British officers who were still unofficially on active service with the Cossacks. This Riza Khan declared to be equivalent to selling to foreigners 'the soul of the nation', which was the army.[70] Forcing Sayyid Ziya into exile, Riza Khan peremptorily dismissed the British officers serving with the Cossacks. The British officers with the SPR soon followed them, as did the remaining Swedes. With all the foreign officers and the remnants of the foreign missions gone, Riza Khan was finally able to embark on the task of building a unified national army, on the European model, but free from foreign control.

## Conclusion

In assessing the consequences of the long Qajar dalliance with foreign military missions, two broad issues arise: the first concerns the role played by the foreign officers themselves, the second, the general impact of the missions on Iran's construction of a modern army.

Explanations for the failure of military reform in nineteenth century Iran have usually focused on the overall weakness of Qajar reform efforts, on the only fitful interest of the shahs and the unpredictable rise and fall of their reforming ministers, on internal opposition, on poor governance and maladministration. Yet it seems clear that the foreign military missions, far from being disinterested and professional, were themselves haphazard and chaotic, often lacked the consistent backing of their governments, were riven by internal conflicts, among the officers and very frequently between the officers and their own diplomatic representatives, and entirely contingent upon the European diplomatic context. The missions aggravated and galvanized European rivalries and aroused intense professional resentment and political hostility among Iranians.

Until the arrival of the Russian mission in 1879, none of the foreign missions had remained long in Iran, either disintegrating through Iranian ambivalence or collapsing as a result of international complications. Not only were they too short-lived to make any real progress but the countries from which the missions were sought constantly changed, as Iran tried to navigate through the complexities of great power diplomacy and avoid unwelcome political entanglements. With each new mission, weapons, methods of training and tactics and uniforms changed accordingly, creating confusion and even havoc, troops engaging on operations while armed with a variety of weapons requiring different types of spare parts and ammunition. Occasionally missions from different European countries were in Iran at the same time, leading to political and professional tensions. The Austrians and Italians imported their conflict from Europe, and relations between the second Austrian and the Russian mission were tense as a result of rivalries in the Balkans. A much more serious danger from the presence of rival foreign missions arose in the twentieth century. Iranian fears of the partition of their country between the British and the Russian Empires, sharpened by the Anglo–Russian Convention of 1907, were given further substance as the Russian-officered Cossack Brigade and the Swedish Gendarmerie were confined to different 'zones' of the country, adding a military reality to diplomatic spheres of influence.

Much historical writing about Qajar efforts at state-building has been dominated by a 'catastrophist' perspective which has encouraged a view of all nineteenth-century reform as futile and hopeless, leading only to a deepening crisis. Certainly the serial efforts to use foreign military missions to produce an Iranian army which exactly resembled the armies from which the European officers were themselves drawn, whether British, French, Austrian or any other nationality, failed, as did the comprehensive schemes for reform within which these efforts were embedded. It may even be argued further that the establishment of the *nizam* regiments actually contributed to Iran's deteriorating military and financial situation. Before Abbas Mirza's reforms, Iran relied for defence and internal security largely on tribal irregulars who made few active demands on the treasury, khans being recompensed by an accounting device, by deductions in the revenues they owed. By contrast, the maintenance of vast numbers of regular troops, most of whom had little or no real existence but the cost of whom was always met in full, the pay of foreign officers themselves and the purchase of weapons from abroad, amounted to a crippling expense. It was indeed an expense which increased throughout the century as ever more regiments were raised, each with large numbers of salaried but otherwise inactive Iranian officers, and ever more foreign missions arrived, even though Iran's financial position deteriorated as it became integrated into the global economy. Rather than the *nizam* regiments dragging Iran towards a wider modernization, the regiments themselves became assimilated to the decaying Qajar order, the conditions of officers and men, far from being maintained at the level prescribed by Abbas Mirza at the time of the Napoleonic wars, worsening as the century progressed. By the end of the nineteenth century Iran's military forces were much weaker vis-à-vis European armies than they had been in the time of Abbas Mirza.

Yet there is another dimension to the history of Qajar military reform. Two foreign missions, although very different in character and context, were successful in producing military forces which were to have a defining impact on Iran's history in the twentieth century, the Government Gendarmerie and the Cossack Division. Both forces carved out an existence in isolation from any wider attempt at modernization. Both were financed without any radical restructuring of domestic taxation, the bulk of their cost borne by one or other foreign power, both were armed by the largesse of Britain and Russia, both sidestepped any use of the unwieldy and inefficient *bunichah* system of recruitment, remaining small and enlisting mostly volunteers, and both relied on diplomatic support to face down their domestic critics and enemies.

The Gendarmerie constituted the most successful in the Qajar period's attempts to build a modern army with the help of foreign officers. In the 1920s the Gendarmerie provided Riza Khan with a human resource, the military expertise and experience of the Gendarme officer corps, vital to the construction of the new army. The Cossack officers for their part provided him with a bedrock of political loyalty on which he secured not just the new army but also his dynasty. Crucially, however, although the officer corps of both forces were incubated by foreign missions, it was only after the marginalization or removal of these missions that the Gendarmes and Cossacks were freed to assume a national political role.

There was in fact a fundamental conflict at the heart of the relationship between Iran and the foreign military missions. All the various Iranian individuals and groups who embraced the concept of military-led modernization, first the shahs and their reforming ministers, then constitutionalist and nationalist political circles, hoped to build an army on the European model in order to defend Iran against Europe. This was not an objective that was shared by any of the foreign military missions, with the partial exception of the Swedish mission established under constitutionalist auspices. The major imperial powers, especially Britain, Russia and France, engaged in the game of army reform in order to augment their own influence over Iran and its government, and in order to deny the field to their European enemies. Their degree of commitment was determined by the imperial context and their missions were intended to further their own political, diplomatic and military objectives, were, in fact, merely another card in the 'Great Game'. Far from enabling Iran to assert its sovereignty with greater strength, the missions were a device to increase European hegemony and Iran's dependence. This was symbolized by the way in which the troops were armed. At the beginning of the nineteenth century, Iran's military forces possessed weapons which were of good quality and produced locally.[71] During the course of the century Iran began what was to become a chronic reliance on the purchase of weaponry in Europe, a reliance which endured throughout the Qajar era and re-emerged under the second Pahlavi Shah, which became an enormous drain on national resources, and which made the army's very existence contingent upon foreign industries and governments.

The conflict between European and Iranian objectives found expression in the perpetual struggle for control which afflicted every foreign mission. The foreign officers constantly complained that they were treated as instructors only, lacking wider powers and at the mercy of the Iranian authorities while the latter, in thrall to the notion of scientific methods of organization and warfare but fearful of the consequences of deeper imperial involvement, alternately invited and resisted the European presence. The Russian military mission finally cut the Gordian knot, gave up any pretence of deferring to Iranian control or even supervision and operated entirely independently.

Iran's experience with the Cossack Brigade, in the last quarter of the nineteenth century, revealed starkly the dangers of foreign missions. By this time, Iran had not only failed to strengthen itself against European encroachment but also, after decades of modernization schemes, had become relatively much weaker, in economic as well as military terms, and ever more vulnerable. Since the early nineteenth century various European powers had involved themselves sporadically and unsuccessfully in Iran's attempts to build a modern army. None of the missions had survived the vagaries of European rivalries and Iranian ambiguity. The Russian military mission of 1879 was a turning point. After its arrival, Iran found itself with a regular cavalry force, but one which was permanently lost to Iranian control and which was, in 1908, to overthrow the institutions of constitutional government on the orders of a Russian officer. During the years of the Russian mission's presence, and indeed partly because of the character of that presence, Iranian attitudes towards foreign military missions were transformed. From actively seeking the help of such missions, Iran began a long struggle to resist their imposition and to have removed those who remained.

Iran's struggle to rid itself of the Russian military mission was to endure until 1920, and was only to be achieved then by British power in pursuit of British goals. However, in the two decades before the 1921 coup, not only did Iran face the unrelenting determination of Russia to retain its mission, but also faced a newly aggressive approach from Britain. For much of the nineteenth century, Britain's interest in Iran's attempts at army reform had been desultory, periods of activity sparked off by a desire to deny the French or the Russians any advantage, and never lasting longer than the specific episodes of imperial rivalry themselves. During the constitutional period, however, burgeoning British interests in the Persian Gulf and southern Iran, especially its interests in oil, concentrated attention on security and defence. Britain now repeatedly offered, and finally threatened, that if Tehran could not maintain order in the south, Britain would itself raise and officer a force. With the example of the Cossack Brigade before its eyes, Britain, at its imperial zenith, embarked on a deeper and more complex involvement in Iran's military modernization. This involvement, however, coincided with the birth of modern nationalism in Iran and made the British determination to guide and control Iran's military forces a point of intense conflict. Britain first sponsored the Gendarmerie, which it hoped would act as a counterweight to the Cossack Brigade. After this catastrophic experiment, Britain lost patience with neutral officers. During World War I, British and Russian determination to impose their own officers increased, as did Iranian reluctance. In 1916 Britain and Russia imposed the Sipahsalar Agreement on a helpless government, providing for a substantial increase in the number of Russians serving with the Iranian Cossacks, and for the establishment of a British military mission. The SPR was established in a deliberate British effort to wrest control of southern Iran from the nationalists and the Gendarmes, and was seen by Iranian opinion not as an instrument for the realization of national aspirations but of their frustration. After the 1917 revolution removed the

Russian imperial presence, Britain, in a bid to establish its sole hegemony over Iran, first adopted the Cossack Division, then sponsored a broader scheme to build a national army led by British officers as part of the Anglo–Iranian Agreement of 1919. The British insistence on imposing its officers and Iranian resistance culminated in a protracted political crisis over the Anglo–Iranian Agreement. The presence of a British military mission charged with reorganizing, training and officering the Iranian army was a pivotal element in the Agreement and caused deep resentment, contributing materially to its eventual rejection.

For much of the nineteenth century, the shah and the reforming elite had seen foreign assistance with army reform as essential, indeed they had no other perspective than simply to copy European models in dress and drill in the hope that European military strength would follow by some still mysterious process. As the century drew to a close attitudes began to change. The foreign missions had always aroused a degree of resentment, religious disquiet mingling with political distrust among both elite and popular classes. Now, however, the growth of modern nationalism and a clearer understanding of the mechanisms of European tutelage, coupled with the actual experience of the Russian military mission with the Cossack Brigade, made it impossible for an emerging Iranian public opinion to tolerate Russian and British officers in command of the army. In this new climate, the Iranian political class lost its appetite for foreign military missions which were now clearly understood to be a harbinger of more general political tutelage. But by now, Britain and Russia were as determined to impose their officers on Iran as Iranian nationalists were to refuse them.

In the nineteenth century the Qajar shahs and their ministers had been free to invite foreign officers as they wished. However, in addition to the unacknowledged contradiction between the motives of Iran and the agenda of the foreign missions, there was another conflict at the heart of the reforming project. The Iranian state was never an abstraction, but an embodiment of particular social forces. Military modernization was couched in terms of improving the state's ability to defend the country against foreign aggression but an equally important objective of army reform was to strengthen the monarchy in order to enable it to impose its will on other social groups within the country which were, either actually or potentially, contending for power. Until the late nineteenth century, the state was in practice identified with the shah and the dynasty and the foreign missions were in Iran in the service of the shah, a position highlighted by their role in safeguarding the dynasty by enforcing acceptance of the succession of Muhammad Shah in 1834 and Muzaffar al-Din Shah in 1896. But support for the shah inevitably involved suppressing his enemies. In the nineteenth century this might mean, for example, action against rebel princes who disputed the succession. The foreign officers, further, inevitably became entangled in domestic power struggles taking place between factions at court, each faction possessing its own position to defend, its own orientation towards one or other imperial power, and with a pro- or anti-reform inclination. In the twentieth century, foreign military missions became drawn into a new and much wider battle between the monarchy and Iranian nationalism. By the constitutional period, the shah had come to be held responsible not for the strengthening of the state but rather with its weakening, and identified with the loss of sovereignty and the spread of foreign influence, a phenomenon perfectly illustrated by his reliance on the Cossack Brigade. State-building opinion now defined progress in terms of limiting royal despotism and resented accordingly foreign attempts, through military missions as well as in other ways, to shore up the shah's power and frustrate their own ambitions.

The reaction against the Qajar experience with foreign military missions led to a resolute refusal by the soldier Riza Khan to countenance such experiments. It was, ironically, only after the removal of the missions that Iran was able to succeed in building a modern army. For the 20 years between 1921 and 1941 no foreign military missions came to Iran.[72] In fact, of all the rulers of Iran since the early nineteenth century down to the Revolution of 1979, Riza Shah was unique in resisting the temptation to allow foreigners control of the army.

After Riza Shah's abdication in 1941 the struggle between the monarchy, now buttressed by the immediate arrival of new foreign military missions, and the nationalist opposition, determined on their removal, resumed in earnest. Within a greatly weakened political context, the new power in Iran, the US, was once again able to insist on missions of its officers serving in the country.[73] As in the late Qajar period, so now, it was the shah, Muhammad Riza (1941–79) who accepted this imposition against nationalist opinion, and suffered accordingly. Once again, as in the years before 1921, the foreign military missions, although intended to further imperial objectives, in fact provoked intense Iranian resentment, constituting a factor of major significance in bringing about another dramatic political rupture, the revolution of 1979.

# CHAPTER 3

# Building and Rebuilding Afghanistan's Army
## An Historical Perspective

After the invasion of Afghanistan in 2001 and the overthrow of the Taliban,[1] the US and its NATO partners became drawn in to the project of rebuilding the Afghan state, and in particular to the creation of a modern army capable of supporting that state. The creation of such an army was, from the beginning, critical to the success of the long-term US strategy: the establishment of a stable pro-Western democracy in Afghanistan which would be both willing and able to deny a safe haven to America's enemies. From 2006, as the insurgency intensified and the security situation deteriorated, the effort to raise, train and equip an Afghan army assumed even more urgent dimensions, coming to occupy a pivotal position in any future exit strategy.[2]

Yet the possible conflict between the state-building and the democratic elements of this project typically evident in much historical experience across the region was apparently not taken into account. The US and its Western allies quickly discovered that, while destroying a regime is relatively straightforward, building a state is complex and uncertain of success. Recreating a modern army in Afghanistan, in particular, proved to be more difficult than at first envisaged. The US and its allies became committed to training and financing the Afghan military on an unprecedented scale, its projected strength being more than twice as large as any previous Afghan army. What was more, they hoped to accomplish this in the midst of a raging civil war, of a kind which might be expected to place strains on the most cohesive and well-integrated of military forces.

Since 2002 the Afghan military has absorbed massive and ever-increasing quantities of cash, while its Western mentors have encountered a range of problems familiar from the past, including problems of recruit-ment and troop retention, of force loyalty, cohesion and discipline, and of training and education. Furthermore, so intractable have these problems proved to be that the Afghan government and its Western advisors have seemed increasingly inclined to resort to a solution also familiar from the past: an ever-greater reliance on local, non-state elements, tribal groups, militias and warlords, a reliance which is inevitably at the expense of the state-building project itself, although this is rarely acknowledged.[3]

The post-2001 Western-sponsored project of establishing an Afghan National Army (ANA), as part of a wider programme of institution-building, is by no means the first such attempt to reconstruct the Afghan army following its collapse under the impact of foreign invasion and civil war. These efforts have all been fraught with difficulty. All have unques-tioningly adopted a Western model for which neither the fiscal, human nor bureaucratic resources were readily available while Afghan state-building, including army reform, was always obliged to contend with difficult polit-ical, regional and economic environments. Nonetheless, despite periodic ruptures, as the twentieth century progressed Afghanistan began slowly to overcome this unfavourable context. Not only did the Afghan state solidify and expand, but wider developments, especially in the field of education, began to transform Afghan society. Yet, by the 1970s the very successes achieved in state and army-building were producing tensions which culmi-nated in a military coup by the pro-Soviet People's Democratic Party of Afghanistan (PDPA) in 1978. The decision by the US to arm and finance the opponents of the PDPA, as part of a global strategy of confronting the USSR, was catastrophic for Afghanistan. It disrupted a state-building tradi-tion which stretched back to the beginning of the nineteenth century and destroyed the social forces which had provided the engine for decades of reform. The US is still grappling with the political and military conse-quences of this decision which led to the creation of a 'failed state' in Afghanistan, the 2001 invasion, and its own reluctant involvement in the attempt to put the Afghan state back together again.

The history of modern Afghanistan may be understood as resembling a repeated cycle of failed state-building. The cycle begins when a programme of centralization and modernization, at the heart of which is the crea-tion of a standing army on the Western model, is initiated by the state. As the programme is implemented, it arouses increasingly strong opposition from elements, typically with a rural power-base, hostile to aspects of the proposed change or its general implications. Neighbouring states take the opportunity presented by domestic fracturing to meddle with the object of protecting or furthering their own interests and strategic ambitions. Finally the state, still relatively weak in relation to its combined domestic and foreign enemies, succumbs and the state-building project collapses, to be followed by a period of violent political conflict and anarchy. This cycle does not end with merely a return to the status quo ante. On the contrary, the strength of autonomous and centrifugal forces grows as a result of every failed state-building effort. After their successful overthrow of King Amanullah in 1929, for example, the military capacity of the tribes was significantly strengthened by their capture of the army's weapons, including its heavy weapons, while their political power and their cultural and ideological attraction was enhanced by their victory and its impact on public opinion.[4] Similarly, of the most profound future significance was the immense strengthening, in arms, money and political and diplomatic support, of tribal and rural militias which took place as a result of their conflict with the PDPA and the USSR in the 1980s. Moribund tribal and militia power was once again revitalized by the strategy adopted by the US to overthrow the Taliban after the attacks of September 2001.

Throughout the nineteenth and twentieth, and into the twenty-first, centuries, this cycle of conflict between state-builders and their opponents has typically collapsed into a war between urban and rural Afghanistan. State-building emerged as and remained essentially an urban phenomenon encompassing both the political right and the left: the monarchy, elite modernizers such as prime minister and later president Muhammad Daud, the leftist PDPA, and even elements of the Islamist movement. Ranged against this trend were the various components of rural society, tribal chiefs and their followers, sometimes settled, sometimes nomadic, landowning notables, village elders and a dependent peasantry, and religious figures including mullahs, sayyids and sufi *pirs*.[5] To these 'traditional' rural groups was added, as society was transformed in the 1980s under the impact of war, a new category, that of militia commander or warlord, the 'new khans'.[6]

Afghanistan's cycle of failed state-building began in the nineteenth century, the efforts of a succession of Afghan amirs to strengthen the

authority of the state being lost in a welter of domestic antagonism intertwined with foreign invasion. It continued in the 1920s with the radical King
Amanullah, overwhelmed by a tribal uprising coupled with discreet British
hostility, found a cautious champion in Prime Minister Muhammad Daud,
and reached its apogee in the years 1979–92 with the protracted struggle
between the urban-based and Soviet-backed PDPA and the predominantly
rural mujahideen supported by the US. After the collapse of the regime in
1992 the Afghan state disintegrated altogether. Although the Taliban, themselves essentially of rural origin, provided a kind of rudimentary domestic
order, they were uninterested in the development of modern institutions,
including an army. Since 2001 the government of Hamid Karzai and its
Western sponsors have once more begun to think in terms of the building
of a modern state, but in a context where the power of tribal and militia
leaders, forces still essentially antithetical to this project, has again been
greatly enhanced and legitimized and even embedded within national institutions, including the army itself.[7]

The comprehensive failure or frustration of Afghan state-building
efforts contrasts starkly with the relative success of its regional neighbours,
who began in scarcely more favourable circumstances. At the beginning of
the nineteenth century, the social and political arrangements in the territory which became Afghanistan did not differ greatly from those pertaining
in, for example, neighbouring Iran. There too the population was overwhelmingly rural, consisting of pastoral nomads and semi-settled or settled
peasants, and was also predominantly tribal. Poverty and illiteracy were
universal among the rural population. The significant power in the countryside was not the state but the tribal khans and the landowners. Towns
and cities were small and vulnerable to wider political conflicts, while
rulers, often basing themselves on tribal support, periodically seized power
through violence and exercised authority through minimal state institutions. These rulers possessed no standing armies but relied for coercive
strength on tribal contingents or the retainers of great lords. Nonetheless,
despite these inauspicious beginnings, as the nineteenth and then the twentieth centuries advanced, Iran and an array of other Middle East states,
although forming in very different contexts, consolidated themselves,
establishing institutions, including military institutions, which reached
over their populations and throughout their national territories.[8] By the

twentieth century the Afghan state alone had been unable permanently to alter the balance between its own power and that of the kaleidoscopic social groups, especially the tribes, over whom it claimed authority.

## Nineteenth-Century Military Reform: Amirs and Imperialists

The Afghan state was created in the mid-eighteenth century by Ahmad Shah, a cavalry commander in the disintegrating Iranian empire and a Pashtun tribal chief who founded the Durrani dynasty which was to rule Afghanistan until the 1970s.[9] The first efforts to build a modern army in Afghanistan took place in the early nineteenth century when a new ruler, Amir Dust Muhammad Khan (1826–39, 1843–63), threatened by domestic rivals and the rise of new regional powers, took tentative steps towards organizing his troops on the European model.[10] Up until this time, Afghan rulers had relied exclusively on tribal chiefs to supply irregular light cavalry and militiamen, as and when required, the tribal chiefs being rewarded with land grants, remission of taxes, and as much plunder as they could take. Indeed, the Afghan monarchy was itself a 'plundering polity',[11] the ruler, always drawn from the Durrani tribal confederation, first among tribal equals.[12] In the context of eighteenth-century warfare in the region, Afghan tribal cavalry was undoubtedly an effective fighting force and had acquired a formidable reputation, Afghan mercenaries being in great demand.[13] However, although well suited to a particular type of predatory warfare outside Afghanistan, these tribal forces were deeply inimical to stable centralized government.[14] In the 1830s Amir Dust Muhammad, wishing to free himself from his dependence on the powerful tribal leaders, began to raise and train regular army units, using as sources of advice and assistance European adventurers and renegades and Iranian and Indian Muslims who had been trained in the new disciplined forces.[15] In adopting this novel and controversial approach, the Amir was deeply influenced by the army reform then being undertaken by neighbouring states. Afghanistan was surrounded by local rulers engaged in frenetic efforts to Europeanize their military forces. To the west, the Ottoman sultan-caliphs, figures of great prestige within the world of Sunni Islam, had already begun to build regular standing armies with the help of European mercenaries and renegades. Closer to home, so too had states bordering Afghanistan whose rulers were direct contenders for regional power, including the shahs of Iran and Ranjit Singh in the Punjab. Sharpest of all was the example of the disciplined sepoys of the East India Company, trained in the tactics of regular warfare and the use of modern weapons.[16]

In his modest efforts to create regular military units, Dust Muhammad was launching a 'military revolution' in Afghanistan, exactly replicating the processes then underway across the Middle East and South Asia. Such military revolutions had been pioneered in Europe and involved the introduction of new technologies and military tactics which then necessitated broader innovations, specifically the creation of bureaucratic tax and administrative structures for financing the army and organizing recruitment.[17] In the Middle East and South Asia, these 'revolutions' involved a transformation of the existing military–fiscal relationships, specifically the replacement of 'feudal' troops, maintained and supplied by tribal chiefs and landowners in return for land grants or remission of revenue, with a regular standing army, supported by the state and paid directly in cash.[18] In Afghanistan, as elsewhere but to a more dangerous extent, such a centralization of revenue collection and military provision inevitably provoked the resentment, and eventually the subversion and resistance, of those tribal chiefs and landlords whose privileges and positions were threatened. The weakness of the Afghan state vis-à-vis tribal power rendered the military reforms of successive rulers fraught with tension and persistently frustrated any possibility of a successful and thorough-going Afghan military revolution.

In the 1830s Dust Muhammad's new advisors drilled troops in Kabul and gave them uniforms, but little was achieved before a political crisis of unprecedented dimensions put an end to the fledgling experiment and introduced a more determined reform agenda, but one tainted by foreign authorship.

By 1839 the British had come to see Dust Muhammad as a threat to its expanding imperial reach. They invaded Afghanistan, deposed the Amir and installed on the throne a new ruler, Shah Shuja (1803–9, 1839–42). During this first Western occupation of Afghanistan, the British pursued an agenda of imperial paternalism which was to become paradigmatic. Afghanistan would become a viable and modernized buffer state, theoretically sovereign but under the ultimate control of Britain, the inevitable opposition of the Afghan elite neutralized by support from the urban merchants and artisans and the peasantry, won over by a British-sponsored programme of reform.[19]

Military reform was a key element of the British plan for creating a stable Afghan government and binding it to their own interests. Their plan was a more radical version of the measures already tentatively adopted by Dust Muhammad and involved the abolition of the tribal cavalry and its replacement by regular forces under the direct control of the state and paid through the treasury, with the intention of creating a more effective and politically reliable support for the pro-British ruler. For the British in Kabul in 1839–40, the creation of these new forces, which would enable Shah Shuja to maintain himself in power, was a key exit strategy, permitting the immediate withdrawal of their own troops.[20]

However, from the beginning recruits were difficult to find and the British scheme was both massively expensive and profoundly unpopular. The tribal chiefs in particular correctly appreciated the threat to their own position and privilege represented by the regular regiments, rejected the opportunity to serve in them as salaried officers, and fought back with the help of the ulama who preached that the uniform and discipline of the new units were contrary to the teachings of Islam. Far from approaching the point at which they might safely withdraw their forces, the British were drawn ever deeper into shoring up an unpopular ruler and suppressing resistance to his government. Finally, in late 1841, the tribal chiefs put themselves at the head of a tribal uprising which succeeded in driving the British out of Afghanistan.[21] The success of the Afghan tribal forces, mobilized by calls to jihad against an infidel enemy and using guerilla tactics, led to the restoration of Amir Dust Muhammad and the enhancement of the prestige of tribal military power and the ideological appeal of Islam.

The restored Amir Dust Muhammad and his successor, Amir Sher Ali Khan (1863–6, 1868–79), both continued to try to imitate European methods of military organization.[22] Despite their troubled relations with Britain, both amirs relied on British subsidies to implement their reforms.[23] The amirs raised and drilled a number of regular infantry and cavalry units, clothed them in an approximation of a British uniform, and provided them with some modern weapons.[24] Yet in practice both were obliged to continue to rely on irregular tribal cavalry and militia while the tribal chiefs guarded jealously the fiscal advantages they enjoyed under the existing system. Indeed, they continued to manipulate it to their own advantage by, for example, inflating muster rolls and claiming the pay of 'ghost' soldiers.[25] The reformed regiments managed to survive but experienced severe problems. Recruitment was difficult, conditions harsh and service unpopular.

In 1879–80, within the context of the 'Great Game', a Russian approach to Amir Sher Ali led to the second Anglo–Afghan war, in which another British invasion of Afghanistan was again defeated by tribal irregulars under the leadership of their chiefs, mobilized by calls to jihad from the mullahs. In this, as in the first Anglo–Afghan war, the regular units played little or no part, the only exception being at the battle of Maiwand, where Afghan regular artillery, backed up by irregulars, inflicted a crushing defeat on a British force which fled in disarray to Kandahar.[26] Most of the regular regiments had fallen to pieces on the outbreak of the conflict, and although the regular troops continued to fight, they did so by abandoning their uniforms and reverting to irregular tactics and their Afghan clothes, fighting alongside the tribal forces.[27]

After this second British withdrawal, a new amir, Abd al-Rahman Khan (1880–1901), ascended the throne.[28] Inheriting, like his predecessors, a country devastated by foreign invasion and civil war, he, like them but with greater determination, tried to equip himself with a reliable regular military force.[29] Abd al-Rahman's military reforms were based on the same principles which had governed previous schemes, and centred on forming regular regiments on European lines, financed and controlled directly by the state – that is, by himself. Using the model closest to hand, the Indian army, and again using as advisors Indian Muslims who had served in that army, he organized his regular units into infantry, cavalry and artillery, every regiment having a mullah, a physician and a surgeon.[30] Adopting the same approach as his predecessors, Abd al-Rahman encountered similar problems: inadequate financial resources, an uncertain supply of reluctant manpower, and a complete lack of trained officers. Nonetheless, he pressed ahead with the creation of reformed regiments, relying, like Dust Muhammad and Sher Ali, on British subsidies to pay the new troops.

Although the new units were nominally on European lines, in fact they continued to exhibit typical tribal features. Some regiments were still composed of men of a single tribal origin, disputes between officers and troops from different tribes were common, and there were even different tiers of payment for those of the same rank but of different tribal origin.[31] The regular units only ever approximated the appearance of a modern army. They carried a variety of weapons, drill was ragged and uniform haphazard. Some battalions wore cast-off red tunics of British troops, others wore 'old green coats, dirty white trousers, and flat-peaked Russian caps'.[32] Although the regular units now received their pay in cash, they were permitted, like the irregulars, to loot defeated tribes and villages. In other respects, military discipline was harsh, offences such as the use of narcotics or insubordination receiving severe punishments.[33]

Abd al-Rahman's most significant military innovation was a form of conscription, introduced in an effort to regularize the supply of manpower and improve the quality of recruits. In the past troops for the regular units had been raised more or less by impressment, sometimes directly by the state, sometimes through the agency of tribal chiefs. After a number of experiments, in 1896 Abd al-Rahman introduced the *hasht nafari* system, whereby one in eight men was liable for military service.[34] For the remainder of his reign, Abd al-Rahman struggled to impose this system on the tribes, often against strong resistance, and in practice it was really only ever imposed on those regions and populations most securely under Kabul's control. Despite his soubriquet, 'the Iron Amir', Abd al-Rahman's centrepiece military reforms were modest. He made no attempt to undermine either the irregular tribal cavalry and militias or the privileges of the tribal chiefs. His regular army would, rather, exist in parallel to the tribal system and the tribal levies remained as important as ever to the enforcement of his authority. [35]

## Modernism and the Tribal Response: The Collapse of the New Army

By 1900, after seven decades of the monarchy's modernizing reforms, Afghanistan possessed only a fragile shadow of a modern state and army. On the contrary, the two Anglo–Afghan wars, and success in driving out the British, had increased Afghan confidence in their traditional military methods and tactics, while rural mullahs and their interpretation of Islam had begun to take on the mantle of defenders of Afghan independence. The political and diplomatic isolation of Afghanistan, the tenuous hold of state institutions, cultural and educational decline and the vitality of tribal ideological, military and political power contrasted starkly with other parts of the Muslim world in the same period.

One of the most serious difficulties faced by successive Afghan rulers in building a modern army was a lack of professionally trained officers. Officers were 'often of the lowest birth' and completely illiterate.[36] Drawn from the same tribal environments as their men, they gained promotion through family or tribal connections while their only access to modern military ideas was through translations and from their Indian Muslim advisors whose own professional knowledge was extremely limited.[37] At the beginning of the twentieth century, Afghanistan's educational system was still primitive and illiteracy was universal outside the tiny elite. Other Muslim states had, during the nineteenth century, taken practical steps to remedy similar deficiencies, especially in the military field. In Iran, Egypt and the Ottoman Empire, military schools had been established to acquaint future officers with European military sciences, missions of European officers imported to provide instruction, and groups of students sent to Europe. In 1904–6 Afghanistan was finally placed on the same path when the new amir, Habibullah (1901–19), founded the Military Academy. Previous amirs had steadfastly rejected British, or any other European, military missions which might compensate for Afghanistan's own lack of professional officers out of a fear of a consequential political subservience.[38] Now Habibullah asked the Ottoman Empire to provide officer-instructors and in 1907 an Ottoman military mission arrived in Kabul.[39] The choice of Ottoman assistance was astute. The Ottomans had acquired a reputation for successfully adopting Western scientific and technological knowledge without compromising their political independence and cultural integrity, and thus offered an appealing example to Afghan opinion, while the employment of Muslim Ottomans would avoid the contamination of direct infidel contact, and the political and religious hostility that such contact would engender. The establishment of the Military Academy was a step of the most profound future significance. The new institution would go on to produce generations of professional officers who would play a leading role in Afghan politics.

The succession of King Amanullah (1919–29) marked a new phase in Afghan 'top-down' modernization. Supported by a newly forming circle of modernist and nationalist intellectuals, the new amir embarked on a reform project of unprecedented scope.[40] Amanullah immediately launched a bid to end Afghanistan's subservience to British domination, resulting in the third Anglo–Afghan war. Despite experiments with creating mixed regiments of regular soldiers and untrained recruits, in this war, as in previous conflicts, the regular army proved to be of very limited military value.[41] The fighting was again conducted mainly by irregular tribal forces, with Amanullah proclaiming a jihad to secure mass popular support.[42]

Amanullah then began a sustained effort to transform Afghanistan into a modern state, building on the fragile but nonetheless real administrative and political achievements of his predecessors. His reforms, however, especially of the tax system and his secularization measures in education and justice, threatened the position of the old religious, tribal and landed interests who accordingly resented and, where possible, resisted them.[43]

Military reform in this period did not appear to occupy the same centrality as it had under previous amirs, yet Amanullah's modest plans for the army clearly revealed the contours of profound underlying difficulties. With the European and especially the Turkish model uppermost in the nationalist imagination, Amanullah hoped to create a modern army which was efficient, cohesive, professional and disciplined, capable of maintaining internal security and, above all, loyal to the state rather than to tribe or tribal chief. He was supported in this by a Turkish military mission, which had superseded the old Ottoman mission at the Military Academy.[44] The presence of the Turkish officers with their Kemalist background, their schemes for the rapid modernization of the army, the enthusiastic encouragement of the most advanced Afghan nationalists, and the gradual arrival in the officer corps of young Afghan officers with some professional training, acquired either at the Military Academy or abroad, usually in Turkey, began to transform the leadership of the Afghan army. In another step of great significance for the future, Amanullah laid the foundations of a modern air force. He had been impressed by the destructive power of the British aeroplanes deployed against his own government in 1919, and during the 1920s began to acquire both planes and pilots, mainly from the Soviet Union. From now on, Afghan governments were increasingly to resort to air power against tribal resistance in moments of crisis while the air force attracted the best educated recruits and acted as an incubator for political activism.[45]

Resistance to the speed and scope of Amanullah's reforms soon appeared, both inside the army and beyond. The proposals of the Turkish advisors for reforming the officer corps by weeding out the older and untrained officers gave rise to the first signs of a conflict within the officer corps that was to persist for several decades. A schism and then a struggle for power developed within the army between the new type of officer, who tended to espouse radical modernizing views of the type then common among army officers in neighbouring Iran and Turkey, and older untrained officers, who owed their position primarily to their tribal and family connections and who wished modernization to proceed slowly, if indeed at all, and without undermining the existing social order. The latter group was strongly of the view that the Turks profoundly misunderstood Afghan society, a society imbued with tribal values which rejected the notion that officers of good standing should be deprived of rank and salary simply on the grounds of the supposed lack of an alien professionalism. In fact, little was actually accomplished in terms of forcing the older officers into retirement or resignation, and most held on to their posts where they nursed a bitter and corrosive resentment, eventually finding a champion in the minister of war, Nadir Khan, of the Musahiban family.[46]

Other reforms proposed by the Turkish officers had an equally ambivalent impact; for example, pay was cut and soldiers promised, in return, barracks and rations, but the money saved went into the pockets of corrupt officers, and demoralization, already rampant in the officer corps, spread to the ranks. The Turkish officers succeeded in forming model battalions with new recruits and trained officers but their performance against tribal rebels was poor.[47] When, in 1924, the first serious armed rural resistance broke out, Amanullah had no choice but to resort once more to calling on friendly tribal levies and the proclamation of jihad.

Although the attack on the officers of tribal origin by Amanullah and his Turkish military advisors had alienated tribal society, the military measure which had the sharpest impact in the 1920s was the enforcement of a new system of conscription. Most of Amanullah's reforms barely affected the rural areas. However, his changes to the *hasht nafari* system of recruiting created an immediate, strong, and entirely negative impression across rural and tribal Afghanistan. Instead of requiring chiefs and elders to choose one man in eight for military service, the new system introduced a ballot, the names of all men of military age written on pieces of paper and lots drawn, the new system known as *pishk*.[48] Amanullah had two reasons for making this change. He wished, firstly, to place the supply of manpower on a fairer and legal footing, and to make it independent of village elders and tribal chiefs, thus avoiding the foisting of the weakest and poorest youths onto the army.[49] Secondly, he wished to use conscription, as his contemporaries Mustafa Kemal and Riza Shah were doing, as a method of inculcating a sense of loyalty to the state and of national consciousness into rural populations to whom these notions were still quite alien.[50]

Previous rulers, including the cash-rich British in 1839–40, had struggled to secure an adequate supply of the right kind of recruit to the regular army. Throughout the nineteenth century, government efforts to widen the scope of conscription had met with bitter, and often armed, resistance. Even the *hasht nafari* of Abd al-Rahman had only ever been imposed on settled areas under government authority. Down to the 1920s, recruitment continued to resemble a form of impressment, even if one carried out through the agency of village elder and tribal khan, rather than directly by the army.

Amanullah's new system of conscription by universal lottery not only removed control of the selection of recruits from the village and tribal elites, but also augured the integration of the recruited youth into an institution, the reformed, national army, from which tribal influence was being rapidly purged. An indication of the attitude of the younger army officers to the tribal khans may be seen in the fact that recruiting officers often gave the most menial work to the conscripted sons of tribal aristocrats.[51] The resentment thus aroused was compounded by the fact that the recruitment boards were notoriously corrupt, prone to blackmail and open to bribery.

In 1928 serious tribal hostility to Amanullah began to gather speed. The state in the tribal areas was still too fragile to put up determined resistance and, as the initial tribal successes led to the spread of the tribal insurrections, the army surrendered largely without a fight. The regular units, including the model battalions, quickly disintegrated altogether, mass desertions were frequent and sometimes, especially where they had found themselves confronting their own tribal kin, individual soldiers and sometimes entire units defected to the tribes, taking their weapons with them.

The army very quickly became irrelevant to the struggle for power in Afghanistan. After the first few weeks, the tribe–state confrontation degenerated into a tribal conflict, each of the contenders dependent on the military support they could muster from the tribes and such religious sanction as they could obtain.[52] Finally, after a disastrous interregnum of pure reaction under the Tajik bandit known as the Bacha-i Saqao (son of a water-carrier), a new ruling family, the Musahiban, led by the former minister of war, Nadir Khan, emerged from the chaos, rallying enough tribal support to take control of Kabul and, with British backing, proclaimed Nadir (1929–33) the new king. The consequences of the tribal victory were not simply a return to the status quo ante. The tribal chiefs had freed themselves from the very light touch of the central government, while their success constituted a warning to any future state-builders who sought to restrain them. Tribal power had in fact taken on a new vitality and boldness. It had acquired a reinforced legitimacy, a political role vis-à-vis the new Musahiban regime, and was greatly strengthened militarily, the tribal *lashkars* (fighting units) having looted most of the army's weapons, including its artillery, and having been reinforced by soldier-deserters with a rudimentary amount of modern training.[53] The new army, on the other hand, had been completely discredited.

## Afghanistan under Musahiban Rule:
## Officers and Politics

In the two decades following Amanullah's overthrow, Musahiban rule was both authoritarian and conservative and was careful to do nothing to antagonize the tribal or religious leaders, whom it actively attempted to associate with its rule. Amanullah's fate seemed to have demonstrated conclusively that neither the state nor its army was strong enough to assert its authority over the tribes but would court disaster in the attempt. The regime, its principal personnel in any case themselves still possessing a tribal identity, was accordingly content to leave the tribal areas to the rule of the chiefs. In these years both government and army responded to the inevitable intertribal feuds and raiding with negotiation and compromise rather than suppression. Although low-level tribal conflict was continuous, and army intervention frequent, such conflict was not directed at and presented no threat to the state itself. Indeed, negotiation and the management of conflict inevitably involved the threat of coercion, yet this was part of the process of compromise, designed to maintain, not destroy, the balance between state and tribal power.

Meanwhile, urban Afghanistan was changing. Modest educational reforms were producing an intelligentsia eager for reform, while a growing urban middle class began to demand more insistently some participation in politics. These developments were reflected within the officer corps of the army. An educated, professional officer corps came into being, produced by the Military Academy and training in Turkey, and epitomized in the Kabul Army Corps, which shared its civilian counterparts' desire for political and social modernization.

After its disintegration in 1929, the army was gradually reconstructed around a nucleus of tribal recruits and received substantial assistance in money and weapons from British India. Throughout the 1930s and 1940s it maintained a strength of around 70,000 men while Musahiban military policy explicitly recognized a military role for the tribes, especially in border defence, and officially sanctioned the chiefs' command of their tribal *lashkars*. Down to the 1950s the Afghan army continued to calculate the military capacity of the tribes as an integral feature of its own strength. A purely tribal Gendarmerie/militia system maintained a semblance of order in some regions of the country, particular the eastern and southern tribal areas, which were still, in the 1950s, completely off limits to the army.[54]

The life of the Afghan soldier in these years remained a miserable one. One observer commented that, 'Judged by modern European standards the conditions of service for the men are appalling, but…a slight improvement on the standard of life prevailing in the rural areas'.[55] Their pay, clothing and equipment were entirely inadequate. Soldiers were unable to send any money to their families, leaving their dependants destitute and reliant on the charity of relatives or the village. Some soldiers resorted to begging.[56] Their shabby and ill-assorted appearance reflected their low morale and they were generally treated with contempt by both civilian officials and their own superior officers and even by the armed tribesmen. Illiteracy was almost universal and desertions common if the conscripts were needed as agricultural labour by their families at harvest times.

By the 1950s the overall efficiency and fighting capacity of the troops still remained very weak and discipline brittle. Their morale was low and their loyalties were still to their family or their tribe rather than to army or king.[57] Their willingness to fight depended not on the orders of their own officers but on the attitude of the tribal chiefs and mullahs, and on the course of operations, military successes, especially opportunities to loot, encouraging them, any reverse likely to lead to mass desertions.[58]

The rank and file, both in Kabul and in the provinces, was hardly touched by the changes which were beginning to affect their officers deeply. Although conditions of service, pay and prospects for the troops changed little, if at all, between the early 1930s and the early 1950s, the officer corps, or at any rate that of the Kabul Army Corps, was changing rapidly and profoundly. In this, both the speed of the transformation and its confinement to Kabul and other major cities, the army was a microcosm of wider Afghan society. The Afghan army was beginning to look as if it were composed of two entirely self-contained elements, the officers of the Kabul garrison, professional graduates of modern officers' colleges, both in Afghanistan and abroad, and the conscripts and older officers, especially in the provinces, tribal in loyalty and unschooled in modern methods of warfare.

Exemplifying the new type of officer was the politically engaged and ambitious Muhammad Daud Khan, himself a member of the ruling Musahiban family, but of its younger generation. Daud rose rapidly through the senior ranks of the army in the 1930s. By the end of the decade he was heading one of the two factions which had emerged, or more accurately re-emerged, within the army, the other faction based around Shah Mahmud Khan, Daud's uncle and the minister of defence. These two factions represented a continuation, within the military, of the broad schism which had emerged during the 1920s over the scope and pace of reform. The group around Shah Mahmud, which had the support of other members of the Musahiban ruling family, including the prime minister, Hashim Khan, was cautious in its proposals for the army, believing that Afghanistan was too poor to embark on building a large regular army equipped with modern weapons, and that the government should continue to rely on its natural allies among the tribes, who should be conciliated and integrated into plans for internal stability and national defence.[59] Muhammad Daud and his supporters among the younger and better-educated army officers wished, on the contrary, to move quickly and to reorganize and re-equip the army on European lines. Like their contemporaries in Iran and Turkey, they wanted to see the army and the air force strong and efficient enough to enable the government to compel the tribes, by force if necessary, to submit to the law, especially in those areas most distasteful to them, conscription, education, and the collection of taxes and customs duties. In general, these officers regarded both the tribes and their mullahs as the enemies of education, reform and every kind of progress.[60]

During the 1930s, the dominant personality in the Afghan army had been Shah Mahmud Khan, the minister of defence. Up to 1939 his control of the army was undisputed and he ran it largely as a personal concern. He also headed the key Tribal Directorate, which was responsible for the administration of the predominantly Pashtun tribal areas in the eastern and southern provinces and he typified the Musahiban approach to the tribes, his caution, tact and respect making him popular with them.[61] His faction amongst army officers, which was large, reflected his position. His supporters were those officers who were themselves drawn from a tribal background, and many of his senior officers had been given their promotion due to their tribal or family influence rather than their efficiency. He was as unpopular among the younger educated officers as he was popular amongst the tribal.[62]

In the late 1930s to early 1940s, however, the balance within the army between the two factions began to change rapidly, with Daud clearly in the ascendant. In 1939 Daud was given command of the Kabul Army Corps, apparently in an attempt by his uncles, the minister of defence, Mahmud, and the prime minister, Hashim, to placate him and satisfy his own personal ambition as well as the desire of the younger Afghan officers for more rapid progress. He was provided with his own budget and the prestige of his command was greatly augmented when it was allotted the major portion of the more modern armaments and equipment possessed by the army. His Kabul Army Corps now became the principal striking force in the country. Furthermore, in an appointment which immensely strengthened his influence over the officer corps, especially in Kabul, he was placed in control of the army educational and training establishments and their budgets, all of which were located in the capital.[63]

Once in command of the Kabul Army Corps, Daud began to gather round him the younger and better-educated officers, who were increasingly impatient for change, and also worked closely with the officers of the Turkish military mission, who had remained in Kabul despite the fate of their first patron, King Amanullah. By the mid-1940s the Kabul Army Corps was visibly improving. With Daud in charge of the army's educational and training establishments, the influence of the Turkish officers, employed as instructors in these institutions, also increased. The numbers of cadets undergoing training increased, the syllabus was updated and courses of instruction in various subjects for junior officers and NCOs were begun.

Daud, his circle of supporters among the Afghan officer corps, and the Turkish officers remained convinced, as Amanullah had been in the 1920s, that it was essential to rid the army of the older, tribal, officers, for reasons of both military efficiency and politics. Free of the incubus of the older officers, the Afghan army could become truly modern and professional and also a vehicle for driving Afghanistan rapidly along a path to modernization, centralization and secularization. Accordingly, Daud launched a sustained campaign to force these officers into retirement. He met, however, equally sustained resistance. The unwanted officers owed their appointments to powerful tribal or family connections, which the government had no desire to alienate, and many were the personal protégés or friends of the Defence Minister.[64]

Frustrated in their efforts to rid the army of the uneducated officers, Daud and the Turkish instructors turned their attention to producing a new generation of younger officers who might gradually replace the older type. To this end they concentrated their efforts on military education and Daud concentrated on consolidating an officer corps which shared his own state-building, centralizing and secularizing agenda.

A military career in Afghanistan had traditionally lacked prestige and remained distasteful to the elite. The army therefore found it difficult to attract young men with sufficient education for training as army officers.[65] Illiteracy or semi-literacy was a serious impediment to officer-training. In one instance, 15 out of 20 junior officers detailed to attend a course in minor tactics and map reading were found to be incapable of reading their training manuals in the Persian language, or of writing intelligible notes in Persian during lectures.[66]

The Turkish instructors adopted a twin-track approach to this problem. They continued to send officers abroad, especially to Turkey, while within Afghanistan, in an attempt to circumvent the extremely low level of national educational provision and the reluctance of the better-off, they created an entirely self-contained system of military education, selecting boys throughout the country for military school at the ages of 11 to 12.[67] This had the advantage of not only improving general educational levels, but of removing future officers entirely from their tribal backgrounds. By the mid-1940s the majority of cadets were drawn from the military schools. Attention was also paid to providing the rank and file in the Kabul Army Corps with some rudimentary education. In 1943–4 platoon and company commanders, who themselves had received their education in the military schools, were made responsible for teaching their men how to read and write, with the objective of thereby spreading literacy throughout the country. The men received about one hour's instruction a day in reading, writing and simple arithmetic.[68]

In more general terms, however, further fundamental reforms remained blocked. The successful resistance of the tribal populations to conscription remained particularly irksome to the professional officers. The conscription system remained steeped in bribery and all sorts of wangling while the law provided an institutionalized form of avoidance in that the better-off were allowed to pay large sums for the provision of substitutes. Recruits were drawn from communities, including tribes, under government control, while most of the mainly Pashtun tribes in the eastern and southern provinces adamantly refused to provide conscripts at all.[69] The Musahiban government's desire to avoid provoking the tribes, especially the Pashtuns, meant that the tendency to over-recruit from areas under government control persisted, giving rise to resentment and discontent, and an utter opposition to any increase in the period of service, an increase the army authorities deemed essential if education and training were to be improved. In practice, separate systems applied to tribes and districts under government control and those autonomous of it, although both played a military role, the former by providing conscripts, the latter irregular forces as and when required and on their own terms. In the mid-1940s the government launched a concerted effort to compel the tribes in the eastern provinces to accept conscription but the strength of tribal resistance combined with the weakness of the army led to the rapid abandonment of this attempt.[70] This episode, and particularly the humiliation inflicted by tribal defiance, had a deep effect on many army officers, and contributed to their resolve to confront the tribes as soon as the army was strong enough.[71]

By the early 1950s there had been a marked improvement in the bearing and discipline of the Kabul Army Corps but, elsewhere in the country, the provincial divisions, still under older tribal officers, had experienced little or no change. The army had also been hit hard by the consequences of the emergence of the Pashtunistan issue following the partition of India and the creation of Pakistan in 1947. The fixing of the frontier between the new state of Pakistan and Afghanistan along the Durand Line seemed to confirm the partition of Pashtun tribal territories, and Afghanistan refused to recognize its new boundary.[72] As a result of its stand on this issue, an embargo was placed on arms exports to Afghanistan by Western countries.[73] This embargo was a key factor in explaining Daud's turn to the USSR for assistance, including military aid.

At the end of World War II, the political order established after the overthrow of King Amanullah had begun to unravel. At first, this was visible only in a reshuffle among Musahiban family members. In 1946 Shah Mahmud, until then minister of defence, became prime minister while Muhammad Daud became the new defence minister. Although this appeared initially to enhance Daud's power, in fact it served rather to aggravate tensions within the ruling family. Shah Mahmud retained his title of army commander-in-chief and the control of the immensely important Tribal Directorate, and tried to limit Daud's independent access to the King. Daud bitterly resented these efforts to curb his power and, after holding his appointment only from May to July 1946, he went into semi-retirement.[74] The rift within the ruling family was concealed although the potential gravity of a dispute between Shah Mahmud, who still had a considerable following amongst senior officers in the army, and his nephew, who had the support of practically all the officers of the Kabul Army Corps and the military training establishments in Kabul, was to become only too clear within a few years.[75]

1946 also saw the beginning of a period of relative liberalization, with growing demands from the intelligentsia, the bureaucracy, and other urban elements such as the merchants, for the opening up of the political system. In 1952, however, the senior members of the Musahiban family reached the limits of their tolerance of political dissent, banned political organizations, closed down independent newspapers, suppressed the fledgling students' union and imprisoned many critics.

These years also saw the army enter a period of crisis. Despite Daud's reforms, many older untrained officers remained in senior positions, while the younger better-educated officers were frustrated and discontented both at their own poor pay and prospects and at the lack of progress made in reforming the army, and at the slow pace of wider political and social change.[76] The army coup of 1952 which brought Nasser and the Free Officers to power in Egypt was apparently much admired by junior officers who wished to emulate the example and the idea of a republic was especially widespread. Army officers shared the frustration and anger felt by politically active elements in Kabul at the 1952 crackdown. This frustration, combined with resentment at the deteriorating condition of the army itself, due to corruption, incompetence and the attitude of the West to the Pashtunistan question, produced within the officer corps an unprecedented politicization and a readiness to support Daud when he moved against the government.

Although Daud was in unofficial retirement, he had nonetheless remained the real power in the defence ministry and also retained his base in the Kabul Army Corps. He tried to continue with his military reforms; in August 1951, for example, the army received a 50–100 per cent pay rise while training was stepped up; in mid-1952 the training hours of conscripts was doubled. Yet the army could not be re-equipped due to the arms embargo over the Pashtunistan dispute and a general lack of financial resources was beginning to have a serious impact. Conscripts, still the socially marginal and physically weak foisted onto the army by their own community leaders, were formally enlisted but then allowed to go home again and there was a substantial overall reduction in numbers while the air force carried out even less flying training than in previous years and enlisted no new pilots.[77] While the army was beginning to disintegrate, it was estimated that around half of the military budget was disappearing in corruption and waste.[78]

In 1953 Daud made his move. He obtained the support of the king, Zahir Shah (1933–73), who was, like himself, a member of the younger generation of the Musahiban family and a product of the Military Academy, and who shared his concern with the condition of the army. Zahir was already chafing at decades of control by his senior relatives and apparently sympathetic to ideas of reform. With his support Daud, in a palace coup, forced Shah Mahmud to resign and took over the office of prime minister.

With Daud as prime minister, both Afghanistan's domestic politics and its foreign relations underwent a transformation.[79] Indeed, the two spheres were intimately linked, as the rapid social and economic development and strengthening of the central government envisaged by Daud was only possible with substantial foreign financial, material and technical aid. His approaches to the US, now firmly pro-Pakistan, rebuffed, he turned to the USSR which responded eagerly. In 1955 the USSR announced a massive aid programme, and in 1956 the two countries adopted an ancillary agreement providing for the USSR to re-equip the Afghan armed forces.

The USSR having a monopoly of military assistance, within a decade the Afghan army became largely Soviet trained and equipped. Until the mid-1950s, the army had changed little, the desperately slow pace of reforms merely serving to highlight to younger officers the enormity of the task still to be accomplished. Now, however, a modern army of the type sought by successive Afghan rulers began to come into existence. Pay was raised, schools and specialist courses for artillery, tank and radar training were established with Soviet instructors, Soviet technicians arrived to maintain the newly delivered equipment, and the air force, in particular, was revolutionized by the receipt of modern aircraft.[80]

By the early 1960s the Soviet bloc's military aid to Afghanistan was estimated at about one-third of all total Soviet aid.[81] The number of Soviet military advisors was around 400 of whom some 250 were directly engaged in training the Afghan armed forces including in the basic training of the troops, and the chief of the Soviet military mission in Afghanistan was of the rank of general. Many of the officers of the mission and their wives were from the Central Asian republics of the USSR and knew at least one of the local Afghan languages. Special courses in the Russian language were organized in the divisions and officers successful in these language courses received monthly bonuses in addition to their regular salaries. The air force received special attention. A team of about 70 Soviet air force personnel provided training, including radar training, to Afghan pilots and airmen at the new Kabul Air Academy. The air force was equipped with Soviet jet bombers and fighters and new Soviet-built military airfields at Bagram and Shindand.[82] The care lavished by the Soviet advisors on the more sophisticated and technically advanced elements of the Afghan armed forces, especially the air force and the tank corps, led to the development of especially strong leftist sympathies among their personnel and they were to play a leading role in the Saur (April) Revolution of 1978.

Large numbers of Afghan officers visited the USSR every year to receive military training. In addition to the many courses offered, a general six-month course was organized for all new graduates of the Military Academy in order for them to train with Soviet weapons and equipment. Afghan officers were invited in groups for a six-week tour of the Soviet Union in order to familiarize themselves with the Red Army, the travel expenses of all officers met by the Soviet Union.[83] In general, the Soviet authorities did their best to gain the sympathy of Afghan officers with various plans for housing projects and medical aid schemes. Officers were also sent to the USSR for medical treatment at Soviet expense. The involvement of the USSR continued to grow throughout the 1960s and early 1970s and by 1973 around a quarter of the Afghan officer corps on active duty had been trained in the Soviet Union.

At the same time, Afghanistan's intelligentsia and urban middle class, especially its younger generation educated in the new schools and Kabul University, was growing in self-confidence and moving leftwards.[84] Many Afghan army officers, who had already formed a generally positive view of the Soviet Union, shared the political radicalization taking place among the civilian intelligentsia, and leftist sympathies became widespread in the armed forces.[85] By the early 1970s sympathy for the pro-Soviet People's Democratic Party of Afghanistan (PDPA) was strong among the officer corps.[86] Indeed, PDPA recruitment had proceeded even faster among army officers than among the general population because, in addition to the material benefits of Soviet assistance, the officer corps now had a tradition of support for state-building policies stretching back to the 1920s and a long record of hostility to the tribal chiefs and mullahs.

Yet these developments still largely affected the officer corps. It was they who benefited from Soviet perks, and who shared the political and cultural preoccupations of the civilian intelligentsia. The rank and file, drawn mainly from the rural areas, remained unaffected by the changes of these years. They were still usually illiterate, their mental world that of the family, tribe or village, their authority that of chief or headman. The modest reforms of the 1960s and 1970s barely reached the rural areas, the government avoiding any confrontation with the tribal chiefs.[87] The chiefs' autonomy within their own areas remained unchallenged and the countryside continued to atrophy. Indeed, in the absence of any significant development, rural self-reliance remained an essential mechanism for survival and social bonds were strong in proportion to the state's weakness. During these years, not only was the gap between rural and urban Afghanistan not bridged but tribal society was increasingly estranged from a small but educated and increasingly sophisticated Kabuli elite. This gap was as marked, if not more marked, within the army as in civilian life.

In 1963 Daud had resigned but by the early 1970s he was ready to make another bid for power, this time with the support of the growing pro-Soviet left. The PDPA had split into two wings, the more moderate Parcham, led by Babrak Karmal, and the radical Khalq, led by Nur Muhammad Taraki and Hafizullah Amin. In the early 1970s Daud had begun cultivating close links with the left-leaning nationalists of the Parcham faction of the PDPA and with Soviet-trained army officers. The civilian Parchamis and the leftist officers shared much with Daud: his nationalism and his desire to build a strong central government, his objectives of rapid social and economic development, his aggressive secularism and his aim of marginalizing Islam and the mullahs, his entire programme dependent on the suppression of tribal political and military power. The officers were also particularly aggrieved over the contrast they had observed between levels of development in the Soviet Central Asian republics and in Afghanistan, and were professionally frustrated by the King's control of senior appointments in the army and his open preference for his own kin.[88] In July 1973 Daud launched a coup supported by key military officers and Parcham's rank and file. The King abdicated; Daud became president and formed a new government, appointing many Parchamis to high office.

The period of Daud's presidency saw support for the PDPA continue to grow, but now it was the more radical Khalq faction which predominated, especially within the army, where Khalq concentrated its recruiting.[89] By the mid-1970s Daud, in the context of a general pro-Western realignment, had begun to turn against his erstwhile allies. Wishing to reduce his dependence on the Parchamis and the USSR, Daud moved to improve relations with the US and with pro-Western regimes in the region, including in Pakistan, Iran and Egypt. He also attempted to consolidate his own domestic position by making a series of appointments from within his own family and his immediate circle.[90] Not only were the leftist army officers of both factions alarmed and dismayed at these developments, but a wider resentment also simmered at the fact that, despite all the modernization of the previous years, under Daud advancement in the armed forces still often depended more on ethnic and tribal (Pashtun) connections than on merit. A political crisis developed which led in 1978 to the Saur (April) Revolution. Khalqis and Parchamis in the Tank Corps and the air force carried out a successful coup. Daud was killed and the soldiers immediately handed over to the civilian PDPA leaders.

Since the 1830s the creation of a strong army had been a constant preoccupation of successive Afghan amirs and kings. With the death during the coup of Daud, although a president yet also the last representative of the Durrani dynasty, two centuries of Durrani rule in Afghanistan was ended by the very army that successive Durrani rulers had done so much to create.

## The Democratic Republic of Afghanistan and the Afghan Army

At the beginning of its period of power the PDPA was located firmly within the Afghan tradition of state-building. Its programme called for the rapid and forcible centralization, secularization and modernization of Afghan society, and it was determined in particular to end the 'feudal' rule of rural khans and landowners. Just as the PDPA's agenda had many features familiar from the past, so too did the opposition which it provoked. In its implementation of its programme, the PDPA found mobilizing against it forces similar to those which had destroyed previous state-building campaigns, most notably that of King Amanullah in the late 1920s. As past experience had repeatedly demonstrated, the extension of state control into areas previously autonomous, and the introduction into the rural areas of reforms conceived by urban political trends, resulted in the immediate emergence of armed opposition. In the 1980s, as in the past but to an even greater extent, the conflict between Afghan state-builders and their opponents was not only a domestic conflict. It was now profoundly shaped by the regional and international context of the Cold War. The arrival of Soviet troops in December 1979 reinforced the Afghan army, but the immense amount of aid, financial and military, which began to reach its mujahidin opponents also transformed them from a collection of tribal militias into a military force of some effectiveness.[91]

Although the state was still weak in 1978, and the possession of the state apparatus by the PDPA fragile, nonetheless the new regime launched an unprecedented reform drive in the rural areas, in the hope of solidifying support before a counter-revolution could mobilize itself.[92] Previous state-building efforts having left rural Afghanistan largely untouched, neither the PDPA, an urban political formation, nor the broader state institutions had the implantation in the countryside necessary to enforce the envisaged rural transformation. Led by a variety of local rural leaderships, counter-revolutionary outbreaks, especially in the tribal areas, followed in rapid succession, leaving the internally fractured regime in an apparently terminal crisis, from which it was only rescued by the arrival of Soviet forces.[93]

The years of political crisis and civil war which followed the formation of the Democratic Republic of Afghanistan in 1978 resulted in the severe disorganization, but not the disintegration, of the Afghan army. For the first time in its history, the Afghan army did not collapse under the weight of foreign intervention and domestic upheaval. The army's ability to survive after the traumatic first months of the Saur Revolution, and its subsequent relatively successful reconstruction by the PDPA and its Soviet advisors, was based on decades of state-building activity. From as early as the 1920s, a majority of Afghan officers had identified themselves with a programme of modernization articulated first by King Amanullah, then Muhammad Daud and finally by the PDPA. Until 1992 the Afghan officer corps largely retained its loyalty to the army as a symbol of the Afghan state.

The rapid reconstitution of Afghan military capacity was a cornerstone of Soviet policy in Afghanistan and a key exit strategy. The Saur Revolution had at first produced a severe depletion of military manpower, while the very arrival of Soviet troops itself caused further waves of desertion. The surviving elements of the Afghan officer corps and their Soviet advisors found themselves faced with the urgent task of preventing the collapse of the entire military structure and then rebuilding it, organizationally and politically.

The PDPA–Soviet strategy involved holding the urban areas, strategic points and key routes while the Afghan army was rebuilt to the point where it would be strong enough to guarantee security itself and suppress opposition in the countryside. At first, the Afghan army was quite unequal to the task allotted to it, and Soviet forces found themselves drawn deeper into a rural counter-insurgency. Nonetheless, even at the time of its deepest crisis, the Afghan army always constituted at least a token presence on operations. Gradually, as it recovered, the Afghan army, supplemented by sarandoy (ministry of interior troops) and informal militias, took over the fighting and the Soviet role was reduced. By the mid-1980s Afghan troops comprised the bulk of those involved in most operations.[94]

Nonetheless, despite a degree of relative success, the army was ultimately unable to establish itself as an institution capable of independent survival and failed to stabilize PDPA control of the country. The army never resolved a range of problems familiar from the past and, over time, rural-tribal hostility sustained by foreign support crucially weakened both the regime and its army.[95] This, combined with financial dependence on a Soviet support which was suddenly withdrawn with the collapse of the USSR in 1991, finally proved fatal.

Despite the sympathy within the officer corps for the egalitarian goals of the Saur Revolution, the gulf between it and the rank and file, in outlook, background and day-to-day conditions, remained vast. The ordinary conscript often remained not only outside the ideological vision of his officers but actually alienated by it.

Differences in morale and attitude between the officers and their men were, for example, clearly revealed by desertion rates. In elite units and the officer corps in general, the military reforms of the previous decades had left a deeper impact. Although the ordinary conscript's integration was still fragile and easily abandoned, desertions from elite units where PDPA allegiance was stronger were much rarer, and were especially low from the air force, while officers in general showed little inclination to desert.[96] Even after the withdrawal of Soviet troops in 1989, the morale of the officer corps remained intact, even raised by its freedom from the taint of foreign support, and many of its officers were eager to carry on the fight.[97]

Among the rank and file, on the other hand, military service was as unpopular as ever and desertion, individual and collective, especially when troops faced active service, was common. Since the nineteenth century, the Afghan army had relied on conscription, only ever partially imposed on a reluctant population, for its manpower. In the 1980s the army continued to conscript in the cities and rural areas held by the government. Resistance to the draft was widespread, yet the army found the problem of 'the massive' desertions much more difficult to combat.[98] As in the past, soldiers usually deserted in order to get away from the fighting while the continuing pre-eminent importance of kinship ties was shown by the high rate of desertions which occurred when units were ordered into action against their own kinship groups.[99] The regime first tried to address this problem by indoctrination and strengthening party control over the troops, on the Soviet model. It quickly discovered, however, that the most effective response to both difficulties in recruiting and desertion was the introduction of economic incentives, huge pay rises and privileged access to food and fuel rations.

Another endemic problem in the Afghan army was that of a lack of force cohesion. This too had a different impact on the conscript troops and the officer corps. For much of the rank and file, tribalism and Islam remained at the core of personal identity, while national consciousness and an over-arching sense of loyalty to the state remained weak, especially among the conscript troops. Meanwhile, the newly forming officer corps had become deeply politicized, this giving rise to new sources of conflict and faction-alism which overlaid the old, but still real, divisions of tribe and ethnicity. Personal and family connections and patronage networks continued to be vital determinants of rank and position.[100]

The elite modernizer Daud, the Parchamis, who had once supported him, and the more radical and plebeian Khalqis, had all competed for the support of army officers since the 1950s, and factions had formed among the officer corps around both programmes and personalities. The competition between these factions was intensified by the fact that they shared many broad and basic objectives, and a common enemy in the form of Islamist/fundamentalist political groupings. After the Saur Revolution, and the seizure of actual power by the PDPA, the problem of Parchami–Khalqi factionalism erupted into widespread violence and purges and counter-purges, which badly affected the officer corps of the army. The adoption of a nationalities policy on the Soviet model by the PDPA, which contributed to the emergence of a new sense of ethnic identity, also tended to undermine military cohesion and was a specific source of tension among officers.[101] Under the Pashtun nationalist Daud, the Pashtun identity of the officer corps had been clarified and strengthened.[102] During the 1980s the PDPA challenged Daud's efforts to stamp an overt Pashtun identity on the officer corps and there was a visible increase in the numbers of Tajiks at senior levels, further alienating the majority Pashtuns. This situation eventually produced, in March 1990, a coup attempt. In the context of intensifying ethnic conflicts after the Soviet withdrawal, pro-Khalqi Pashtuns in the army, led by the Defence Minister and former Chief of Staff, Shah Nawaz Tanai, reached an understanding with the Pashtun-dominated mujahidin faction of Gulbuddin Hekmatyar and attempted a military coup.[103]

Throughout the 1980s military development continued to be hampered by the consequences of Afghanistan's generally low cultural level and lack of development. This profoundly affected all levels of the army. Problems of education and training remained acute, a direct result of the still rudimentary primary and secondary education system in the country. Around 60 per cent of the troops were illiterate, giving rise to particular difficulties in training specialists such as tank crews and artillerymen. Very great efforts were made to compensate for Afghan educational deficiencies by training large numbers of military personnel in the USSR but the officer corps nonetheless showed a marked qualitative decline as the army expanded and there was also a shortage of leaders at junior officer and NCO levels.[104]

One of the most intractable problems facing Afghan state-building projects, including army reform, had been the difficulty of finding the necessary financial resources. Funding an army able to combat the multiple rural insurgencies of the 1980s was completely beyond the capabilities of the Afghan state. As in the past, so too for the PDPA, the only means by which the Afghan state could pay for military expansion was through foreign assistance and the USSR provided both cash and weapons for the Afghan army. Given the depth of the crises which the regime faced, there was little opportunity for contemplating the longer-term future, beyond a belief that general economic development, with Soviet assistance, would follow military success and the stabilization of the country. The commitment of the Soviet Union to the survival of the PDPA regime freed Afghanistan from the impossible task of raising sufficient financial resources internally to support the military, in a country poor in exploitable economic resources and where the fiscal base of the state was fragile, indeed shrinking, with rural areas controlled by the mujahidin outside the fiscal framework altogether. Although assistance from the USSR meant that the army was paid and equipped, when that aid was suddenly and unexpectedly terminated in 1991, the Afghan government was left with no means of sustaining either the army or the militias on which it had become increasingly reliant. The collapse of both army and state quickly followed.

Since their earliest formation in the nineteenth century, regular army units, hampered by Afghanistan's lack of roads and poor communications, had rarely succeeded in defeating tribal irregulars, whose guerilla tactics exploited to the full the country's terrain. In the 1980s, too, the military confrontation between the PDPA and the tribal-Islamist opposition was largely inconclusive. The mujahidin, due partly to the limitations of their military capability and partly to their political disunity, were never able to defeat the PDPA regime. Equally, the government, through much of the 1980s, was unable to impose a decisive defeat on the mujahidin. The PDPA and its army benefited from Soviet support, but at the cost of a rapidly deteriorating international context and the Afghan conflict's acquisition of the status of cockpit of the Cold War.

Throughout the 1980s, foreign support was crucial to sustaining the mujahidin. Pakistan, hostile to Kabul over the Pashtunistan dispute, and its president, Zia al-Haq, keen to advance his own Islamist agenda, eagerly embraced the opportunity to assist Afghan Pashtuns who took sanctuary across the border. The triumph of the Iranian Revolution in 1979 brought another enemy to the PDPA's door in the shape of Khomeini, who offered ideological encouragement and some material aid to Persian-speaking and Shi'a elements. Even China became involved in the anti-PDPA campaign, as part of its bid to gain influence in the Central Asian republics to its south, and its wider rivalry with the USSR.[105] However, the decisive support for the anti-PDPA forces came from Saudi Arabia and the US.

In addition to foreign support, the tribal fighters were also provided with ideological coherence by the arrival in their midst of Islamist radicals from the urban areas, such as Gulbuddin Hekmatyar, Borhanuddin Rabbani and Ahmad Shah Masud. Afghan Islamists had been increasingly fearful of the direction taken by the government since Daud's coup of 1973. Daud himself was resolutely hostile to their agenda and to all manifestations of religious influence and their dislike of him was aggravated by his intermittent collaboration with the Parchamis, with whom he shared a secular outlook. In 1975 the Islamist radicals tried to launch an uprising in the tribal areas against the Daud regime, but it was a fiasco.[106] After the Saur Revolution, and especially after the arrival of the Soviet army, they grasped a new opportunity. The tribal opposition and the urban Islamists who hurried to put themselves at its head were transformed after December 1979 by the provision of American political and diplomatic support, and American and Saudi material aid, including military supplies, channelled through Saudi Arabia and Pakistan. The concomitant ability of the Saudis and Pakistanis to mould the politics of the Afghan counter-revolution thus helped to increase the weight of a conservative Islamic ideology well suited to reinforcing tribal traditionalism. During the 1980s, the old rural authorities of tribal khan and village elder were first reinforced, then supplanted by a new type of leadership, that of militia commanders and warlords. Although the Afghan opposition was presented to international opinion as a resistance movement, the actual course of the war indicated its essentially tribal character; tribal militias frequently changed sides, hedged their bets by negotiating simultaneously with both government and mujahidin, were riven by clan rivalries, accepted material inducements and followed the dictates of political opportunism.

Given the military deadlock between Kabul and the mujahidin, the PDPA, aware from quite an early stage that no purely military solution was possible, began to make military, political and ideological concessions to the tribes. At first slowly, and then much faster from the mid-1980s under the leadership of a new president, Muhammad Najibullah, the balance between the state and the unstable coalition of its enemies in the countryside, tribal chiefs, Islamist radicals, militia commanders and warlords, began to alter.

In the military field this changing balance was best exemplified by the growth of the militia system, which complemented and reflected Najibullah's policy of National Reconciliation, both policies reflecting a broader strategy of winning over, rather than defeating, any militias or warlords who seemed amenable.[107] From its very early days, the PDPA had tried to utilize friendly or bribable tribal forces to combat the mujahidin. From the mid-1980s, a reliance on tribal militias became an even more marked feature of the Najibullah regime. They were useful in military terms, able to confront the mujahidin more effectively than regular troops, and politically, in an increasing reversion to Afghan nationalism, they could be represented as part of Afghanistan's traditional means of defence. As the militia system waxed, so the army, to some extent, waned. Militiamen were paid much more than regular soldiers, and joining a pro-government militia was often an attractive alternative to conscription. In order to consolidate their support, the government diverted military resources, including artillery and tanks, away from the army to the militias, and kept them well supplied with money and consumer goods. By the late 1980s, throughout the country, both pro-government and pro-mujahidin tribal fighting groups were transformed into well-funded and well-equipped militias, and tribal khans and village elders were correspondingly superseded by militia commanders and warlords.

After the Soviet withdrawal in 1989, Najibullah, with both regular and irregular forces, avoided the universally predicted defeat. Yet, although Najibullah appeared to be consolidating his position, the urban populations backing him out of fear of the consequences of a mujahidin victory, power was draining away from the state.[108] The actual balance of power between the army and its militia allies had shifted decisively in favour of the latter, which were beyond the control of the military authorities and on whose fragile and contingent support Najibullah was now dependent. It was, however, the sudden termination of all Soviet aid, economic and military, to Afghanistan at the beginning of 1992 which caused the Najibullah regime to collapse. Pro-government militias abandoned Najibullah and, under strong pressure from their patrons in Saudi Arabia and Pakistan, a collection of warlords, including Hekmatyar, Dustum and Masoud, in a temporary and unnatural show of unity, marched on Kabul.[109]

## The Afghan National Army

After 1992 not only the government of Najibullah, but the Afghan state itself collapsed and the army disintegrated.[110] Armed groups proliferated throughout the countryside taking advantage of the opportunities for profit presented by the absence of state and army. Although the Islamist leaders had originated from within an urban tradition of religious reform, during their rise in the 1980s they had been absorbed into a tribal military movement that owed little to ideology. The majority of the thousands of minor mujahidin commanders had little or no political or social vision beyond the maintenance and aggrandizement of their own power. To such figures, the state represented only a threat, while the mujahidin leaders in Kabul, for whom the state represented a potential prize, proved able neither to transform their militias into disciplined forces nor to rebuild institutions of government.[111]

The scale of foreign support for the mujahidin in the 1980s had been unprecedented. The arrival of cash and weapons in such massive quantities, and without accountability, had now produced a novel situation: the emergence of an entrepreneurial approach to the war, a vested interest not in winning, but in simply ensuring the maintenance of the conflict, and the concomitant continuation of opportunities for accumulating wealth and local political power. The chaos and violence was gradually reduced as the Taliban, a new movement of largely rural and refugee origin, extended its power and in 1996 drove the competing warlords from Kabul. The Taliban, however, did not locate themselves within the Afghan state-building tradition, their mechanisms for ruling the country consisting of a network of *shuras* (councils), and friendly tribal militias.[112]

The collapse of the state after 1992 was of a much more fundamental and dangerous character, and the task of reconstruction more difficult, than in previous similar episodes. In the nineteenth century and even by the late 1920s, state institutions were still rudimentary and flimsy, and most Afghans were hardly touched by them. The impact of their temporary disappearance was therefore limited, and the task of reconstruction similarly straightforward. By the latter part of the twentieth century, however, the Afghan state had assumed a much more significant role, and its collapse removed the basic economic, political and social framework within which most Afghans lived, leaving them obliged to look to warlords, khans and militia leaders for protection and sustenance. During the 1980s a wide range of anti-state forces, tribal, ethnic and warlordist, had been armed and financed and brought to new levels of political activism, but the social forces which had previously formed the backbone of the state-building enterprise were significantly weakened. By the 1990s, much of the urban elite, especially the intelligentsia, had fled into permanent exile, while significant sections of the army had switched allegiance to regional militias, where they gradually succumbed to the stronger tribal environment. The post-1992 disintegration also presented a novel danger in regional terms. In the past, Afghanistan had been isolated from a wider regional context by imperial strategy and geography. By the 1990s, in a new context of globalization, post-Cold War regional uncertainty and with a highly mobilized and politicized Afghan population, the consequences of state collapse were regional and international as well as domestic.

After the attacks of 11 September 2001, the US made the decision to overthrow the Taliban but the methods employed contributed once more to strengthening tribal-warlord power. Wishing to avoid committing American troops to a ground attack on the Taliban, the US opted for channelling cash, weapons and political support to militias and warlords remaining outside and hostile to Taliban control, principally the Northern Alliance led, until his recent assassination, by Ahmad Shah Masud.[113]

This sudden cascade of money and arms was successful in mobilizing a force capable of driving the Taliban from Kabul but it also necessarily revitalized local armed groups and their commanders who had been subdued or co-opted by the Taliban. By 2002 Afghanistan was once again home to hundreds of thousands of active militiamen.[114] Although a government was formed around the technocrat Hamid Karzai, the militia commanders and warlords were, from the beginning, an integral part of the new regime. The Karzai government, in the absence of any national army, was at first entirely dependent on the militias of the Northern Alliance, hastily constituted into the Afghan Military Forces. The constituent and *ab initio* role of warlords and militias within the new regime was exemplified by the appointment as minister of defence of Muhammad Qasim Fahim, a Tajik warlord who proceeded to stuff the defence ministry and senior ranks of the army with his own Tajik dependants and followers.

Despite an initial international euphoria, the leading part played by the US in overthrowing the Taliban and bringing Karzai to power, and the new government's association with warlordism in general, and with the Northern Alliance in particular, meant that the legitimacy of the new regime was from the beginning compromised. For certain sections of Afghan society, the new government's connection to foreign support was even greater than that of the PDPA had been. Although the PDPA had lost much of its legitimacy in nationalist eyes after the arrival of Soviet troops, it had not itself been brought to power by a foreign force.

The new government, together with its US and other international sponsors, rapidly drew up proposals for a new army. The Afghan National Army (ANA) was to be a completely new, regular, professional army, with only the minimal recruitment of former mujahidin, most of whom were to be demobilized and reintegrated into civilian life. The new army was to be ethnically balanced and democratically accountable, funded, as this became possible, from the Afghan government's own revenues.[115] This blueprint was based on an uncritical adoption of foreign models of military organization, with apparently little or no consideration of the realism of these models in the Afghan context, or the difficulties arising from the absence of the necessary fiscal and administrative base.

Between 2001 and 2006, the task of building the army progressed very slowly, partly because of US indifference, its attention having turned to Iraq, and partly due to the resistance of the newly revitalized militia commanders. Militias and their commanders began to hide themselves within the new Afghan forces, and to turn themselves into the private security companies on which the government was to come to depend. Problems inherent in the new army remained submerged due to the relatively localized and low-level insecurity. Meanwhile, the early post-Taliban consensus was masking deep differences between the US and Afghan officers and defence officials over the new army, its size, function and methods of recruitment. These were not merely straightforward disagreements about organization but concealed fundamentally different conceptions of the place of the army in state and nation.

At first the US had envisaged a small, cheap, volunteer army for Afghanistan, its strength eventually reaching no more than 70,000 men. According to this view, the army's only task was to ensure internal security, while international forces and diplomatic support guaranteed the country's borders and regional defence needs. The Afghan government, however, saw the army differently, as a symbol of sovereignty and an instrument of national integration. Senior Afghan army officers and officials in the Afghan Defence Ministry, basing their approach on a long Afghan nationalist tradition, repeatedly called for increases in numerical strength and for the reintroduction of conscription.[116] Although they often argued for conscription on economic grounds, conscript soldiers being cheaper than volunteers, undoubtedly their emphasis on conscription arose from wider concerns.

For the advocates of conscription, its reintroduction would have addressed a number of problems which the new Afghan army was beginning to experience. For past nationalist regimes, in Afghanistan and throughout the region, conscription had been a key strategy for incubation of national cohesion, identity and loyalty. For countries where primary loyalties were still to tribe or kin and where government was remote, the experience of service in a national institution, especially one where 'modern' attitudes were paramount, was crucial in promoting new ways of comprehending the relationship between the state and the individual.

The economic argument for conscription was perhaps the least compelling. Although it was true that conscript pay might be much lower than that of volunteers, the policy had other costs. As well as administration and enforcement, economic incentives might still be necessary. During the 1980s, for example, although the PDPA had implemented conscription, with a good deal of success, it had also been obliged to introduce such incentives to deter desertions. But in terms of producing an army which might be perceived as truly 'national', conscription had clear advantages. It would avoid the difficulties found in recruiting sufficiently large numbers of volunteers, especially when combat operations were fierce. It would produce recruits from different ethnic, religious and tribal groups in proportion to the size of their communities, thus avoiding the perception, especially widespread in the early years, that minorities were over-represented in the Afghan army at the expense of the majority Pashtuns. Furthermore, since only those with few or no other opportunities enlisted voluntarily, conscription would also offer the possibility of enlisting the better-educated and less desperate.

The US, however, remained resolutely opposed to conscription and consequently a range of policies had to be adopted to address these difficulties. Successive and increasingly substantial pay increases were introduced to attract volunteers.[117] To try to ensure an ethnic balance in volunteers, ethnic quotas, rather reminiscent of the PDPA nationalities policy, were instituted and, in order to prevent infiltration by insurgents, a 'vouching system' was introduced by which village or tribal elders guaranteed the reliability of new recruits. These policies produced very uneven results.[118]

By 2009 the pay of a soldier had reached the sum, enormous by Afghan standards, of 165 US dollars per month.[119] Yet both recruitment and retention continued to be hit hard by the high salaries offered by both private security companies and insurgent groups eager to recruit trained Afghan soldiers. In general, voluntary enlistment did not attract a high quality of recruit. On the contrary, although recruitment was variously assessed as fairly easy, due to the dire lack of employment opportunities, to slow, there was agreement that the quality of recruits had been poor, and had declined further as recruitment rates intensified.[120] Recruits tended to come from the poorest and most marginalized communities; illiteracy among them, for example, was estimated at 90 per cent, much higher than in the general population, and drug use was widespread.[121] Most of the recruits had had no experience of structured environments such as schools, and found adjusting to military life difficult.[122] Morale remained low and the army encountered high rates of attrition, through soldiers going absent without leave or deserting altogether and refusing re-enlistment. Rates of absence without leave and desertion varied wildly, but reached very high levels when troops were faced with combat operations and were usually motivated by a desire to avoid the fighting altogether rather than by dissident political or religious loyalties.[123] In the absence of census data, neither the US/NATO nor the Afghan government formed a clear idea of what the ethnic balance in the army ought to be, but were agreed that the force was not ethnically balanced and that recruiting had been especially difficult in Pashtun areas.[124] The effort to achieve an ethnic balance remained a 'significant challenge' with an under-representation of some groups, including Hazaras and Uzbeks, and an over-representation of others, such as Tajiks.[125] Ethnic rivalries within the army remained intense and since 2008 it became increasingly clear that efforts to prevent infiltration into the army by insurgents had not succeeded, with attacks on International Security Assistance Force (ISAF) troops by Afghan soldiers increasing steadily.[126] Between 2009 and early 2013, a total of 24 British soldiers were known or suspected to have been killed by allied Afghan forces in so-called 'green on blue' attacks, forcing NATO-led troops to scale back joint patrols and change strategy.[127] The prestige and morale of the army was further undermined by corruption at all levels, and by a record of human rights abuses.[128]

In many respects the weaknesses visible among the rank and file of the ANA resembled those of past Afghan armies. The reconstituted cadre of officers and NCOs also manifested similar problems but on a scale magnified by the social disintegration of the past three decades.[129] Furthermore, the weakness of the officer corps, to a much greater extent than that of the rank and file, had profound implications for the future of the army. The quality of ANA officers remained a major, perhaps the main, impediment to force expansion and operational efficiency.[130] During most of the twentieth century, a system of military training was laboriously created in Afghanistan, at its apex the Military Academy, which slowly created an educated and trained officer corps. From the mid-1950s to 1989, officer training was further enhanced by Soviet assistance, both within Afghanistan and in the USSR. A small but developing Afghan education system contributed to the emergence of suitable human material from which a modern officer corps might emerge. After 1992, this entire structure collapsed. Post-2001, the new ANA was obliged to begin to recreate officer training facilities from scratch, while potential officers lacked the skills and literacy levels common among their predecessors. The production of an adequate number of officers to command the ever-expanding army proved completely beyond the capacity of the newly established Kabul Military Academy. In 2009 an estimated 50 per cent of officers were still illiterate and the corps continued to be divided by ethnic, political and personal rivalries. The corps suffered from old problems such as the ubiquity and rivalry of patronage networks, and from new, for example the hostility between uneducated former mujahidin commanders and the more competent but less well-connected Soviet-trained officers who formerly served in the army of the PDPA.[131]

Between 2002 and 2006 both state-building and army reform progressed haltingly. Meanwhile, legitimacy was draining away from the Karzai government which seemed unable to provide either basic security for the population or any hope of economic improvement. ANA morale and prestige inevitably suffered from the decline in popular support for and legitimacy of the Karzai government and from a 'plummeting' of popular support for US and ISAF forces.[132] From 2006 the insurgent challenge rapidly gathered speed.

The imperative need to confront the insurgency led to an abandonment by the US of its original hope for a small army. The projected numerical strength of the Afghan army was repeatedly revised upwards, to 80,000 in February 2008, jumping to 134,000 and then again, in January 2010, to 172,000, US commanders expressing the belief that a force of 270,000 was necessary while Afghan officers held out for even larger numbers.[133] The army struggled to meet its expanding recruitment targets by voluntary enlistment. By June 2009 numbers had reached 86,558, but this was still only half the number projected as necessary in early 2010.[134]

The cost of the army rose commensurately and the expanded projections led to the surfacing of serious doubts about fiscal sustainability. In June 2008 the (US) Government Accountability Office estimated the cost of maintaining both army and police at around 2 billion dollars per year. In fact, almost half of all US funding to Afghanistan between 2002 and 2009 had gone towards building the army and police forces.[135] Projected requests for US funds for security forces rose to astronomical levels while the prospects of ever meeting these costs out of Afghan revenues receded accordingly. The costs mushroomed due to the need to recruit, train and arm an army much larger than originally envisaged, coupled with the necessity of providing the army with the more expensive equipment required to confront the insurgency. Thus was the Afghan state launched on its current 'unsustainable trajectory'.[136]

The dramatic rise in projected numbers magnified difficulties, in recruiting, retention, training, ethnic balance, morale and discipline, which had until now been partially submerged. In general, despite the urgency of the security situation, progress in building the army was so slow that, by June 2008, it was reported that less than 2 per cent, only 2 of 105, army units were fully capable of conducting their mission.[137] Although ANA participation in operations had been important in propaganda terms, its actual military role and effectiveness remained very much in doubt. Since 2006 the army has been directly targeted by insurgents and has had some difficulty even in protecting itself. In this respect its experience contrasts with that of the PDPA army which was much more successful in reconstituting its military capacity in both organizational and operational terms.

In the context of these ongoing and unresolved difficulties, the US, although making a commitment to increase the Afghan army, at the same time began openly and actively to empower local militia groups. The Soviet experience, however, and the record of NATO thus far, tends to suggest that the second of these strategies will inevitably be at the expense of the first, reducing the pool of available manpower and further undermining the control of the state.

Between 2001 and 2008 little was accomplished in reducing the sway of tribal militias. On the contrary, local government figures and private security companies, and even ISAF itself, continued to make extensive use of them, many militias simply turning themselves into private security companies.[138] However, until 2008, NATO army commanders had officially opposed any deliberate policy of employing and strengthening tribal militias for fear of creating rivals to the army and the state. From 2008 onwards, the US, attempting to replicate the apparent success of a similar orientation towards the tribes in Iraq, increasingly articulated a policy of building on existing tribal structures and arming local tribal forces in order to compensate for the slow and uncertain progress made in rebuilding the ANA. This policy, known as the Community Defence Initiative, appeared in tandem with a broader approach, also reminiscent of the Najibullah era, of seeking an accommodation with, rather than confronting, elements within the Taliban and other hostile groups.[139] The Afghan army from top to bottom appeared to be unhappy with the new utilization of militias, seeing it as a return to the failed strategies of the Soviet Union during the 1980s.[140] By duplicating the methods of the last years of the PDPA, the Karzai government was widely feared to be leaving itself vulnerable to similar results.[141]

# Conclusion

The predicament in which the new Afghan army found itself reproduced, in certain respects, past Afghan state-building dilemmas. The creation of an effective military force remained crucial to the viability of the regime which, however, lacked the necessary resources, fiscal, material and human. It consequently found itself reliant on the support of a contested foreign presence, a reliance which appeared to increase its power vis-à-vis its domestic enemies but actually reduced its legitimacy. The dilemma confronting the US and NATO also recalled past foreign involvements. For them, standing up an Afghan army remained a key exit strategy, reminiscent of the exit strategies of the British in 1839–41 and the Soviet Union in the 1980s.

The difficulties experienced by successive Afghan governments, whether royal or republican, left or right-wing, in building an army have been remarkably similar and have their origin in the fragility of the broader state-building effort and the concomitant inability of the Afghan state to prevent the linking up of domestic and foreign opposition. This linkage has been crucial in destabilizing the Afghan state. Whereas foreign opposition alone merely provoked resistance, religious and/or nationalist, domestic opposition to state-building on its own lacked sufficient unity and coherence to offer a real alternative national strategy.

The Afghan state and its army has always relied on the prop of foreign support, whether British subsidies to the amirs in the nineteenth century, Turkish advisors to Amanullah and the Musahiban, Soviet assistance to Daud in the 1950s–70s and to the PDPA in the 1980s, or US/NATO sustenance now. Even the Taliban owed much of their successful rise to Pakistan. Opposition to the state has also, at different moments, drawn strength from foreign sources which was crucial to its success. States such as the US and Britain have alternated, depending on the context, between support for the state and support for its enemies.

In Afghanistan and other countries of the region, foreign involvement has often been unpredictable in its alignment with domestic political forces and has collaborated both with state-building and even nationalist trends and with their opponents. The varying possibilities open as imperial strategies are revealed by a comparison with the neighbouring state of Iran where Britain's attitude was diametrically opposite to that which it adopted towards Afghanistan. In the 1920s, in both Iran and Afghanistan, nationalist regimes had come to power which saw the suppression of autonomous tribal power as key to their own sovereignty. In pre-1921 Iran, the great tribal confederations of the south were not only autonomous of the central government but also benefited from the patronage, political and financial, of the British imperial presence. For Britain the tribal leaders provided a mechanism for securing a base in southern Iran, independent of the weak and unreliable government in Tehran. The dangers inherent in this situation were only too obvious to Iranian nationalist opinion which viewed the suppression of tribal power as synonymous with a blow against British domination of their country. The new nationalist regime which came to power after the coup of 1921, headed by Riza Khan (later Shah), was determined to end the power of the khans and to integrate the tribal populations into a newly homogenized and Westernized population. In this, the Iranian regime espoused a rather stronger, but essentially similar version of the state-building project adopted at the same time in Afghanistan by King Amanullah. In Iran, as in Afghanistan, the new government encountered tribal and religious opposition. However, when a particularly dangerous moment was reached in the mid-1920s, Britain abandoned its *quondam* tribal clients in favour of supporting the new central government, believing that Riza Shah was now the most reliable guarantor of its strategic interests. Again, when Iranian tribal groups rebelled in 1929, exactly contemporaneous with the fatal revolt against Amanullah, Britain backed Tehran. Had Britain not thrown its weight behind Riza Shah and against the tribal opposition in 1924–5 or 1929, his fate may well have resembled that of his Afghan contemporary. The British decision to opt for Riza Shah and a unified Iran in preference to its older tribal clients assured for Tehran a secure space in which to implement its broader state-building agenda.[142] Regarding Afghanistan, on the contrary, Britain was never able to overcome its suspicion of Amanullah and withheld its approval and support. The Musahiban victory in 1930, with discreet British backing, restored tribal ascendancy and delivered a major blow to nationalist opinion.

In more general terms, the state-building balance-sheet of Iran and Afghanistan presents a stark comparative contrast.[143] By the twenty-first century, Iran had come to resemble a 'leviathan' state, with a massive apparatus capable of extending its reach into the most remote corners of the country and of projecting its military power on a regional scale. In Iran the state now plays a major economic role, directly employs millions, and enforces a high level of control over the individual lives of its citizens. It has grown steadily since 1921, with only one significant disruption during World War II. Even the 1979 revolution did not weaken but rather immensely strengthened the state, albeit with a new elite in command. Afghanistan, by contrast, has barely possessed a state at all for the last three decades, and even during the long periods of relative stability, for example from 1930 to 1978, was prepared to trade the imposition of rural transformation for social peace.

State-building came later to Afghanistan and remained weaker than in any comparable country within the region. Nonetheless, in the first two decades of the twentieth century, the outlook in Iran was scarcely more favourable. Not only had nineteenth-century efforts at modernization largely failed, but the radical reform of the Constitutional Revolution (1905–11) had further weakened the Iranian state to the point where it appeared likely either to fragment or to fall under full imperial domination. By 1921 tribal power was once more in the ascendant across most of the country.

Yet nineteenth-century Iran had seen certain significant changes in the tribe–state relationship. The ruling dynasty of the Qajars was as tribal in origin as the Durrani monarchy.[144] Yet the Qajars, equally reliant on tribal military support, nonetheless moulded tribal power to suit a modest state-building agenda, specifically by creating large tribal polities with hereditary chiefs which were more amenable to central control. The modern Pahlavi state, building on the slender achievements of its Qajar predecessor, was able to break the power of the tribal khans and ultimately to co-opt them, turning them into instruments for the execution of its policies over the tribal populations, including disarmament and settlement. It similarly succeeded in securing the acquiescence to this agenda of the urban-based senior ulama, among whom in any case a modernist vision was taking hold which, far from making them enemies of state-building, finally enabled them to take command of the state in 1979. In Iran, oil revenues provided cash for the army, while broader economic development absorbed the tribal population driven off the land and the expanding state bureaucracy and private sector offered opportunities to tribal elites. The process of detribalization, operating at different speeds and in different ways but in evidence among all layers of the tribal pyramid, was massively accelerated by the land reform of the 1960s while the accompanying 'White Revolution' ended the power of the khans in rural areas. After the 1979 revolution the Islamic Republic, although it valued the historical enmity of the tribes towards the Pahlavis, redefining them as 'treasures of the revolution', its assertion of its own political supremacy in the tribal areas was absolute. In the chaos of the post-revolutionary period, some of the khans had tried to reposition them-selves as political leaders of the tribal populations, but they had met with little success. The tribal khans' attempt to mount a political and military challenge to the revolution signally failed to attract the support of the rank and file, now reaping the benefits of state attention in the form of education and health care, and ended in utter disarray.[145]

Both the persistence and strength of tribal power and the strategies adopted towards it by the state differed profoundly in twentieth-century Iran and Afghanistan. Afghanistan's rulers, failing to create any effective military strength of their own, were forced into an ever-deeper reliance on the tribes, to defend themselves against domestic rivals and the country against foreign invasion. Furthermore, no significant modernist movement arose among Afghanistan's ulama which might assist in the strengthening of national institutions, although the political salience of Islam and the status of religious figures among the tribes and in the rural areas more generally were enhanced by the calls to jihad which accompanied tribal mobiliza-tions. Insufficient economic development failed to disrupt patron–client tribal relationships, neither did a modernizing state bring the advantages of development, education, health care and better communications, to the rural populations, thus tempting them into its support and weaning them away from their old authorities. In contrast to Iran, the Afghan state made no decisive break with its tribal past but continued to waver in its tribal policy, successive rulers understanding the threat to their supremacy repre-sented by khans and chiefs, yet too weak to act against them. Unlike Iran, the Afghan state never disarmed or conscripted much of the tribal popula-tion; on the contrary, it still included more than a million armed tribesmen in its plans for military defence in the 1950s. From the first cautious efforts of Amir Dust Muhammad in the early nineteenth century until the premiership of Daud in the 1950s, successive Afghan governments shied away from imposing their authority on the tribal leaderships, preferring to 'encapsulate' them in their rural fastnesses. Their ambivalence contrasts starkly with the practice of other modernizing states in the Middle East, not only Pahlavi Iran but also Kemalist Turkey, which rejected any survivals of tribal power.

It was only with the arrival of Muhammad Daud as prime minister in 1953 that the Afghan state rejected its symbiosis with tribal power. Even then, however, this rejection remained largely theoretical and Daud's position weaker than army officers-turned-politicians elsewhere in the region. By this time the Afghan officer corps had become widely and deeply politicized and bent on rapid change, with itself in the vanguard. Ever since its emergence in the early twentieth century, the modern officer corps of the Afghan army had seen itself as spearheading the modernization drive. Indeed, it was perhaps the most modern institution in the country. Its eagerness to drag Afghan society into a wider modernity, and its specific hostility to khans and mullahs explains the readiness with which it embraced the doctrines of the PDPA. Yet the civil war which broke out in 1978 revealed the consequences of past state-building failures and the gulf which existed between the urban leftist officers and the rural populations at whom their reforming agenda was directed.

In this context, even the PDPA fell back on the deployment of tribal militias. No Afghan government has yet been able to construct a regular army capable of guaranteeing its sovereignty against co-ordinated foreign invasion or domestic opposition. Similarly, no Afghan government, finding itself in difficulties, has yet been able to resist the temptation of harnessing tribal military power. Some, such as the Musahiban regime between 1930 and 1953, did so willingly, some, such as that of Amanullah in the 1920s reluctantly. Inevitably, in the long run the result has been the same: a further weakening of the state, the enhancement of tribal political culture and its ideological hegemony and a strengthening of autonomous and centrifugal local powers, sometimes to the point where they could destroy altogether the government which originally mobilized them. There is no evidence that, in the absence of a transformation in political, economic and social relationships in the countryside, the current US/NATO strategy will have a different outcome.

Throughout the modern Middle East, the construction of a regular national army, capable of acting as a symbol of the state and of enforcing state authority within the national borders and against foreign threats, was deemed a quintessential element of the wider state-building project. Both Iran and Afghanistan embarked on the path of forming regular army units at the same time. Both adopted the same models and encountered similar difficulties. The very adoption of a European template invited suspicion in both countries, the diversion of resources to the new troops aroused jealousy and resentment among existing elites and neither country was able to develop the fiscal base nor state institutions necessary to support a regular army. A deficiency in human and material resources afflicted both countries throughout the nineteenth century. Neither found a solution to the problem of financing modern units from their own resources, and neither possessed sufficient personnel with a modern education to constitute a modern officer corps. The strategies they adopted were very different. Iran embarked on a long experiment with a succession of foreign military missions and allowed the financial strain of financing their recommendations to contribute to a growing danger of bankruptcy.[146] Afghanistan, on the other hand, refused to countenance the presence of foreign advisors with the army altogether, and protected the state from the financial effects of military reform by relying on British subsidies. Despite their contradictory strategies, both entered the twentieth century without effective modern military forces.

Yet by the early twentieth century, modest state policies were beginning to take effect in both countries. This was particularly true in the field of education, and specifically military education, where new institutions began to produce a modern officer corps. The experience of both Iran and Afghanistan in this period highlights the complexities of the role played by foreign military missions. The Ottoman and Turkish military missions to Afghanistan appear to have aroused little controversy. Although the Turkish officers' advice to Amanullah was unpopular with more conservative elements, it was the advice, and not the foreign officers themselves, which was the target of criticism. Religious opinion was neutralized by the fact that the Turkish officers were Muslims, albeit secular in their outlook, while nationalist currents found their presence and their Kemalist background a source of ideological reinforcement and practical assistance. In Iran foreign missions played a more complicated role. The European officers who had been employed with the Iranian army during the nineteenth century had usually been drawn from countries with strong imperial ambitions, especially Britain and France. The missions had been haphazard and chaotic, riven by internal conflicts and entirely contingent on the European diplomatic context. The Russian military mission, which arrived in 1879, was, for both religious and nationalist opinion, the perfect embodiment of malign foreign domination and the force it established, the Iranian Cossack Brigade, a byword for brutal domestic reaction. Yet, in 1910, the new constitutional authorities themselves invited foreign officers to organize a Gendarmerie. Sweden was chosen as a source of officers due to its neutrality, and the new force quickly became identified, despite its foreign leadership, with the most advanced trends in Iranian political life.[147] Both the Ottoman/Turkish mission in Afghanistan and the Russian and Swedish missions in Iran presided over the birth of a modern officer corps. In Afghanistan the Turkish mission remained until finally displaced in the late 1950s by the USSR. The officers produced under its tutelage strongly replicated their mentors' Kemalist outlook on politics, society and the role of the military, were secularist and centralizing and determined to reduce the role of the tribes and the ulama, and constituted a natural constituency for the ambitions of Muhammad Daud. In Iran, neither the Swedish nor the Russian missions survived the coup of 1921. For Riza Shah, Iran's military self-sufficiency was an article of faith, and his army, although its officers were sent abroad for training, a symbol of a more general independence. Iranian officers, like their Afghan and Turkish counterparts, saw themselves as spearheading a political, social and cultural transformation, enabling their country to take its place in the new post-World War I community of modern nation-states.

In the period after World War II, Iran and Afghanistan's experience of foreign military missions diverged significantly. In Afghanistan, the elite modernizer Muhammad Daud was able to invite a Soviet military mission to lead the reorganization of the Afghan army without compromising his regime's legitimacy. The Soviet mission worked with the grain of the prevailing secular Afghan nationalism, and was able to rely on the support not just of Daud and his immediate circle, but also of the wider trends of left-leaning Afghan nationalism rapidly gaining strength among both civilians and army officers. The Soviet mission in Afghanistan prior to 1978 attracted little of the opprobrium endured by US missions in Iran. There the arrival of US military missions from the 1940s onwards provoked an intense political reaction. Muhammad Riza Shah accepted the US missions in the teeth of nationalist opinion, and both he and the army suffered accordingly. American military personnel in Iran, and their extraterritorial privileges, enraged both the religious and the secular opposition who identified their presence not as a buttress to, but as a betrayal of, Iran's independence and sovereignty.

The popular view of Afghans is of a people incorrigibly and impartially opposed to foreign involvement. Yet, as Afghanistan's experience of foreign military missions shows, their attitudes are considerably more nuanced and relate not simply to the fact of foreign involvement, but rather to its character and objectives and the broader context, while the impact of the foreign presence has also been very varied. The defining issue appears to have been the perception of various strands of Afghan nationalism of the role of the foreign missions. Although in the early stages of military reform, neither successive Afghan rulers nor public opinion would tolerate European Christian advisors to the army, the later arrival of the Ottoman and then the Turkish military missions was enthusiastically endorsed by nationalist opinion. In the nineteenth and early twentieth centuries both Britain and Russia were distrusted as imperial powers determined to impose their own control. The Afghan policy was to do everything possible to keep them at their distance, even at the cost of delaying Afghanistan's entry into the world of modern states and its continuing diplomatic and increasing cultural isolation. The Ottoman and Turkish advisors, however, in addition to being fellow Sunni Muslims, were not suspected of harbouring wider ambitions in Afghanistan. From this perspective the acceptance of a massive military mission from the USSR in the 1950s–60s appears puzzling. Yet the Soviet presence was tolerable to most of Afghan opinion because it appeared to be supporting, rather than subverting, a nationalist dynamic. Elite modernizers such as the right-wing President Daud, and the growing Afghan Left, both within the army and in civilian circles, perceived the Soviet presence as beneficial to the state-building project. These perceptions of the legitimacy of Soviet assistance were transformed after 1979 by the ability of the PDPA's opponents to portray the regime as lackeys of an occupying foreign power.

All states are vulnerable to fragmentation and collapse if the pressure placed on them is sufficiently intense. In the late 1970s, after defeat in Vietnam, the US was faced with an 'arc of crisis' stretching from the Horn of Africa to Iran and Afghanistan and was unable, owing to domestic opposition, to commit ground troops to any of these conflicts.[148] Locked in a global confrontation with the USSR, it therefore opted to support indigenous insurgencies against regimes which it considered pro-Soviet.

Angola was another case in point and shows that the Afghan war of the 1980s was not unique but, in its intersection of domestic and international forces, was paralleled by other conflicts across the world. In post-independence Angola, an urban-based left-wing government, the MPLA (Popular Movement for the Liberation of Angola), supported by Cuban troops, engaged in a bitter and protracted conflict with its domestic enemies, backed by the US and South Africa and entrenched in parts of the rural areas. The success of Cuban troops in sustaining the MPLA and allowing it to consolidate its authority in the 1970s was an encouraging precedent for the USSR's intervention in Afghanistan. The Angolan President, during the 1980s, underwent an evolution similar to that of the PDPA, and both gradually distanced themselves from Marxism. After 1992 Angola established excellent relations with the US. It is ironic that Najibullah, had his regime survived the collapse of the Soviet Union, might have become an ally of US interests and, in particular, a regional bulwark against 'global jihadism'.

The encouragement of ethnic, tribal and religious insurgencies resulted in a proliferation of failed states when the end of the Cold War led to a loss of Western interest. Afghanistan was a victim of such a global strategy. By its decision to back the mujahidin after the Saur Revolution, the US and its allies empowered elements opposed not just to the pro-Soviet PDPA but to the entire state-building project. After 2002 the Karzai government was unable to resolve definitively doubts about its own legitimacy and the character of its reliance on foreign assistance, especially military assistance.[149] Indeed, despite the belated adoption of an overt 'hearts and minds' approach, such doubts have grown and spread. Although the hydra-headed insurgency never possessed the capacity to defeat Western and ANA forces in Afghanistan, it has prevented them from winning. This was sufficient in military terms for a kind of victory, creating a space within which, after the withdrawal of US and British troops, the Karzai government might slowly implode.

# CHAPTER 4

# The Iranian Army under Monarchy and Republic

## State-Building, Empire-Building and Revolution

Muhammad Riza Shah, like his father, Riza Shah, controlled and dominated but also mortally feared his army and its officers, especially its senior officers.[1] Like both shahs, British and American diplomats in Iran also saw the army as a source of potential political opposition. Especially after the wave of coups d'état which swept through the Arab world from the 1950s, both Muhammad Riza Shah and his Western supporters were vigilant, ever on the alert for the emergence of an Iranian version of the Egyptian Colonel Nasser or the Iraqi Colonel Qasim. Yet this obsession with the danger of a coup, emanating from the higher ranks of the army, colonel and above, turned out to be entirely misplaced. Under both shahs, the majority of the high command remained loyal, their own positions inextricably linked to the fate of the regime, even the most ambitious of Iran's colonels, brigadiers and generals, exemplified by General Ali Razmara, offering only sporadic and contingent opposition. Yet the measures taken to avert any challenge from this quarter rendered the high command of the army impotent in the face of the real threat to the monarchy which emerged in 1977–8. A comment from a US embassy report, that the conscript was of no political importance, summed up this mistaken assessment.[2] In fact, when the crisis came, it was indeed to be the hundreds of thousands of rank-and-file soldiers who, by defecting or simply deserting, were key in determining the outcome of the struggle between the Shah and the revolutionaries, while it was the non-commissioned air force officers, the *homafars*, who dealt the *coup de grâce* to the imperial regime.

The experience of the Iranian army in the pre-revolutionary and revolutionary periods conformed to the classical revolutionary model. Although conventional assessments have conceptualized the army in Pahlavi Iran as a monolithic bastion of the monarchy, it was in fact throughout its life riven by political fissures and social tensions, between left and right, communist, nationalist and royalist, and between the most senior officers, their middle-ranking subordinates, and the rank and file. The break-neck modernization of the 1960s and 1970s in particular saw a dangerous widening of the gap between senior and junior officers, and between the officers and the rank and file, this gap perhaps best illustrated by the case of the *homafars*, highly politicized air force technicians from humble back-grounds, whose professional frustrations combined with the revolutionary susceptibilities of the newly educated lower middle classes to produce an incendiary cocktail.

Under intense pressure from the revolutionary movement which was rapidly gaining hegemony over the wider society, the army began to frac-ture. The rank-and-file soldiers, conscripted from the urban and especially the rural poor, brought with them into the army the attitudes of the social layers from which they were drawn and which, by the late 1970s, also popu-lated the vast slums and shanty towns surrounding the major cities and especially the capital, Tehran. As the anti-Shah protests grew from tens of thousands to hundreds of thousands, it was such slum-dwellers who were drawn onto the streets and upon whom the conscripts were ordered to fire. The soldiers' class solidarity, as well as their receptivity to the increas-ingly religious tone of the protests, proved far stronger than any superficial monarchist indoctrination to which they had been subject once conscripted. They too, furthermore, shared the wider resentment of the newly urban-ized poor at the corruption and luxury of the ruling elite, this elite perfectly exemplified by their own officers.

During 1978 the Shah made sporadic attempts to use his massive army, equipped with the most sophisticated equipment petrodollars could buy, to suppress the growing revolutionary fervour, but both the Shah and his high command were aware that, while their jet fighters and Chieftain tanks were reliable, the men who operated them were not. As the crisis devel-oped, the army began to disintegrate, troops fraternized openly with demonstrators and desertions rocketed. Within the revolutionary context, the stark, political, economic and social divisions within the army took on a fatal significance. Caught between the mutinous rank and file and a demoralized high command, the middle ranks of the army simply retreated into neutrality or requested leave or early retirement.

Throughout the unfolding of the revolutionary period, the senior officers failed to act coherently to defend the regime which had succoured them, and this lack of leadership was crucial in determining the allegiance of the middle ranks of the officer corps. Certainly the intensity of the revolutionary pressure affected the high command, many senior officers in awe of the extraordinary power manifested on the streets and split between those who believed that concessions were unavoidable given the condition of the army, and those who still advocated repression. Undoubtedly too, the generals were perplexed by the Shah's vacillation and lethargy. But the main explanation may be found in the very measures which the Shah had put in place to control his generals, of whom he exhibited an almost pathological jealousy. The rigidly authoritarian hierarchy, built around the person of the Shah, the stimulation of rivalries, the pervasive atmosphere of suspicion and distrust, the material rewards for subservience, all served to undermine any capacity for counter-revolutionary action as the regime unravelled.

Thus the senior officers' failure to defend the monarchy in 1978–9 was the result of the very character of monarchical rule. Indeed, in other respects too it was the very policies adopted by the Shah which created the forces within the army which were to turn against him. His manic acquisition of technology led to the creation of a military layer, the air force *homafars*, who, in an action of immense symbolic as well as practical significance, defeated the Imperial Guards, the so-called Immortals, in February 1979, a final act in the life of the monarchy. In more general terms, it was the Shah's insistence on a particular model of military development, the building of a large army based on conscription, which proved to be his downfall, as a small, volunteer professional army would surely have proved to be much less vulnerable to external social and political pressures, more loyal to its creator and more effective in purely military terms. In an even wider sense, it was the Shah's land reform, the very centrepiece of his modernization project, which brought the rural poor into Tehran's shanty-towns, later to constitute a political force which overwhelmed the conscript soldiers.

In fact, and in contrast to the officer corps of neighbouring Arab states, the Pahlavi army possessed no real tradition of coup-making. In the years down to 1979 it never developed a corporate and independent identity, and made no bid for power on its own account. There had, of course, been two coups, one in 1921, and one in 1953. Both had, however, been incubated by foreign sponsorship, Riza Khan's seizure of government control in 1921 orchestrated by the British alone, General Zahidi's overthrow of Musaddiq in 1953 by the US with British assistance.[3] Such foreign sponsorship was essential to both interventions. Indeed, the CIA's own account of the situation prevailing among Iranian army officers in the months prior to the 1953 coup reveal an almost farcical incompetence, especially on the part of Zahidi himself, which was only overcome by determined coaching and pressure from the real authors of the coup. In late 1978 and early 1979, army officers, uncertain of the US attitude and without any significant domestic backing of the kind from which they had benefited in 1953, proved incapable of a repeat of the action that had rescued and restored the Shah in 1953. Although the American general Robert Huyser had arrived in Iran with the objective of encouraging the army to intervene, this was far too little and far too late, and in no way compared with the nursing of the coup preparations carried out by the CIA in the earlier period.

Nonetheless, the fear of a possible coup, of disloyalty in general and of politically ambitious generals in particular, dominated both Pahlavi shahs, and both put in place mechanisms designed to atomize the high command. In fact, however, those very politically ambitious generals, Ali Razmara, Fazlullah Zahidi and Taymur Bakhtiyar, largely sought to advance their careers by serving the Shah, not opposing him.[4] The 1953 coup itself was undertaken not to overthrow the old order, as was the case in the Arab world of the 1950s, but rather with the express objective of restoring the rule of Muhammad Riza Shah. Although both Muhammad Riza Shah and US officials spent much time searching for a potential Nasser or Qasim, the position of the Iranian army vis-à-vis the regime was not analogous to that of the pre-coup Egyptian or Iraqi armies, nor were the shahs perceived in the same way as had been King Farouk or the Hashemites. In particular, the Iranian army had experienced no shock of the kind delivered to Arab armies by their defeat in the 1948 Palestine war, a defeat which discredited not just the army leaderships but the entire political and social order. Neither Riza Shah nor Muhammad Riza Shah were, like the Egyptian and Iraqi monarchies, identified unambiguously as representing the 'old social classes'.[5] On the contrary, they were seen as often acting against the interests of these classes, as in, for example, the land reform of the 1960s, while in many respects they personified the rapid modernization on Western models which dominated the secular nationalist discourse in the Middle East for decades. Throughout the Pahlavi period, therefore, army officers tended to share the regime's ideology of secular nationalism and modernism, indeed they constituted its advance guard in this respect.[6]

Nonetheless, and although the majority of the high command remained wedded to the regime, attitudes throughout the wider officer corps towards the monarchy, and the persons of the shahs, were more complicated. Such critical attitudes were conditioned by both politics and professionalism. Dislike of the dictatorial modes of both shahs and a preference for constitutionalism were often to be found among officers, especially at the middle and junior levels, as were concerns that corruption, nepotism, the unchallenged whims of the shahs and the general backwardness of society were retarding specifically the progress of military modernization. Sometimes, these attitudes combined in a particularly dangerous conjunction. In fact, a tradition of opposition to Pahlavi rule may be discerned within the Iranian army, beginning as early as the foundation of the new regime in 1921. This opposition was both elite: Colonel Pasyan in 1921, the constitutionalist Gendarmes such as Major Mahmud Puladin of the 1920s, the pro-Musaddiq Generals Taqi Riahi and Mahmud Afshartus and the Patriotic Officers in the early 1950s, General Valiullah Qarani later in the decade; and subaltern: Major Lahuti in 1922, the radical mutinies of 1926, Lieutenant Muhsin Jahansuz in the late 1930s, the Tudah Military Organization in the 1940s to 1950s, the *homafars* during the revolution. Yet this opposition never expressed itself through the mobilization of the army in a military coup, and rarely even thought in these terms, tending to act, rather, in support of and in concert with civilian political activity, and through legitimate political channels. The pro-Musaddiq Patriotic Officers group, for example, may be taken as typical of this mentality. In general, discontent within the Pahlavi army, at the dictatorship constructed by Riza Shah and reconstructed by his son, at the latter's perceived subservience to the West, at the petrodollar-funded luxury and corruption of the court, was persistent, although driven underground by fear of SAVAK[7] and by the material rewards which were the return for loyalty. When the historic challenge came, neither officers nor men rallied to the defence of the monarchy. The rapid disintegration of the officer corps and the rank and file was finally consummated first by the military's declaration of neutrality, and then by an institutional switch of allegiance from shah to Islamic Republic.

The Iranian army under each of the Pahlavi shahs exhibited certain similar defects which ultimately made it unable to carry out the task for which it was fundamentally intended, that of guaranteeing the dynasty. Many of the problems which first manifested themselves in the 1920s and 1930s not only remained, but became magnified in the Muhammad Riza Shah decades. Under both shahs, military spending was always too high in relation to income and rational national priorities. Disproportionate amounts of money were spent in acquiring technology which was beyond the capacity of the army to use. The army tended to fragment in moments of political crisis, the officer corps dividing into those prepared to defend the Shah at (almost) any cost, those who hesitated, and those who went over to the opposition. In this sense July 1952 was a dress rehearsal for the much graver internal crisis which the army experienced in 1978–9. Both shahs exercised a highly personalized control over the army, were mortally afraid of coups, and created a military culture of corruption, rivalry and insecurity, periodically demonstrating their power by abrupt dismissals, anti-corruption drives and prosecutions. As individuals, both were central to the military systems over which they presided. After the disaster of 1941, both army and dynasty were, thanks to the Allied occupation, able to reconstitute themselves. No such favourable context existed in 1977–9 and the army, fracturing along several different faultlines, finally abandoned the dynasty which had created it.

## The Era of State-Building: Organizing the New Army, 1921–41

The creation of an army modelled on European lines, as part of a general programme of defensive modernization, had been a central objective of Iranian reformers since the early nineteenth century. By 1900, repeated initiatives aimed at military renovation had, however, ended in a generalized failure, with only the Russian-officered Cossack Brigade providing a modicum of order in Tehran and protection for the Shah. During the constitutional period (1905–11), the revolutionaries struggled to combat the consequences of the defencelessness of the new institutions of representative government, their only significant measure of military reform producing the Government Gendarmerie, while the years of World War I threatened Iran with internal disintegration and foreign occupation. Finally, in February 1921, a Cossack officer, Riza Khan (later Riza Shah),[8] cut the Gordian knot and seized power in Tehran through a military coup. Ruling Iran first as war minister, and from 1925 as shah, he embarked on a concerted effort to implement the state-building agenda, at the heart of which was a modern army, which had come to hegemonize elite discourses of reform over the previous century.

Riza Shah's determination to build a national army in Iran has generally been seen as the centrepiece of the entire state-building project of the period, the needs of military modernization determining both the scope and the character of much of the wider programme of reform and development. According to this view, interwar Iran's experience closely resembled the model of the 'military revolution' which had so captured the imagination of Middle Eastern rulers since the early nineteenth century. Yet the massive effort undertaken in these two decades to build a new professional army organized on European lines, capable of asserting Iran's regional ambitions, possessed profound flaws. By 1941 the new Iranian army was militarily ineffective, structurally weak, deeply politicized, and expensive beyond the capacity of the economy to sustain. Conscription, for example, had encouraged an embryonic process of national integration and had certainly produced an impressively large army, but the resulting force continued to possess serious military and operational inadequacies. Furthermore, the vast amounts of money spent on acquiring the most up-to-date weaponry from abroad resulted in a distortion of military priorities and led to unrealistic and complacent assessments of the army's strength. The Shah himself, whose increasingly arbitrary rule had brought about his own isolation, simultaneously relied upon, yet mortally feared, his own army, and its increasingly disillusioned officer corps. By 1939 Iran had acquired a dazzling facade of military strength. But the conscript army of the 1930s was a parade-ground army, largely untried in battle. In 1941, when it met its first real test, it collapsed, only able to offer sporadic resistance to the Anglo–Soviet invasion.

From the beginning of the new Pahlavi regime's life in 1921, it was clear that the needs of the military were, and would remain, Riza Khan's first priority. Immediately after becoming war minister, he put forward his plans for building a new army. His objective was to create a unified, centralized, national army, modern and modelled on European lines but free of foreign officers, the core of this new army to be constituted by his own old corps, the Cossack Division.[9] At the end of 1921 the two existing forces, the Gendarmerie and the Cossack Division, were amalgamated, and in January 1922 the new army was organized into five divisions, each division with the target strength of 10,000 men. In 1923 the Northern Independent Brigade, responsible for the Caspian provinces, was added to the five divisions. This military agenda was, however, immediately stymied by serious difficulties in finding new recruits, either in sufficient numbers or of the right type. Although energetic efforts were made to bring the divisions up to strength, with constant public exhortations from the Ministry of War, the provincial divisions remained considerably below their targets of 10,000 men each. By early 1926 the army still numbered barely 40,000.[10]

Iran's still rudimentary administrative and bureaucratic framework meant that initially the Iranian military authorities had no choice but to continue to rely on recruiting procedures inherited from the past. These included a continued reliance on the *bunichah* system, whereby each village provided recruits according to the amount of land under cultivation, supplemented by voluntary individual enlistment and the permanent incorporation of small tribal contingents.[11] The new divisional officers were no more successful in raising *bunichah* soldiers from the peasantry than had been their Qajar predecessors; their efforts were met with resistance and flight and produced only poor results. Exasperated with these antiquated methods, between 1923 and 1925 Riza Khan, supported by the modernist reformers of the Revival and Socialist parties, forced a conscription bill through the Majlis. Universal military service had emerged in the constitutional period as a state-building policy central to programmes of reform and, for the nationalist elite of early Pahlavi Iran, as elsewhere in the interwar Middle East, conscription was vital not only for the construction of a strong army but also for the creation of an integrated, homogeneous and modern society. Religious opposition having been neutralized by a concession granting exemption to all religious students, the conscription bill was passed by the Majlis in June 1925.[12]

Yet, although conscription was ardently advocated by elite opinion, wherever it was actually imposed it provoked intense hostility. In the cities of southern Iran in 1927 and in Tabriz in 1928, massive movements of opposition appeared, led by the ulama, while fear of the recruiting commissions was an important factor in the major tribal revolts of 1929.[13] Nonetheless, Riza Shah was determined to force conscription upon the population of Iran and he provided both the requisite political will and the necessary financial resources. The introduction of conscription was the single most significant measure of military reform introduced by the new state. By 1930, with all manifestations of organized resistance ruthlessly crushed, the way was clear for a massive expansion in the army's manpower. The army mushroomed from about 42,000 men in 1930 to an estimated 105,451 in 1937, reaching, by 1941, 127,000 men organized into 18 divisions, with a total mobilizable force of 400,000, an enormous number given a national population of less than five million economically active males.[14]

Although the army produced by conscription was certainly large, it remained deficient in competence and low in morale. Despite the huge amounts of money spent annually on the army, the conscripts themselves endured extremely harsh conditions. In 1931 their pay was only a paltry 7 *qirans* per month (volunteers received 45 *qirans* per month). Their physique and stamina were reported to be unsatisfactory; they were worked hard in all weathers, badly fed and housed, with inadequate medical and sanitary arrangements.[15] The poor morale resulting from bad material conditions was compounded by a lack of proper training programmes and the atmosphere of arbitrary terror which the Shah fostered within the army and which pervaded all ranks from the lowest to the highest. In general, the largely illiterate conscripts lacked confidence in their officers. Such an army was naturally of only limited use on active service and throughout the 1930s the military authorities continued to raise tribal levies for the small-scale operations which were its only occupation.[16] Fortunately for the regime the very pacification of the country which made the imposition of conscription possible also meant an end to the tribal campaigning which had typified the 1920s.

The ranks of the new army were eventually filled by reluctant conscripts, taken predominantly from the settled peasantry and the urban poor. The construction of a modern officer corps presented different difficulties. In 1921 Riza Khan at first relied on material bequeathed to him by the past, merging Cossack and Gendarmerie officers who had been trained by the Russian and Swedish military missions and in the respective cadet schools and officers' colleges of those forces. Some of these officers had also, on their own initiative, acquired some military education in European countries, especially France and Russia, and in the Ottoman Empire. In the early 1920s Riza Khan established a unified system of military education inside Iran, including a cadet college structured on modern European lines, and introduced a scheme for the training abroad of Iranian officers, the first party leaving for France in 1923. However the training received at St Cyr was frequently inappropriate and irrelevant to Iranian conditions; its application in the Iranian army was resisted by the entrenched conservatism of the senior commanders, and it often proved difficult to integrate the young officers effectively into the army on their return. In the mid-1930s, in another drive to improve clearly deficient military education, Riza Shah temporarily suspended his hostility to foreign military advisors and a French military mission arrived to act as instructors at the cadet college and the staff college.

Riza Khan's new army was an enormously expensive undertaking and from the very beginning the war ministry absorbed the lion's share of the national revenue. In the early 1920s the army already accounted for approximately 40 per cent of budget expenditure. Riza Khan's plans for building a new army took little cognisance of Iran's financial realities and, at first, the government experienced great difficulty in providing the military with the cash they demanded. As the decade progressed, however, the position of the Treasury improved. Dr A. C. Millspaugh, the American advisor who had been engaged to reorganize Iran's finances, was able to furnish the Ministry of War regularly with the funds sanctioned in the budget.[17]

During the 1930s the army, as an institution, continued to be immensely privileged by the Shah. Money, raised through draconian fiscal policies, especially astronomical rates of domestic taxation, was lavished on it and it was made into a showcase for the regime, expressing most perfectly the ideology of secular nationalism on which the Pahlavi monarchy based its

legitimacy. During the 1930s the army and military expenditure underwent a relentless expansion. Conscription was enforced with increasing
effectiveness as the decade progressed and resources devoted to the army
increased even faster than its numerical growth, the Shah being especially
keen to acquire the latest and most expensive military hardware. Although
exact calculations are difficult, it is clear that throughout the Riza Shah
period, the Ministry of War's budget allocation was far higher than that
of any other government department and that spending on the army grew
steadily, nearly quadrupling between 1930 and 1941.[18] The Ministry of War,
even in the early 1930s, a time of dire financial crisis, always had ample
funds at its disposal.

Furthermore, in addition to its official budget allocation, the Ministry
of War also received, directly from oil revenues, the enormous sum of about
2 million pounds annually during much of the 1930s for the purchase of
up-to-date and sophisticated military equipment from abroad, including
aeroplanes, artillery, machine-guns and mechanical transport.[19] By 1937
weapons of all kinds were pouring into the country, to such an extent
that the quantities of tanks, artillery and other material were beginning to
unsettle neighbouring countries. The new air force was particularly expensive.[20] Riza Shah was convinced of the indispensability of air power for both
tribal pacification and the prestige of the state, and by 1936 the Iranian air
force possessed 154 aircraft and was still placing orders for more. Yet the
Shah's obsession with acquiring the most advanced military technology
turned, paradoxically, into a weakness. According to an observer, having
completely neglected the proper training of their men, the General Staff had
'allowed themselves to be dazzled by mere possessions; they have erected an
imposing facade of guns for which there are no shells, of aeroplanes they
cannot maintain, of vehicles they cannot drive, and of mechanical devices
they cannot comprehend...their passion for purchase has exhausted their
means of maintenance.'[21]

The largesse bestowed on the army notwithstanding, difficulties had
quickly emerged relating not only to the apparent insatiability of the high
command's appetite for cash but also to internal financial procedures.
The tenure of the financial advisor, Dr Millspaugh, was dominated by a
struggle, sometimes open, sometimes covert, between himself and Riza
Khan over control of military expenditure. Riza Khan was determined

to keep complete control of the army budget and consistently refused to submit the accounts of the war ministry for inspection by the Ministry of Finance. Despite persistent efforts, neither Dr Millspaugh nor the Ministry of Finance were ever able to establish or exercise any control over the budget of the Ministry of War. Finally, Riza, now Shah, forced Millspaugh to leave. After his departure, the finance ministry gave up the struggle and the army remained a law unto itself, free of even the threat of audit. The consequences of this situation, in embezzlement and corruption, periodically threatened to engulf the officer corps.

In interwar Iran, the army was oriented exclusively towards domestic security. Its overwhelmingly important military task in these two decades was the extension and maintenance of the authority of the central government throughout the country, the suppression of alternative sources of authority such as autonomous local rulers and tribal chiefs, the disarmament and pacification of the civilian population and the maintenance, once established, of internal security. All the campaigns undertaken by the army in the period 1921–41 fell into this category. The army's second function, the protection of Iran from external aggression and the defence and assertion of its regional position, remained purely theoretical.

Yet, despite the immense effort put into the organization of a regular army, and the regime's aggressive anti-tribal discourse, in fact the bulk of the actual fighting in the many campaigns of these years was still actually carried out not by the regular troops but by irregular tribal levies, raised and disbanded as occasion required. The military authorities, as far as possible, utilized negotiation, bluff and intrigue rather than fighting, tried to win over sections of tribes to the side of the government, raised tribal levies to give assistance to the regular troops and used traditional leaders, whom they were often still too weak to crush, to maintain order.[22] The government frequently achieved its objectives by one or more of these methods rather than through conventional military victories by the regular army. The army's record when these tactics were exhausted and it was obliged to undertake real campaigning against the tribes was often dismal, characterized by reluctance and retreat and often by actual surrender or defeat.

Yet, if the reality of Riza Shah's tribal policy was one of pragmatism and co-option, yet the regime's discourse of legitimacy presented the role played by the army in an altogether different light. This discourse emphasized the imperative of confrontation, defined the tribes as presenting an existential threat to national survival, and insisted on the necessity of building up military strength and authoritarian state structures capable of containing and eventually eradicating this threat. The tribal problem was used to justify the primacy of the army in the national budget and the installation of military rule in the provinces while any politically popular victories, however achieved, were invariably presented as military triumphs, and used to burnish the credentials of both the army and its commander, the Shah.

In general, throughout this period the army, although of doubtful conventional military capability, was extremely successful in advancing, not merely the power of an impersonal state, but the political ambitions of its own chief, Riza Khan/Shah. In his rise to power, between 1921 and 1925–6, Riza Khan used the army both to intervene directly in Iranian politics and to manipulate, in a more subtle way, the ideological and cultural context. His direct military intervention had begun, of course, with the 1921 coup d'état itself. In 1922 and especially after the failure of the republican movement in 1924, he used the army to intimidate the Majlis, while growing military control over elections fatally compromised the independence of that institution. The army, at Riza Khan's behest, orchestrated political campaigns such as the republican movement and prepared the ground for constitutional change, from the Qajar to the Pahlavi dynasties, at the end of 1925, martial law a key mechanism in ensuring this transition. Riza Khan systematically promoted the military at the expense of the civilian authorities throughout the country, and placed army officers in control of defeated tribes. He also used the army to promote an image of his regime appealing to modern nationalism, strong, independent and modern, technologically advanced and educated in European sciences.

From the very beginning the entire fabric of the new army had very much centred around Riza Khan personally.[23] He had always insisted that all matters of military importance should be referred to him, determining administrative detail as well as broad policy, and reducing his senior commanders to complete dependence on his favour. It was Riza Khan himself who determined the character of the developing military culture and the senior commanders took their cue from their chief. It was he who had set a spectacular example of contempt for the civil authorities, had been principally responsible for creating an atmosphere of intrigue and insecurity within the high command and, having personally amassed wealth by questionable methods, allowed his senior officers to do the same, believing he could thus buy their continued support. After his accession to the throne, the new Shah continued to retain full control of the army in his own hands, devoting a great deal of his time and personal energy to every detail of military administration. Far from relaxing his hold on the army, as the 1920s turned into the 1930s, he seemed rather to be tightening his grip. He held to his habit of making unheralded descents at dawn upon units, arsenals and military schools. By these visits and his behaviour on them, including his 'vindictiveness, petulance and impatience',[24] he engendered considerable fear throughout all ranks of the army. The higher command in particular existed 'entirely on the pleasure' of the Shah, and functioned 'on a wholesome fear of his displeasure'.[25]

By the late 1920s, however, the Shah was beginning to fear his own creation. Although attempting to ensure the loyalty of his officers by bestowing positions of power and permitting widespread corruption, Riza Shah was far from complacent about the ambitions of his immediate subordinates. As the army had grown and become established throughout the country and opportunities for the acquisition of wealth and power had increased, so ambition and jealousy in the upper echelons of the officer corps had also intensified. This phenomenon was made particularly serious by the senior commanders' tendency to adopt strategies of discrediting their rivals, making accusations of political unreliability and disloyalty to the Shah. Furthermore, this tendency was encouraged by the ease with which the Shah could be convinced of the existence of conspiracies and subversive activities. Indeed the atmosphere within which this intriguing flourished had been established and fostered by Riza Shah himself who seemed increasingly unable to tolerate any prominence other than his own and who simultaneously depended upon, and feared, his own senior officers. Gradually, both the army itself and the regime which had been built around it became suffused with suspicions of treason and betrayal. The Shah watched his senior officers closely, maintaining control by abrupt dismissals, of those whom he thought becoming too rich or too powerful, and reinstatements, of those whom he had previously disgraced.

Yet, in reality, and notwithstanding the Shah's perennial suspicions, throughout the 1930s the high command was consistently loyal to the regime. In becoming shah, the former Cossack officer had distanced himself from his senior commanders and made a challenge from any one of them more difficult. However, any residual hesitancy felt by his erstwhile equals from the Cossack Brigade regarding his pre-eminence was more than neutralized by their awareness of the extent to which their individual position relied upon the maintenance of a nationally organized, centrally controlled and politically coherent military structure. Senior officers tolerated the insecurity of their position, and their occasional humiliation, in return for prestige and wealth, and even welcomed the Shah's capriciousness when it resulted in the downfall of rivals. Nonetheless, throughout the 1930s the high command continued to be periodically convulsed by the Shah's arbitrary purges which destabilized and disorganized the command structure, creating a climate of uncertainty, insecurity and demoralization throughout the officer corps.

As his isolation had become more complete, so the Shah had abandoned his trust in his own army. Although the army had been, and still was, useful in the rural areas for tribal management, and might still be used in cities, especially provincial cities, as a tool of coercion in times of crisis, it was of little use as a guarantor of political security and might even be a source of political opposition. The pampered and privileged army became itself an object of the Shah's suspicion, and the civilian political police were deployed to keep watch on army officers. By the 1930s the army had been superseded by the police as the key internal guarantor of the maintenance of the regime and the personal safety of the Shah.

During the 1920s the army had been constantly engaged in tribal campaigning but, as the 1930s advanced and the objectives of tribal pacification and settlement were achieved, active operations became fewer and ever more minor in scope. Since much of the training of the rank and file had always consisted of actual participation in campaigning, and no adequate substitute was devised, the deleterious effect of this decline in active service on the already problematic military capacity of the army was plain. The absence of any military challenge also fostered complacency and encouraged the high command to develop unrealistic assessments of the army's strength and to devise fantastic strategies for national defence. The consequences of this approach became all too obvious in 1941.

With the outbreak of World War II in 1939, the Shah's first response was a desperate effort to preserve Iran's neutrality. Successful for the first two years of the war, this policy was doomed by Hitler's attack on the Soviet Union in June 1941. Following the launch of Operation Barbarossa, the Shah's fears of an invasion from the north intensified and the army drew up grandiose plans for resisting attack. But the British minister in Tehran, Reader Bullard, was well aware of the lack of realism in the plans of the General Staff, his view being that the Shah and his military advisors took too optimistic a view of the ability of the army to offer a successful resistance to serious invasion.[26] When, on 25 August 1941, the Anglo–Soviet armies descended on Iran, the resistance put up by the army was even less effective than had been anticipated. This was largely due to its own lack of morale, but there had also been an almost entire lack of serious defensive preparations, to the extent that it appeared that the military had never had any serious intention of resisting.[27] The Shah had apparently remained confident up to the last moment that Britain and the Soviet Union would not resort to military action and this optimism had reflected itself in the complacency of the army. When the invasion began, on 25 August, the first aerial bombardments created panic, which spread rapidly to the headquarters of military units. These had retreated at speed, their troops promptly disintegrating. The causes of the poor morale of the troops were familiar from previous years: the rank and file were underfed and underpaid, the senior officers corrupt, they had received no training for modern warfare nor in the use of their expensive weapons, and there was an almost complete absence of supply arrangements.

The army in the field disintegrated from the top down, the rank and file dispersing after their officers had fled. Demoralization, which began among those divisions on the front line, quickly spread throughout the army, to troops who had not been engaged on operations. By 30 August 'complete chaos' reigned in Iranian military circles.[28] As large numbers of officerless troops deserted, they usually managed to take with them their rifles, ammunition and equipment, which they sold to the tribes in order to be able to buy food. By the time the situation began to stabilize, little was left of the army.

# The Era of State-Building: Political Opposition within the New Army, 1921–41

Riza Shah built his new army around a core of his old comrades from the Cossack Division who remained largely loyal to him throughout the life of his regime. Nonetheless, from the moment of its foundation Pahlavi rule was subject to challenges from elsewhere within the new army. In the first half of the 1920s, before the consolidation of his dictatorship, Riza Khan experienced a number of challenges from constitutionalist and nationalist officers. By mid-decade, conditions within the new army were provoking a different kind of opposition, whereby political disaffection fused with material hardship to produce armed mutinies among the junior officers and the rank and file. In the late 1930s a more modern ultra-nationalist group of officers, from provincial middle and lower middle-class backgrounds, seemed to be a harbinger of an Iranian 'Free Officers' movement, raising the possibility that the regime might, then or in the future, be at risk from a military coup.

In 1921 Riza Khan erupted into Iranian political life. During the next five years he consolidated his power, destroyed the Qajar dynasty and placed himself on the throne. In realizing this project, he based himself on the army, or more precisely on a section of the army, having originally come to power via a military coup. However, the army's support for its chief in this period was not, as is often assumed, always united or unwavering. In fact at certain key moments, such as the crisis resulting from the republican agitation in 1924, the force was wracked with dissension to the point where senior commanders openly defied Riza Khan's orders and it seemed possible that the army might split apart.

In the circumstances of domestic political weakness and threatened imperial domination which characterized Iran during and immediately after the Great War, the source from which a leadership with the requisite determination was most likely to emerge was the military. In 1920–1, however, it was by no means clear which element within Iran's disparate armed forces might posit itself as the instrument of national salvation. Although, as a result of the later consolidation of Pahlavi rule, Riza Khan's military pre-eminence by 1921 seems established, in fact military rivals to his ascendancy, both individual and collective, still flourished. The establishment of his own supreme power, both within the army as well as over state and society generally was, at the time of the coup, still a matter awaiting accomplishment. The liquidation of his most serious military rival, the nationalist Gendarme officer, Colonel Muhammad Taqi Khan Pasyan, and the suppression of any overt challenge from the Gendarmerie, were key episodes in this process.

Throughout 1920–1 the Cossack Division and the Gendarmerie were contending, sometimes covertly, sometimes overtly, for military supremacy in Iran. The Gendarmerie, imbued with the spirit of constitutionalism and with a strong nationalist record, offered a sharp contrast to the Cossack Division, long identified with the most reactionary tendencies in Iranian society. In order to assert his hegemony in both the new army and the regime being constructed around it, Riza Khan was obliged to reduce the independence, appeal and prestige of the Gendarmerie and this he was able to accomplish by degrees during 1921.[29]

During the spring and summer of 1921, the obstacle to Riza Khan's pre-eminence represented by the Gendarmerie was starkly illustrated by the regime then firmly entrenched in Mashhad under the leadership of Colonel Pasyan.[30] The colonel had seized power in Mashhad in early April as part of the wave of such actions in the provincial capitals which had accompanied the February coup in Tehran. Although elsewhere Gendarme officers quickly ceded power, Colonel Pasyan remained obdurate in Mashhad. His regime implied a grave political, ideological and military threat to Tehran and highlighted the fragility of Riza Khan's grip on power in the immediate post-coup period. Pasyan presided over a prolonged period of tension, between the central government and provincial radicalism, between the opposing military and political agendas of the Gendarmerie and the Cossack Division, and between his own personal ambitions and those of Riza Khan, which was only ended with the physical liquidation of the Gendarme regime in Mashhad.

Pasyan's destruction freed Riza Khan to adopt unchallenged the mantle of nationalism among the military and to fashion the army in his own image. By the end of 1921 the Gendarmerie found itself submerged, politically and militarily, by Riza Khan's Cossack Division. By a combination of co-option and repression Riza Khan ensured, both in the new army and in the regime constructed around it, his own supremacy and the ascendancy of his comrades from the Cossack Division, triumphing over the leadership offered by the officer corps of the Gendarmerie and the political traditions represented by the force. By late 1921 Riza Khan had clearly emerged as the single most powerful personality within the Iranian army and was able to pose as the saviour of the Iranian nation, presenting a new-found, but undoubted, appeal to nationalist elements.

Yet opposition to Riza Khan continued within the new army, and in the years of political contest, 1921–5, fell into three broad categories. In the first category were the cluster of oppositional activities which had their origins in the long-standing rivalry between the two elements which mainly comprised the new army, the Gendarmerie and the Cossack Division. The second category included the various types of disaffection which arose as a result of Riza Khan's attempt to replace the Qajar dynasty with a republican dictatorship. The final category comprised the military mutinies which broke out in 1926 and which possessed an explosive combination of ideological opposition to the regime and severe material grievances relating to pay and conditions.

However, the phenomenon of military disaffection within the new army should not be exaggerated in relation to the key question of the survival of Riza Khan and his regime. Only over one issue, that of republicanism, did the army appear to be in real danger of fissuring while the disintegration of 1926 was essentially an exasperated reaction to intolerable conditions. On the whole the bulk of the army, particularly its ex-Cossack upper echelons, remained staunchly loyal to its chief throughout these years. Never before had the army occupied the dominant position throughout Iran which it achieved in the early 1920s. Senior officers saw opening up before them spectacular opportunities for the acquisition of wealth, opportunities of which they took full advantage. The most powerful officers in the army, all ex-Cossacks, knew that they owed their new eminence to their chief and they repaid him with political subservience. Furthermore, notwithstanding various degrees of doubt about Riza Khan's personal and political ambitions, many ex-Gendarmes also offered their broad support to the regime's nationalist agenda, finding especially appeal in its avowed aim of creating a strong and modern army. Many ex-Gendarmes survived, and even thrived, in the new army, although they could not aspire to the highest posts.

The formal unification of the two forces at the end of 1921 immediately resulted in an outburst of military disaffection which entwined itself with an existing political radicalism in the city of Tabriz in early 1922. The rebellion was led by the Gendarme Major Abul Qasim Khan Lahuti, who was later, while in exile in Soviet Tajikistan, to become one of the foremost literary figures of his generation.[31] Although Lahuti himself was motivated by wider aims, using the insurrectionary period in Tabriz to put forward an agenda of radical political reform for the whole country, the majority of his followers among the Gendarmes, mostly NCOs and ordinary soldiers, had been provoked into mutiny by resentment at the fact that junior Cossack officers had been promoted over the heads of more senior Gendarmes, and that pay had been issued to the Cossacks, but not to the Gendarmes, who were already seven months in arrears.[32] The rebellion was brief, and crushed by a Cossack force commanded by an ex-Gendarme, Brigadier Habibullah Shaybani, after it signally failed to evoke any significant support in the wider country.

During the 1920s, the ex-Gendarmes remained the object of official suspicion and the focus of a series of alleged plots and conspiracies against Riza Khan.[33] There was, however, considerable public scepticism about the plausibility of these conspiracies, and suspicion that they had been embellished, or even manufactured, by the chief of police, Colonel Muhammad Dargahi. But opposition to Riza Khan among military officers did not find expression merely in conspiracies and assassination plots, real or imaginary. Perhaps the clearest example of open, organized and coherent dissent within the army emerged vis-à-vis the movement to establish a republic in Iran in 1924. Although the republican movement in both the capital and the provinces was initiated and sustained largely by the military authorities, nonetheless deep divisions existed within the army regarding the legitimacy of this movement and again the ex-Gendarme officers, fearing the republican movement was a mask for the further ascendancy of Riza Khan, provided one nucleus of discontent.[34]

The ex-Gendarme officers were not the only opponents of the republican movement within the army. There was considerable royalist sentiment among both the officer corps and the rank and file and strikingly, and perhaps uniquely, his espousal of republicanism deprived Riza Khan of the support of some of his closest ex-Cossack comrades. The participation of the rank and file in anti-republican meetings within the army provides a rare glimpse of the attitudes of this layer of the army. Although the ordinary soldiers showed little interest in politics, they took a keen interest in religious questions and were unquestioningly loyal to the monarch. They became overtly anti-republican when the ulama assumed the leadership of the opposition to Riza Khan.

In early April 1924, as it became clear that the republican movement was collapsing, Riza Khan resigned as prime minister, reverting to the tactic of direct military intimidation, in an attempt to break the political deadlock resulting from the failure of the republican movement. The Majlis was immediately bombarded by telegrams from the provincial divisional commanders, some expressing regret at Riza Khan's resignation and requesting the Majlis to ask him to return, others more menacing, yet the army commanders knew that they did not have the unequivocal support of either their officers or their men. It seems that Riza Khan had been forced to retreat on the issue of republicanism not only by the vehemence of civilian opposition but also by the depth of discontent among the military and by his fear that to persist with the project might actually lead to a split within the army. The fiasco of the republican movement produced a marked demoralization in the army. This demoralization in turn was reflected both in disasters on the battlefield and in a rash of plots during the summer and autumn of 1924.[35]

During the remainder of 1924 and early 1925, Riza Khan succeeded in regaining the political initiative, using the imposition of martial law following the murder of the US vice-consul, Major Robert Imbrie, to suppress opposition. With the army in control in Tehran, public assembly was banned, a military censorship imposed on the press, and mass arrests carried out. Finally, with the deposition of Ahmad Shah at the end of 1925, the struggle between Riza Khan and the Qajars was resolved. This removed the dilemma experienced in previous years by certain sections of the army as to where their loyalty was due and thus eased, to some extent, the internal tensions characterizing the previous period. Indeed the accession to the throne of one of its own was a source of intense pride to much of the army. Nonetheless, 1926 was to see a renewed outburst of disaffection, provoked now largely by the deteriorating material conditions inside the army, particularly as these affected junior officers and the rank and file.

Despite the fact that military expenditure absorbed so much of the budget, from the very beginning of the life of the new army the troops had been constantly in arrears of pay; corruption, embezzlement and financial malpractice of every kind abounded. These endemic problems were intensified after Riza Shah's accession to the throne. Late 1925–6 saw senior officers, left more or less to their own devices, using their new ascendancy to amass as much wealth as possible, as quickly as possible, using part of their new-found fortunes to retain their positions by placating the new Shah's demands for money.

Inevitably, provoked beyond endurance, units of the army began to mutiny, the two most serious outbreaks both being led by junior officers. The first episode occurred towards the end of June at Salmas, in Azerbaijan.[36] It was an apparently spontaneous affair caused by discontent at non-receipt of pay and hatred of the commanding officer, Colonel Yusuf Khan Arfa, who had become deeply unpopular due to his severity and harsh notions of discipline.[37] A few days after the Salmas mutiny a more serious insurrection broke out, again led by a lieutenant, this time in the Eastern Division, at the remote frontier post of Maravah Tappah. Here one of the spontaneous protests by the troops at deteriorating conditions developed into a full-scale rebellion which was only liquidated by the arrival of fresh, regularly paid troops from the Shah's loyal Tehran Central Division.[38]

In the years between 1921 and 1926, before the effective consolidation of the new Shah's dictatorship, the spirit of political and intellectual independence instilled in sections of the officer corps by their experiences during the constitutional period and the Great War remained alive. By the late 1920s, however, the same pall of silence that was covering civilian politics had settled also over the army. The Shah had persistently tried to insulate the army from political activity and, by a combination of harsh repression, political co-option and the guarantee of material privilege and social prestige, had succeeded in acquiring the support, or at least acquiescence, of the majority of the upper echelons of the officer corps. Any political dissent took place in secrecy, fear and isolation. Indeed the entire army, from the most loyal commander downwards, functioned in an atmosphere of sporadic terror, an atmosphere deliberately cultivated by the Shah as a means of control.

The 1930s was a decade of intense political repression in Iran. This repression, together with unpopular measures such as the new oil concession negotiated with the Anglo–Iranian Oil Company and the regime's blatant corruption, increasingly alienated nationalist opinion. As the 1930s wore on, Riza Shah lost the support of the older generation of the intelligentsia, who sank into passivity or disgrace during the early 1930s. The younger generation of intellectuals, however, felt no such ambivalence towards Riza Shah and, from the perspectives usually of the political left but also sometimes of the right, were more forthright in their condemnation of the regime. It is in this context that a new type of disaffection emerged within the army, best exemplified by the Jahansuz group.

In the autumn of 1939 a group of junior officers and cadets and a number of their civilian associates were arrested. They were accused of having links with foreign powers and with plotting an armed revolt against the Shah and his dynasty. After a brief and secret trial many received lengthy prison terms while their leader, Muhsin Jahansuz, was sentenced to death and shot.[39] The actual activities in which the Jahansuz group engaged were trivial in terms of any threat offered to the regime's security and the episode was hidden from contemporary public knowledge by heavy press censorship and the circumstances of the group's court-martial. The Jahansuz group has been described as having a right-wing, pro-fascist or Nazi tendency. This characterization, however, derives largely from Jahansuz's translation of extracts from Hitler's 'Mein Kampf' and has been greatly exaggerated, although the appeal of Italy and Germany for nationalist intellectuals, and especially army officers, in the interwar Middle East was considerable. In general terms Jahansuz and his associates were modernists, socially conscious, advocating rapid industrialization and technological advance and an end to poverty and the subordination of Iran to the imperial powers. Furthermore, in their strong secular nationalism these radicals of the right shared the official ideology of the regime. It was precisely what they saw as the regime's departure from these values which inspired their opposition. It was Riza Shah's failure to carry out effectively his own programme, of nationalist modernism, and his perversion of its key tenets, which impelled them into active hostility.

By the 1930s the army was equipped with a dazzling array of weaponry and the officer corps occupied a position of material privilege and social prestige.[40] Nonetheless, there were ample reasons for discontent within the army. There was widespread resentment at the military clique which monopolized power within the army, at the prevailing uncertainty and insecurity caused by the erratic and arbitrary exercise of power and disgust at the spectacular corruption. Junior conscript officers did not share in the opportunities and benefits available to career officers, and they and the rank and file appear to have been unfavourably impressed by the contrast between the lavish wealth of the senior commanders and the devastation and destitution which the regime's economic policies had wrought on the rural areas from which most of them came. The acquisition of immense landed wealth by both the Shah and his military favourites was a keenly felt grievance among these rural and provincial recruits. Furthermore, conscripts, although they now received their meagre pay and rations regularly, were generally treated extremely harshly.

The existence of organized disaffection within the army was a matter of profound political anxiety for the Shah. The presence of such a group within the army, the quintessential institution of Pahlavi Iran, showed that even this prized and pampered institution was neither immune nor invulnerable to dissent. Although far too junior to pose a threat as coup-makers, the discovery of the Jahansuz group came as a shock to the Shah, reviving his perennial fears of assassination and renewing his doubts regarding the ultimate reliability of the army as guarantor of his dynasty. Although the Shah tolerated, indeed encouraged, corruption among his senior commanders and expected armed tribal rebellion, the existence of political opposition among cadets and young officers he construed as representing not just a threat to himself but also to the existence of his dynasty.[41] Since his accession to the throne, political control of his senior generals had been essential to Riza Shah, not just in order to safeguard his own position but also to guarantee the smooth and unchallenged succession of the Crown Prince. In fact the Shah had little fear of any rival to himself, but was extremely conscious of the vulnerability of the succession. The precedent which he himself had set by rising to power and to the monarchy itself through his control of the army haunted him. He encouraged the Crown Prince to take a great interest in military matters and the young Muhammad Riza had already become well known in the Tehran garrison, but the Shah knew that it would be some years before the young man would, in the event of his own death, be able to establish himself on the throne without both a struggle and the support of a senior general. He openly spoke of the importance of his living long enough to ensure the succession.[42] The Shah had always particularly feared assassination[43] and his concern for his dynasty now added new urgency to that fear. Although he knew that none of his senior officers possessed either the courage or the wider political support necessary to offer a challenge to his own power, he was aware that the sudden propulsion of the young and inexperienced Crown Prince onto the throne would present an ambitious general with an almost irresistible opportunity. He feared that such a general might aspire to the throne himself, launch a military dictatorship or become regent on behalf of the Crown Prince.

Accordingly the presence of radical opposition within the army appeared to the Shah to represent a real threat to his dynasty. The Jahansuz group also seemed to threaten the realization of another major danger, that of the military coup. He had even begun to suspect that Germany, which he had cultivated throughout the decade, might now be tempted to dispense with him altogether and install an overtly and unambiguously pro-German regime in Iran based on Nazi sympathizers within the army.

The investigation into the alleged conspiracy was handed over to the chief of police, General Rukn al-Din Mukhtar, a key figure in the Shah's apparatus of political repression. In Mukhtar's hands it was almost inevitable that any sign of discontent among junior officers would become a plot against the Shah's life. Jahansuz and his fellow officer cadets had done nothing more than criticize the regime in discussions among themselves, but the Shah was determined that Jahansuz should be executed. The court-martial which tried the accused duly complied with the Shah's orders, sentencing Jahansuz to death and many of the other accused to long terms of imprisonment.

However, Riza Shah himself had only a year and a half of power remaining to him. The harsh treatment meted out to his critics within the army made his own position no stronger, nor did it enable him effectively to control the pro-German inclinations of the officer corps or to channel these tendencies into support for his regime. When, after the German attack on the Soviet Union in June 1941, the Allies invaded Iran, they did so not only in order to open a new corridor to Russia and to secure the expulsion of German agents, not only to oust the procrastinating Shah, but also to forestall a coup by pro-Axis officers of the kind that had occurred earlier in the year in Iraq and which had dealt such a serious blow to Allied morale and prestige.

# The Nationalist Challenge, 1941–53

The disintegration of the Iranian army on contact with British and Russian troops in August 1941 was a traumatic episode for nationalist opinion in general and particularly for the officer corps of the army itself. Prior to the invasion, defensive preparations had been desultory and erratic, reservists had only belatedly been called up and throughout all ranks morale was at rock bottom. Senior officers were divided in their strategic assessments and all were in mortal fear of the Shah's reaction to their proposals. On 25 August, during the Iranian month of *shahrivar*, British and Soviet divisions crossed into Iran, the British from the south and the Soviets from the north. Although there were pockets of resistance (the British described, for example, how the soldiers at the Abadan oil refinery 'fought with tenacious gallantry',[44] while the naval commander, Admiral Ghulam Ali Bayandur, was killed in the defence of Khurramshahr), most of the military units, even those not engaged in active operations, simply melted away, the officers fleeing, leaving their abandoned men to survive as they could.

Riza Shah, isolated from political and military realities for many years and apparently surprised by the invasion, was unable to formulate a coherent response. He ordered a cease-fire which further accelerated the army's disintegration, countermanded the orders of his own senior officers, and physically attacked and threw into prison the Minister of War and the chief of staff, ordering the courts-martial of five more generals. Within a couple of days the entire military organization was in chaos, a political crisis was developing in Tehran, and loyal remnants of the army were engaged in suppressing a mutiny by pilots at an air base near Tehran.[45] On 16 September the first step towards stabilizing the situation was taken when Riza Shah abdicated and went into exile. With this action, he succeeded in preserving his dynasty, his son, Muhammad Riza Shah, ascending the throne.

Meanwhile, tens of thousands of starving but well-armed conscripts and reservists were roaming the country. These men, no longer of any value in preserving even internal security, were now rapidly becoming a menace on their own account. The situation was perhaps at its most desperate in western Iran. In Kirmanshah, Major-General Hasan Muqaddam's negotiation of the cease-fire with his British opposite had been followed by mass desertions, those of his officers still at their posts making little or no effort to prevent the deserters taking with them their rifles and ammunition. These weapons the soldiers, without food for three days, promptly sold to the Kurdish tribes, who immediately launched attacks on remaining military units and entered and occupied the towns on the Sanandaj–Tabriz road.[46] Meanwhile, a wave of acute apprehension was rolling over the populations of Kirmanshah and the surrounding area, who feared attacks by ex-soldiers, transformed into bands of brigands, on the city and especially on the scores of isolated and exposed villages throughout the countryside.[47] Although the situation in Kurdistan had immediately become serious and was continuing to deteriorate, the General Staff offered only the opinion that to order troops in their present state against the Kurdish tribes was merely to present the tribesmen with more rifles. Eventually the British occupying forces, to the further humiliation of the local Iranian army commanders, acted to restore some semblance of security. Throughout the country, the collapse of the authority of the central government represented in the rural and especially the tribal areas by the army and the Gendarmerie, the acquisition by the tribes, only recently and with great cost and difficulty disarmed, of thousands of modern rifles, the return of their khans and aghas, and the danger posed by deserter-bandits, appeared to augur a return to the pre-Pahlavi era of *harj o marj* (chaos and internecine strife).[48]

Military disintegration continued unabated throughout October. The situation was as bad in the capital as in the provinces. The General Staff stated that, of the original 50,000 men of the 1st and 2nd Tehran Divisions, for example, only about 12,000 remained. In fact the General Staff even expressed their despair that they now had no reliable troops at all.[49] The military authorities felt themselves to be powerless to stem the flood of desertions as absconding troops were able to find sanctuary once through Soviet army lines where they could not be pursued. In any case, the army no longer possessed sufficient reliable troops to form parties to pursue deserters. The safety offered by the Soviet zone caused a particular haemorrhaging from the Tehran divisions, which drew their men largely from the northern provinces, especially Azerbaijan.

After recovering from the shock of the events of late August, and freed from their debilitating fear of Riza Shah, the General Staff began to grapple with the task of reconstituting their forces. The youthful new Shah, himself an army officer since 1938 and now surrounded by officers who had risen to high command under his father, immediately indicated that he intended to follow his father's example in assuming personal leadership of the army. The Shah and his senior officers together reasserted their belief in restoring the old military system, a large army based on conscription, with the Shah at its apex. Such an army had been the linchpin of Riza Shah's state, and had provided the environment which had nurtured both his son and his generals. For these circles, Pahlavi rule and the army appeared to exist in symbiosis, any alternative hardly conceivable, a large army deemed essential for providing the monarchical system with a strong institutional base, as well as for guaranteeing internal security, external defence, and prestige.

The most pressing problem facing the generals was that of reassembling their manpower. With a disregard for military realities which was to become typical, the Shah expressed the desire to rebuild the army to pre-war levels, 300,000 to 400,000 mobilizable men.[50] This was to be achieved, furthermore, through reviving one of his father's most hated policies, conscription. His senior officers argued that, even if the army were to be reduced considerably below its former strength, it could not be maintained by voluntary recruitment. Offering rates of pay high enough to attract recruits would be too costly and even then it would be the unemployed in the towns who would enlist and not the peasants, who were the best material. In their advocacy of this plan, the Shah and the army came up against determined opposition. The British took exactly the opposite view. Fearing the troublemaking potential of a discontented rank and file and a pro-German officer corps, they advocated the replacement of what they described as an inefficient and underpaid conscript army with a smaller volunteer force, tasked solely with the maintenance of internal security.[51] The British proposed an army of about 42,000, a number which even they conceded represented a drastic reduction and which, of course, horrified the Shah. There was also intense domestic opposition to Muhammad Riza Shah's military policy from both broad layers of the political class, newly liberated by Riza Shah's abdication and prepared to denounce the old army both for its corruption and oppression and for its recent disgraceful dereliction of duty, and the wider population, who feared the return of conscription. In fact, resistance to the restoration of military rule, in any form, was one of the few notions unifying much of society in the chaotic new political context.

Although opposition was strong, the Shah and his generals won this first skirmish and got their way in the matter of conscription. Under intense Allied pressure, the army made an attempt, 'no one can say how serious', to find voluntary recruits, but the results were hopeless and the country duly returned reluctantly to conscription.[52] But owing partly to the prevailing disorder, especially in the tribal areas, and partly to the Soviet refusal to allow the policy to be applied in their areas, the army was only able to take recruits from relatively restricted areas. Nonetheless, by the end of the year the situation was beginning to stabilize. The pace of desertions slowed and recruits began to come in, although slowly and unwillingly and although the Soviet zone remained a haven for those preferring flight.

In fact, the tussle over the restoration of conscription was the overture to a long struggle between the Shah and his generals, on the one hand, and his domestic opponents together with the British and the Americans, on the other, over the size, structure and mission of the reconstituted army. Finance was to be a key weapon in this struggle. The army had succeeded in restoring conscription, but for the remainder of the war years the Shah's increasingly grandiose plans for the expansion of the army were to be constantly frustrated by parliamentary and foreign control of government financial resources.

By early 1942 the contours of the new domestic political configuration in Iran were emerging more clearly. Over the next few years these contours were to become ever more starkly delineated as the army became the focus of a nexus of conflicts, between the Shah and individuals and cabals among his senior officers who believed themselves able to dominate him; among the senior officers themselves, who competed for the Shah's favour and the patronage of one or other foreign embassy; between the Shah and his generals and the Powers, British, Soviet and American, temporarily allied against Germany; between the Shah, the Majlis and the various factions among the political elite; between the left, especially the Tudah Party, and nationalist and rightist political tendencies, all vying for influence over the officer corps; and between the Shah and the general population who were determined to prevent a return to royal dictatorship exercised through the army.

The young and inexperienced Muhammad Riza Shah, his grip on power fragile, attempted to navigate these multiple conflicts by positioning himself, in imitation of his father, as both nominal head and actual commander of an army which he sought to make as large and well armed as possible. Like his father, Muhammad Riza Shah relied on coercion, in the form of conscription, to provide the army with recruits. His generals, on whom he depended, he tried to protect, both from retribution for their actions under Riza Shah and from efforts by the post-1941 civilian authorities to rein in their power, but junior officers continued to suffer from poor pay and conditions and a lack of opportunities for advancement on merit. At all levels of the army, discontent was rife. The conscripts viewed their service as tantamount to a prison sentence while junior officers became increasingly receptive to nationalist and Tudah propaganda. Even some senior officers of the army were ambiguous in their attitudes to the Shah and *in extremis* unreliable. Although the upper echelons of the army, inherited from Riza Shah, generally regarded the monarchy as indispensable to the maintenance of the system which guaranteed their own privilege, for many years the Shah was unable to assert his own unchallenged pre-eminence over his generals. He was rather obliged constantly to contend with their ambition, political independence and jockeying for power, repeatedly promoting and purging in an effort to maintain control.

Thus, during the 1940s and early 1950s, the Shah was obliged to engage in repeated twin struggles, firstly to prevent any challenge to his position emerging from within the army and, secondly, to prevent civilian political power from intruding into his control of the army. However, just as the Shah was determined to consolidate his own control over the army, so his civilian political opponents were determined to wrest it from him. This struggle found its focus in the position of the minister of war. The Shah had preserved his father's military chain of command which transmitted orders from the palace directly to the General Staff and then to the field, marginalizing completely the civilian war ministry, always holding to the belief that the Ministry of War had no other purpose than simply to supply the needs of the army as determined by himself as commander-in-chief. Between 1942 and 1953 the constitutional position and actual power of the minister of war became the site of a bitter contest between the Shah and a succession of prime ministers, beginning with Ahmad Qavam and ending with Muhammad Musaddiq.

This conflict over who should control the army, which was not to be resolved until after the 1953 coup, first burst into the open in late 1942. In the summer of that year Ahmad Qavam, a *bête noire* of the Pahlavis, had become prime minister.[53] He had immediately announced that he would keep the portfolio of war minister for himself, insisting that in future the Chief of the General Staff should report to him and not to the Shah.[54] This was the opening volley of a direct attack on the Shah whom Qavam continued to try to weaken over the next few months. In December the Shah, who loathed Qavam and who was quite unable to tolerate the threat to his control of the army being proffered by his father's old enemy, seized an opportunity to act. Taking advantage of Qavam's growing unpopularity, the palace encouraged an eruption of rioting on the streets of Tehran.[55] The Shah openly allied himself to anti-Qavam sentiment in the Majlis and called on Qavam to resign. This manoeuvre was successful. Qavam survived in office for a few more weeks but was fatally weakened and finally resigned in early 1943.

This episode demonstrated the danger to any Iranian government of attempting to establish anything more than a semblance of control over the army, and also made clear the Shah's determination to maintain the army's loyalty to his own person rather than to the institutions of the state.[56] It illustrated dramatically the sensitivity of the Shah, even at this early stage of his rule, to any civilian challenge to his unfettered control of the army and further produced early indications of his broader contempt for civilian government and his views as to the political role which the army might possibly play. He openly advocated 'a revolution from above', ostensibly to obviate a revolution from below, while General Jahanbani, a member of the Shah's military cabinet, asked the Soviet ambassador, while the rioting was in full swing, what his view would be were the Shah and his generals to take public affairs in hand for a while.[57] Bullard, the British ambassador, concluded that this amounted to a proposal for a coup d'état, and illustrated the Shah's 'dangerous passion for playing at soldiers'.[58]

So central was the army to Muhammad Riza Shah's understanding of his own position that, from the very beginning of his reign, he showed an acute sensitivity to, and deep resentment of, any criticism of his officers, whether this came from domestic or foreign sources. Nonetheless, the Allied powers, and particularly the British, were determined that the

Iranian army should submit to foreign advice and assistance. The British initially hoped that their own officers might provide this assistance but then, in a concession to the realities of their wartime alliance, briefly considered a British–Soviet mission.[59] The officer corps of the Iranian army, however, led by Riza Shah-era generals including Fazlullah Zahidi, Murtaza Yazdanpanah, and Ali Riazi, was still seething with resentment and humiliation over the disaster of *shahrivar*. A large number of officers clung to their pre-war admiration for Germany and covertly hoped for an opportunity to seek revenge on the Allies. They were intensely anti-British, their hostility increased by their belief that the British were responsible for bringing the Russians into Iran. Neither the Shah nor his generals had been made more receptive to Allied advice by the wording of the Tripartite Treaty of Alliance which formalized the Allied occupation in early 1942 and which assigned the Iranian army only an internal security role. Many officers, including the most senior, interpreted the treaty as a refusal to treat Iran as an ally and as a continuation of the humiliation of defeat and occupation.

The proposal of British military advisors was therefore extremely unpopular among Iranian army officers, this unpopularity aggravated by their knowledge that Britain advocated only a very small volunteer army, while Soviet advisors were completely unacceptable. The Shah, under intense pressure, finally acquiesced to the least objectionable option and accepted US missions to both the army and the Gendarmerie. In fact, the Shah's suspicions about US involvement had already been partly allayed when Iran was declared eligible for US Lend Lease Aid in March 1942, and were now further modified by the hope that the arrival of the American missions would encourage the US to become the suppliers of the weapons necessary to equip an army of the size and type he desired.

Although the Shah had been seduced partly by the vision of American supplies, his officer corps remained resolutely opposed to Allied control of the army. With the arrival of the US missions, Colonel H. Norman Schwartzkopf to the Gendarmerie in August and Major-General Ridley to the army in October, it became essential that the core of the remaining anti-Allied opposition within the army be eliminated and the rest of the officer corps rendered more malleable to foreign shaping. Towards the end of 1942, using the anti-Qavam rioting in Tehran as a cover, the British decided to deal with the persistent pro-German sentiment within the army. On 6

December, British military personnel, believing the Iranian government powerless to act against the army, arrested General Zahidi, who headed this current among Iranian offices and was then general officer commanding in Isfahan. Also arrested were a number of other army officers, some of high rank, and civilians believed to be sympathetic to the Axis Powers and to be co-operating with tribal insurgents among the Qashqai.[60] These arrests dealt a further blow to morale among officers. Although they were ostensibly aimed at removing the active pro-Axis leadership within the army, they also removed the most determined opponents of foreign military missions.

From the very beginning, the Shah and his generals were ambivalent towards the American missions. The Shah was anxious that his control of and influence over the army might be restricted as a consequence of their presence and was averse to giving the Americans any wider remit than the minimum insisted upon by the Allies. He was in particular disappointed by General Ridley's failure to give succour to his more grandiose plans. Ridley rather inclined towards the British view, proposing an army of ten divisions, totalling only 53,000 fighting men, with recruits, staffs, services and training establishments bringing this to 86,000 although even this modest project would require an increase in the budget of 100 per cent.

The Shah's struggle with and over the American advisors was underway in earnest by June 1943 and became entangled with his desire to resist any encroachment by the civilian authorities. He continued to insist on his right to exercise executive control of the army, even in matters of detail, and on the direct responsibility of the General Staff to him as commander-in-chief rather than to the government. The Chief of the General Staff, General Yazdanpanah, taking his cue from the Shah, was at daggers drawn with the Minister of War, and this conflict was expressed in sharply differing attitudes to the US mission. The chief of staff was determined to limit the role of the US advisors to the minimum that was necessary to avoid their resignation while the Minister of War took precisely the opposite position, welcoming at least a degree of control by the Americans that would establish oversight of the disbursement of army funds and would restrict the untrammelled power of the General Staff.[61]

The Shah's attitude was born of both his extreme sensitivity to criticism, even as implied in the presence of foreign advisors, his determination to remain supreme within the army, and his paradoxical fear of incurring the resentment of his own senior officers, whose attachment to himself he was convinced was essential to the maintenance of his position. The generals were themselves at least as eager as the Shah to remain beyond the control of both the government and the US mission, their submission to the young Shah largely nominal and their influence over him real and far-reaching.

Indeed, it seems that by mid-July 1943 the frustration and exasperation of certain cliques within the army were reaching breaking point. At least one, and possibly more, coups were actively being planned. The most significant, possessing a vaguely nationalist character, was directed at the old guard among the senior officers and at the generalized corruption prevailing among the political class. The plotters hoped to use the Shah as a legitimizing figurehead but believed that he could be 'eliminated' if necessary. The conspirators struggled to obtain the support of General Razmara, who was worried about the Soviet reaction, and the plot appears to have fizzled out without any action being taken.[62]

As 1943 progressed, the struggle ebbed and flowed. The Majlis passed bills giving its official imprimatur to the engagement of 30 American officers as advisors to the army and of eight to the Gendarmerie, and of the American police expert, Timmerman, as director-general of the police. Public opinion forced the Shah to sign, very reluctantly, a decree making clear that the Minister of War was responsible for the army, that the Chief of Staff was subordinate to the Minister, and that his own powers were limited to certain prerogatives of approval. Yet the Shah never accepted the curtailment of his powers expressed in the decree and he began to organize a counter-attack.[63] Opposition to the US mission within the army was undiminished and was beginning to be able to draw on support from the Soviets who were suspicious of any extension of American influence and who refused to allow American officers to be stationed at divisional headquarters within their zone. The Shah appointed to his personal staff two senior officers, General Yazdanpanah as his aide de camp, and General Razmara as chief of his military secretariat, both of whom had recently occupied the post of chief of staff but had resigned owing to their unwillingness to subordinate themselves to the minister of war. They were both famously hostile to foreign influence in the army and were able to rely on a staunch following in the army among those opposed to the Americans. This move by the Shah further strained relations between himself and his minister of war and tilted the balance within the officer corps once again away from the government and towards the court.[64]

Nonetheless, a certain vacillation might be detected in the Shah's attitude to the US mission. Although he disliked the American advisors, he tolerated them in the hope that they would become a channel through which would eventually pour American arms and military equipment. Yet he also feared the implications of American support for the constitutional authority of the Ministry of War and their resistance to his plans for military expansion. His dislike extended organically to their colleagues, the American financial advisors led by the recently returned A. C. Millspaugh, the same official who had proved such a thorn in his father's side and whose restrictions on the army budget allotment now represented the most concrete brake on the Shah's goals.[65] The British and the Americans held to the view that the Shah's plans for the army bore no relation whatever to the needs or resources of the country.[66] By the end of 1943, the army still possessed a fighting strength of only 53,000, with a total manpower of 86,000. It remained 'demoralized, underpaid, underfed and discontented', senior officers embezzling unchecked while the junior officers 'steal what they can to keep themselves and their families alive'.[67] In July 1943 it suffered a spectacular reverse, a detachment of some 900 men defeated by a tribal force of Qashqai and Buyir Ahmadi at Semirum, with charges of treachery, cowardice, incompetence and neglect of duty leading to a number of courts-martial.

During 1944 the triangular struggle between the Shah and his officers, the American military and financial advisors, and the government and Majlis continued unabated, leading to practical paralysis. Meanwhile, Dr Muhammad Musaddiq had already emerged in the Majlis as an outspoken critic of the army, pointing out that the Shah had no constitutional right to interfere in the affairs of the government or individual ministries, while four changes in the post of minister of war and five in the post of chief of staff produced bewilderment among both military officers and civilian officials. The Shah continued to seek absolute personal command unhampered by parliamentary or public criticism or financial constraints, yet his 'fear of such criticism and his own personal weaknesses' prevented him from exercising effective command while his jealousy and suspicions led him also to oppose the exercise of authority by either the Minister of War or Chief of Staff.[68]

The Shah's hostility towards the US mission had been mellowed by the hope that a certain degree of outward support would succeed in securing supplies of weapons. Yet by early 1944 he was becoming increasingly frustrated at the American resistance to his schemes while certain of his generals remained implacable in their hostility to the US mission. Opposition to Ridley's mission within the army was led by Generals Razmara, Hidayat and Yazdapanah, who also encouraged the Shah in his belief in the need for an army of at least 110,000 men. Gradually, these officers moved into the ascendant and senior officers sympathetic to the US mission were removed from their posts.[69] The pro-British General Hasan Arfa was removed from command of the 1st Tehran Division and General Amirahmadi lost his position as minister of war while Amirahmadi's rival, General Razmara, was made chief of staff. This last appointment, however, merely changed, rather than relieved, the Shah's anxieties, turning his resentment of the Americans into fear of his ambitious new chief of staff. Nor did the Shah's perennial suspicions of the Minister of War subside. Even though the new civilian minister of war, Ibrahim Zand, was originally a nominee of the Shah, he quickly aroused the Shah's jealousy, the Shah making his usual accusation that Zand was attempting to be commander-in-chief as well as minister of war.

The Shah's doubts about the American officers were exacerbated by the attitude adopted by Dr Millspaugh. Just as his father had fought with Millspaugh over the army budget, so now did Muhammad Riza Shah. Millspaugh insisted that the army be confined to internal policing and he encouraged both the government and the Majlis deputies to resist the Shah's demands for an increased budget allotment for the military and even urged them to consider an actual reduction in its strength in order to make funds available for better pay for officers and men and more modern equipment. General Ridley signally failed to champion to Millspaugh the Shah's case for more money for a large army. In any case, Ridley and the other American officers, anticipating an end to the war and to their mission, had already begun to scale back their activities. Ridley's influence was less and less in evidence, his interest mainly confined to transport and supply.[70] By now both the American officers of the mission and their Iranian counterparts had come to conclude that the mission had accomplished little, its position had remained ambiguous and had not produced the hoped-for supplies. Millspaugh himself was to leave in 1945.

In the early months of 1945 there were further convulsions in the senior ranks resulting from personal rivalries intertwined with political and ideological conflicts. Razmara was replaced as chief of staff by the pro-Allied General Arfa who immediately began to remove all Razmara's friends and substitute his own. Meanwhile, as the deputies continued to criticize the army budgets as being beyond the means of the country, the Shah outlined his idea for the grandiose expansion of the air force on very modern lines, having, apparently, little conception of cost or the long and rigorous training required for air force personnel.[71] Throughout 1945 the army continued to be hobbled by Majlis resistance. The deputies delayed ratification of the military budget, forcing the army to live from hand to mouth on monthly credits equivalent to one-twelfth of the previous year's budget. Political intrigue, favouritism and personal ambition wracked the upper echelons of the officer corps and the uncertainty arising from the ambiguous positions of the Shah and the Minister of War continued to cause confusion and lower morale. Meanwhile, another element was added to the mix. By the beginning of 1945 it was becoming clear that the Tudah Party was increasingly directing its propaganda towards junior officers and NCOs, highlighting their low rates of pay, their slow rates of promotion, and their inability to rise under the dead weight of the 'sloth, ignorance and corruption' of their seniors.[72]

The Tudah Party had been founded shortly after Riza Shah's abdication. In its early years it had attempted to maintain itself as a broad-based organization, including various leftist and democratic currents and advocating a reformist programme, only later crystallizing into an orthodox pro-Soviet Communist Party. During the war years it grew quickly, becoming the only nationally organized modern political party in the country. It created and led trade unions, especially strong in the southern oil industry, established a broad hegemony over much of the intelligentsia and in 1943 managed to secure the election of eight Majlis deputies.[73] In 1944 a network of army officers sympathetic to the Tudah, including Colonel Izzatullah Siyamak, Colonel Muhammad Ali Azar, Major Ali Akbar Iskandani and Captain Khusraw Ruzbih, formed the Military Organization of the Tudah Party of

Iran. These officers had been active in forming leftist cells within the armed forces since 1942 but without any direct contact with the Tudah. It was only in 1944, as a result of Colonel Siyamak's contacts with Abd al-Samad Kambaksh, a former air force officer and now one of the Tudah leadership, that the cells were put in formal touch with the Party and the Military Organization created, with Kambaksh as its party liaison officer.[74]

By the summer of 1945 discontent among junior officers at their conditions was intense while the prestige of the Tudah Party, basking in the glow of the Soviet victory over Fascism in Europe, was at its height. One indication of the strength of support for the Tudah within the army may be found in General Arfa's assertion that, when he became chief of staff in December 1944, he had been given a list of 100 officers with Tudah ties or sympathies.[75] In mid-August in Mashhad, members of the Military Organization decided to act. With Kambaksh's support but apparently without the knowledge of other Tudah leaders, they launched what was soon revealed to be a premature adventure in an effort to spark off a wider rising against the government in the Turkman region close to the Soviet border.[76] Eighteen officers of the Mashhad garrison, led by a lieutenant-colonel, commandeered a jeep and two lorries and seized radio equipment and arms and ammunition. To prevent pursuit they immobilized the remaining army vehicles by removing their ignition keys and by putting salt in their petrol tanks, sugar, though more effective, being too expensive. They made their way towards the Turkman region, reaching Bujnurd, having cut the telegraph lines from Mashhad. On their arrival at Bujnurd they announced that they had come to inspect the cavalry squadron stationed there but they then disarmed the squadron and made for the Turkman steppe. Meanwhile, Mashhad was paralysed with fear at the prospect, fuelled by rumour, of a Turkman descent on the city. The chief of staff in Mashhad, lacking reliable army troops, mobilized the Gendarmerie, a local commandant, a lieutenant, assembling a force at Gunbad-i Qabus, near the Soviet frontier, from the men stationed in scattered posts throughout the area. A confrontation took place, seven of the army officer mutineers being killed and two wounded and taken prisoner. The next day three officers and four men were picked up in an exhausted condition nearby on the Gunbad-i Qabus road. Meanwhile, six officers from the Tehran garrison, led by a lieutenant-colonel on the General Staff, deserted and joined the mutineers just before the skirmish at Gunbad-i Qabus. These seven, together with six of the original Mashhad mutineers, escaped capture, as did two others, from Tehran and Tabriz, who deserted later.[77] This adventure had been led by Major Ali Akbar Iskandani and Colonel Muhammad Ali Azar, Iskandani being killed and Azar and others taking refuge in the Soviet Union.

Although this episode remained a minor affair in its national impact, the army was clearly shaken and carried out a purge. A commission was appointed in Tehran to examine the activities and contacts of all officers of the strategically and politically important Tehran garrison and, as a result, 30 officers were found to have close contact with either the Tudah Party or the Soviets and were arrested while a further ten, less deeply implicated, were posted away from the capital to divisions in the south. Further arrests continued for some time. The government also introduced a bill into the Majlis, in the hope of drawing the sting of discontent among junior officers, promising financial benefits and other improvements in their conditions. Nonetheless, government concern at Tudah influence over the officer corps, especially in the new context of the Cold War, became ever more intense.

The Mashhad fiasco, which appears to have been the project of a radical faction within the Tudah led by Kambaksh, also irritated the Tudah leadership. When it was followed by the Military Organization's provision of aid and officers to the autonomous government of Azerbaijan, the Tudah majority leadership considered disbanding the Organization altogether, or at least severing links with it.[78] Nonetheless, when the dust had settled after the collapse of the Azerbaijan and Kurdistan republics, the Tudah, responding to Soviet pressure, restored its good relations with the Military Organization.

The Mashhad mutiny was closely followed by the collapse of the army in Azerbaijan upon the declaration of autonomy by the Azerbaijan Democrat Party. Since 1941, the Red Army, while in occupation of northern Iran, had restricted the movement of Iranian troops and encouraged leftist and nationalist trends sympathetic to the Soviet Union. As the war ended and the USSR prevaricated over withdrawal, emboldened local radicals in Azerbaijan and Kurdistan seized the political initiative, declaring autonomy and instituting a range of reforms. In December 1945 the Tabriz garrison, under the command of General Ali Akbar Darakhshani, apparently himself a Tudah sympathizer, surrendered to the Azerbaijan Democrat Party, led by the old communist, Jafar Pishivari, an event which caused both shock and alarm to the high command of the Iranian army.[79] One year later, however, Iranian army divisions were able to march into Azerbaijan and Kurdistan to almost no armed resistance, the autonomous republics having already been fatally weakened following the Soviet Union's agreement to withdraw as a result of diplomatic negotiation and an empty promise of an oil concession from Ahmad Qavam, once again prime minister. Once in occupation of the rebellious regions, the Iranian army wreaked a terrible vengeance on the populations, especially the politically active elements.

The restoration of Iranian control over Azerbaijan and Kurdistan in December 1946 following declarations of autonomy by those areas was a key moment in restoring army morale and tilting the domestic balance of forces in favour of the Shah and the army. Although the collapse of the autonomous governments had been brought about largely by political and diplomatic means, the Shah and his generals nonetheless milked the episode for all it was worth, turning it into a major propaganda victory, lauding the patriotism of the army and its vital role in maintaining Iran's sovereignty, this tactic meeting with much success among both public opinion in general and nationalist circles in particular. Seizing his opportunity, the Shah, in the afterglow of 1946, gained Majlis approval for an enlarged army and additional US military assistance. His ancient dislike of Qavam had been intensified by a petulant resentment that the Prime Minister had received too much credit for the Azerbaijan operations at his own expense as commander-in-chief and, in early 1947, he succeeded in forcing his old enemy out of office.

As a result of the events of 1946, the Shah significantly strengthened his domestic position and the standing of the army. As the Cold War began in earnest, Iran along with Greece and Turkey forming the West's 'northern tier' of defence against the Soviet Union, the US began to modify its former cautious approach towards the Shah and his military ambitions. Relations began to grow warmer and closer. The Shah, for his part, had realized that the US had supplanted Britain and was the new global superpower, and was convinced that the construction of a smooth and amicable relationship was now essential. The US reciprocated the Shah's new amiability, seeing Iran as playing a key role in the Truman Doctrine of 1947 which distilled the emerging Cold War trope of containing communism while, in addition to Iran's strategic location, the country literally floated on a sea of oil.[80] Although the wartime US mission to the army under Ridley had achieved little, this strengthening US interest immediately found concrete expression in the October 1947 arrival of an enlarged advisory mission, known by its acronym, ARMISH.[81] Nonetheless, although relations between the Shah and the Americans were undoubtedly warmer, fundamental disagreements over military policy remained. For the Shah, the role of the army in state-building and consolidating the monarchy were paramount. For the Americans, on the other hand, it was the practical contribution which the Iranian army might be able, or perhaps unable, to make to regional security arrangements which was the key consideration.

The Shah understood military strength in terms of numbers and weapons. In order to win over the US to his view and obtain concrete US support, he had therefore constantly to emphasize, and even exaggerate, the threat of Soviet aggression. The US, however, resisted his blandishments, remaining doubtful of the immediacy of any attack, and even more sceptical about the Iranian army's ability to meet it should it occur. The US, with the example of China before its eyes, assessed the communist threat to Iran as rather one of subversion and accordingly emphasized to the Shah that Iran's security would best be guaranteed by real internal reform. In any case, the Americans, including the head of ARMISH, General Evans, believed the army weak and backward, unable to absorb modern weaponry and training and led by corrupt and inefficient senior officers.[82] Although the US began to supply Iran with military equipment in 1947, Iran received only a fraction of that desired by the Shah, indeed it was the minimum deemed sufficient to provide for internal security and frontier control.[83]

By the end of the decade the army had grown and was somewhat better armed, although it continued to find the use and maintenance of its new equipment difficult. It now numbered about 131,500 although this was still 10,000 below the planned establishment. Over half of this deficiency was in officers although there was apparently little difficulty in finding the 25,000 conscripts needed for each half-yearly call-up.[84] American advisors were assisting at the Military College and the Staff Academy and Iranian officers had begun to be sent on courses in the US and, to a lesser extent, in France but the training of conscripts was still being hampered by the shortage of officers and NCOs and the generally low levels of literacy. Every unit contained a high proportion of raw recruits which adversely affected operational efficiency. There were no effective mobilization plans for the recall of reservists and their training was in abeyance due to lack of funds. Morale, which had reached rock bottom during the war years, was still low and it seemed likely that, in the event of any conflict, the action of provincial forces would be determined by the whim of individual commanders 'who might jump whichever way appeared most favourable to the time'.[85] Corruption remained endemic. The price for a colonel to be promoted to a brigadier, for example, was apparently 50,000 riyals plus a pair of silk rugs.[86]

In addition to his problems with the intractability of the US and ARMISH, the Shah was facing another problem connected to his army: the rise of General Razmara.[87] In 1946 Razmara had managed, once again, to obtain the appointment of chief of staff. Both the minister of war, General Amirahmadi, and the Shah himself had recently expressed strong doubts about Razmara. The Shah, jealous of Razmara's prestige as commander in the campaigns against the Azerbaijani and Kurdish autonomists, had described him as 'disloyal, dishonest and little better than a Russian agent', stated that he would never consent to his reappointment and that he regarded him 'as a viper that must be crushed'.[88] Yet Razmara succeeded in ingratiating himself with the Shah, assisting in the ousting of Qavam in 1947, and consolidated his position. In contrast to previous incumbents, who had lasted only months, he remained secure in his post as chief of staff, exercising supreme authority over the army under the aegis of the Shah and to the complete exclusion of the Minister of War. By 1949 the power accumulated by Razmara was becoming as much a menace as a support to the Shah. Whatever his private plans for further advancement, he was certainly assembling the elements necessary for a coup. Occupying 'the position of a dictator in the army', the Minister of War confining his activities mainly to financial matters,[89] Razmara was also in command of the navy and the air force. During 1949, the greater part of the Gendarmerie and its responsibility for internal security was transferred to the army, adding to his influence. He was popular in some quarters, and in the central military police, which had a strength of about 5,000 and considerably outnumbered the civil police of Tehran, he had a force capable of assuming control in the capital. He was openly ambitious to become prime minister.

By 1949 the Shah was also facing organized nationalist opposition, in the form of the National Front, led by Dr Muhammad Musaddiq. The National Front was motivated by two essential concerns, the desire for constitutional government and the hope of regaining control of Iran's oil from the Anglo–Iranian Oil Company. The Iranian government had recently negotiated a new, but flawed, supplementary agreement with the oil company, but it was profoundly unsatisfactory to the National Front which, in 1950, called for the nationalization of the oil industry. The Shah thus found himself caught between his powerful military subordinate, General Razmara, and the National Front, certainly fearing the former as a more immediate threat. However, Razmara was popular with all three key foreign powers, Britain, the US and the Soviet Union, this in itself a sign of his political astuteness, and as a result the Shah, his jealousy notwithstanding, agreed to his appointment as prime minister with the objective of pushing the supplementary oil agreement through the Majlis. In March 1951, his popularity waning as a result of widespread hostility to the oil agreement, Razmara was assassinated by a member of the radical Islamic group, the *Fida'iyan-i Islam*. The Shah was popularly believed to have had a hand in the assassination and, at any rate, was certainly relieved at the removal of his principal rival for the army's loyalty. In fact he seems to have believed strongly that Razmara himself was on the point of carrying out a coup. Soon after Razmara's assassination, the Majlis passed Musaddiq's oil nationalization bill and in May 1951 Musaddiq himself became prime minister. So far as the army was concerned, its reaction to Razmara's assassination was perhaps more feeble than might have been expected, senior officers in Tehran seeming to have felt more fear than outrage.[90] General Hijazi, commanding the Military College, was made chief of police and military governor of Tehran but his strong measures to maintain security resulted in an attempt on his life also.

From the moment of Musaddiq's assumption of the premiership, relations between the army high command and the government became more and more strained. Musaddiq was well known as a supporter of the constitutional position of the minister of war and as an opponent of the Shah's ambitions, in imitation of his father, to extend military rule. He disliked the cost of military spending, poured scorn on the Shah's pet obsession of a Soviet invasion, and advocated a policy of neutralism, his views necessarily undermining any argument for a large, powerful army. As soon as he became prime minister, Musaddiq acted to neutralize opposition from all quarters in the army, reshuffling the higher appointments in order to remove the most hostile senior officers. The Tudah, which at first assumed that the oil nationalization was a plot to hand Iranian oil over to the Americans, was also a target and the military authorities took severe action to try to eliminate Tudah influence in the army, particularly in units of the Tehran garrison.

Musaddiq was determined to ensure Iran regain control of its oil industry and also to limit the power of the Shah and the court, objectives which he saw as inextricably interlinked. Months of domestic and international conflict ensued while the Shah and his royalist supporters, and Britain, began to search for a way to remove him. By the summer of 1952 Ahmad Qavam, his old enmity towards the dynasty notwithstanding, had emerged as the most viable conservative candidate to replace Musaddiq.[91] In July the simmering crisis came to a head, finding a focus in the perennial dispute over the post of minister of war. Forming a new government after elections to the seventeenth Majlis, Musaddiq, prompted by the Patriotic Officers, opposed the Shah's attempt to appoint a general to the post. When the Shah insisted on his customary, although not constitutional, right to make the appointment, Musaddiq resigned and the Shah appointed Ahmad Qavam as prime minister. On 21 July the population offered its response in the form of an uprising in the capital and other major cities. Qavam was dismissed by the Shah and Musaddiq reappointed, taking for himself the portfolio of minister of war, later symbolically renamed minister for national defence.

The intensification of the political crisis had exacerbated tensions within the army, which began to emerge into the open. Officers who supported Musaddiq but were not sympathetic to the Tudah had now formed themselves into a loose organization known as the Patriotic Officers. This group comprised many senior officers in the army and the air force, including at least six brigadier-generals, was led informally by General Mahmud Afshartus, and its objectives were broadly constitutionalist and democratic.[92]

The events of 21 July (30 Tir) were a key turning-point both in the general struggle between Musaddiq, the Shah and Britain, and, more specifically, in the relationship between the regime and the army, or at least its upper echelons. Before these events, the army had held together, the senior commanders still confident and the troops prepared to obey orders to act against the growing power of the 'street'. Even up until midday on 21 July, the Tehran garrison had stood firm against the demonstrators. However, by this point the Shah's hesitation and uncertainty as to how he and his army should react was beginning to manifest itself. He feared the consequences of military repression and had given General Alavi Muqaddam, the military governor of Tehran, orders to use minimum force, orders at which the general had protested strongly. Furthermore, the Shah, even at this critical moment, appeared to harbour reservations regarding Qavam and to be intriguing against him with elements of the National Front.[93] In these circumstances, the General Staff were unable to respond coherently, General Garzan, the chief of staff, was reported to have completely lost his head at the height of the riots, although by now the high command probably realized that the Shah lacked the resolution necessary to prevail. This uncertainty over the attitude and behaviour of their royal commander-in-chief paralysed the high command. Especially after the politically radical and anti-Western Ayatullah Kashani issued a fatwa calling on soldiers to join the popular struggle, fraternization between troops, particularly tank crews, and the demonstrators became increasingly common and younger officers openly spoke of defying the authorities. Later in the day, after Qavam's resignation, the Shah, fearing that the Patriotic Officers group within the army and especially in the air force was preparing to act against him, ordered that all security forces be removed from the streets in order to avoid the risk of any further disintegration. By the evening General Garzan, now relieved of his post as chief of staff, and General Alavi Muqaddam, formerly the military governor, were under house arrest in the Officers' Club.

The events of 21 July dealt a potentially fatal blow to the Shah's standing as commander-in-chief with his senior officers, and a rapid deterioration in the loyalty of the army to the Shah took place throughout all ranks, affecting particularly the Tehran garrison which had been in closest contact with the demonstrations of 21 July.[94] As a result of Ayatullah Kashani's exhortations to military personnel, officers were advised not to wear uniform in the streets while both officers and troops were spat at and refused lifts in public buses. At the same time, Tudah activity among junior officers and NCOs increased, meeting with considerable success.

On returning to his post as prime minister, Musaddiq, advised by the Patriotic Officers group, made a number of important changes to the army high command, immediately removing the most incorrigible and beginning a process of retiring a large number of royalist senior officers. Amongst the first to go were Marshal Shahbakhti and Generals Garzan, Alavi Muqaddam and Hijazi. Following reports of anti-Musaddiq coup-plotting within the

Tehran garrison, the 1st Division was broken up into its component brigade groups, the divisional commander, General Aryana, dismissed and posted to Paris as military attaché, and the divisional staff dispersed.

At first Musaddiq found it difficult to stabilize the high command. He initially appointed General Yazdanpanah as chief of staff but he resigned almost immediately. Musaddiq then appointed General Baharmast, an officer trusted by the Shah, but after his involvement in the 'proto-coup' of February 1953, he was superseded by General Taqi Riahi, of the Patriotic Officers.[95] Afshartus was also made police chief. Musaddiq, a little later, formed a Security Council to advise him on army matters, consisting of Generals Baharmast, Naqdi, an ex-minister of war, and Aqavli, the head of the Officers' Bank. The Patriotic Officers pressed for large numbers of retirements, dismissals and even prosecutions but Musaddiq and the Security Council eventually agreed on a final list of only 136 retirements on full pension.[96] This resulted in many fiercely pro-Shah officers remaining on active service, while those retired, led by Zahidi, were free to organize themselves into the Retired Officers' Club, a centre of anti-Musaddiq activism.

The British were particularly alarmed by the effect of 21 July on the army, identifying the Shah, and what they described as his 'weakness and well-nigh treachery', as the key factor demoralizing the senior officers and creating disillusionment with the monarchy.[97] Adopting a rather hysterical tone, the British reported that the morale of the Tehran garrison had collapsed catastrophically while loyalty to the Shah had fallen to zero.[98] Their concern was sharpened owing to the fact that, by the autumn of 1952, they had already begun to plan, together with the Americans, covert operations against Musaddiq, involving the co-operation of senior military figures, especially a core composed of those forcibly retired by Musaddiq, and most notably General Zahidi.[99] General Hijazi, for example, had already begun intriguing more or less openly, and in October was arrested for plotting to put General Zahidi in power as prime minister, while the alleged conspiracy within the Tehran garrison was believed to have been at the instigation of the British. On 22 October Musaddiq announced the rupture of diplomatic relations with Britain.

Preparations for a coup continued throughout the first half of 1953, the US moving into the lead role and in late June giving a green light to the CIA, now in charge of the operation, and its Iranian collaborators, civilian and military. There had already been one false start and one fiasco, General Zahidi, who had been provided with substantial sums of money with which to organize a network of army officers, at the centre of both. In February Ayatullah Kashani, who had now moved into the anti-Musaddiq camp, organized large crowds to attack Musaddiq's home in a 'proto-coup',[100] following which Zahidi and other retired officers were briefly arrested. In April, in another botched coup attempt, General Mahmud Afshartus, Musaddiq's chief of police, was kidnapped and murdered.[101] A number of senior officers, all retired, again including General Zahidi, and several anti-Musaddiq civilian politicians, were deeply implicated in this episode.[102]

The practical difficulties facing the CIA in its efforts to shape the disparate anti-Musaddiq elements in Iran into an organization capable of carrying out a coup were enormous. When, in the early summer of 1953, CIA paramilitary warfare expert George Carroll began planning the military dimension of the proposed coup, he discovered, firstly, that the US had little or no concrete and reliable information about the Iranian army and, secondly, that the CIA actually possessed no military assets in Iran.[103] Neither the US embassy in Tehran nor the CIA and Pentagon in Washington had so far bothered to collect any detailed information on Iranian military figures. In June the CIA began the task of intelligence gathering on the Iranian army. The reports of their operatives in Iran were not encouraging. The CIA was informed that the chief of staff, General Riahi, and all his staff, drawn primarily from the pro-Musaddiq Iran Party, were loyal to Musaddiq. Furthermore, Tehran was garrisoned by five brigades, three infantry mountain brigades and two armoured brigades, and at least three of these five brigades were firmly under General Riahi's control. British military intelligence (the Special Intelligence Service, SIS or MI6) reported that Colonel Ashrafi, the military governor of Tehran and commanding officer of the Third Mountain Brigade, was in favour of coup action but this was later proved to be incorrect.

In the early part of July, the CIA drew up a plan designed to neutralize the Tehran garrison and to isolate all other brigades in Iran. This plan was based on the supposed co-operation of the commander of the Third Mountain Brigade in Tehran but was criticized by Carroll as flimsy and unworkable and later had to be abandoned altogether when it became clear that Colonel Ashrafi was not, as had been claimed, a British agent. The CIA therefore began to make a concerted effort to develop new assets among the Iranian military. The CIA and SIS agreed that if the coup, now code-named Operation AJAX, were to succeed, the CIA would have to 'start from scratch and work quickly to find powerful friends among Iranian troop commanders'.[104] Their instrument for this task was Colonel Abbas Farzanagan, an assistant Iranian military attaché in Washington, who was directed in July to go to Tehran and renew his old contacts within the Iranian army. Yet extreme anxiety remained that the CIA and SIS both lacked military assets capable of being organized into an effective fighting force and that the cultivation of new assets would take too long.

Meanwhile, the CIA's specific fears regarding General Zahidi's alleged military assets were confirmed.[105] For some time the CIA had been trying to persuade General Zahidi, the central figure in any coup-planning, to list his military assets and to indicate how he hoped to use them. When he finally reported, he admitted he had none of the five brigades in the capital. His plan assumed he might be able to use only the Imperial Guard, commanded by Nimatullah Nasiri, some troops from the Department of Army Transport and elements from the Police and the Armed Customs Guard. He also hoped that Colonel Taymur Bakhtiyar might be able to bring troops from Kirmanshah to the capital. The CIA concluded that 'it was disappointing to learn that Major General Zahidi, prime minister designate under TP-AJAX, possessed almost no military assets. General Zahidi, therefore, could not be relied on to execute his own staff plan'.[106] Carroll concluded further that the Shah would never sign a *firman* dismissing Musaddiq while Riahi's control over the Tehran garrison remained unbroken.

Zahidi had, furthermore, failed to organize, as requested, a military secretariat, thus Carroll had no representative with whom to meet and co-ordinate when he arrived in Tehran on 21 July. As the CIA later admitted, because of Zahidi's 'manifestly weak position among the military men then on active duty' and because it had become apparent that the CIA would itself have to seize the initiative and furnish Zahidi with both plans and men, Carroll accordingly decided to step up the development of two officers whom Colonel Abbas Farzanagan had identified as potential coup leaders, General Nadir Batmanghilij and Colonel Hasan Akhavi.[107]

Colonel Akhavi's inadequacies as coup-maker quickly became apparent. His first plan called for a military coup without explaining how it might be accomplished. After Colonel Farzanagan exhorted Akhavi to be more realistic, the latter came up with a plan which was 'more specific but still pitifully inadequate…[it] was nonsense'.[108] In his discussions about a coup with Carroll, Akhavi did not even mention Zahidi and did not seem to be in touch with him. In discussions between Carroll and Akhavi it soon became apparent that Akhavi was not himself in a position to command anything and only hoped that he might persuade his friends to act. At this time, the Shah too admitted that he did not possess any important military assets.

Up until this point both the planning of the coup and the activities of the key personnel had been almost farcical. But from early August the CIA began to impose greater coherence. Carroll met with a friend of Akhavi, Colonel Zand-Karimi, who claimed a long list of sympathizers within the Tehran garrison, principally among deputy commanders of brigades and regimental commanders. Carroll began to plan on the basis of the assets claimed by Zand-Karimi, the latter apparently in touch through these officers with every infantry battalion commander in Tehran and with most of the company commanders. These officers, however, had no organization and were in no position to challenge Chief of Staff Riahi's control of the Tehran garrison which he exercised through the brigade commanders. Carroll concluded, with some prescience, that the fate of the planned coup would depend on whether Riahi 'succeeded in arresting our friends before we arrested his'.[109]

Over 11, 12 and 13 August the coup-planning went ahead predicated on the mobilization of 40 line commanders within the Tehran garrison. Akhavi also finally met Zahidi although Zahidi, despite the fact that he was now taking charge of the military side of the coup, still knew none of the other younger officers central to the plot. It was decided that the coup should begin within 48 hours of the Shah signing the *firman* dismissing Musaddiq and that the *firman* should be delivered to Musaddiq by Colonel Nasiri of the Imperial Guard.

Persuading the Shah to sign the *firman* was another obstacle. The Shah vacillated, tormented by his own doubts and fears, as well as by his specific hostility to the notion of General Zahidi as prime minister.[110] Eventually, after the US resorted to threats as well as blandishments, the Shah signed two decrees, one dismissing Musaddiq, the other appointing Zahidi.

On 15 August the first attempt to execute the coup was successfully frustrated by Riahi who mobilized the commanders of the five Tehran brigades who deployed troops throughout the city.[111] As Carroll had earlier predicted, Nasiri was indeed arrested as he tried to arrest Musaddiq and the coup network began to disintegrate. Next morning, with Tehran securely in the hands of pro-Musaddiq forces, arrests began of those suspected of involvement in the coup, including General Batmanghilij and Colonel Zand-Karimi, and the Shah fled the country. At the same time, the CIA and Zahidi were attempting to recover the situation, taking a series of steps to organize public support, or the appearance of it, for the Shah and hostility to Musaddiq. Riahi in control in Tehran, they decided to mobilize pro-Shah units outside Tehran. The Isfahan commander refused to join, but Colonel Bakhtiyar in Kirmanshah agreed. On 17 August Musaddiq made a futile attempt to regain the political initiative and control of the streets and ordered his chief of police to break up crowds of demonstrators, thus demobilizing his own supporters. On 19 August, chaotic and violent pro-Shah demonstrations sponsored by the CIA were held in Tehran, with mid-ranking army officers in the lead. Finally a decisive conflict took place at Musaddiq's own home between the Imperial Guard and loyal military units, the latter only defeated after a bloody battle. Meanwhile, Zahidi had emerged from hiding and broadcast a statement over Radio Tehran stating that he was the legally appointed prime minister and his troops now controlled the city.[112]

During the coup, the Tudah Military Organization remained inactive. Relations between Musaddiq and the Tudah had always possessed a degree of tension, the Tudah, at least at the beginning, sceptical of Musaddiq, suspecting that the oil nationalization was a ruse to hand control of Iranian oil to the US. Nonetheless, as the anti-British protests got underway, the Tudah played a major role in organizing industrial action and mass support on the streets. Although the Tudah was now defending the nationalization of oil, their growing influence caused tensions within and defections from the pro-Musaddiq coalition to increase, particularly after 21 July 1952. By the time of the coup, the number of officers involved in the Military Organization was estimated by some at 466, the lowest figure, while other sources believe it was as high as 700. Some 243 officers were stationed in the crucial Tehran units, but of these only three or four were serving in the Imperial Guard while most were in non-combat positions. During 1952 and 1953, the Organization had been on the alert. Through an intelligence network in the army, it had helped uncover plots against the Musaddiq government. It was aware of the 1953 coup plot and had warned party leaders and notified them that they were ready to take immediate action.[113] When the royalist officers acted, however, the Military Organization did not mobilize. The Tudah later argued that the Military Organization, given its size and the location of its members, was unable to take any meaningful action to prevent the coup. Many years after the events, certain of those who had been Tudah officers criticized the Military Organization's passivity, pointing out various, if limited, military steps it might have taken. But these steps, such as distributing weapons to Tudah Party members, would have involved a challenge so profound it would have amounted to a bid for power. This was a step the party leadership, whose strategy, like that of its mentors in the Soviet Union, was essentially defensive and who were profoundly suspicious of the nationalists, was not ready to take. Furthermore, the leadership possibly hoped that it would be able to survive the coup intact, preserving its underground organization for the post-Musaddiq period. In fact, the Tudah's inability or unwillingness to use its Military Organization to do what it could to defend the nationalist government was an historic mistake. Its failure at this key moment contributed materially to its being discredited in the eyes not only of the current generation, but of the next generation also, while it found itself subject to the most extreme repression by the post-coup government, its membership inside the country decimated and its leadership forced into exile. Severely damaged politically and organizationally, it was largely superseded by new leftist groups and condemned to marginality as the revolutionary movement erupted in the late 1970s.

## The Era of Empire: Hubris and Nemesis, 1953–79

Immediately after the coup, the Shah established a new intelligence unit with CIA assistance under General Taymur Bakhtiyar who had marched his troops from Kirmanshah to Tehran to assist the coup-makers. This unit was, in 1956, to be expanded into SAVAK. In August 1954 it uncovered the Tudah Military Organization. More than 450 military personnel were arrested, ranging in rank from colonel to sergeant, and tried by military courts. Of these 27 were executed and 144 sentenced to life imprisonment. Even after this, a remnant survived under the Organization's intelligence chief, Captain

Khusraw Ruzbih, but his arrest and execution in 1958 put an end to organized Tudah activity of any real significance inside Iran until the revolution.[114]

As well as hunting down Tudah activists, the post-coup regime also turned its sights on nationalist elements within the army. The armed forces were purged while some 1,800 pro-Zahidi officers were promoted. The officers who had been centrally involved in the CIA planning enjoyed a meteoric rise. Zahidi, of course, became prime minister. General Batmanghilij was made army chief of staff and later minister of the interior. Colonel Farzanagan also became a government minister while Colonel Bakhtiyar was promoted to general and made military governor of Tehran, and later first head of SAVAK. Colonel Nasiri was also promoted to general and later also headed SAVAK.

The success of the coup enabled the Shah to purge the army of all those he suspected of offering their loyalty to Musaddiq or the Tudah, but it failed to make him secure regarding his own supporters among the military. His reluctance to see a powerful general like Zahidi become prime minister had made him dangerously hesitant over signing the decrees necessary to secure military support for the coup, and within a month of the overthrow of Musaddiq he was again openly voicing his jealous resentment of any possible encroachment by Zahidi on his position as commander-in-chief. The Shah expressed himself with a vehemence on this point that alarmed his British interlocutor, saying that he would not 'have the impression created that I am a puppet of General Zahidi's'.[115] He anxiously continued that he must retain effective control of the armed forces or he would sink into insignificance and eventually be forced to abdicate. He further revealed that he also lacked confidence in some of Zahidi's colleagues, including the Minister of Defence. In general, the British observed that the Shah was 'not unduly grateful' to those officers who had acted to restore him to his throne, taking their loyalty for granted.[116] They concluded that he was living in a 'dream world', believing that his restoration was the result of his own popularity and resenting the suggestion that any group in particular, including the army, had assisted him. For his part, Zahidi was already finding the Shah's habit of issuing orders and making military decisions without consulting him 'intolerable'.[117] Zahidi was also at odds with the chief of staff while there were dissensions among the senior officers between those who had supported the Shah throughout the crisis and those who had wavered. Zahidi survived as prime minister only until April 1955, when he was dismissed by the Shah, going into virtual exile in Switzerland.

Although, after the coup, the Shah's suspicions of his most senior officers remained, his relationship with the American advisors of ARMISH/
MAAG[118] was transformed, his former ambivalence towards them
vanishing. They had played a role in the US coup preparations, General
Robert McClure, the head of the mission, helping to recruit Iranian
commanders while the mission also distributed supplies to pro-Zahidi
military units.[119] After the coup, the mission found its position greatly
enhanced. Operating from within the Ministry of Defence, it came to
permeate most branches of the General Staff, while McClure apparently
had great influence over the Shah, whom he met frequently.[120]

After the coup, all ambiguities, and any hint of neutralism and non-
alignment disappeared from Iranian foreign policy, the Shah aligning Iran
closely with the US, politically, militarily and strategically. In 1955 Iran
joined the Baghdad Pact, the Shah using this new strategic commitment to
pressure the US into providing greater quantities of the most modern military equipment while also beginning to plan to raise the strength of the
armed forces to 200,000 by March 1956. In 1959 Iran and the US signed a
bilateral defence agreement.

In addition to the new clarity regarding Iran's international orientation,
the domestic political configuration was also stabilizing around the personal
rule of the Shah. Having been restored to his throne by one coup, the Shah
was determined to avoid another. Officers of the Tehran garrison, key to
any bid for power, were carefully chosen for their loyalty to the Shah while
the Shah was himself commanding officer of the 1st Corps in Tehran, all its
officers especially close to royal circles.[121] Taymur Bakhtiyar, a close relation
of the Shah by marriage, had crushed political opposition, including within
the army, in Tehran while military governor after the coup, and now, as
head of SAVAK, kept a close watch for any sign of dissent, including among
officers. Indeed, the Shah's determination to establish and maintain his own
personal control of the army was becoming one of its major weaknesses. All
decisions about military policy were made by him alone, and he made all
senior appointments and promotions, with the result that officers rose to
high rank on the basis of their loyalty rather than their professional merit.

Despite the consolidation of the control of the post-coup regime over
the army, subterranean discontent continued to exist. Although their conditions were improving slowly, junior officers were still unhappy at their

material conditions, salaries poor in relation to the cost of living, inflation high and housing inadequate. To this was added a specific professional frustration in the relative slowness of promotion, the upper ranks of the army choked with colonels and generals, and the necessity of possessing the right contacts.[122] But the main cause of dissatisfaction among junior officers was dislike of the character of the emerging monarchical dictatorship, a dislike which they shared with their civilian counterparts. According to a profile of the officer corps produced by the US embassy in Tehran in 1957, at least half, and probably more, of the junior officers in the army were middle-class civilians in uniform, sharing the political views of that class, the cradle of the Musaddiqist nationalist movement. These officers were critical of the upper class, considered the generals part of the 'reactionary' or 'British-loving' ruling elite, and emphasized their corruption. They were, furthermore, becoming increasingly professionalized in their approach to the army and to the wider society, and becoming impatient at the slow pace of change in both. Disillusioned with Musaddiq himself, this group was also susceptible to Tudah influence. Even the smaller group of junior officers from upper-class backgrounds, who possessed greater loyalty to the Shah and integrated themselves more easily into the Shah's political machine, tended to be critical of the upper class and the political situation. Although it was true that the longer officers of any background served in the army, the more they tended to become professionalized, this did not mitigate their discontent, since their professional frustrations were very much seen as a product of existing political and social conditions, and they saw themselves as reformers and agents of change.[123] Indeed so Westernized and 'modern' did they see themselves, that they were apparently particularly susceptible to Baha'ism.

The American embassy report considered most of the senior officers, with the rank of colonel and above, to be 'primarily cogs in the Shah's political machine' and loyal to the throne, realizing it to be the keystone of their own position.[124] They enjoyed the prestige and material rewards of high rank, were ready to jockey for lucrative posts and were often corrupt. Only a few had a professional military outlook but were rather army politicians, and they varied greatly in competence. The most important of this group were Generals Taymur Bakhtiyari, head of SAVAK, Mahdi Quli Alavi Muqaddam, head of the national police and bitter enemy of Bakhtiyar, and Ali Alavi Kia, head of military intelligence and the Shah's check against

Bakhtiyar. The Shah placed great reliance on this triangle of power, but was careful to keep the corners of the triangle at each other's throats.

Even amongst the senior ranks, however, the US report detected some dissatisfaction. There were groups smaller than the first which included those whose approach was primarily professional, who tended to avoid politics and who lacked any particular enthusiasm for the Shah, those who came from and identified with the landed upper class and disliked the Shah accordingly, and those from a middle-class background who continued to share the nationalist aspirations of that class. In general, although it was certainly the case that the predominant trend within the army was one of support for the regime and reasonable, though not last-ditch, loyalty to the Shah, a significant number of junior officers and a few of their seniors would welcome the return of a nationalist regime.

As far as the wider society was concerned, in the years after the coup the army was profoundly unpopular. To the rural poor, the army meant the hated conscription. To the urban middle classes it was the visible representation of the pro-British reaction to the Musaddiq era, symbolic of the Shah and the upper class and the embodiment of arrogant and thoughtless conservatism. To many among the upper classes themselves, the army was a danger, reverting to the role it had played in the Riza Shah era of usurping the traditional influence and perquisites of the big landlords and merchants.

The 1950s was a decade of nationalist, sometimes left-leaning, coups in the Arab world. The American and British embassies in Tehran were, accordingly, on the lookout for potential coup-leaders in Iran. The political context was, however, very different. The reputation and prestige of the Iranian army was low. It had recently participated in the Western-led overthrow of a nationalist figure whose stature was growing with the passage of time. In military terms, most educated Tehranis and even many officers and soldiers themselves considered the army to be a joke, the officers with no stomach for fighting and ready to run in every direction. It was further widely believed that the army was corrupt, especially in the upper ranks, and that it was brutal towards civilians and conscripts alike.[125] No individual Iranian army officer enjoyed any broad base of support in society and, in general, the senior officers were not the kind of men considered able to 'lift up a country by its bootstraps'.[126] In August 1959 the American embassy concluded that, although there were several generals who might be able to mobilize support within the army for political change, there was no figure now identifiable among the lesser military figures who might emerge as Iran's Qasim, the radical leader of the recent coup in Iraq.[127]

Towards the end of the decade, dissatisfaction seemed to be increasing. Junior ranks were increasingly disgusted at the extent of the corruption and dishonesty which existed at all levels of government and especially within the army, and there was a growing feeling that this situation must change. The other main cause of discontent was the belief among younger officers, ranking from lieutenant to major, that their commanders were chronically inefficient, and that military progress depended on their being replaced with better-trained and more professionally competent personnel. Some even advocated across-the-board reductions of all senior officers in the interests of a more realistic officer corps structure. Most younger officers had no confidence in their commanders. They were seldom given the opportunity to take responsibility and initiative was stifled whenever a younger officer was apparently becoming overly ambitious, too clever or attempted improvements contrary to the wishes of the leadership. In addition, the cost of living was constantly increasing while the pay of junior officers and soldiers remained low. Officers viewed with distaste the corruption of the court and the 'thousand families', many of whom were the very leaders in the army whom they would like to see removed, and they resented the prevalence of family and patronage networks from which they were excluded. In fact, the American embassy reported that as many as 2,000 of the 10,000 officers on active duty, at the coup-making ranks of lieutenant-colonel to brigadier, might be described as nationalists – that is, reformers who wished to raise the standard of living of the mass of the population, eradicate corruption and restore constitutional government.[128] The informal leader of this group was General Riahi, formerly Musaddiq's chief of staff. A degree of solidarity arose from the fact that most were connected by ties of family, education or friendship. Furthermore, although no Tudah organization survived within the army, the nationalists included Tudah sympathizers while many former Tudah officers who had been sentenced to imprisonment had served their terms and been released, and still had many contacts in the army.[129]

In early 1958, the manifold discontents simmering within the officer corps burst into public view when General Valiullah Qarani, head of the intelligence staff, was arrested on the charge of engaging in political activity, which was forbidden for all army officers.[130] A large number of officers and civilians were also arrested or interrogated by SAVAK in connection with Qarani's activities. It was officially alleged that Qarani and his collaborators had been conspiring with a foreign power, unnamed but assumed to be the US, against the Shah and his government. Qarani was put on trial in the summer of 1958 and sentenced to three years in prison.

Qarani, then with the rank of colonel, had joined the anti-Musaddiq royalist forces in August 1953 and had been briefly dismissed by Musaddiq's chief of staff General Taqi Riahi. After the coup, he was promoted to the rank of brigadier-general and appointed head of military intelligence. Within a short time after the coup, Qarani appears to have developed doubts about the new regime. Influenced by the moderate reformist outlook of civilian acquaintances such as Hasan Arsanjani, Qarani became increasingly concerned at the widespread corruption and political repression, and impatient at the pace of change, identifying the underlying cause as the continuing dominance of the old landed upper class, represented by former prime minister General Zahidi, the current prime minister, Manuchihr Iqbal and, within the army, by his rivals Generals Bakhtiyari, Kia and Alavi Muqaddam. Qarani concluded that the political and social deadlock could only be ended by forcing the Shah to act against the upper class, restore constitutional rule and implement wide-ranging reforms, but undoubtedly he was also motivated by the dynamics of his rivalries with his brother generals.[131]

Qarani's activities remained very limited in scope. He was well connected among the political elite and he mainly concentrated on trying to cultivate and win over potential supporters among this elite and also to sound out the US with a view to gaining American backing. His main goal was to bring pressure to bear on the Shah, from both domestic sources and from the US, to appoint a reforming government. He also appears to have made vague plans to foment disturbances or carry out a coup, but only as a last resort and in unspecified circumstances. Qarani claimed to his American contacts that he was supported by a group of 'patriotic officers' and he indeed seems to have forged a loose association in the army consisting of some 70 officers.[132] This grouping included several senior officers but mostly consisted of junior officers from the Tehran garrison. Qarani appears to have engaged only in talk with his military and civilian sympathizers. He quickly and inevitably came to the attention of SAVAK, leading to his arrest and the disintegration of his networks, such as they were. He alone was brought before and sentenced by a military court, this leniency towards his sympathizers and even, in his relatively short sentence, towards Qarani himself, perhaps indicating the Shah's desire to play down any public awareness of dissent within the army and between himself and the Americans.[133] The next year, in what was interpreted as an attempt by the Shah to purchase the loyalty of the officer corps, a formidable list of promotions was published which included the creation of eight new lieutenant-generals and many more major-generals and brigadiers.[134]

After the 1953 coup, the Shah had moved Iran decisively into the Western camp. Nonetheless, despite Iran's adhesion to the Western bloc and the new harmony between the Shah and ARMISH, fundamental differences in approach and perspective between the Shah and the US remained. The American willingness to maintain contact with Qarani indicated an ongoing uncertainty on the part of the US about the character of the Shah's regime, its ability to survive in the long term and its reliability as a bulwark against communism and the Soviet Union. In general, US officials had always believed and remained convinced that the Shah's future depended on his introducing substantive reforms which would provide him with a real political base in the country. The Shah for his part, aware of American ambiguity and their contacts with his opponents, even at the highest levels of his own army, found his perennial fears and suspicions intensified. His instinctive reaction was to reject any concession to reform and to place ever more emphasis on the security environment, both domestically and regionally. These differing perspectives had repercussions for military planning and tensions persisted between the Shah and the US military mission regarding the size, organization, composition and mission of the armed forces, the amount and type of military equipment, and the nature of the external threat.[135]

Nonetheless, the Shah was eventually obliged, by domestic political discontent and American pressure, to begin a programme of economic, political and social change which became known as the White Revolution. The launch of this programme, which included free elections and land reform, led to the open eruption of the discontent which had simmered since the 1953 coup and which had since been aggravated by political frustration and economic failure. The secular and religious opposition united in a popular uprising in Tehran which reached its peak on 5 June. In response, the Shah once again brought the army onto the streets of the capital, offering a military response to a political problem. The government estimated the resulting loss of life at 90, the opposition at several thousands. The army's deployment on this occasion was brief, and it held together with no open dissent or refusal to obey orders. The suppression of this uprising, known, by the name of the calendar month in which it took place, as the 15th Khurdad, was the last time the army was used on the streets of Iran's cities until 1978 when its experience was to be very different.

The years between the 15th Khurdad and the beginning of the revolution constituted an entirely novel period in Iran's politics and also, and accordingly, in the development of the army. During the 1960s and early 1970s, the role of the Iranian army was redefined. It continued to act as a practical support for the Shah and as a symbol of the Pahlavi monarchy, but it now also became an instrument for buttressing the Shah's ambitions to assert Iran's regional hegemony and his ever larger foreign policy objectives. This redefinition was made possible by the Shah's now unchallenged construction of a personalized and highly centralized mode of rule, by opportunities arising from changes in the regional context, and by the rise in the price of oil, this last creating a lucrative Iranian arms market, all of which encouraged the US in the direction of an increasingly uncritical pro-Shah orientation. Within the Iranian army, dissent was silenced by a deluge of material privileges.

Scepticism in the US State Department about the Shah's obsession with numbers and with weapons, although it remained latent, was rapidly overruled in the face of Iran's utility as a pro-Western pillar adjacent to a rapidly radicalizing Arab world coupled with the quantities of cash which became available as a result of oil price rises, especially after the 1973 October War. The US was by far the most important arms supplier in this period, although the Soviet Union, Britain and France also rushed to join the bonanza.

The growth in men and material was extraordinary. The rising trend was already apparent in the 1960s, Iran's military expenditure rising from 203 million dollars in 1957 to 752 million dollars a decade later.[136] Military expenditure as a proportion of GDP also rose, from 4.2 per cent in 1960 to 6.8 per cent in 1967. The British withdrawal 'east of Suez', announced in 1968 and completed by 1971, opened up huge new possibilities for Iranian hegemony in the Persian Gulf and the Shah expanded his naval capacity accordingly. In 1972 the Shah announced the expansion of Iran's security perimeter beyond the Persian Gulf and into the Indian Ocean. The US now granted Iran the status of one of the 'twin pillars' of its security system in the Gulf, the other pillar being Saudi Arabia. Two further events were of key importance. The first of these was the promulgation of the Nixon Doctrine in 1969, according to which America's allies were to take responsibility for their own defence, itself a reaction to US defeat in Vietnam. As a consequence of this new orientation, in 1972 Nixon informed the Shah that he could purchase any weapons, other than nuclear weapons, which he felt necessary for Iran's defence, thus confirming the final abandonment by the US of any rational calculation of the needs and capability of the Iranian army and of any attempt to constrain the Shah's insatiable appetite for weapons. The second key event was the oil price rise following the October War in 1973. Iran's military expenditure in general, and the upgrading and enhancement of the army's firepower in particular, now took on epic proportions. Between 1970 and 1977 Iran allocated approximately 29 per cent of its total budget to military expenditure.[137] The Iranian defence budget was estimated to have increased from approximately 880 million dollars, in the Iranian fiscal year ending 20 March 1970, to 9.4 billion dollars in the year ending 20 March 1977, an increase of almost 1100 per cent in seven years.[138] Of this expenditure, weapons purchases accounted for about 21.5 per cent, about 5.5 billion dollars for the period 1968–76. All three branches of the armed forces, but particularly the air force, saw enormous numerical and material growth in the 1970s. The Imperial Iranian Air Force had become a separate service in 1955 and was the favourite of the Shah who was himself a pilot.[139] Total military manpower rose from 180,000 in 1965–6 to 413,000 in 1978–9. This total included a rise in the army from 164,000 to 285,000, in the air force from 10,000 to 100,000, and in the navy from 6,000 to 28,000.[140] One detailed study has concluded that, within a decade, Iran had become a middle-level military power, with a largely mechanized army, a sophisticated air force and the core of a 'blue water' fleet.[141] Yet this gives a misleading impression of the degree of coherence and rationality in the Shah's mania for acquisition. In fact, by the 1970s Iran's arms programme was out of control. No US or Iranian government department was exercising oversight, the Shah alone responsible for spending decisions but scarcely understanding what he was purchasing.[142]

While little had been done to address older weaknesses within the Iranian military, the scope and pace of this apparent modernization brought with it new problems. The human resources on which the Iranian army could draw, for both its officer corps and its rank and file, were inadequate, unprepared to cope with the volume and sophistication of the new equipment. In 1966, for example, just before the start of the boom years, still only about 30 per cent of the population over ten years of age was literate. Valuable segments of the conscripts' two years' service had to be spent in providing basic literacy and even, for ethnic minority recruits, a working knowledge of spoken Persian. In general they remained little more than cannon-fodder, unable to earn promotion or a rise in basic pay.[143] The generally low level of educational provision also affected the officer corps, and became more visible as the complexity of the weapons systems increased. The lack of skilled manpower led to the arrival in Iran of vast numbers of American advisors to assist in the operation and maintenance of the imported weapons, a solution which contributed significantly to the unpopularity of the regime. In 1973 there were an estimated 3,600 American technicians in Iran working on defence projects, a number which rose to 10,000 by 1978 as a direct result of the explosion of arms sales.[144] All military personnel were given legal immunity while in Iran and were consequently a particular object of revolutionary propaganda, denounced by Khomeini as symbols of Iran's subservience to the US, becoming a target for the guerrilla campaign of the 1970s. Another solution to the problem of skilled manpower which was adopted was also to prove of fatal significance to the regime. In the 1970s, the air force introduced a new layer into its hierarchy, that of the *homafars*, technicians who were responsible for maintenance. From modest backgrounds and, although technically trained, not educated beyond high-school, the *homafars* were considered unsuitable for integration into the officer corps. Their demands for such integration were consistently refused by the regime and their resulting professional frustration, together with their social origins and outlook, made them especially receptive to revolutionary propaganda.[145]

While accumulating new problems as a result of the breakneck pace of modernization, the army continued to preserve and even magnify many older difficulties and weaknesses. The Shah maintained an iron grip over the officer corps, especially its upper echelons. He continued to employ the techniques perfected by his father, promoting, demoting and dismissing his senior officers at will and, like his father, using charges of corruption as a facade for ridding himself of officers showing signs of becoming independent, over-powerful or popular, thereby gaining for himself some temporary political credit. The Shah was suspicious of Zahidi's ambitions even before the 1953 coup. By 1955 he was gone. In 1961 General Bakhtiyar, a key figure in the post-coup security apparatus, was dismissed as head of SAVAK and accused of plotting against the throne, fleeing into exile. At the same time, as if to demonstrate his total supremacy in the army, the Shah also dismissed General Abdullah Hidayat, chief of staff, and Generals Alavi Muqaddam and Alavi Kia, the latter two, along with Bakhtiyar, key figures in his military-security apparatus. In the previous year the Shah, under intense domestic and international pressure to begin reforms and hold free elections, had carried out a veritable purge, ordering the arrest and prosecution for embezzlement of General Ali Akbar Khudayagan, together with a lieutenant-colonel, two majors, five junior officers and others from his brigade.[146] A few days later, a total of five brigadier-generals, 19 lieutenant-colonels, 37 colonels, 11 majors, 51 junior officers and a number of other ranks, all from the notoriously unpopular department for military conscription, were similarly arrested and charged with corruption.[147] The opportunity for making political capital from these episodes was fully exploited by the Shah while they also served as a reminder that material privilege and position remained entirely dependent on his pleasure.

The entire military edifice was built around and depended upon the personality of the Shah, yet the Shah had never entirely emerged from the shadow of his father and betrayed traits of weakness and vacillation. The practice, which the fearful and insecure Shah had long struggled to impose, whereby even the most trivial matter was referred to him personally, was institutionalized, weakening further the already attenuated ability and motivation of senior officers to take decisions or show initiative. For the court, political considerations were paramount in making military appointments, with the result that loyalty trumped competence and mediocrity found favour. The Shah possessed many mechanisms for ensuring the subservience of the officer corps. No general might visit Tehran or meet with another general without the Shah's personal permission. Officers were watched by the Shah's special Imperial Inspectorate as well as by military intelligence and by SAVAK. Bitter personal and professional rivalries were instigated and encouraged among officers, who were invited to monitor each other's activities, resulting in a pervasive atmosphere of insecurity, jealousy and fear. Senior officers might be humiliated by public scoldings, their postings arbitrarily reshuffled to avoid any risk that they might establish independent power bases or followings. But the carrot as well as the stick was liberally deployed. The Shah bestowed on the senior officers salaries, pensions, benefits, housing, medical facilities, travel abroad and subsidized department stores and appointed them to run provinces, government ministries and state economic enterprises.[148] During the years of expansion in the 1960s, and especially after the beginning of the oil boom, financial opportunities, legitimate and illegitimate, opened up for well-placed army officers.

The malaise affecting the high command percolated relentlessly down. Just as few senior officers were prepared to delegate responsibility, so few junior officers wished to accept it. Since issues were invariably referred upwards, officers, especially staff officers, correctly believing themselves powerless, absolved themselves from any forward planning, all decisions left to the last possible moment, if made at all.[149] Junior as well as senior officers had begun to share in the general largesse but, although all publicly referred to the Shah in godlike terms, there were undoubtedly feelings of frustration at the middle and lower-ranking echelons.[150] Such frustration arose from the very apparent inefficiencies rampant throughout the army and at the monopoly on high rank maintained by those with the right social and political connections. Meanwhile, little had changed for the conscript. Discipline was arbitrary and harsh, and the gulf between officers and men was immense, the conscripts often little more than their officers' servants.[151]

The Shah's imperial ambition to play the role of regional hegemon in the Gulf, and his alarm at the apparent spread of pro-Soviet radicalism in the Arab world, eventually led, in the mid-1970s, to the actual deployment of the Iranian army on foreign soil, the first ever such deployment in modern times. Iranian troops fought in Dhofar between 1973 and 1975 in support of the Omani monarchy's campaign against the rebellion of the leftist Popular Front for the Liberation of Oman. The weaknesses, old and new, which continued to afflict the army were very much in evidence in these, its only significant operations of the period. Although both the Sultan of Oman and the British officers who commanded the Omani army publicly praised the value of Iranian assistance, different opinions were expressed privately. British assessments appreciated the Shah's loan of helicopters, but criticized the troops for relying on massive firepower, lacking initiative, repeating orders down the line parrot fashion, tending to be jumpy and trigger-happy and sometimes firing on each other or their allies.[152]

This was the army which stood between the Shah and the revolutionaries in 1978.[153] Between 1963 and 1978, the army was not seen on the streets of Iran's cities. It was garrisoned near major towns, and was occasionally used in rural areas in support of the Imperial Iranian Gendarmerie, and military officers staffed military courts, a role which contributed substantially to an erosion of the army's legitimacy in the eyes of opponents of the regime of all shades. But it was not the most active element in the Shah's domestic system of control. It was the Gendarmerie which was most significant as a paramilitary rural police force and, after 1971, a counter-insurgency force, while SAVAK, always headed by an army general, was responsible for crushing political opposition. As the revolutionary crisis of 1978 unfolded, however, the army was again brought onto the streets.

An armed guerrilla campaign against the Shah's regime had begun in 1971 but it was only in 1977 that opposition began to take on a mass, and then, in 1978, a revolutionary, character. During 1977, although the protests were growing larger and louder, the government continued to rely on the police to break up meetings, strikes and demonstrations. In early 1978, after the regime launched a personal attack on Ayatullah Khomeini, opposition rapidly radicalized. Troops and tanks appeared first on the streets of Tabriz and then in other Iranian cities, including the capital, and declarations of martial law were frequent. The deployment of the army led to a massive increase in casualties, peaking on 8 September, subsequently known as Black Friday, when troops fired live ammunition into a peaceful crowd, with heavy casualties.

The army was ill prepared to meet civil disturbance. The sophisticated high-tech weaponry so beloved by the Shah was of little use against unarmed demonstrators in urban centres, while the 'stereotyped and mass-production' training of the troops, heavily based on US methods,[154] and the inflexible obedience to orders of all levels of the officer corps, combined to make the army very much a blunt instrument whose deployment on the streets invariably aggravated discontent.

The army's inability to stem the worsening situation led the Shah to succumb to his perennial tendencies towards vacillation. Following Black Friday, he publicly hesitated in supporting his army in its actions, rebuking his generals and singling out for criticism the army commander, General Oveissi. After Black Friday, the army, accustomed to referring every decision upwards, often as far as the Shah himself, became increasingly uncertain whether it should use force or show restraint. The generals began to lose confidence in the Shah. The hard-line General Oveissi tried to steamroller the Shah into appointing him head of a military government by ordering the army not to intervene in major disturbances in Tehran in early November. The Shah did indeed appoint a military government, but one headed by the dovish chief of staff, General Azhari, who represented the opposite current to Oveissi which feared that further repression only might make the situation worse. Azhari's government soon showed itself helpless in the face of the self-confidence of the revolutionaries which had grown as the Shah had faltered.

While the upper echelons of the military, themselves divided between hawks and doves, were confused and demoralized by the Shah's chidings and apparent weakness, lower ranks of the officer corps and the rank and file were becoming actively mutinous. The revolutionaries now in the ascendant among the opposition adopted several different tactics towards the army designed to neutralize and win over the troops. Armed attacks were carried out, these serving to undermine military morale and confidence. Even more effective was the promotion of fraternization and constant exhortations to the military to join the movement to overthrow the Shah. As the demonstrators placed flowers in the troops' gun barrels, and wore white shrouds to symbolize their readiness for martyrdom, the army crumbled, the conscript rank and file particularly susceptible to religious appeals and warnings. In mid-December the Information Ministry issued a series of desperate communiqués denying that the army was on the verge of mutiny.[155] Junior officers and the troops were by now refusing to fire on crowds, even shooting other soldiers to prevent them doing so, and desertions rocketed while air force personnel attended demonstrations in full uniform.[156] Pro-revolutionary fervour even reached the elite Imperial Guard. In early December a small group of officers and men from the Guard attacked the officers' mess, killing more than a dozen officers and wounding many more.[157]

As the revolutionary movement advanced, the class fissures within the military had become more visible. The conscripts, many from the villages and provincial towns, brought into the army the attitudes of the wider population, were more inclined to religious belief than their middle-class urban officers, and were perplexed by orders to shoot at demonstrators very similar to themselves in background, education and culture. Their officers had taken little care during their two-year periods of service to create an esprit de corps, and their pay and conditions were bad, especially when compared to the officers. The gulf was crudely epitomized by pay scales. Whereas a general received a salary of 70,000 dollars per annum, and even a lieutenant 14,000 dollars, a conscript was paid merely one dollar per day.[158] The revolution allowed the ingrained grievances of the rank and file to come out into the open. Equally resentful were many junior and middle-ranking officers. The massive expansion of the military in the 1960s–70s had resulted in the presence within the officer corps of greater numbers of men drawn from the lower middle classes, exactly the social group that was providing the backbone of the revolutionary movement. The appeal of the revolution to such elements was immense, whereas the ideological power of the monarchy–army nexus was revealed as thin and brittle. By late 1978 even middle-ranking officers, lacking confidence in their seniors, indifferent to the fate of the Shah, and in awe of, or even sympathetic to the revolution, withdrew into passivity, or quietly requested retirement.

Azhari's military government was paralysed by internal divisions among senior officers. They were, in any case, hamstrung by habits cultivated over decades, of rivalry, jealousy and mutual suspicion, which prevented the emergence of any co-ordinated policy or any independent initiative, and demoralized by the Shah's periodic arrests of officials and officers intended to placate the opposition. As the Shah's prospects darkened, senior officers also began to fear for their own future, to plan their escape abroad or to calculate the possibilities of making their peace with the revolution. The endgame was finally reached when the Shah dismissed General Azhari and asked the liberal Shahpour Bakhtiyar to form a government, announcing a little later that he himself intended to go abroad on vacation. Bakhtiyar's government was rejected by all shades of opinion, including his own National Front.

Meanwhile, the US had begun to consider its options. Just as the upper echelons of the Iranian army was fatally fractured, so too had internal divisions within the Carter administration further undermined the Shah and energized the revolutionaries. Carter's early espousal of a human rights policy had contributed to the emergence of the revolutionary movement and to the Shah's uncertainty. In early January, the Americans began to hedge their bets. Carter instructed an American air force general with close connections to Iranian air force officers, General Robert Huyser, to go to Iran and to prepare contingency plans with the Iranian army for a military takeover.[159] Huyser was met with suspicion from all sides. Khomeini warned that the Shah was planning a coup and called on 'honourable elements' in the army to prevent 'such a crime' while the Shah believed that Huyser had come to betray him to the revolutionaries.[160] As far as the senior officers themselves were concerned, Huyser found them lacking the initiative or ability for co-ordination, too divided to take power into their own hands, and planning to follow the Shah into exile. They possessed no clue as to how to regain the loyalty, or even obedience, of their men, they disliked Bakhtiyari and had lost confidence in the Shah. The Shah himself, meanwhile, lapsed into resigned passivity.

Neither the generals nor the CIA were in a position to repeat the coup of 1953 which had restored the exiled Shah to his throne. After the Shah's departure, the senior officers began rather to position themselves with an eye to the future. The chief of staff, General Qarabaghi, hoping to preserve the institutional integrity of the armed forces and perhaps also his own position, made contact with Khomeini's aides and, in a practical overture to the revolutionaries, omitted the pledge of loyalty to the Shah from the commissioning oath to graduating cadets.[161]

Meanwhile, their subordinates in the armed forces, led by the Shah's favourite service, the air force *homafars*, had already made their choice. In a perfect illustration of the class conflict within the armed forces being played out during the revolution, the coup de grace was given to the imperial regime by the *homafars* in a bloody conflict with the Imperial Guard. Early in February revolutionary *homafars* seized the air bases at Dushan

Tappeh and Farahabad. In a re-enactment of a classical revolutionary scenario, the *homafars* were joined by civilian revolutionaries and weapons were distributed to the populations who forced Imperial Guard units to retreat. Even some of the Imperial Guard themselves now defected. On 11 February Qarabaghi and his remaining senior officers met and conceded that they could no longer contain the situation. They agreed on a statement declaring the army's neutrality and ordered the remaining military units back to their barracks.

## Conclusion: The Armed Forces and the Islamic Republic

Throughout the revolutionary period, Khomeini and his supporters had carefully adopted the deliberate tactic of trying to win over the army, rather than simply destroying it, issuing appeals to officers as well as to the ordinary soldiers to join the revolution. During 1979 and into 1980 the new revolutionary government struggled both to hold the armed forces together and to assert its own authority over them, Khomeini ordering military personnel to return to work and offering amnesties.[162] But the armed forces were subject to the same strains and fissures that were emerging among society in general after the successful overthrow of the Shah. By July 1979, about 60 per cent of the army had simply disappeared, most simply going home.[163] What remained was under the primary influence of revolutionary councils which advocated the dissolution of professional military hierarchies altogether in favour of popular militias. In the first half of 1979 the new government took several steps to re-establish its control. Although the most senior officers most closely identified with the Shah and who bore the heaviest responsibility for repression were purged, and a small number executed, the government at first retained high-ranking professional officers in command of the armed forces, although only those who had clearly established their revolutionary credentials. These included General Qarani, who had been imprisoned in 1959, and who was appointed chief of staff, and General Taqi Riahi, who had been Musaddiq's chief of staff, as defence minister. Perhaps the most significant measure which the new government took to manage the armed forces was the establishment of the Revolutionary

Guards Corps, also known as the *Pasdaran*.[164] A militia known as the *Basij-i Musta'zafan* (mobilization of the dispossessed) was later created as a reserve for the Revolutionary Guards. A paramilitary organization which functioned in parallel to the armed forces, possessing its own command structure and recruitment, the Corps in its early years represented the Islamic revolutionaries' distrust of the conventional armed forces and their sympathies, which they had learned from the left, for theories of 'people's war'. The Guards were created as an instrument of the Islamic revolution, and were loyal to Khomeini as *vilayat-i faghih* and to the new republican authorities. They played an openly political role, asserting the authority of the new regime against its multiplying internal enemies, and they kept a close watch on the army.

The first purge in the armed forces had been limited in scope, specifically targeting senior officers, brigadier-generals and major-generals, and the Imperial Guard, and mostly involving forced retirement rather than execution, altogether probably around 26 out of more than 200 army generals were executed.[165] In September 1979 a second purge began under the leadership of the new civilian defence minister, Mustafa Chamran. This second purge concentrated on the lower echelons of the armed forces, targeting those who were merely suspect rather than actually guilty of counter-revolutionary crimes, and bore down most heavily on the officer corps of the army. This purge, which was directed at both royalist sympathizers and at leftists who had been active in the soldiers' councils,[166] resulted in the removal of substantial numbers of officers, especially in the ranks of major to colonel, and also of NCOs.[167] Although the purge, which continued until the end of the summer of 1980, eliminated from the army some oppositional elements, from both left and right, and therefore solidified the control of the new regime, it left the Iranian armed forces to face the Iraqi invasion with a leadership which had been 'ravaged by a combination of revolutionary zeal and suspicion'.[168]

The domestic conflicts of this period, which often overlapped with the activities and propaganda of exile groups, tended to confirm the authorities' belief that the army was replete with counter-revolutionary conspiracies. Indeed, although the officer corps had been unable and indeed unwilling to put up any systematic opposition to the revolution, elements within the army did strike back against the consolidating Islamic Republic at several points during 1979–80. In May and June 1980, for example, two coup plots were discovered linked to the exiled General Oveissi and dozens of military personnel were arrested. Most significant, however, was the so-called Nuzhih plot of July 1980.[169] In an illustration of the shifting alignments resulting from the emergence of new post-revolutionary political realities, this episode brought together two currents which had been on opposing sides prior to 1979, pro-Shah military officers and the secular nationalists. In early July 1980 several hundred Iranian paratroopers approached Nuzhih air force base near Hamadan with the objective of launching a coup. The authorities, who had learned of the plot, were prepared and arrested many as they reached the base and several hundred more in the days following. Many were later executed. The coup involved army officers still in Iran, formed into a secret group called the *Nizaiyan-i Vatanparast* (Patriotic Officers), civilian dissidents, exiled politicians such as the Shah's last prime minister, Shahpur Bakhtiyari, and even Iraqi intelligence. The numbers of military personnel implicated in the plot, 700–750, indicated the solid opposition towards the Islamic Republic in some quarters of the armed forces, and heightened the regime's belief that it was under siege and its determination to eradicate opposition. The purges were stepped up, leaving Iran even more vulnerable to the Iraqi invasion, which came in September 1980.

Iraq had supported the Nuzhih plot in the hope of weakening Iran even further prior to launching its invasion. Certainly in September 1980 all of Iran's forces were unprepared for war, their command structures shaken by purges, their equipment allowed to deteriorate and their general organization in chaos. Nonetheless, the eight-year war with Iraq gave the Iranian armed forces the opportunity to restore their prestige and legitimacy. After the initial shock of the invasion, the Iranian armed forces regained their equilibrium and finally fought back, seizing the initiative in late 1981 and driving the Iraqis out of Iran by the summer of 1982, gaining a sliver of Iraqi territory as they advanced.

The war years saw the Iranian military transformed not only into an effective fighting force but also into an institution of the Islamic Republic, although friction persisted between the regular services and the *Pasdaran* and *Basij*. Iranian mechanics became adept at cannibalizing damaged equipment and kept at least some of the sophisticated weaponry imported by the Shah operational for far longer than Western observers had predicted to be possible while vast improvements were made in the ability of the officer corps at the planning, co-ordination and execution of operations.[170] The war, which endured until the cease-fire of August 1988, was devastating for both Iran and Iraq. Yet, despite the huge losses in personnel and material, the Iranian armed forces emerged intact and undefeated, with a carefully selected cadre of veteran combat commanders and junior officers able to provide leadership which was competent, experienced and, in general terms, loyal to the Islamic Republic. Just as the exigencies of war had allowed the government of the Islamic Republic to consolidate its authority over state and society, so too was its specific control of the armed forces strengthened and deepened.

After the end of the war, the division between the army and the Revolutionary Guards became further institutionalized, with the Guards the more powerful service. The army confined itself to the conventional duties of national defence against external aggression while the Revolutionary Guards steadily expanded their role as defenders of the Islamic Republic's ethos, both at home and abroad. In general, the military's share of the budget remained much lower than in the Shah's time due to fluctuations in oil revenues and the needs of a growing population, although the latter also ensured the ready availability of conscripts. As a consequence of financial stringency and Western sanctions, the regime, instead of thorough-going modernization, opted for the acquisition of deterrent and retaliatory missile and defence systems.[171] So far, the army has remained immune to political temptations. The Guards, on the other hand, have since 2004–5 become ever more deeply embedded in Iranian politics and the economy. They provided key organizational and financial support, and indeed muscle, for Mahmud Ahmadinejad's elections to the presidency in 2005 and 2009, receiving important political and diplomatic appointments in return, while their international links and their economic power, in the defence industry and far beyond, continued to grow. While the army of the Islamic Republic, in contrast to the Pahlavi army, has confined itself to its narrowly conceived professional role, the Guards have become deeply embedded in both the political and the economic life of the country. But, again in contrast to Pahlavi Iran, the Islamic Republic has cultivated both the rank and file and the officer corps of the Guards, and the force has shown no inclination to develop any corporate identity or agenda independent of the regime.

As it consolidated its power, the Islamic Republic was confronted with a multiplying number of enemies. The state, however, did not disintegrate. On the contrary, the Islamic Republic used the very domestic and international conflicts in which it was embroiled to rebuild its institutions, especially the military. Rather than destroying the Pahlavi state, the revolutionary authorities took over the institutions of the Pahlavi era, including the army, and, by a combination of purging, replacing of leaderships and ideological offensives, transformed these institutions into loyal branches of the new regime. Although under enormous centrifugal pressures after the revolution, the state apparatus survived and then thrived. In contrast to neighbouring countries such as Iraq and Afghanistan, which had also undergone convulsive political changes, by the twenty-first century the writ of the Iranian state, enforced by its army, ran unimpeded through the entire country and encompassed the lives of the entire population.

# CHAPTER 5

# Tribes, Coups and Princes
## Building a Modern Army in Saudi Arabia

In the decades following World War I, countries such as Iran, Iraq and Afghanistan used the creation of a modern army as an engine for wider processes of change. Such military-led state-building followed a precedent established in the previous century by Egypt and the Ottoman Empire. In these countries, military revolutions involving the introduction of new technologies and military tactics made essential broader transformations in tax, administrative and educational structures to finance the army and provide literate manpower. In Saudi Arabia, however, no such military revolution, dragging society in its wake, took place. Military expansion was funded not by domestic taxation but by oil royalties provided by a foreign concession, recruitment remained voluntary, avoiding the administrative centralization and bureaucratic rationality demanded by conscription, while both the integrative function of conscription and the emergence of a professional officer corps were both sacrificed to the imperative of sustaining the tribal and family ascendancy of the al-Saud. The Saudi army remained a small volunteer force, while surrounding countries built mass armies. The Saudi army also, although mobilized, held back from significant practical participation in the wars of 1948, 1956, 1967 and 1973. Thus, although especially the experience of 1948 had a profound impact on the then still tiny number of officers, the country largely avoided the political trauma which resulted from military defeat in other Arab countries. In contrast to its regional neighbours such as Iran and Iraq, Saudi Arabia used the mechanism of building an army not to transform society but rather to maintain the existing social order. Thus Saudi Arabia entered the twenty-first century having experienced not military modernization but rather military modernization in reverse, the strength of tribal and family ties and patronage not weakened but rather embedded ever more deeply within a system of patrimonial rule.

Military-led state-building began much later in the Arabian peninsula than in other parts of the Middle East. Indeed, the first steps in this direction were taken by Abd al-Aziz ibn Saud as much as a century after a state with an equally low fiscal and administrative base and a similarly predominantly tribal social structure, Afghanistan, had embarked on this path. The absence from the Arabian peninsula, until the mid-twentieth century, of the state-building agenda which had hegemonized the modernist discourse across much of the wider region, was due to the apparent poverty of indigenous economic and political resources and, a corollary of this poverty, to the resulting lack of interest on the part of the imperial powers, European and Ottoman. Britain was content to assert its imperial supremacy in the Persian Gulf through the use of naval power and agreements with local shaikhs along the Gulf littoral, while the Ottomans maintained their control of the key cities of the Hijaz, Mecca, Medina and the port of Jidda, through the intermediary of urban notables possessing religious prestige, the most important of whom was the Sharif of Mecca, the Hashemite Husayn ibn Ali. The process of centralization and modernization which had transformed the Ottoman central administration and army in the nineteenth and early twentieth centuries only impinged to the lightest degree on the Hijaz, and not at all on Najd.

By the late 1930s the modern state and army building, which the surrounding countries of Iraq, Iran and even Transjordan had begun in earnest, could no longer be ignored by Abd al-Aziz ibn Saud, now king of a newly stabilized Saudi Arabia. At the same time, the new kingdom, or more specifically its possession of significant oil resources, was intruding with increasing urgency into the consciousness of outside powers, old and new. In 1938 oil production commenced, the oil concession operated initially by Standard Oil of California and then by the great oil company formed in 1944, Aramco, and by the early 1940s the US was showing a strong official interest in Saudi state-building, particularly in the sphere of military reform. Nonetheless, the first foreign involvement came from Britain. Yet, the presence of the British military mission in the late 1940s and early 1950s was in reality an anachronism. It resulted from Saudi displeasure at the US role in the creation of Israel and from Ibn Saud's fixation with his supposed enemies and rivals in the Hashemite Kingdoms of Iraq and Transjordan, British officers having acted as advisors to the armies of both states. The presence of the British military mission temporarily concealed the new reality. After a flirtation with Egyptian military assistance in the early 1950s, the Saudi reliance on the US emerged clearly, only to deepen as the decades passed. Ibn Saud's meteoric rise had been partly due to his ability to manoeuvre between several imperial powers. After his death, Saudi Arabia gradually lost this relative freedom of action, its dependence on US advice, training and supply turning eventually into an unequal equation, Saudi military subordination enmeshed in numerous defence agreements with the US and underpinned by the US arms industry.

Despite the import of huge quantities of military equipment and of large numbers of foreign advisors, and the export of students and cadets to train abroad, all at vast expense, the Saudi armed forces failed to achieve a systematic modernization of the kind being instituted elsewhere. The army was modelled, in theory, on the national institutions typical of a modern state. In practice, however, the army, and most significantly its officer corps, remained unrepresentative of the country at large while an additional new force, the National Guard, was created precisely in order to reflect and sustain the tribal and patrimonial character of the Saudi monarchy. By the twenty-first century, Saudi military forces, after 70 years of moderniza-tion and despite the possession of the latest high-tech military technology, remained tied to the tribal and regional bases of the Saudi royal family. Indeed, both the general direction of Saudi state-building, and the specific development of the military, including the army, the National Guard and the air force, avoided any challenge to tribalism but rather embedded it within the new institutions. Tribal and family connections, for example, continued to play an integral role in military recruitment and promotion. This actually amounted to a kind of military modernization in reverse. Elsewhere in the Middle East, tribalism had been weakened or suppressed altogether. In Saudi Arabia, on the contrary, it had been reinvigorated and modernized, becoming a central organizing principle around which the new institutions of the state, both civil and military, were constructed. For example, whereas in the 1950s princes had only occupied the very apex of the various military and defence institutions, the numerical expansion of the royal family and its access to the best education meant that by the 1990s all three services and the defence ministry found their entire upper echelons increasingly dominated by an ever-growing pool of officers of royal birth.

Just as the military was ultimately bound to reproduce the characteristics typical of the regime which created it, so too did army opposition echo that found in Saudi society. As in the wider Middle East, so too in Saudi Arabia, the 1950s and 1960s saw the rise of pan-Arabism and Nasserism among the most forward-looking elements, among civilian opposition groups and in the army. Yet, the social groups for whom these ideologies held appeal were themselves small, weak and fractured, and such currents in the army had the power only to express themselves in coup attempts with little wider support, let alone hope of success. As the growing oil wealth increasingly enabled the regime to buy off opposition among the better-educated, so a social and ideological trauma resulting from that same oil wealth led to the emergence, among the poorer tribal groups and in the National Guard, of a different kind of dissent, now with a strong religious revivalist character. Here too, the Saudi experience echoed that of the wider Middle East, where various kinds of Islamic politics had largely supplanted secular nationalism by the 1980s. The fear of religious opposition within the National Guard produced a crisis within the regime regarding its military. Having ardently desired a modern army to provide the panoply of military strength deemed necessary to defend themselves against their old dynastic rivals, the Hashemites in Iraq and Transjordan, the al-Saud had then created the National Guard to defend themselves against the army. Having created two parallel forces, the Guard to keep watch on the army and ultimately protect the royal family from a coup, by the time of the siege of the Grand Mosque in Mecca in 1979 it appeared that the al-Saud could no longer rely on either of its principal forces. For a brief period, the Saudis seemed to be opting for abandoning their own military altogether in favour of Pakistani mercenaries. Nonetheless, with the Gulf increasingly the site of intra-state conflict, the Iran–Iraq war followed by the Iraqi invasion of Kuwait, the Saudis began to pay renewed attention to the army, but in a context where real defence imperatives were to be met through the alliance with the US.

The problems presented to the Saudi system, and the choice made by the Saudi regime to use military modernization as a mechanism to reinforce its own grip on power and the tribal and religious underpinnings of Saudi rule, may most clearly be seen in the debate over conscription. In neighbouring countries of the Middle East such as Iraq and Iran, where the state had been commandeered by radical modernizers, the Ba'th Party or the Pahlavi shahs, conscription had been used to build large armies, and to school a diverse population in the rituals of nationalism and citizenship. In such countries, the nationalist agenda involved the deliberate eradication of tribal, religious and regional particularities. In Saudi Arabia, on the contrary, the state based itself on a particular tribal group, reinforced by a specific religious affiliation. This presented Saudi state-builders with a dilemma. How could modern institutions such as a national army be created without challenging, and possibly undermining, the very basis of Saudi rule? This dilemma had first appeared at the very beginning of the era of state-building, when Saudi princes and officials discussed recruitment with the British military mission in the late 1940s, and raised the possibility of a policy of conscription. Unable to reconcile the consequences of universal military service with the desire to maintain the tribal and religious supremacy of the al-Saud, the debate over conscription simmered unresolved. Recruitment remained voluntary, and thus open to manipulation, but difficult, the army and the National Guard constantly short of men. Conscription continued to be proposed from time to time as a solution to the army's manpower problems, although its implication for the tribal and religious character of the military was never openly confronted. For the al-Saud, it was precisely the integrative function of conscription that they wished to avoid; thus by the twenty-first century, they found themselves still facing an otherwise insoluble military manpower problem.[1]

## Ibn Saud, Tribal Forces and the *Ikhwan*, 1900–30

The first three decades of the twentieth century witnessed the spectacular expansion of Saudi power across much of the Arabian peninsula. An earlier period of Saudi rule had disintegrated in the 1870s to 1880s under the pressure of clan and tribal rivalries, but by the end of the century Saudi power had again revived under the leadership of Abd al-Aziz ibn Saud. His rise, although piecemeal and uncertain at the time, later appeared inexorable. Defeating his most important local enemies, the Rashidis of the Shammar tribe, he captured Riyadh in 1902, an event which occupies a seminal place in the foundational myth of modern Saudi Arabia. Having consolidated his control of Najd (central Arabia), by 1913 Ibn Saud had also established his rule over the predominantly Shi'i area of al-Hasa (the eastern province). During World War I, Ibn Saud continued his skirmishing with the Rashidis, tribal chieftains like himself, but this struggle now became subsumed under the wider international conflict, Ibn Saud receiving British guns and subsidies to fight the pro-Ottoman Rashidis.[2] By 1921 Ibn Saud, benefiting from his connections to the winning side in the global conflict, was clearly signalling his own position as the pre-eminent power in Arabia, consigning the Rashidis to a subordinate position in the emerging political order. In the early 1920s he increased his pressure on the Hijaz, then ruled by the Hashemite King Husayn, another British protégé who had headed the Arab Revolt during the world war and to whose sons, Faysal and Abdullah, the British had allocated the new monarchies of Iraq and Transjordan. Husayn's British connections, though longer and deeper than those of Ibn Saud, were not sufficient to protect him and between 1924 and 1926 Ibn Saud took control of the entire Hijaz, including Mecca and Medina and the port of Jidda. With the annexation of Asir from the Yemenis in 1930 Ibn Saud's territorial expansion had completed the creation of modern Saudi Arabia and in 1932 he declared himself king.

Ibn Saud established his new kingdom on territories encompassing three-quarters of the Arabian peninsula by military conquest yet without the possession of anything resembling a modern army. Similarly, although he undeniably engaged in a state-building process in the 1920s and 1930s, with territorial delimitation, agreements with neighbouring states, and a small degree of administrative centralization, the resulting polity still largely resembled the Saudi emirates of the previous two centuries. It lacked, even in embryo, the typical features of a modern state-in-formation, and was based on the same clan and tribal structures which had supported earlier chieftaincies. With the very partial exception of the Hijaz, all the territories or populations now incorporated into the kingdom of Saudi Arabia had remained isolated from the defensive modernization and associated measures of state-building that had laid the basis for both modern states and modern armies in other parts of the Middle East during the nineteenth century. Consequently, as Ibn Saud carved out his new state, he found himself almost entirely lacking in the building blocks, educational, administrative-bureaucratic, fiscal and military, which other new states in the region, such as Republican Turkey, Hashemite Iraq and Pahlavi Iran, had inherited from Ottoman and Qajar reform efforts. Indeed, Ibn Saud's early state-building efforts began from an institutional base lower than any other major country in the region, including those, like his own, with predominantly tribal populations.

Prior to 1912 Ibn Saud relied on military forces which were composed of members of his own clan and some beduin followers who fought using the only quasi-military methods of which they had any knowledge, those of tribal raiding.[3] These were the techniques of warfare employed generally in the Arabian peninsula and arose organically from a society where both settled and nomadic communities were tribal in social organization, and which included a large beduin population dependent on camel breeding and raiding. Up until this time his campaigns had no especial ideological/religious colouring, despite his family's historical association with Wahhabism and their empowerment of this movement in earlier Saudi-led emirates of the eighteenth and nineteenth centuries.[4] Ibn Saud's military successes were against forces similar to his own, and his victories part of the ebb and flow of power between tribal chiefs.

In 1912–13, however, the military balance between Ibn Saud's military strength and that of his local rivals was fundamentally transformed through his foundation of colonies of *Ikhwan*, beduin who gave up both nomadism and also, nominally at least, tribalism, and took up permanent agricultural settlement. The *Ikhwan* were, through the agency of religious missionaries known as *mutawwa'a*, turned into militant exponents of Wahhabism and provided Ibn Saud with an entirely novel military force, one which was, again at least in theory, loyal entirely to himself rather than to its troops' own minor tribal chiefs.[5] The *Ikhwan* were motivated not only by ideology but also by the opportunity to profit from raiding/military activities, such activities designed to extend the intertwined influence of Wahhabism and the secular power of Ibn Saud and therefore sanctioned by religion and supported by the state. These new shock troops of the al-Saud, barely controllable irregulars indoctrinated with a variant of puritanical

Islam and motivated by the prospects of loot, offered a striking contrast to the new military forces, regular *nizam* regiments modelled on European armies and inculcated with state-centred patriotism, typically created by rulers elsewhere in the Middle East seeking to strengthen both their offensive and their defensive power. Although a new institution and key to the ruler's accumulation of power, the *Ikhwan* colonies were unable to provide a mechanism for national integration. On the contrary, their very ideological extremism, their divisive impact on a society which included substantial non-Wahhabi and even Shi'i elements, and their continuing practical adhesion to and reinforcement of tribal values, gave their activities rather a centrifugal and destabilizing dynamic.

The *Ikhwan* appear to have had, on paper, a relatively well-regulated system of military service. Despite the theoretical abandonment of tribalism, only *Ikhwan* who originated from tribes with military traditions were allowed to participate in campaigns.[6] Those so liable were divided into three categories, those permanently ready for action as soon as a call to jihad should be made, reservists, and finally those who might only be mobilized in an emergency.[7] When called on campaign, the *Ikhwan* came with their own camels, arms and food. It has been argued that the *Ikhwan* colonies provided Ibn Saud with the means to weaken the tribal structure of society, although it appears that in practice tribal affiliation continued to constitute a central organizing principle, determining both the composition of the population of each individual settlement and its internal demarcations and hierarchies.[8] There is no doubt, however, that the system did provide him with a unique and, at least in local terms, highly effective, military strike force. Yet the *Ikhwan*, although their military contribution to Saudi expansion was considerable, were not the only military force at Ibn Saud's disposal. He always drew on other sources of military manpower and, although much of his military success between 1912 and 1926 may be attributed to the *Ikhwan*, his army also included beduin mobilized on a purely tribal basis and significant numbers of Najdi townsmen. With an army so composed, Ibn Saud was able to expand his territory through military conquest. Yet, although his forces acquired a reputation for military prowess, in fact, their successes were only against enemies even less sophisticated than themselves, also lacking modern weapons, methods of organization, and divided along tribal lines.

During the 1920s, Ibn Saud expanded his state through military conquest, acquiring a reputation as the quintessential 'desert warrior' of European imagination, yet in reality his success was due also to his ability to take diplomatic advantage of a favourable international and regional context. Before World War I Ibn Saud had manoeuvred successfully between the declining Ottoman and rising British power in the Arabian peninsula. After the war, recognizing the new configurations of power in the Middle East, he made a pragmatic accommodation with the new state system established under British tutelage. Having annexed the Hijaz, vital to the viability of his new state, Ibn Saud refrained from any challenge to the borders separating his territories from the new British-mandated kingdoms of Iraq and Transjordan to the north, and the British-protected states of the Gulf littoral to the east.

In the 1920s, the expansion of Saudi rule in the peninsula owed much, in terms of ideological legitimacy and the defeat of local rivals, to the fighting abilities of the *Ikhwan*. The *Ikhwan*, however, though possessing certain unique features which distinguished them from traditional tribal forces, nonetheless experienced the same waxing and waning of their fortunes in the context of state-building experienced by tribal forces elsewhere. Having played a central role in the establishment and expansion of the state, the *Ikhwan* then immediately turned into an impediment to the consolidation and centralization of power and, in particular, to the ascendancy of a dynastic leader, albeit himself of tribal origin.[9] This conflict then, as elsewhere, inevitably led to a mortal struggle for supremacy between the new ruler and his *quondam* military base through which the fledgling state might either triumph or collapse.

The establishment of the *Ikhwan* colonies had been intended to attenuate the conflict between the central administration and the tribal nomadic periphery. In this it was partially successful but at the expense of replacing this perennial conflict with a new tension, that between ideological zeal and pragmatic politics and diplomacy. As long as the energies and ardour of the *Ikhwan* were harnessed to territorial expansion, with the accompanying opportunities for raiding and booty, they were a useful component of Ibn Saud's project. By the late 1920s, with the expansion of the state having reached its practical limits and with Ibn Saud himself committed to the newly drawn frontiers of Iraq, Transjordan and Kuwait, the *Ikhwan* had ceased to be a pillar and become instead a threat to Ibn Saud's rule. *Ikhwan* trans-border raiding became an embarrassment and then, as a result of the local and imperial hostility it aroused, a menace to Saudi stability itself. Ibn Saud's consequent prohibition of raiding into Iraq and Transjordan left the *Ikhwan* vulnerable to the economic hardship resulting from failures with camel breeding and agriculture in their settlements.[10] This, together with their frustration at the mundane realities of Saudi rule, their growing alienation from the new, routinizing dynastic administration, and their own subordination and that of the Najdi tribal chiefs in general, combined to produce the *Ikhwan* revolt. The course of the revolt illustrated the military limitations of the *Ikhwan*. Ibn Saud appears always to have nursed some distrust of the *Ikhwan*, a force with a degree of independence, just as the Saudi rulers were later to distrust the regular army. He mobilized a countervailing force drawn from the beduin and settled populations of Najd, whose hostility had been guaranteed by their own experiences, as unsatisfactory Muslims, of *Ikhwan* raiding. Despite the ferocious reputation of the *Ikhwan*, they suffered a series of military defeats, although the success of Ibn Saud's force was crucially dependent on its being armed with some modern weaponry provided by the British and supported by tactical bombing raids by the British RAF stationed in Iraq.[11]

## Early Saudi State-Building and the New Army, 1930–50

The suppression of the *Ikhwan* between 1928 and 1930 paved the way for the declaration of the Kingdom of Saudi Arabia in 1932, its name indicating its status as the dynastic possession of the al-Saud. In 1933–4 a local war was fought between Saudi Arabia and Yemen, both sides relying on traditional forces and tactics, the Saudi victory of little significance in military terms. During the 1930s some formalization and institutionalization of government did take place but it remained extremely limited and Ibn Saud's rule continued to resemble, on a somewhat grander scale, that of a typical beduin tribal chief. All executive, military, legislative, judicial and religious powers were vested in Ibn Saud personally, and he ruled with only the aid of a few advisors, whose status was that of personal dependants of the

King.[12] Throughout this period, although some rudimentary state-building took place, the resulting state was one which still owed more to the past than the future. Indicating the essentially pre-modern nature of the new state, two of the key strategies employed in political consolidation were, firstly, the patronage and co-option of different tribal groups and, secondly, the creation of a stable base for the dynasty through the contracting of marriage ties with a large number of families and clans, especially important tribes but also leading urban and religious families.[13] Through the latter strategy in particular, Ibn Saud was able to create a network of family and blood ties which eventually produced, in the form of his own descendants, a numerically substantial ruling caste which was anchored in tribal values of genealogy and kinship and which provided the bedrock for the Saudi state even as it modernized in the 1960s and 1970s.

By 1940 Ibn Saud still relied heavily on his irregular traditional quasi-military forces. These included a royal bodyguard, mostly black slaves, who were responsible for the personal safety of the King and other members of the royal family, and tribal levies who received a subsidy on condition of being ready for service at any time. The royal bodyguard had no central control or regular organization, the King and the princes each maintaining a small, private armed retinue. The men were paid, fed and provided with rifles and ammunition by their masters but did not carry out any form of training, spending their time 'lounging around the entrances of their master's office or residence', some always accompanying him on journeys.[14] They wore no uniform and many had swords and daggers in addition to rifles. They numbered collectively in the region of 10,000 but they possessed little or no military significance, their main purpose to enhance their master's prestige. The levies were also completely untrained, but had the advantage of being numerous and relatively cheap, the King probably able to mobilize as many as 70,000 men, mounted in twos on camels.[15]

Notwithstanding his continued practical reliance on tribal and personal forces, during the 1930s Ibn Saud had become openly committed to building a modern army for his new kingdom.[16] Indeed, he began to attach great importance to this project, ardently desiring the prestige and symbolic sovereignty represented by a modern army. He was well aware of the power shown by European armies in their operations across the Middle East during World War I and was also, in particular, acutely conscious of the British efforts to assist with the raising of regular armies for his rivals, the Hashemite kings of Iraq and Transjordan.[17] In fact Ibn Saud's desire for a modern army seemed to be driven primarily by his rivalry with the Hashemites. He apparently believed that the main task of such a modern force would be to defend his kingdom against Iraq and Transjordan, whose rulers he believed continued to harbour aggressive intentions towards his country. However, his military plans were also driven by a large element of *amour propre* and he often seemed more jealous than afraid of the Jordanian Arab Legion, itself led by British officers.[18]

A very rudimentary beginning to military modernization had been made in the late 1920s after the absorption of the Hijaz into Saudi territory. With the conquest of the Hijaz, Ibn Saud had taken over a machinery of government which had been organized along Ottoman lines and also the remnants of a regular army, Ottoman-trained officers who had served with the Hashemite Sharif Husayn's British-sponsored Arab revolt in World War I and then with Husayn after he became ruler of the Hijaz. After the final defeat of the Hashemites in the Hijaz, Ibn Saud invited all army officers of the former Hashemite army to enter his service and formed his first regular units from their ranks.[19] In 1930 three regular regiments, infantry, machine-gun and artillery, paraded in Jidda for the first time. During the 1930s some institutional development took place, at least on paper. Officers of Syrian and Iraqi origin were employed in a newly established Directorate of Military Affairs, superseded by a General Staff in 1939, and a military school was founded in al-Taif. Nonetheless, progress of any substance was slow to non-existent. Even states with a more secure fiscal base were finding the cost of building a modern army difficult to bear. Saudi Arabia, in the 1930s, found itself in a continuous economic crisis. With the cessation of raiding after the suppression of the *Ikhwan*, the revenues of the state had dwindled from their already very low levels. Saudi income depended on the religious tax known as *zakat*, customs and the Hajj, but even pilgrimage numbers had been hit by the world depression. With the very partial exception of the Hijaz, the Saudi state lacked any basic framework of centralized administration necessary for a modern army. In particular, again with the partial exception of those officers of Hijazi origin, Saudi Arabia lacked a cadre of officers with any modern training or experience of regular military organization.

By 1940 the Saudi authorities had managed to assemble at al-Taif a force of *nizam* (regular) troops numbering 1,000 to 1,500.[20] Yet the lack of an educated officer corps was making any real progress more or less impossible. Ibn Saud was dependent on the 'military flotsam' of the old Ottoman army, of Turkish and Kurdish as well as Arab origin, and on a handful of Arabs with more recent modern training from other countries of the Middle East.[21] None of these officers had any tie with Saudi Arabia other than their pay, and this was not high enough to attract or keep those of talent. Their conditions of service were also poor. Promotion depended entirely on patronage and there were at least two former generals relegated to subordinate positions. From Ibn Saud's point of view, perhaps the major drawback of such trained officers as he possessed was their former links to the Hashemites, most of the Arab officers in the Ottoman army having defected to Sharif Husayn either before or after 1918. General Hamdi Bey, appointed director-general of military affairs in 1931, was typical. Born in the early 1890s, he was a Kurd from the territories which later became Iraq and had risen to non-commissioned rank in the Ottoman army. Reaching the rank of colonel in the army of King Husayn, he then passed into the service of Ibn Saud and commanded troops at Yanbu before 1928, becoming commander at Jedda that year. He subsequently became director-general of military organization in 1931 and then ADC to Prince Faysal.[22] Other examples included General Ibrahim Tassan, who was to command the Saudi contingent stationed in Egypt after the 1948 Palestine war, and Said al-Kurdi, who was to command Saudi troops during the 1948 war and was appointed the first Saudi chief of staff. Tassan was born about 1893 in Najd but brought up in Asir. He entered the Ottoman army but later joined the Hashemite revolt and was associated with Colonel Lawrence.[23] Al-Kurdi, his name indicating his origin, had also fought, apparently gallantly, for King Husayn against Ibn Saud.

Ibn Saud was aware of the professional weaknesses of the command structure as well as the politically undesirable background of many of its members, and made largely unsuccessful efforts to address the problem. In an effort to raise the prestige of the new force, in 1939 he made his son, Saud, titular head of the army. He installed a new General Officer Commanding, Muhammad Tariq al-Afriqi, an officer untainted by any past Hashemite connections, but this appointment was still not a success. Al-Afriqi had the reputation of being a competent soldier, based on his having trained at the Ottoman staff college in Istanbul, and having seen service in several Ottoman wars and more recently against the Italians in Abyssinia. But, of African descent and black, his ethnicity militated against his acceptance in his new command. Other officers, for whom his appearance recalled the legacy of slavery, resented having to serve under him.[24] Another attempt to address the shortage of trained officers came in the form of an agreement with Iraq which provided for the military training of Saudis in Iraq or by Iraqi instructors in Saudi Arabia, but it too came to nothing, sunk by Ibn Saud's general suspicions about the Hashemite Iraqi regime's policy towards him and his throne.[25]

Ibn Saud's ambitions for military modernization were not confined to the army. As early as the 1920s he had become aware of the value of aircraft in tribal management and internal security generally. In Iraq the British had repeatedly deployed the RAF on bombing missions against recalcitrant tribal groups, and tactical bombing raids had been crucial to the success of the operations against the *Ikhwan*. The lessons of the utility of air power in enforcing the power of the state were then being learnt by rulers throughout the Middle East and beyond. Indeed, the region had had the misfortune to pioneer the new tactic, the very first experiments in aerial bombing having been carried out by the Italians in their 1911 colonial war against Libya.[26] By the beginning of the 1930s concrete steps had been taken in the direction of forming a Saudi air force. In 1930 Britain provided four de Havilland biplanes with British pilots and maintenance crews, while ten Saudis were sent to Italy to study aeronautics.[27] During the 1930s, further planes were presented by the French and Italian governments and an Italian air mission arrived to take charge of the air force project.[28]

By 1939, however, the construction of a Saudi air force, which had in any case proceeded very slowly, was thrown into disarray by the outbreak of World War II. The British were desperate to get rid of the Italian mission and in the spring of 1939 succeeded. In return for Ibn Saud's dismissal of the Italians, Britain arranged for a few Saudi pilots to continue their training in Egypt.[29] Although Ibn Saud, having lost the Italians, now put immense pressure on Britain to provide assistance with his air force, he received little encouragement, the British themselves daunted by the lack of educated young men, of mechanics, of a proper budget, and of comprehension on the part of the ruling family of the requirements of such a large technical undertaking.[30] Even the Saudi pilot, Abdullah Mandili, who was placed in command of the air force, had little knowledge of technical matters.[31] By 1946 the air force still languished, consisting only of a few fighters based in Dhraran.

Although any such progress as was being made towards military modernization was halted during World War II, these years were nonetheless a turning point for Saudi Arabia. During the war years Ibn Saud was again provided with a British subsidy to preserve his neutrality and to enable him to survive given the further declining revenues resulting from disruption to the Hajj. Yet, British subsidies notwithstanding, this period saw a major change in Saudi Arabia's international orientation. Signalling a broader post-war shift in the Middle East away from the old imperial powers of Britain and France towards US hegemony, in the early 1940s the American role in Saudi Arabia began to grow exponentially. The burgeoning new relationship was most obviously illustrated by the establishment of Aramco in 1944 to operate the Saudi oil concession. This shift, however, was temporarily disrupted by US support for the establishment of a Jewish state in Palestine in 1948. A few years earlier, in 1943, Ibn Saud had secretly granted the US the right to build a military airfield at Dhahran and in the same year the first formal US military mission had arrived, although it did little beyond hold discussions.[32] After the war, however, with Saud–US relations suffering from the Palestine crisis, it was to Britain that Ibn Saud turned for help in reorganizing the army.

Ibn Saud was well aware of the steps being taken, with British help, by his rivals, the Hashemite rulers of Iraq and Transjordan, to modernize their armies, and he now requested British assistance to create a Saudi force of about 10,000 men along the lines of the Arab Legion established by British officers in Transjordan.[33] In 1947 a British military mission arrived in Saudi Arabia, closely followed by an Air Training Team. These missions, in the few years of their existence, faced political hostility and immense organizational and financial difficulties, and made only very limited progress.

Although Britain had been preferred to the US as a source of military assistance for purely political reasons, the mission still found itself operating in a difficult political environment. The King particularly disliked British support for the Hashemite dynasties in Jordan and Iraq, its control over the smaller Gulf states, and its influence over the new Arab League. The mission found its work hampered by the fallout of this ongoing political friction, its sphere of activity confined to al-Taif and Jidda and its members forbidden access to the rest of the country.[34] Resentment at Britain's wider role in the Middle East combined with religious and national sensitivities to produce a considerable amount of latent opposition to the mission among officers and civilian officials. In fact, the more senior officers avoided the mission as much as possible and made little attempt to co-operate or even liaise effectively. Officers and officials raised difficulties to any suggestions from the British mission and 'signs of welcome from these quarters were conspicuous by their absence'.[35] The British officers of the mission were very conscious that their enemies would exploit to the full any false step while the mission received little support from the Saudi rulers. Prince Mansur, the head of the newly formed defence ministry, took only a fitful interest in the activities of the mission, visiting its base at al-Taif rarely and only for short periods.[36] In general, the patrimonial system of governance, where all the emerging ministries were controlled by sons and grandsons of the King, left the mission floundering, frustrated and uncertain, its progress dependent on the whim of Ibn Saud and his sons who themselves seemed to lack any real grasp of the magnitude of the task in hand. An indication of the King's only very partial comprehension of the implications of the military project upon which he had embarked occasionally surfaced in his clinging to the view that beduin irregulars were a match for any trained troops.

In addition to the difficult political environment, the British mission found its work impeded by financial constraints in both the UK and Saudi Arabia. Having constantly to importune a cash-strapped post-war government in London, the British officers also struggled to persuade the Saudis to accept the cost and regularize the payment of the new force. Just as the administrative framework of government in general, and the army in particular, was extremely flimsy, so its fiscal base was very low. The Saudi economic crisis of the war years having been ameliorated by British subsidies and US loans, from 1944 oil production began to rise. However, it was only from the 1950s onwards that oil revenues were to be available in sufficient quantities to finance the expansion of the state. In the late 1940s, the British mission, too early for the oil bonanza, struggled to recruit, retain and train both officers and men.

The British officers and the Saudis were separated by profound disagreements over the appropriate method of recruitment to the new army. Saudi officers and senior officials as well as the Saudi princes periodically raised the possibility of conscription, a system with which they were familiar from the Ottoman past and which they knew to be in operation in neighbouring countries. Their advocacy of conscription, however, took no account of the expense of implementation and the complete lack of any remotely suitable administrative framework. The British, more sharply aware of the financial constraints which were already hampering their very modest efforts, advocated voluntary enlistment encouraged by offers of the best possible terms and conditions.

During its first year, the British mission repeatedly drew the attention of the defence minister, Prince Mansur, to the shortage of volunteer cadets for the new military school and the entire absence of new recruits to the army, explaining that the main reason for the reluctance of recruits to present themselves was poor conditions of service. Living conditions of the existing soldiers were poor to the point where they undermined morale, no system was in place for granting leave or promotion, and the men reacted by desertion, the incidence of which was very high indeed.[37] In addition, the British officers found the available raw material unpromising, believing the urban population unsuitable for military service and the beduin unlikely to take easily to the discipline of a modern army. To address these difficulties, they recommended pay increases for both officers and men, increased ration allowances, and the issuing of fixed regulations for promotion. By November 1948 they had succeeded in persuading the Saudi authorities to raise pay by 150 per cent over the old rates and the mission began to see an improvement in enlistment.[38] The increased rates of pay resulted in an influx of recruits to al-Taif, over a thousand within a couple of months, the new recruits coming from across the country, from tribes opposed to the al-Saud such as the Shammar as well as from the pro-Saud Ruwallah and Anizah and from towns as far apart as Jawf in the north, Medina in the Hijaz, and Abha and Jizan in the south-west.

Other, perhaps more serious problems, remained. The training of the new recruits presented enormous difficulties. Not more than 1 per cent of the recruits was literate and instruction was necessary in reading and writing before any could be trained for technical roles. There was, furthermore, a shortage of NCOs who might supervise their basic training. Yet, from the beginning, the British mission identified the officer corps as the true Achilles heel of the new force. There was an acute overall shortage of officers while those in post were described by the British as old, uninterested, untrained and illiterate.[39] But the mission was aware that it was neither possible nor desirable to dispense with them in large numbers until others, better trained, were available to take their place. Progress was therefore likely to be slow, the speedy production of competent officers hindered by the general lack of primary and secondary education and by the absence of sufficient military instructors.

The mission adopted a two-part solution to the problem presented by the weakness of the officer corps. The first part of the solution involved the establishment of an efficient, functioning military school in al-Taif; the second involved arranging for the training of the best officer cadets abroad. The mission considered the military school, with its task of training the officers of the future, to be one of the most important institutions in the Saudi army.[40] By 1949 the mission reported that the school had made progress but was being severely hampered by the lack of funds and the consequent insufficiency of proper accommodation and training facilities. There were, for example, no modern rifles. Those issued were of British manufacture but dated from between 1894 and 1908.[41] The mission also singled out Prince Mansur, complaining about his lack of active encouragement, his inclination to parsimony and his reluctance to be hurried into anything. In addition to the military school, the mission also organized courses of instruction for the most promising Saudi officer cadets abroad, at Sandhurst in the UK, and at the Egyptian military school and with the Egyptian army.

The choice of Egypt as a destination for officer cadets was to be of incalculable significance. The experience of the Saudi cadets in Egypt was electrifying. They returned appalled at the state of their own country's military capability but, even more than this, they had imbibed some of the nationalist fervour then sweeping through Egyptian military and civilian circles and which was soon to result in the Free Officers' coup of 1952.

The year 1948 brought another significant radicalizing experience to the new Saudi army with the participation of Saudi units, two battalions, in the Palestine war. Ibn Saud had, during the 1920s and 1930s, demonstrated no particular interest in the fate of Palestine and, by 1948, still remained deeply reluctant to become involved in this conflict. Indeed, his main concern appeared to be his fear that his Hashemite rival in Transjordan, King Abdallah, would seize the opportunity presented by the war to strengthen his own position. Nonetheless, under intense pressure from the Arab League, and concerned at the loss of prestige that would result from the failure of the 'Custodian of the Two Holy Mosques' to act over the fate of Jerusalem, the King agreed to a token involvement. The Saudi government issued a declaration that the country would join in the defence of Palestine to protect its Arabism and to prevent its partition and the establishment of a Jewish state.[42] About 1,000 men, plus a few volunteers, were deployed to the Palestine front to operate under Egyptian command. The Saudi military contribution was negligible; the units had been hurriedly formed, a considerable number of the officers and men had received little or no tactical training and few had even fired their weapons. Equipment was lacking and both administrative and medical arrangements were nonexistent, the troops not possessing a haversack or even a water bottle.[43] There was no means of intercommunication or control and the commander had been out of touch with military action or even training since 1924 when he fought on the side of King Husayn against Ibn Saud. Only the second-in-command was a competent officer, himself a Palestinian who had been attached to the British mission as an interpreter and who had then accepted a commission in the Saudi army.

Nonetheless, these difficulties notwithstanding, the prospect of serving in Palestine aroused immense enthusiasm within the ranks of the Saudi army. The officers of the British mission, having failed to persuade the Saudis against involvement and with a scepticism of Saudi military capacity born of intimate experience, seemed surprised at the passionate commitment displayed by the fledgling troops. One British officer commented: 'It is difficult to describe the feelings of relief and delight shown by the selected few or the obvious despair of those left behind. As the troops left Taif large numbers of officers and men, convinced that the war would be over before they could get to Palestine, were weeping profusely and asking to be allowed to go. In fact a few managed to jump onto the lorries surreptitiously.'[44]

The Saudi contingent, as predicted, made little contribution to the military progress of the Arab cause in Palestine. Yet for the Saudi army, service in that war produced a similar reaction to that experienced by other Arab armies. The rank and file awoke to a new knowledge of the wider Arab world and their own relative poverty and backwardness, while the officers shared in the region's humiliation and in the resulting determination to end the political status quo in their own countries which was widely believed to have caused it.

## New Army, New Politics, 1950–70

The impact of the shock produced by defeat in Palestine and contact with Egyptian Free Officers was not to show itself for several years. In 1949–50 the British mission reported its belief that it was making steady, if slow, progress, lamenting that it was difficult for anyone who had not seen the Saudi army to appreciate the extent to which it was ill equipped, untrained and lacking in organization.[45] The King and his advisors remained firm in their determination to build up and equip the army, taking every opportunity to emphasize the necessity of this step. By the late 1940s, the King was also openly envisaging the use of the proposed army for internal security. The wave of military coups which was to break across the Arab world was only just gathering strength, and the role of army officers as the spearhead of Arab nationalism and modernism was only just starting to become apparent. As yet, therefore, Ibn Saud could contemplate the development of his army without fearing its officer corps as the harbinger of radical political transformation.

All this was to change, however, in the coming decade. The early 1950s saw the US replace Britain, definitively and permanently, as Saudi Arabia's key international partner, a shift which was subsequently replicated across the Arab world and exemplified most sharply by the Suez crisis of 1956. The mid-1950s also saw the arrival of military coup attempts in Saudi Arabia, a trend which had already manifested itself in a number of Arab countries.

By the late 1940s Saudi revenues from oil, produced through the operations of the American company, Aramco, had begun to rise rapidly. After the end of the Palestine war, diplomatic relations between Saudi Arabia and the US, damaged but never broken off, began to improve again. Military links inevitably followed. In 1951 an agreement was concluded which allowed the US to continue to use Dhahran as an air base and establish a permanent

US military mission in Saudi Arabia.[46] Indeed, the King used the negotiations over Dhahran to put considerable pressure on the Americans to agree to supply modern weapons to his new army, an institution still close to his heart.[47] Ibn Saud agreed with the US that the military mission would organize, equip and train an army of 17,342 men, and that the US would also assist with the development of an air force, continuing the work done over the previous few years by the British Air Training Team.[48] As links between the Saudis and the US grew stronger, so those with Britain declined and the British military mission, still in the country, found itself increasingly irrelevant. Saudi unease over a number of British policies, especially Britain's closeness to the Hashemites and to the rulers of the small Gulf states, came to a head in the early 1950s over the al-Buraymi border dispute between the Saudis and Abu Dhabi and Oman, in which Britain sided with the latter two states. The mission, unable to work effectively in this context, left Saudi Arabia, although Sandhurst continued to receive a small number of Saudi cadets.

It was, however, not the new influence of the US, but the rather older connection with Egypt which was to exercise the most dramatic influence on the Saudi army in the 1950s. During that decade Egypt was both the main destination for Saudi officer cadets and the heart of pan-Arab nationalism, with Gamal Abd al-Nasser in power since the Free Officers coup of 1952 had overthrown the monarchy. Saudi Arabia itself was also beginning to experience dramatic changes. Oil revenues more than quadrupled in the first few years of the decade, enabling the expansion of the state in general, and freeing military planning in particular from its former financial constraints. In 1953 the King died and was succeeded by his son, Saud, ending the relative coherence of Ibn Saud's personal rule and giving rise to struggles over the division of the Saudi patrimony, especially between Saud and his brother Faysal, which were to plague the kingdom's politics for years to come. A younger generation of Saudis, better educated and with greater experience of the world beyond the kingdom, began to appear, and they were joined by an influx of highly qualified and sophisticated Arabs from elsewhere in the region, creating small, politically vulnerable but receptive civilian and military milieux for the new ideas that were sweeping across the Arab world.

The new king, Saud, continued his father's policy of cultivating friendly relations with Egypt and concluded a mutual defence treaty in 1955.

Although Nasser's regime was repugnant to the Saudis, the country was valuable as a counterweight to the Hashemites in Jordan and Iraq. Expanding military links complemented the diplomatic connections. Officers and NCOs went to Egypt for training in much larger numbers and in January 1955, reflecting a certain desire to distance Saudi Arabia from the US, Saud invited an Egyptian military mission and 200 Egyptian military advisors to the kingdom. Saudi officers were exposed to an ever-increasing extent to ideological influences emanating from Free Officer circles. However, Nasserite and more generally nationalist sympathies had already, over the previous few years, penetrated the officer corps and inevitably led to the eventual appearance of plots and coup attempts. The first such recorded event occurred in the early summer of 1955 when a Saudi 'Free Officers' movement along Egyptian lines and led by a young lieutenant who had studied in Egypt, Abd al-Rahman al-Shamrawi, was discovered and crushed with an unknown number of executions.[49] This plot is often attributed to direct Egyptian instigation. Although Egypt was undoubtedly the ideological and political inspiration for this movement, yet it is highly unlikely that the new Egyptian military mission played any direct role in its germination. The mission had arrived only months before the plot was discovered and in any case the Egyptian regime was not, at that stage, actively engaged in seeking to overthrow the al-Saud. Nonetheless, rumours of plots and coup attempts, often with Egyptian involvement, continued unabated.[50]

Nasserite sympathies were not the only current to find support within the Saudi military. Even before the discovery of the Saudi Free Officers, in early 1955 radical pro-Communist literature had been found circulating among police and army units in the oil province of al-Hasa. This was undoubtedly a consequence of the industrial militancy and political radicalization which was making the Saudi oil industry in those years the principal site of social conflict in the country and which illustrated the emergence of new social forces capable of united action which might seriously challenge Saudi rule. In general, discontent within the Saudi army emerged in tandem with and mirrored that slowly forming within civilian circles.

Dissent within the officer corps arose from a number of sources. The dynamism of Nasserism contrasted with the weakness of Saudi political, social and economic development, the modest origins of the Free Officers with the corruption, nepotism and patrimonial authoritarianism of the

Saudi rulers, and Egypt's embrace of modernism and nationalism with the self-serving manipulation by the Saudi royal family of tribal and religious conservatism. Army officers also had specific grievances. As in other Arab armies, morale in general had been dealt a blow by failure to prevent the Palestinian catastrophe of 1948. Within the officer corps, those of Hijazi origin, by far the best educated and most sophisticated element, suffered systematic discrimination due to their supposed insufficient loyalty to the al-Saud, while the entire officer corps found the most senior positions barred to merit and education and reserved for those with royal connections, whether of blood or patronage.

Evidence of dissent within the armed forces transformed the attitude of the al-Saud towards the project of military modernization begun by Ibn Saud. With the *Ikhwan* long subdued, and the tribes and their shaikhs either suppressed or, more usually, co-opted, the beduin began to seem a more reliable prop than the army, whose officers were so clearly susceptible to nationalist, republican and even very mild socialist ideas. For the al-Saud, the army, of which they had initially been so proud, had suddenly ceased being a symbolic and physical bulwark for the regime and had become instead the incubator of a threat.

Having learnt well the lessons of the fate which had befallen the Egyptian King, and which they were soon to observe overtake the Hashemite dynasty in Iraq, the al-Saud turned away from the modern regular army back to its tribal bedrock. As late as the 1940s Ibn Saud and his sons and grandsons had relied heavily for personal security on the royal bodyguard, extravagantly armed but entirely untrained personal retainers, who offered a visible symbol of royal power and inviolability. This body of men, which had fallen into neglect as the attention of the King and his sons had been captured by the regular army, was now revived and turned into a regiment of tribal troops. A step of even greater significance was taken with the formation of the National Guard. Ibn Saud, despite his fascination with military modernization, had never entirely abandoned his belief in the military efficacy of tribal irregulars. In the 1940s and earlier, the al-Saud had been able to mobilize, when necessary, tribal levies who received a subsidy in return for being ready for service. These tribal levies now became the basis for a paramilitary force first known as the White Army, its name deriving from the colour of the robes worn by its soldiers, and subsequently as the National

Guard. The White Army/National Guard was composed in roughly equal numbers of full-time regular soldiers and part-time irregulars, the latter mobilized as and when needed. Both the regular and irregulars were drawn mainly, if not exclusively, from Najdi tribes loyal to the dynasty. Indeed, many recruits to this force were actual descendants of those who had fought with Ibn Saud in his wars of conquests or were the sons or relatives of pro-Saudi tribal leaders. Indeed, the tribal chiefs played a central role in recruiting for the White Army and the force functioned as much as a mechanism for rewarding the loyalty of key tribal intermediaries as an effective military or paramilitary body.[51] Service in the White Army/National Guard offered access to the new oil wealth, distributed in salaries and pensions, and the Saudi elite thus expanded and reinforced its social base.

From now on, the White Army/National Guard, whom the al-Saud believed was immune to the political contagion which appeared to be spreading through the regular officer corps, was to act as a counterweight to the army and to take on primary responsibility for internal security and for the defence of the expanding numbers of the royal family. Yet with the creation of this force an ambiguity entered the Saudi military project which was to become an enduring dilemma. A regular army continued to constitute, for the royal family and the Saudi elite in general, an indispensable component of the wider modernist project.[52] All the advice which the Saudis received from their foreign advisors and the example of the nationalist regimes which surrounded them argued that such a modern army was essential for the defence of the country. Yet the experience of the 1950s had implanted in the Saudi rulers a distrust of their own officers which they could never overcome. Thus they created an alternative force which, however, undermined the national character of the military, absorbed scarce manpower, failed to achieve a capability equal to that of the army and which eventually, in complete negation of its sole *raison d'être*, itself proved susceptible to political dissent.

The Saudi suspicion of Egypt and specifically of the activities of the Egyptian military mission grew rapidly from the mid-1950s. Although King Saud mobilized the regular and tribal forces in defence of Egypt during the 1956 Suez crisis, he acted only under intense pressure from his advisors who feared the damage to Saudi prestige which would result from a failure to act in support of the Arab cause and against Israel. A post-war rapprochement between Saudi Arabia and the US strengthened Saud's hand and the discovery of another army plot, in which the Egyptian military attaché in Jidda was implicated, finally destroyed the Egyptian military mission.

The improvement in US–Saudi relations after Suez had a significant military dimension. The US promised to assist in doubling the size of the regular army from its existing very approximate and probably exaggerated number of 15,000, and to provide supplies of modern arms, while the Saudis agreed to a five-year extension of the US lease on Dhahran. The US also offered assistance in modernizing the air force and in creating a navy. However, the US advisors soon found, as the British military mission had found before them, that the low level of general and especially technical education among the Saudis meant that the arrival of sophisticated equipment increased, rather than diminished, Saudi dependence on foreign support. The modernization of the army was further hampered by the continuing patrimonial structure of Saudi rule, which meant that leadership in every sphere was confined to the royal princes, regardless of merit or talent, while the intensifying conflicts among those princes turned the army and the National Guard into tools of a factional struggle. In 1964 this factional struggle, personified by King Saud and his brother, Prince Faysal, was finally resolved by the complete victory of the latter and his accession to the throne.[53] The National Guard and the Royal Guard played a role in the ebbs and flows and final resolution of this internal conflict, but it was a minor role, as an adjunct to the more significant social forces of ulama and tribes, and as an instrument of one or other bloc of princes. Saud relied on the Royal Guard, although he lost its support at the last moment, and Faysal on the National Guard, the reaction of these two forces being essentially a reflection of the shifting allegiances of their tribal officers and rank and file. The army seems not to have been drawn into this factional conflict but to have remained aloof throughout. No army officers asserted an agenda of their own nor did they make any bid for power on their own account.

Within the army, oppositional or overtly pro-Nasser tendencies remained significant. Although these tendencies were deeply concealed in peacetime, for fear of savage punishment, the Yemeni civil war forced them into the open. In 1962 a Free Officers' military coup in North Yemen established the Yemen Arab Republic. In the ensuing civil war, the republican side looked to their fellow nationalist officers in Egypt for help while the Yemeni royalists turned to Saudi Arabia and Jordan. Saudi support for the Yemeni royalists provoked an immediate and starkly negative reaction in military circles at home, especially within the air force, expressed by the defection to Egypt of several pilots. A Saudi cargo plane with supplies for Yemeni royalists flew instead to Cairo where its crew of three immediately entered the Egyptian air force and the next day two more pilots defected on a training flight.[54] This was the first recorded manifestation of political discontent by Saudi air force officers. In Saudi Arabia, as elsewhere, the air force attracted many of the most well-educated candidates, demanded the most sophisticated skills and offered the best training, including training abroad. Across the region in this period, the air force tended to provide the vanguard of the modernizing and nationalist tendency.

Nationalist and pan-Arab sympathies remained present within the army and especially within the air force throughout the 1960s. Nothing was openly articulated other than loyalty to the royal family but opinions held privately, and sometimes expressed in conversation, revealed a different picture. Admiration for Nasser remained widespread, especially among officers and pilots who had received training in Egypt, and the desire for faster modernization, within the army but also in the country more generally, was also prevalent. Middle-ranking military officers educated abroad were conscious of the unimpressive condition of their own country and resentful of the difficulties in the way of their own advancement represented by the tribal and family monopoly on power, well-educated officers often having to rely on old and illiterate 'beduin' generals for recommendations for promotion. The grievances of officers of Hijazi origin were particularly acute in this respect. Political loyalty, conflated by the al-Saud with family and tribal loyalty, indicated that officers and NCOs be found from among Najdis. In general, however, the Hijaz produced potential recruits of better training and education and wider experience than the less-developed Najd. The army accepted Hijazis but only made very halting efforts to end discrimination against them in promotion and recognition of merit. Even those Hijazis who joined the army possessing no particular animosity towards the regime soon found this situation a source of discontent. Furthermore, the stranglehold of the royal family on key military and defence ministry positions had not abated after Faysal replaced

Saud on the throne. In fact, upon his accession, King Faysal immediately replaced Saud's family dependants and supporters with his own in key military appointments, thus changing the personnel but not the patrimonial character of Saudi military leadership. The slow progress of military modernization was also a specific concern within the army. By 1962 the regular army still numbered only about 18,000, with another 18,000 full or part time in the National Guard. By 1967 the army reached perhaps 25,000, and the National Guard about 31,000. In 1967 the Saudis were given a sharp reminder of their weakness. The disaster suffered by the Arab armies in the June war caused many of the younger Saudi officers to feel ashamed of how little help Saudi Arabia had given to Egypt and the wider Arab cause in the struggle with Israel.

In 1969 the Saudi authorities decided to nip these manifold discontents in the bud. Following numerous civilian arrests, between June and September a large number of army and air force officers, perhaps eventually more than 130, were also taken into custody. Further arrests took place the following year. Air force officers figured particularly prominently among those arrested. Of the first 70 officers arrested, 38 were from the air force and 30 from the army, with the service of two unknown.[55] Some of those arrested held senior appointments. This pre-emptive strike by the authorities was described by contemporary observers as 'the severest possible blow to the two major services and particularly to the air force'.[56]

The Saudi regime had meted out harsh punishment, including execution, to previous military conspirators. But now, buoyed up by ever-increasing oil revenues, it appears to have been moving towards the adoption of a different approach to dissent, seeking to mollify and co-opt opponents rather than repress them. The officers arrested in 1969 and 1970 were kept in relative comfort. No charges were brought and they were gradually released without any official comment within a year or two. Aided by the propaganda value of a Saudi air force victory over forces from the People's Democratic Republic of South Yemen in a skirmish at the frontier post of al-Wadiah in late 1969, the regime opted for a charm offensive towards its officers.

The Saudi state, financed by its oil revenues, expanded rapidly from the late 1950s, and this expansion, in turn, transformed Saudi society. Saudi defence spending, especially after the oil price rise following the 1973 Arab–Israeli war, reached astronomical levels, accounting for more than one-third of the Saudi budget in the 1980s.[57] This largesse enabled the Saudi authorities to implement systematically a strategy of buying off, rather than repressing, political dissent, including dissent within the army. From the 1970s onwards, the Saudi military were pampered and cosseted, with extraordinarily high salaries and extravagant privileges. Fitful efforts were even made to integrate the Hijazis more successfully. By the early 1970s this strategy was clearly paying dividends and gradually the army made its collective peace with the regime. There were now few signs of unrest. Occasionally officers were heard to voice mild exasperation at the slowness of promotion and the lack of opportunity but there was little apparent evidence of great frustration or dissatisfaction.[58] This sense of contentment trickled down to the rank and file, who shared in the general prosperity and who were even less inclined to question the regime's view of itself and of its armed forces.

The air force resisted the regime's blandishments rather longer than the army. Air force officers felt, much more acutely, the barrier to their own careers and to the development of the force represented by the princely domination of the upper echelons, particularly as fighter pilots. Nonetheless, even here resentments were subdued by generous financial rewards and the expansion of the service, which created more opportunities for those without connections.[59] A final manifestation of organized opposition appeared within the air force in 1977, when a rather half-hearted coup attempt by some Saudi air force pilots, funded by Libyan intelligence, was easily thwarted.

## The National Guard and the neo-*Ikhwan*

Although the type of dissent which had emerged within Saudi military circles in the 1950s and 1960s was, by the 1970s, disappearing, the al-Saud continued to harbour a mistrust of the army. This mistrust was not concealed but was, on the contrary, very evident. It showed itself in general terms in the regime's clear preference for the National Guard, and also in such specific measures as the deployment of most of the army to remote areas of the kingdom, well away from the capital and other cities, the immobilization of quantities of its vehicles and weaponry and the inaccessibility to military personnel of stocks of ammunition.

Shocked by the appearance of nationalist and republican sentiments amongst the officers of the prized new army, in the 1950s the al-Saud had turned back to their tribal support, organized into the White Army. In 1963 another British military mission, consisting of three senior officers, arrived to reorganize the White Army, which was renamed the National Guard. It was now, in effect, a second army, with its own headquarters, and its commander, Prince Abdullah, ranking as a minister.[60] Indeed Abdullah seemed to view the National Guard as a personal fiefdom and used it to jockey for position within the circle of senior princes. Recruits increasingly came not just from loyal Najdi tribes but from tribes directly under Abdullah's control while his attempts to bolster the National Guard, and to make it an open rival to the army, created friction within the royal family. Abdullah considered his control of the National Guard vital to the advancement of his wider political objectives, specifically his ambition to become crown prince and eventually to accede to the throne. His position as commander became a touchstone for the wider conflict among the many sons of Abd al-Aziz ibn Saud, who had broadly divided into two factions based on matrilineal descent: those, including Abdullah, linked through their mothers to the Jiluwi family and Shammar tribes, and the 'Sudayri seven', those sons born of Hussa bint Ahmad al-Sudayri.[61] Abdullah retained the command of the National Guard until 2010, even after becoming king in 2005, finally relinquishing it to his son, Mutaib.[62]

In 1970 the British mission produced a comprehensive plan for the reorganization of the National Guard which, from 1971, also received US assistance. The British plan, drawn up with the approval of the Saudi leadership of the National Guard itself, provided for a small, highly mobile and efficient force for internal security requirements.[63] Yet the 1970s saw little progress towards this goal. Under British supervision, links with loyal tribes were strengthened further but manpower problems remained acute. Recruiting was tightly controlled. Sponsorship by their tribal shaikh or an influential relation or friend was an essential prerequisite for both officers and men.[64] In general, the Saudi insistence on recruiting from Najdi beduin meant that National Guard personnel, both officers and men, were among the least educated and least familiar with modern methods in Saudi society. The rank and file lacked the education to absorb even simple systems while compensation had to be made for the weakness of the officer corps by an increasing reliance not only on British officers but also on large numbers of Jordanian and Pakistani military advisors brought in by the British mission. Training was minimal, and only about half of the complement was present with their units at any one time, strength fluctuating as soldiers took leave, with or without permission, to attend to their own financial affairs, take up more lucrative employment or harvest their crops.[65] The strength of the Guard was officially given as 50,000 but the actual number was probably not much more than half this estimate. A National Guard cadet school was eventually established and officers began to arrive in the US for training, but the force remained essentially based on tribal recruitment and imbued with a tribal ethos.

The National Guard's main tasks were to keep a watchful eye on the army and to act as a defence for the royal regime against its internal enemies. It was therefore mainly stationed, in contrast to the army, near centres of population, especially the capital. Yet, when it faced its major test in 1979, its military efficiency was shown to be severely limited and even its political loyalty to be less than complete.

The 1970s had seen a number of accelerating changes in Saudi society. Although state services such as health and education expanded exponentially, the impact of the sudden influx of massive oil wealth on a society in which two-thirds of adult males were still illiterate had been traumatic, resulting in social and psychological dislocation and disorientation. One response, especially among the poorer Saudis where tribal ties had remained strongest, had been to turn to a form of neo-Wahhabism highly critical of the laxness and corruption of the royal family. The appeal of this trend was especially strong to those very social groups who had provided the backbone of the Saudi regime since the suppression of the *Ikhwan*. In November 1979 these *neo-Ikhwan* struck, seizing the Grand Mosque in Mecca and holding it during a prolonged siege by the army and the National Guard.

The insurgents were religious *ultras* and, in a feature particularly worrying for the regime, many came from the Utaybah and Qahtani tribes, traditional sources of manpower for the Royal Guard and the National Guard. Indeed, one of their leaders, Juhayman ibn Muhammad al-Utaybi, had until recently been a corporal in the National Guard. Although these tribal groups had been of key importance in the development of the Saudi security apparatus, it was now suddenly remembered that they continued to harbour resentment of Ibn Saud's suppression of the *Ikhwan* in the late 1920s, both the Utaybah and the Qahtani having fought for the *Ikhwan*. The names of two leaders of the attack on the Mosque, Juhayman ibn Muhammad al-Utaybi and Muhammad ibn Abdullah al-Qahtani, indicated their tribal origins and the tribal allegiances which they shared with many of their followers.[66]

The first regime response to this attack came not from the army but from the National Guard. This was the first serious action in which the National Guard had been involved and its manifold practical weaknesses became rapidly apparent. Chaos resulted from unserviceable vehicles, shortages of weapons and faulty ammunition. Logistical neglect and tactical incompetence, combined with the lack of training of the troops and the poor performance of the officers, led to the Guard taking heavy casualties.[67] The tribal structure of the Guard, believed by the Saudis to be its primary political strength, was soon shown to be a serious military weakness, with Guardsmen refusing to obey orders from senior officers unless they came from those in their very own unit. Added to this general military incompetence was a degree of panic among the Saudi authorities about the possible disloyalty of the Guard. Rumours were rife that the Guard was itself implicated in the attack, these rumours being partly fuelled by panic checks on the whereabouts of men on leave and on weapons' holdings.[68]

The extent of support for the insurgents within the National Guard was never revealed although reports suggested that their political message was sympathetically received by fellow tribesmen in the force. It was, however, clear that the attack on the Mosque found little significant support among the tribes in general. Nonetheless, the siege of the Grand Mosque marked a watershed in terms of the perception and the reality of the internal security threats to Saudi rule. Pan-Arabism and radical Arab nationalism were rapidly becoming spent forces, to be replaced by various brands of Islamic politics.

Eventually the army took over the operation from the National Guard and succeeded in retaking the Mosque although again not without heavy casualties and constant friction between the commands of the two forces. Although the army had struggled to overcome the insurgents, there was no doubt that its performance had been greatly superior to that of the Guard and its reliability in this case greater too, neo-Wahhabism having made little impact on its officers and men.[69] The effectiveness of the army in internal security, supposedly the preserve of the National Guard, and its relative imperviousness to religious extremism caused the Saudis to reconsider their former inclination towards the Guard as the main security pillar of the regime. In fact, it seemed for a while that the fiasco of the siege of the Grand Mosque was resulting in a general Saudi loss of confidence in their own armed forces. In 1979 they thus went so far as to bring in 10,000 Pakistani troops not as advisors or support staff but actually to serve in the army, half of this contingent providing all the necessary manpower for the 10th Armoured Brigade.[70]

In one important respect, however, the National Guard retained and reinforced its position as a key pillar of Saudi rule. The 1970s had seen discontent reframed, secular Arab nationalism largely displaced by an Islamist discourse. In Saudi Arabia the Islamic politics of disaffection mobilized not only neo-Wahhabis but also a Shi'i community newly energized by the Iranian Revolution of 1979. Used systematically to suppress the Shi'i opposition, the National Guard were able to regain some of their reputation as a reliable instrument of royal rule. However doubtful the National Guard may have been in confronting their fellow Sunni tribesmen, they constituted a loyal and brutal tool to be used against demonstrations and strikes among the Shi'a in the eastern oil province of al-Hasa in 1980.

## New Wars, New Empires, Old Problems, 1980–2011

By the late 1980s none of the Saudi military and paramilitary forces had succeeded in becoming truly national institutions, all continuing to suffer, in different ways and to different degrees, from tribal, regional, religious and class distortions. The National Guard remained firmly tied to its tribal base, its command structure reflecting the connections between the tribal leaderships and the senior princes and, in a context conditioned by the Iranian Revolution, came to be seen increasingly as an anti-Shi'a sectarian force. The upper echelons of both army and air force consisted of members of the royal family, which now numbered as many as 20,000 people, combined with a layer of military professionals who owed their appointments to royal patronage. Not only did this block advancement to talent but it also introduced an element of chaos into the command structure, even subaltern royal officers able to trump the orders of their professional superiors. The army too, in marked contrast to neighbouring countries, had failed to become an engine of national integration. It remained a volunteer force, and Hijazis were still only imperfectly incorporated into the officer corps and rank and file, while Shi'a were almost completely excluded. Reflecting the new concern for the army evident in the 1980s, and with manpower ever less available owing to the expansion of more lucrative job opportunities in the wider economy, a decision in principle in favour of conscription was announced. Nonetheless, the attitude of vacillation prevailed in practice, and no action was taken towards implementation.[71]

After the disastrous performance of the National Guard in 1979, and the outbreak of the Gulf wars in the 1980s and 1990s, the Saudis once again began to prioritize the army. But the Saudi army continued to fall far short of the numbers projected as necessary by its foreign advisors; in 1990 it still numbered only about 45,000 men.[72] Nor could the Saudis compensate for a lack of manpower by developing a small, highly technically trained and equipped force as technically competent and politically reliable Saudis were in short supply and the army unable to compete with the private sector. The numbers of foreigners employed in the kingdom on defence contracts had, however, grown to fantastic proportions. By the mid-1980s it was thought that, for an army estimated at 45,000, there were approximately 30,000 American, 4–5,000 French and 2–3,000 British advisors training the various military forces, as well as the 10,000 Pakistanis serving in the 10th Armoured Brigade.[73] The Saudi army's dependence on foreign assistance for training and logistic support was increasing rather than diminishing, equipment purchased abroad with petrodollar wealth becoming ever more sophisticated. Naturally the Americans played the greatest role in servicing Saudi military modernization and a new awareness of the risks involved in the strategy of reliance on the US and subservience to its strategic and arms industry imperatives began to permeate the Saudi officer corps. The accuracy of these fears was thrown into sharp focus in 1991 with Saddam Hussein's occupation of Kuwait. The Saudis were forced to face the fact that their massive military expenditure, about 3 billion dollars over the previous 20 years, had left the country practically defenceless. The seriousness of the situation was later admitted when the Saudi high command admitted that during the first week of August the Iraqi Republican Guard could have occupied al-Hasa province in six hours.[74] The Saudis were obliged to appeal to the US for direct protection and King Fahd's invitation to US troops to defend Saudi soil inaugurated a prolonged political crisis in the kingdom.

Just as the National Guard had been little engaged on actual security operations prior to the Grand Mosque attack of 1979, so too the army had had almost no battle experience before 1991. Although it had been mobilized in 1948, 1956, 1967 and 1973, its actual participation in operations in these conflicts had been practically non-existent. The army was therefore facing a novel test in its participation in Operation Desert Storm from which it did not emerge with credit. The US advisors themselves did not have high hopes of the army's ability and, although some units, particularly from the National Guard, occasionally showed determination, in many respects Saudi forces performed even worse than expected.[75] Even the prized and much lauded air force showed itself to have serious limitations. The war also revealed starkly the dependence of all the services on foreign support. Saudi troops had almost no capacity to handle their modern weapons, purchased at such tremendous cost, despite the decades of training, and they relied on foreign technicians for even the most basic equipment maintenance. All the Saudi military operations were planned by the US, and for intelligence, logistics, communications and air defence, again they relied entirely on foreigners.[76]

The arrival of very large numbers of US troops in Saudi Arabia during and after the 1991 Gulf War created intense political problems for the al-Saud, contributing to a crisis of legitimacy and the rise of Islamist opposition in general and of al-Qaida in particular. The basic parameters of Saudi military development, however, the failures of which had been partially responsible for the arrival of foreign troops in such massive quantities, remained largely unchanged. In fact, the multiplication of perceived security threats, to the Saudi regime as much as or more than to the country itself, led to an even greater emphasis on close co-operation with the US. Not only was the bilateral military relationship with the US not reviewed, but rather it was expanded and deepened. Defence expenditures continued to rise. By 2007 Saudi military expenditure had reached 33.8 billion dollars, making it eighth in the world in military spending.[77] The cascade of sophisticated weaponry requiring foreign technical expertise continued unabated and the gap between Saudi technical capacity and the sophistication of the equipment grew ever wider. The strength of the various military and paramilitary units also continued to expand; by 2008 the regular army numbered 75,000 and the National Guard 100,000 full and part time. Nonetheless, recruitment remained skewed and the forces unrepresentative of Saudi society. Both Saudi army and National Guard still recruited under severe constraints. The Hijazis continued to harbour various discontents, the Shi'a were deeply suspect, and even the traditional recruiting base of the army and National Guard in Najd had been shrunk by the rise of neo-Wahhabism among the poorer tribal Saudis. Not only was the integrative effect of military expansion absent from the Saudi experience, but such expansion actually tended to contribute to, rather than mitigate, an alienation stimulated by political crisis.

By the twenty-first century Saudi Arabia had in practice abandoned the goal of creating an army strong enough to defend its borders from external aggression. Such national defence was essentially now in American hands.[78] The massive expenditure on defence showed no signs of slowing and, its military utility revealed as marginal by the Gulf War of 1991, operated as a mechanism for recycling petrodollars to the advantage of the Saudi elite and the Western arms industry. Indeed, Saudi defence spending served to cement its political and diplomatic relationships with the West, especially with the US, rather than to improve the actual performance of its armed forces. The Saudis also, after decades of debate, finally decided against using conscription to achieve the integration of its diverse population and the inculcation of a mentality of loyalty to the state. On the contrary, the National Guard in particular remained emblematic of the personal rule of the al-Saud and their tribal and religious exclusivity. Indeed, in 2011 Saudi military forces took a further step towards embodying the sectarian and tribal status quo in the Gulf when the Saudi National Guard entered Bahrain at the invitation of the ruling al-Khalifa family, whose repressive apparatus was even more skewed than that of the al-Saud, to suppress pro-democracy demonstrations which had broken out in response to the 'Arab Spring' then sweeping across the Middle East.[79] Having surrendered the responsibility of national defence to the US, the Saudi National Guard appeared content to take on the role of peninsula policeman.

# Conclusion

The Middle East entered the twenty-first century with authoritarian, strong (or perhaps only hard or fierce)[1] states supported by large, expensive armies, all, with the exception of the somewhat peculiar Arab Gulf states, manned by conscript troops, their officers highly educated and often strategically located within the commanding heights of politics and economy.[2] This may be seen as the culmination of a process which had begun in earnest in the late eighteenth/early nineteenth century, when a range of Arab, Ottoman, Iranian and Afghan polities began what was to be a protracted experiment with army reform.

Can it be concluded then that the project of 'military modernization' upon which the rulers of the nineteenth century embarked with such enthusiasm, has proved successful? How can we reappraise the utility of the application to the Middle East of the 'military revolution' hypothesis which has been widely applied to analyses of European state-building?[3] David Ralston has cogently summarized the key tenets of this hypothesis. According to Ralston, the new dynastic monarchies of sixteenth-century Europe increasingly relied on organized bodies of men on foot, a new trained infantry, which proved superior to the hosts of feudal cavalry typical of the immediate past.[4] As the new dynastic monarchies emerged across Europe, they gradually transformed their military organization, moving from the ad hoc raising and disbanding of armies for specific campaigns with the assistance of military contractors and mercenaries and loans from the great banking houses, towards the maintenance of permanent standing armies financed through the mobilization of domestic revenues. This novel form of organization then necessitated an ideological and cultural shift, away from aristocratic notions of individual valour towards collective discipline and obedience. Such a transformation also necessarily depended upon an equally, or perhaps an even greater, transformation of the bureaucratic, administrative and fiscal resources at the disposal of the state. The army, furthermore, now armed with the new weapons of portable firearms, required much greater training, this eventually leading, via the establishment of new specialist schools for the production of personnel for the military and bureaucracy, to the creation of a professional officer corps. These changes inevitably involved ever-greater state centralization and also the imposition of greater legal uniformity and discipline upon not just the soldiery, but upon the wider society, a process which, unsurprisingly, often generated considerable resistance, at both elite and popular levels, the new armies themselves the principal instruments by which such resistance might be suppressed. In the process of such suppression, the centralizing state increased its own absolute power while simultaneously weakening the capacity of the general population to offer resistance. Ralston concludes that the standing army was, 'by the demands it created and the social pressures it caused…one of the major forces behind the almost revolutionary transformation of European society between 1500 and 1700'.[5]

By the early nineteenth century the military revolution had reached the Middle East. From Morocco in the west to Afghanistan and the Punjab in the east, rulers emerged, resembling or trying to resemble the dynastic monarchies of early modern Europe. Although much emphasis has been put on the emulation or imitation by Middle Eastern rulers of European political and military organization, in fact the almost simultaneous emergence of centralizing dynastic monarchies across the region appears to have been generated by indigenous pressures and to have had an organic connection to the local social and political context. These rulers, sultans, khedives and amirs, in the search for political consolidation, then embarked on a transformative process similar to that undertaken by Gustavus Adolphus in Sweden, Louis XIV in France and Peter the Great in Russia. Each ruler in turn abandoned the old ad hoc military forces, furnished by quasi-feudal khans and landowners, and replaced them with a standing army, eventually based, at least in theory, on conscription. Across the Middle East, new dynastic states created new educational institutions, new bureaucracies and new administrative machinery to organize conscription, raising new taxes to pay for it all.

In the Middle East, however, the results and consequences of the attempted military revolutions of the nineteenth century were very different from the achievements of enlightened despotism in Europe. By World War I and after a century of such experiments, many Middle Eastern states found themselves at a greater disadvantage than ever in relation to Europe. The costs of the new *nizam* armies had proved ruinous and their martial abilities uncertain while the search for military expertise had resulted in the arrival of foreign military missions, undermining sovereignty and often presaging full colonial control. The failure of Middle Eastern states to solve the problem of financing the new armies was perhaps most obviously central to the wider failure of the military revolution. Across the region, economic development lagged by comparison to nineteenth-century Europe, was indeed distorted and derailed by aggressive European economic penetration, and no agricultural or industrial revolution took place capable of generating an economy, and therefore a level of revenue, able to support the new military expenditure. The military revolution thesis, as applied to Europe, has marginalized economic development as a motor for change, but it may well be argued that it was the Middle East's relative economic weakness, and particularly the weakness of indigenous capitalism, which undermined its state-building efforts in the nineteenth century, and not its administrative, educational or technological deficiencies. The military revolution arrived in the Middle East a little too late, local states already being subject to enormous economic, political and military pressure from a young European imperialism in its most energetic phase. Forced to try to compress into a few decades what had taken a century or more in Europe, most Middle Eastern rulers could never catch up, their military reforms always lagging behind an industrializing and aggressively expansionist Europe.

The state-building project which underlay the military revolution provoked intense hostility across early modern Europe, from both remnants of the old order, displaced by rising social forces, and from the mass of the population, conscripted and taxed in order to maintain the new armies. Yet, in these domestic conflicts which reproduced themselves from country to country, the balance of power lay with the centralizing state which represented the most modern form of political organization. This was not so in the Middle East. As rulers began to implement the basic policies which comprised the military revolution, they encountered fierce resistance from still powerful pre-modern social formations, which had so far been little undermined by broader economic or political change. They also, however, and crucially, very quickly began to face opposition not from declining, but from rising social groups. As political hostility to the dynastic monarchies and their apparent submission to Europe grew, Middle Eastern rulers faced a challenge unknown to their earlier European counterparts, that of being outflanked by the emergence of oppositional political forces with a more coherent and consistent claim than themselves to the mantle of modernism and nationalism. In 1864 the Tunisian countryside rose in revolt, successfully derailing the *nizam* project of the Beylical dynasty but unable to propose any strategic alternative. By 1880, the khedivial family in Egypt found itself facing not only remnants of the old order but, of much greater significance, the nationalist, anti-imperialist and populist revolt of Urabi Pasha, while the Ottoman Sultan, a little later, was to be marginalized by his own modernist officer corps.

As Middle Eastern rulers began to attempt a military revolution, they were already struggling with a growing penetration of their economies and polities by a voracious European presence. In their drive to control territory and resources, European empires sometimes imposed full colonial control, but often sought rather the cheaper and easier option of the exercise of informal influence over local states and rulers. Military missions were a perfect mechanism for the extension of such informal influence. Given local rulers' desperate desire to strengthen themselves against domestic opposition, against regional rivals and against the menace of imperialism in general, the offer of military advice from one or other European power was frequently eagerly embraced. However, just as European loans to finance *nizam* troops led to bankruptcy and the weakening or even the loss of independence, so too did the foreign missions, meant to strengthen the army, often lead rather to a parallel undermining of sovereignty. The assessment of the experience of one country, Qajar Iran, confirms the generally deleterious impact of the presence of foreign military missions. European military missions succeeded each other in Iran with dazzling speed. Yet by the end of the nineteenth century Iranian military capacity was weaker than ever, while its military forces had become ruinously expensive. Far from enabling Iran to assert its sovereignty, the missions functioned as a device to increase European hegemony and Iranian dependence. Although Iran maintained its hold on a formal sovereignty throughout the nineteenth century, the changing character of the foreign missions clearly delineated the growing influence of imperial power. At the beginning of the nineteenth century, Abbas Mirza had exploited the European conflicts of the Napoleonic era to begin building a military force with which to consolidate his own domestic position and attempt to regain territory lost to the Russian empire. By the end of the century and then World War I, the presence of the Russian officers of the Iranian Cossack Brigade, and the British officers of the South Persia Rifles had, on the contrary, come to represent the almost complete subordination of shah, court and country to imperial control.

If the nineteenth-century military revolution failed to produce the state-building achievements in the Middle East which it had produced in Europe, what was the experience of the twentieth century? To what extent do the histories of individual armies, the Iranian and Afghan formed after the watershed of World War I, the Saudi after World War II, shed light on the interplay of state-building and military reform and the role of Western assistance in the twentieth century?

Although the tradition of military reform, along with the authoritarian modernization within which it was embedded, may be traced back to the late eighteenth to early nineteenth century, the three states examined above all began their state-building projects in earnest only after World War I. Perhaps surprisingly, Afghanistan was among the earliest of the states in the region to embark on a military revolution. Yet, by 1900, after seven decades of experiments, Afghanistan possessed only a fragile shadow of a modern state and army. It was only with the advent to power of King Amanullah in 1919 and the attainment of formal independence after the third Anglo–Afghan war, that modernist activism seized a degree of state power in Afghanistan. In Iran too, military reform had its origins in the early nineteenth century, but the state-building project was only launched in any effective sense after Riza Khan's coup of 1921. Saudi Arabia came much later to forming a regular army, only beginning this task after World War II. Yet, whatever the historical period in which each state launched its project, the project itself remained remarkably similar.

As the Middle East emerged from the wreckage of World War I, military development quickly became central to the state-building projects of all the new states in the region and also key to the nationalist ideology which buttressed them. Authoritarian and modernist regimes such as that established in the new Iraq were perfect illustrations of this phenomenon. Even nationalist movements which lacked states, most notably the Palestinian, forged a discourse of state-building and expressed a denied national identity through military organization and action.[6] This was equally true, of course, of the pre-state *Yishuv* in Palestine and later in Israel, where the army possessed an almost sacred status. Even states which explicitly rejected the nationalist discourse in favour of tribal and religious tropes, such as Saudi Arabia, were forced initially to follow the same path, such was the dominance of the modernist discourse, although the Saudi awareness of the potential dangers of an educated officer corps and of conscript troops ultimately caused them to reconfigure their project.

As the narratives of Iran and Afghanistan given above demonstrate, the construction of large armies based on conscription was widely accepted by modernizing elites as essential to both state-building and social development. Such a discourse pervaded the Middle East from the 1920s onwards.[7] The imposition of conscription, however, upon a population unaccustomed to the direct intrusion of the state and often still armed, proved a serious challenge to the new regimes.[8] It was, nonetheless, a challenge which the ruling nationalist elites of countries like Iran, Turkey and Iraq were determined to overcome. Although the success of universal military service in inculcating notions of patriotism, loyalty to the state and citizenship has been questioned, the example of Iran would seem to argue in its favour.[9] In the turmoil of the revolutionary years, 1978–9, the army certainly disintegrated, but it fractured along class and ideological, not ethnic or regional, lines. The history of conscription in Afghanistan and Saudi Arabia, however, reveals a different dynamic. In a sign of the failure of the ruling Musahiban dynasty in Afghanistan to confront the stark realities of state-building, with its inevitable confrontation with competitors for power, especially in the rural fastnesses, the modernizing Afghan state finally shied away from imposing the policy. Conscripting only the urban population and submissive tribal and peasant groups, the Afghan monarchy admitted the historical limitations of its own hegemony. The fate of conscription in Saudi Arabia is also indicative of the more general characteristics of state and society. The Saudi royal family, like the Afghan, feared the consequences of the impact of conscription, but for different reasons. As a result, service in the Saudi army, and in the other Arab Gulf states, perhaps uniquely in the Middle East, remained voluntary. The administrative centralization and bureaucratic rationality demanded by conscription were avoided, while both the integrative function of conscription and the emergence of a professional officer corps were both sacrificed to the imperative of sustaining the tribal and family ascendancy of the al-Saud. Throughout the decades of high modernism in the Middle East, the Saudi army remained a small volunteer force, while surrounding countries built mass armies. Indeed, a comparison of Iran and Saudi Arabia suggests that the Saudi royal family, by eschewing conscription and 'coup-proofing'[10] itself by creating a counterpoise to the army in the shape of the National Guard, has learnt well the lessons of state-building in the Middle East. The Shah may well have found that a small professional army would have remained loyal to its master and held together as a repressive tool in a way that a conscript army was never likely to do.

Indeed, from the 1960s, a solution to manpower and reliability problems began to be adopted by the Arab Gulf states which was altogether contrary to the dynamic implied by conscription. During the 1970s British advisors had introduced into the Saudi army a substantial number of Pakistani officers. These Pakistani officers came as part of a contingent which included Jordanian officers. In fact, the Jordanian army, still heavily influenced by Britain, the ousting of Glubb Pasha notwithstanding, had pioneered the employment of Pakistani Muslim officers, brought in after Jordan's humiliating performance in the 1967 war with Israel. Just as in Afghanistan in the nineteenth century, so now too it was hoped that the presence of Muslim officers would mitigate local hostility to a foreign presence with the military. After the siege of the Grand Mosque in Mecca in 1979 the al-Saud took this idea one very significant stage further, bringing in 10,000 Pakistani troops not as advisors or support staff but actually to serve in the army, half of this contingent providing all the necessary manpower for the 10th Armoured Brigade.[11] By the twenty-first century, other Arab Gulf states had enthusiastically followed where the Saudis led, recruiting their military and paramilitary forces largely from Pakistani Muslims, thus creating a mercenary force with no domestic loyalties other than to the dynasty, and avoiding the 'democratization' of the army implied by conscription.

In the nineteenth-century Middle East, military defeat seemed intimately linked to the emergence from within the officer corps of radical political challenges. In the twentieth century, the coups of the 1950s have been famously attributed to the trauma dealt to Arab nationalism by defeat at the hands of Israel. The Saudi army, although theoretically mobilized, held back from practical participation in the Arab–Israeli wars of 1948, 1956, 1967 and 1973, thus avoiding the dramatic political upheavals which resulted in other Arab countries from military defeat. Nonetheless, the Saudi officer corps of the 1950s and 1960s shared to some extent in the radical nationalism percolating through the officer corps of other Arab armies. In the case of Iran and Afghanistan, it is striking that radical and revolutionary challenges developed inside and outside the army without the stimulus of military defeat. The Pahlavi army avoided altogether any significant military conflict, its Dhohar operations of the mid-1970s the only minor exception and in any case presented as successful. Although the humiliation of occupation in 1941 had lingered, the absence of any serious military test muted any political challenge to the Shah from within the army. Although dissent certainly existed in the army of early Pahlavi Iran, and 'Free Officer' tendencies may be detected among the supporters of Musaddiq and in the early 1960s, no challenge to the monarchy was able to crystallize within the army. It was only as the civilian revolutionary movement demonstrated its strength in 1978 that the army began to crumble, and then it was from the bottom up, even at that stage, the officer corps lacking both the capacity and the will to take power into its own hands. The Afghan army remained even further from any engagement outside domestic tribal management. Yet here, although in general modernism and nationalism had arrived later and remained weaker than elsewhere, revolutionary political ambition was born and matured among the intelligentsia and urban middle class, especially as these groups were represented within the officer corps, finally producing the PDPA coup of April 1978.

The role of the air force in this period in incubating the most advanced political tendencies across the region is in particular remarkable. This service attracted many of the most well-educated and ambitious candidates, demanded the most sophisticated skills and offered the best training.

Hafiz al-Asad used his position as commander-in-chief of the Syrian air force to play a key role in the 1966 Ba'thist coup; air force personnel were a leading element of the 1979 coup in Afghanistan; and even in Saudi Arabia air force officers demonstrated marked Nasserist sympathies. In Iran too, a subaltern layer within the air force, technicians known as *homafars*, was central to the revolution of 1979.

In the nineteenth century, the arrival of Western military advisors and missions compromised the sovereignty and undermined the legitimacy of local states and rulers, and also distorted military development, moulding it to suit imperial needs rather than local agendas. This only worsened in the twentieth century. The connections between official military assistance and the needs and wishes of the US and British defence industries shaped an attitude of political indulgence towards Muhammad Riza Shah, allowing him to develop a repressive apparatus financed by petrodollars and staffed by US personnel immune from the Iranian legal system, and unpopular regional ambitions and alliances, all of which contributed to his own fatal loss of domestic support. Military sales and thus recycling of petrodollars to the benefit of Western defence industries has, the fate of Iran notwithstanding, only accelerated in recent years, contributing to the elaboration of a largely religious critique of Saudi rule. On the other hand, the Afghan experience with a Soviet military mission remains a puzzle. Apparently eliciting little hostility, the character and impact of Soviet military assistance to Afghanistan in the 1960s and 1970s, before the invasion of 1979, continues to await a scholarly appreciation.

The conflict habitually breaking out between local elites and foreign advisors is well exemplified by the battles over conscription. Everywhere in their old and new imperial possessions, the British had advocated small, volunteer, professional armies. Such forces had the advantages of being cheap, and also manageable in terms of any possible political ambitions. In Egypt after the Urabi Revolt, Britain allowed only a small army to be reconstituted, with mainly policing functions, all the higher officers, including the commander-in-chief, the *sirdar*, being British. Although the Egyptian army later proved useful in the reconquest of the Sudan after the Mahdist Revolt, the army remained sidelined until at least the late 1930s, resentment at their professional marginalization contributing to the growing nationalism of the officer corps. Britain took its dislike of large, expensive conscript armies, with their tendency to produce politicians in uniform, into its new mandates. The case of Iraq provides a classical example of the radically divergent views over conscription held by British officials, principally concerned with internal and imperial security, and Iraqi nationalists, wanting to use the army as a 'school of the nation' in the Prussian tradition. Similar clashes took place in Iran after 1941 and in Saudi Arabia after 1945. Even in Afghanistan in 2012, the debate continued to rage between Afghans who understood conscription as a state-building component and Western military advisors preoccupied with cost and military efficiency.

If a key tenet of the military revolution in Europe was the notion that armies capable of defending the national territory and the sovereign state would be financed by the mobilization of domestic resources, principally taxation, then the three case-studies above, of Iran, Afghanistan and Saudi Arabia, show that this feature was largely absent from the Middle Eastern experience. Afghanistan was always unable to raise cash for a regular army. The transition from semi-feudal levies to a standing army created a perpetual crisis for the nineteenth-century Afghan state which could only be resolved through a reliance on British subsidies. After World War II the dire condition of the Afghan army and the US refusal of military assistance led directly both to Daud's coup and to Afghanistan's turn to the USSR. Indeed the USSR continued to support Afghan military development until its own collapse in 1991. In both Iran and Saudi Arabia, money for the army came not through taxation based on economic development but from oil revenues. Although Riza Shah had been brutally effective in raising revenue in the 1930s through domestic taxes on basic foodstuffs, his new army, especially its enormously expensive weapons procurement programme, was always financed directly from oil revenues. His son followed his example, although of course the resources from oil were infinitely greater by the 1970s. Saudi Arabia too, of course, avoided the strains likely to result from taxing the population by exploiting its massive oil reserves to finance both state and army. In fact these examples illustrate perfectly the two paths open to most Middle Eastern states: dependence on foreign assistance or, where possible, in the Gulf states, including Iran and Iraq, a delusion-inducing reliance on oil revenues. Iran indeed made an almost seamless transition from recipient of military assistance in the 1950s to provider of petrodollars to Western defence industries by the 1960s–70s.

Turkey is perhaps the most important example of a country which managed to avoid these extremes. Although Turkey, like Iran, was allotted a role in the West's 'northern tier' of defence against the Soviet Union, and was designated a recipient of special economic and military assistance under the Truman doctrine, it lacked the oil wealth which so distorted military policy in the Gulf region, while its relatively independent political posture avoided a debilitating dependence on foreign military aid and assistance.

Middle Eastern armies have proved surprisingly durable in both political and military terms. Both the Iraqi and the Iranian armies remained organizationally and politically intact during the long war of 1980–7, despite the high casualty rate. The Afghan army also maintained a degree of structural cohesion and ideological consistency as it battled a combination of domestic, regional and international enemies during the 1980s, only itself collapsing after the withdrawal of all support from its sole ally, the Soviet Union. In Iraq the army did not disintegrate after the trauma of the 2003 invasion, but had to be disbanded by the new coalition authority. Even in Syria, after 18 months of civil conflict, the army has failed to oblige the almost universal predictions of its disintegration.

Yet, as the case of Afghanistan demonstrates, the state-building process can be reversed. Any state, whether in the Middle East, Europe, or any other part of the world, may prove vulnerable to fragmentation and collapse if the pressure placed on it is sufficiently intense. Whereas the relatively smooth transitions in Egypt and Tunisia in 2011 left both army and state intact, the Iraqi state has still not recovered from the effects of the 2003 invasion and occupation, while Syria, bearing the weight of a struggle of regional and global significance, and post-Ghadafi Libya both appear to be on the road to becoming failed states. Although the US and its Western allies appear to have concluded that such failed states are preferable to hostile regimes, the experience of Afghanistan detailed above would seem to indicate otherwise.

The ever-present potential, in a region subject to highly unusual levels of political stress and tension, of a reversal of the state-building process should also be borne in mind when assessing the success of any individual project. In fact, the historiography of state-building in the Middle East has in general been characterized by a marked teleological bias. For example, in the cases of Iran and Afghanistan, the historical experience has been interpreted, to an extraordinary degree, from the perspective of the present.

In Iran, the state remaining intact, progress from fissiparous fragility to strength and hegemony is seen as natural and inevitable and opponents of the central government, including the tribes, as an unavoidable casualty of modernity. The literature on Afghanistan, also using the present as a guide to the past, has reached opposite conclusions, emphasizing the significance and vitality of tribal life and magnifying the mistakes of state-builders, most notably of King Amanullah and of the PDPA.

In the twentieth century, Middle Eastern armies remained marked by their origins as instruments for the consolidation of domestic state power in general and dynastic rule in particular. In Europe, a developing special-ization and professionalization increasingly clearly demarcated the roles of internal security, the responsibility of police and sometimes paramili-tary police forces, and external defence, the army. Although Middle Eastern armies grew enormously in the twentieth century, unlike their European counterparts they remained largely focused on internal security. This was facilitated by the fact that, apart from the brief and unequal Arab–Israeli wars, the Middle East was free from intra-state conflict in the decades after the post-World War I settlement until the outbreak of the Iran–Iraq war in 1980. Even in the twenty-first century, Middle Eastern armies, as the conflict in Syria unfolding in 2011–12 demonstrates, retained a primary function as guarantors of state and regime security. Paradoxically enough, it was the Iranian army which had first, during the 1960s and 1970s, begun a reorientation away from domestic security towards playing an external power-projection role. Yet it was to be precisely this army which was to face, and then fail to meet, a test of a rare magnitude in the form of a mass revolutionary upheaval at home.

Whatever their capacities as instruments of domestic political power, Middle Eastern armies were, by the twenty-first century, still weak when measured against a Western standard. Middle Eastern rulers, engaged in desperate efforts at military reform during the nineteenth century, had found themselves falling ever farther behind an industrializing and impe-rial Europe. Despite the enormous resources devoted to armies across the region during the twentieth and twenty-first centuries, this gap in mili-tary capacity between the Middle East and the West continued to grow. In the nineteenth century, the most effective resistance to Western encroach-ments had been offered, not by the *nizam* regiments with their professional officers, but by irregular forces often with a religious leadership. In the twentieth and twenty-first centuries, this tradition continued, exemplified by Hizbullah's defeat of the Israeli attack in 2006.

As the US and its allies have discovered in Iraq and Afghanistan, and as the nationalist elites of the Middle East found before them, the tensions between state-building and democratic governance are profound and complex, and not easily resolved. None of the Middle Eastern states discussed above have managed to integrate these two elements in a stable combination. So intractable did these tensions appear to be, indeed, that earlier modernist ideologues occasionally resorted to the construction of a discourse that explicitly valued strong leadership, even dictatorship, over popular political participation.[12] Every regime, pro-Western or nationalist, Islamic or secular, has taken an authoritarian path of state-building, indeed the more dynamic the phase of transformation, the greater was the curtailment of democratic rights and freedoms, confined as these were to the elites. Pahlavi Iran or Kemalist Turkey may be contrasted with the earlier constitutional period, Nasserist Egypt with the 'Liberal Experiment'[13] of the 1920s–30s, and Ba'thist Syria and Iraq with the previous rule of the notables. Armies have been central to this modernist project, so much so that they have, in bouts of frustration at the slowness and compromise of civilian politics, sometimes literally taken command of the project themselves, thus falling prey to the corruption and degeneration which they so criticized in their civilian predecessors.

For much of the twentieth century, Middle Eastern armies had an uneven record as guarantors of regimes, generating challenges as often as suppressing them. By the end of the century, however, the old image of the army as a vehicle of change in the region appeared to have become outdated. In general, the armies of the region, or at least their professional officer corps, seemed to have instead transformed themselves into corporate institutions intent only on defending their own interests. By the twenty-first century, however, the broad consensus about the role of the military in Middle Eastern politics proved to have been premature. The actions of the Egyptian army in 2011 and especially in 2013 demonstrated that the apparent withdrawal of the army from active and direct political intervention was a trajectory capable of abrupt reversal. The age of the coup was not in fact over. Nonetheless, in contrast to the Free Officers of 1954, the Egyptian army in 2011 and 2013 acted essentially out of a conservative desire for self-preservation and as guardians of the old secular order, not, despite the dreams of the people of Tahrir Square, as an ally of the revolutionaries.

In its authoritarianism, the Middle Eastern state-building experience chimes with that of Europe. The emerging dynastic monarchies of early modern Europe, and the enlightened despotism of the eighteenth century, were top-down institutions and ideologies *par excellence*. Only in a later historical period, with the state-building enterprise largely complete, did Europe begin its long experiment with democracy. In the Middle East, recent events across the region have shown that the era of state-building and national consolidation is far from complete. In this context, experiments with parliamentary institutions, appropriate to societies with high levels of social peace, have proved problematic, exacerbating ethnic and sectarian tensions rather than providing mechanisms for their resolution, and failing to address revolutionary demands for social and economic, as well as political, change. Inevitably, into the vacuum created by the mass popular challenge offered to discredited regimes has stepped the army, once again presenting itself as a uniquely pre-eminent national institution.

# Notes

## Introduction

1 Maha Azzam, 'Egypt's military council and the transition to democracy', Chatham House Briefing Paper, May 2012, p. 3. Available at www.chathamhouse.org/publications/papers/view/183547, accessed 8 April 2013.

2 See Ahmed S. Hashim, 'The Egyptian military, Part One: from the Ottomans through Sadat', Middle East Policy Council, September 2011. Available at www.mepc.org/journal/middle-east-policy-archives/egyptian-military-part-one-ottomans-through-sadat (accessed 8 April 2013); Stephen H. Gotowicki, 'The role of the Egyptian military in domestic society', FMSO Publications, 1997. Available at http://fmso.leavenworth.army.mil/documents/egypt/egypt.htm (accessed 8 April 2013).

3 Azzam, 'Egypt's military council', p. 3.

4 See Robert Springborg, 'Roundtable: rethinking the study of Middle Eastern militaries', International Journal of Middle Eastern Studies 43/3 (2011), pp. 397–9.

5 For an account of the military in Tunisia, Morocco and Algeria see Michael Willis, Politics and Power in the Maghreb: Algeria, Tunisia and Morocco from Independence to the Arab Spring (London, 2012).

6 Ibid., p. 116.

7 Ibid., p. 117.

8 Ibid., p. 117.

9 Anthony H. Cordesman, A Tragedy of Arms (Westport, CT, 2002), pp. 216–20; Kenneth M. Pollack, Arabs at War: Military Effectiveness, 1948–1991 (Lincoln, NE, 2004), pp. 358–446.

10 Pollack, Arabs at War, p. 447.

11 The phrase is Hanna Batatu's. See Hanna Batatu, The Old Social Classes and the Revolutionary Movements of Iraq: A Study of Iraq's Old Landed and Commercial Classes and its Communists, Baathists and Free Officers (Princeton, NJ, 1979).

12 Raymond A. Hinnebusch, Authoritarian Power and State Formation in Ba'thist Syria: Army, Party and Peasant (Boulder, CO, 1990), pp. 156–65.

13 Ibrahim Al-Marashi and Sammy Salama, *Iraq's Armed Forces: An Analytical History* (Abingdon, 2008), p. 205.

14 Ibid., p. 201.

15 Steven A. Cook, *Ruling but not Governing: The Military and Political Development in Egypt, Algeria and Turkey* (Baltimore, 2007), p. 15.

16 Manfred Halpern, *Middle Eastern Armies and the New Middle Class* (Princeton, 1962). See also, for example, Sydney Fisher, *The Military in the Middle East: Problems in Society and Government* (Columbus, OH, 1963); James A. Bill, 'The military and modernization in the Middle East', *Comparative Politics*, October 1969; J. C. Hurewitz, 'Soldiers and social change in plural societies: the contemporary Middle East', in M. E. Yapp and V. J. Parry (eds), *War, Technology and Society in the Middle East* (London, 1975). For a more recent assessment see Elizabeth Picard, 'Arab military in politics: from revolutionary plot to authoritarian state', in A. Hourani, P. S. Khoury and M. C. Wilson (eds), *The Modern Middle East* (London and New York, 1993), p. 552.

17 Al-Marashi and Salama, *Iraq's Armed Forces*, p. 143.

18 Picard, 'Arab military in politics', p. 554.

19 Ibid., p. 554.

20 Anthony Sampson, *The Arms Bazaar: From Lebanon to Lockheed* (New York, 1977); Edward Posnett, 'Treating His Imperial Majesty's warts: British policy towards Iran, 1977–79', *Iranian Studies* 45/1 (2012), pp. 119–37.

21 See, *inter alia*, Donald Stoker (ed.) *Military Advising and Assistance: From Mercenaries to Privatization, 1815–2007* (London, 2008).

## Chapter 1: The Military Revolution in the Middle East

1 Although the role of military reform in generating a dynamic for a wider state-building agenda has long been acknowledged, studies of the new armies of the nineteenth-century Middle East and North Africa are few. Among the most important are Stanford J. Shaw, 'The origins of Ottoman military reform: the nizam-i cedid army of Sultan Selim III', *The Journal of Modern History* 37/3 (1965), pp. 291–305; L. Carl Brown, *The Tunisia of Ahmed Bey* (Princeton, 1974); M. E. Yapp, 'The modernization of Middle Eastern armies in the nineteenth century: a comparative view', in M. E. Yapp and V. J. Parry (eds), *War, Technology and Society in the Middle East* (London, 1975); Wilfrid J. Rollman, *The 'New Order' in a Pre-Colonial Muslim Society: Military Reform in Morocco, 1844–1904*. PhD dissertation (University of Michigan, 1983); Khaled Fahmy, *All the Pasha's Men: Mehmed Ali, his Army and the Making of Modern Egypt* (Cambridge, 1997). Recently attention has turned away from the reforming Westernizing elites and refocused on military modernization as experienced 'from below'. See Fahmy, *All the Pasha's Men*; Erik J. Zürcher (ed.), *Arming the State: Military Conscription in the Middle East and Central Asia* (London and New York, 1999); Odile Moreau and Abderrahmane el Moudden (eds), 'Réforme par le haut, réforme par le bas: la modernisation de l'armée aux 19e et 20e siècles', *Quaderni di Oriente Moderno*

(special issue) (Rome, 2004). For an interesting discussion of Western perceptions of non-European armies see Patrick Porter, *Military Orientalism: Eastern War through Western Eyes* (London, 2009).

2 Abderrahmane el Moudden, 'Looking Eastward: some Moroccan tentative military reforms with Turkish assistance (18th to early 20th centuries)', *The Maghreb Review* 19/3–4 (1994), pp. 237–45.

3 See John P. Dunn, *Khedive Ismail's Army* (Abingdon, 2005).

4 This has been most extensively documented, especially in its negative aspects, by Fahmy, *All the Pasha's Men*.

5 Jeremy Black, *War and the World: Military Power and the Fate of Continents, 1450–2000* (New Haven, CT, 1998), p. 45.

6 Virginia H. Aksan, 'Ottoman military recruitment strategies in the late eighteenth century', in Zürcher (ed.), *Arming the State*, p. 30.

7 For a discussion of military technology transfers, see Black, *War and the World*.

8 Ibid.

9 An elite caste of slave soldiers of non-Muslim, non-Arab origin.

10 James Morier, *A Second Journey through Persia, Armenia, and Asia Minor, to Constantinople, Between the Years 1810 and 1816* (London, 1818), p. 211.

11 Stephanie Cronin, 'Deserters, converts, Cossacks and revolutionaries: Russians in Iranian military service, 1800–1921', in Stephanie Cronin (ed.) *Iranian–Russian Encounters: Empires and Revolutions since 1800* (Abingdon, 2012), pp. 143–8.

12 Amira K. Bennison, 'The "New Order" and Islamic Order: The Introduction of the *Nizami* Army in the Western Maghrib and its Legitimation, 1830–73', *International Journal of Middle Eastern Studies* 36/4 (2004), pp. 591–612, p. 603.

13 Wilfrid J. Rollman, 'Military officers and the "Niẓām al-Ǧadīd" in Morocco, 1844–1912: social and political transformation', in O. Moreau and A. el Moudden (eds) *Réforme par le haut*, p. 217.

14 Ibid., p. 218.

15 Driss Maghraoui, 'From "tribal anarchy" to "military order": the Moroccan troops in the context of colonial Morocco', in O. Moreau and A. el Moudden (eds) *Réforme par le haut*.

16 S. Tanvir Wasti, 'The 1877 Ottoman mission to Afghanistan', *Middle Eastern Studies* 30/4 (1994), pp. 956–962, note 3, p. 961.

17 Vartan Gregorian, *The Emergence of Modern Afghanistan* (Stanford, CA, 1969), p. 184.

18 Rollman, 'Military officers and the "Niẓām al-Ǧadīd"', p. 218.

19 Stephanie Cronin, *The Army and the Creation of the Pahlavi State in Iran, 1910–1926* (London, 1997), pp. 27–8.

20 Avigdor Levy, 'The officer corps in Sultan Mahmud's new Ottoman army, 1826–1839', *International Journal of Middle East Studies*, 2/1 (1971), pp. 21–39.

21 Dunn, *Khedive Ismail's Army*.

22 Cronin, 'Deserters, converts, Cossacks and revolutionaries'; Bennison, 'The "New Order" and Islamic Order"', p. 599. The presence of European adventurers and mercenaries in the nineteenth-century Middle East and North Africa surely anticipates the mushrooming of the security industry of the late

twentieth/early twenty-first centuries. See Donald Stoker (ed.) *Military Advising and Assistance.*

23 Surprisingly, in the light of the amount of material, memoirs and diplomatic correspondence which they generated, the European missions of the nineteenth century have attracted relatively little interest. The German missions to the Ottoman Empire have received the most detailed attention. See the four early articles by Robert J. Kerner, 'The mission of Liman von Sanders: 1, its origin', *The Slavonic Review* 6/16 (1927), pp. 12–27; 'The mission of Liman von Sanders: 2, the crisis', *The Slavonic Review* 6/17 (1927), pp. 343–63; 'The mission of Liman von Sanders: 3', *The Slavonic and East European Review* 6/18 (1928), pp. 543–60; 'The mission of Liman von Sanders: 4, the aftermath', *The Slavonic and East European Review* 7/19 (1927), pp. 90–112. See also Ulrich Trumpener, 'Liman von Sanders and the German–Ottoman alliance', *Journal of Contemporary History* 1/4 (1966), pp. 179–92; Glen W. Swanson, 'War, technology and society in the Ottoman Empire from the reign of Abdulhamid II to 1913: Mahmud Şevket and the German military mission', in M. E. Yapp and V. J. Parry (eds), *War, Technology and Society*. Morocco's interesting experiment with an Ottoman mission is dealt with by el Moudden, 'Looking Eastward'. For the Austrian mission to mid-nineteenth-century Iran see Borhan Khoschnewis Gawgani, *Die Österreichische Militärmissionen in Persien 1852 bis 1881*. PhD dissertation (Universität Wien, 1978). The Russian Cossack mission to Iran is discussed by F. Kazemzadeh, 'The origin and early development of the Persian Cossack Brigade', *The American Slavic and East European Review* 15/3 (1956), pp. 351–63; Uzi Rabi and Nugzar Ter-Oganov, 'The Russian military mission and the birth of the Persian Cossack Brigade: 1879–1894', *Iranian Studies* 42/3 (2009), pp. 445–63. For the Swedish mission to the Iranian Gendarmerie during the constitutional period, see Markus Ineichen, *Die Schwedischen Offiziere in Persien 1911–1916* (Bern, 2002); Cronin, *The Army and the Creation of the Pahlavi State*, pp. 17–53. For the British mission to the South Persia Rifles see Floreeda Safiri, *The South Persia Rifles*. PhD thesis (University of Edinburgh, 1976); W. J. Olson, *Anglo–Iranian Relations during World War I* (London, 1984), pp. 153–213.

24 See Fahmy, *All the Pasha's Men*, pp. 99–103.

25 David B. Ralston, *Importing the European Army: The Introduction of European Military Techniques and Institutions into the extra-European World, 1600–1814* (Chicago, IL, 1990).

26 Although even they were not immune to the lure of *nizam* forces. For Shamyl's efforts to build regular units, see Stephanie Cronin, 'Deserters, converts, Cossacks and revolutionaries', note 50, p. 181.

27 The effectiveness of such irregular forces in certain precise conditions may be seen across the globe in the twentieth century.

28 Bernard Lewis, *The Emergence of Modern Turkey* (London, 1961), p. 90.

29 Ralston, *Importing the European Army*, p. 63.

30 Ibid., p. 56.

31 See Timothy Mitchell, *Colonising Egypt* (Cambridge, 1988).

32 M. Naim Turfan, *Rise of the Young Turks: Politics, the Military and Ottoman Collapse* (London, 2000), p. 58; Ralston, *Importing the European Army*, pp. 60–1.

33  For the Ottoman system of military recruitment see Erik Jan Zürcher, 'The Ottoman conscription system, 1844–1917', *International Review of Social History* 43/3 (1998), pp. 437–49.

34  Fahmy, *All the Pasha's Men*, p. 93.

35  Ibid., pp. 107–10.

36  Lisa Anderson, *The State and Social Transformation in Tunisia and Libya, 1830–1980* (Princeton, NJ, 1986), pp. 65–70. For Tunisian military reform see also Brown, *The Tunisia of Ahmed Bey*.

37  Anderson, *The State and Social Transformation*, pp. 65–70.

38  Ibid., pp. 142–5.

39  Ralston, *Importing the European Army*, p. 63; Alexander Schölch, *Egypt for the Egyptians! The Socio-Political Crisis in Egypt, 1878–1882* (London, 1981), p. 23.

40  Ralston, *Importing the European Army*, p. 100; Eliezer Beeri, *Army Officers in Arab Politics and Society* (London, 1970), pp. 305–10.

41  Turfan, *Rise of the Young Turks*, p. 60.

42  Ibid., p. 64.

## Chapter 2: Importing Modernity

1  The Safavids claimed descent from the seventh Imam and had ruled an empire which at its height stretched from Baghdad to Herat.

2  Riza Shah, like his contemporary Mustafa Kemal Atatürk, conceptualized the state-building project in terms of consolidating these borders, not on an irredentist challenge.

3  Avigdor Levy, 'The officer corps in Sultan Mahmud's new Ottoman army, 1826–1839', *International Journal of Middle East Studies* 2/1 (1971), pp. 21–39.

4  Rudi Matthee, 'Between sympathy and enmity: nineteenth century Iranian views of the British and the Russians', in B. Eschment and H. Harder (eds), *Looking at the Coloniser: Cross-Cultural Perceptions in Central Asia and the Caucasus, Bengal and Related Areas* (Wurzburg, 2004); 'Facing a rude and barbarous neighbour: Iranian perceptions of Russia and the Russians from the Safavids to the Qajars', in A. Amanat and F. Vejdani (eds), *Iran Facing Others: Identity Boundaries in a Historical Perspective* (New York, 2012).

5  See C. E. Bosworth, 'Army ii: Islamic, to the Mongol Period', in *Encyclopaedia Iranica*, available at www.iranicaonline.org/articles/army-ii (accessed 8 April 2013); M. Haneda, 'Army iii: Safavid Period', in *Encyclopaedia Iranica*, available at www.iranicaonline.org/articles/army-iii (accessed 8 April 2013); J. R. Perry, 'Army iv: Afsar and Zand Periods', in *Encyclopaedia Iranica*, available at www.iranicaonline.org/articles/army-iv (accessed 8 April 2013).

6  Several contemporary accounts of the army in the late eighteenth to early nineteenth centuries have been left by European observers. See, *inter alia*, Comte de Ferrières-Sauveboeuf, *Mémoires Historiques, Politiques et Géographiques des Voyages du Comte de Ferrières-Sauveboeuf Faits en Turquie, en Perse at en Arabie, depuis 1782 jusqu'en 1789* (Paris, 1790); George Forster, *A Journey from Bengal*

to England (London, 1798); Dr G. A. Olivier, *Voyage dans l'Empire Othoman, l'Égypte et la Perse* (Paris, 1800–7); P. A. L. Gardane, *Journal d'un Voyage en la Turquie d'Asie et la Perse fait en 1807 and 1808* (Paris, 1809); James Morier, *A Journey through Persia, Armenia, and Asia Minor, to Constantinople, in the years 1808 and 1809* (London, 1812); James Morier, *A Second Journey through Persia, Armenia, and Asia Minor, to Constantinople, between the years 1810 and 1816* (London, 1818); Moritz von Kotzebue, *Narrative of a Journey into Persia* (London, 1819); J. M. Tancoigne, *A Narrative of a Journey into Persia and Residence in Tehran* (London, 1820); Pierre Amédée Jaubert, *Voyage en Arménie et en Perse* (Paris, 1821).

7  Morier, *A Journey through Persia*, pp. 242–3.
8  For the *zanburaks* see Manoutchehr M. Eskandari-Qajar, 'Mohammad Shah Qajar's Nezam-e Jadid and Colonel Colombari's Zambourakchis', *Qajar Studies* 5 (2005), pp. 52–79.
9  Muriel Atkin, *Russia and Iran, 1780–1828* (Minneapolis, MN, 1980).
10 For a discussion of the respective military strengths and weaknesses of Iran and Russia see Atkin, *Russia and Iran*, pp. 99–122.
11 See Emineh Pakravan, *Abbas Mirza* (Paris, 1973).
12 For an overview see J. Calmard, 'Les réformes militaires sous les Qajars (1795–1925)', in Y. Richard (ed.), *Entre l'Iran et l'Occident* (Paris, 1989).
13 See Pakravan, *Abbas Mirza*.
14 Morier, *A Second Journey through Persia*, p. 211.
15 Ibid., p. 211.
16 In the Ottoman Empire and Egypt, the reform effort could only begin in earnest after the destruction of reactionary military castes, the Janissaries and the Mamluks respectively. In Iran no such action was necessary as no such forces existed, an illustration not of its relatively advanced condition but rather of its primitive civil and military structures.
17 The presence of such a significant number of Russian deserters in Tabriz may be explained by the extremely harsh conditions prevailing in the Russian armies in the Caucasus. See Atkin, *Russia and Iran*, pp. 106–7.
18 Morier, *A Second Journey through Persia*, pp. 211–12.
19 Fath Ali Shah to Napoleon, letter quoted in Atkin, *Russia and Iran*, p. 126.
20 For the Gardane mission, see Gardane, *Journal d'un voyage en la Turquie d'Asie et la Perse*; Alfred de Gardane, *Mission du Général Gardane en Perse sous le Premier Empire* (Paris, 1865). For Franco–Iranian relations, see Iradj Amini, *Napoleon and Persia* (Richmond, 1999).
21 Tancoigne, *A Narrative of a Journey into Persia*. For the regiment of Russian deserters see Aleksandr Kibovskii, '"Bagaderan" – Russian deserters in the Persian army, 1802–1839', *Tseikhgauz* 5 (1996), translated by Mark Conrad. Available at http://marksrussianmilitaryhistory.info/Persdes2.html (accessed 8 April 2013).
22 Accounts of this mission and of the 1833 British mission may be found in Dennis Wright, *The English Amongst the Persians* (London, 1977).
23 Aleksandr Kibovskii and Vadim Yegorov, 'The Persian regular army of the first half of the nineteenth century', *Tseikhgauz* 5 (1996), translated by Mark Conrad,

pp. 20–5. Available at http://marksrussianmilitaryhistory.info/PERSIA.html (accessed 8 April 2013).

24 Kibovskii and Yegorov, 'The Persian regular army'.

25 Henry C. Rawlinson, *England and Russia in the East: A Series of Papers on the Political and Geographical Condition of Central Asia* (London, 1875), pp. 30–1. See also, for example, John Malcolm, *The History of Persia* (London, 1829).

26 For a general discussion of conscription in the Middle East see Jan Lucassen and Erik J. Zürcher, 'Introduction: conscription and the historical context', in E. J. Zürcher (ed), *Arming the State: Military Conscription in the Middle East and Central Asia* (London and New York, 1999).

27 Some observations about the difficulties encountered by the British officers of this mission may be found in Lt-Col Stuart, *Journal of a Residence in Northern Persia and the Adjacent Provinces of Turkey* (London, 1854).

28 Throughout the nineteenth century the shah possessed a number of European officers of a wide variety of nationalities in his service. See, for example, Mansurah Ittihadiyyah and S. Mir Muhammad Sadigh (eds), with an introduction by Jean Calmard, *Zhinral Saminu dar Khidmat-i Iran-i Qajar va Jang-i Hirat, 1236–1266* (Tehran, 1375); Bo Utas, 'Borowsky, Isidore', *Encyclopaedia Iranica*, available at www.iranicaonline.org/articles/borowsky-isidore (accessed 8 April 2013); Jaqueline Calmard-Compas, 'Ferrier, Joseph Phillipe', *Encyclopaedia Iranica*, available at www.iranicaonline.org/articles/ferrier-joseph-philippe (accessed 8 April 2013).

29 See Count F. E de Sercey, *Une Ambassade Extraordinaire: La Perse en 1839–1840* (Paris, 1928); J. Pichon, *Journal d'une Mission Militaire en Perse (1839–1840)* (Paris, 1900).

30 An account of the French mission may be found in Eugene Flandin, *Voyage en Perse* (Paris, 1851).

31 See Abbas Amanat, *Pivot of the Universe: Nasir al-Din Shah and the Iranian Monarchy, 1851–1896* (London and New York, 1997); Shaul Bakhash, *Iran: Monarchy, Bureaucracy and Reform under the Qajars: 1858–1896* (London, 1978).

32 For the Austrian mission see the account by its medical doctor, Jakob Polak, *Persien, das Land und seiner Bewohner* (Leipzig, 1865) and Borhan Khoschnewis Gawgani, *Die Österreichische Militärmissionen in Persien 1852 bis 1881*. PhD dissertation (Universität Wien, 1978). For Austro–Iranian relations see Helmut Slaby, *Bindenschild und Sonnenlöwe: Die Geschichte der Österreichisch–Iranischen Beziehungen bis zur Gegenwart* (Graz, 1982); Helmut Slaby, 'Austria, diplomatic and commercial relations with Persia', *Encyclopaedia Iranica*, available at www.iranicaonline.org/articles/austria-1 (accessed 8 April 2013).

33 For the circumstances of Amir Kabir's fall, see Amanat, *Pivot of the Universe*, pp. 133–68.

34 For a discussion of the Italian interest in Iranian military reform see A. Piemontese, 'An Italian source for the history of Qāğār Persia: the reports of the General Enrico Andreini (1871–1886)', *East and West* 19 (1969), pp. 147–75; 'L' esercito persiano nel 1874–75: organizzazione e riforma secondo E. Andreini', *Rivista degli Studi Orientali* 49 (1975), pp. 71–117.

35 For the Shah's relationship with Napoleon III see Amanat, *Pivot of the Universe*, pp. 352–3.

36 This policy held sway between 1830 and 1870 and concentrated on consolidation in India and a static defence of the Empire.

37 See Piemontese, 'An Italian source'.

38 Guity Nashat, *The Origins of Modern Reform in Iran, 1870–1880* (Urbana, IL, 1882), pp. 55–71.

39 For the early history of the Iranian Cossack Brigade see F. Kazemzadeh, 'The origin and early development of the Persian Cossack Brigade', *The American Slavic and East European Review* 15/3 (1956), pp. 351–63; Stephanie Cronin, *The Army and the Creation of the Pahlavi State in Iran, 1910–1926* (London, 1997), pp. 54–88; N. K. Ter-Oganov, *Persidskaya Kazachya Brigada, 1878–1921* (Moscow, 2012); Uzi Rabi and Nugzar Ter-Oganov, 'The Russian military mission and the birth of the Persian Cossack Brigade: 1879–1894', *Iranian Studies* 42/3, pp. 445–63. Two of the Brigade's Russian commanders have left memoirs: A. I. Domantovich, 'Vospominanie o prebivanii pervoi russkoi voennoi missii v Persii', *Russkaia Starina* (1908), no. 2, pp. 331–40, no. 3, pp. 575–83, no. 4, pp. 211–216; V. A. Kosogovski, 'Persia v kontse xix veka', *Novii Vostok* (1923) no. 3, pp. 446–69; 'Ocherk razvitia persidskoi kazachei brigady', *Novii Vostok* (1923), no. 4, pp. 390–420. The memoirs of Kosogovski have been translated into Persian, *Khatirat-i Kulunil-i Kasakufski* (trans. Abbas Quli Jali) (Tehran, 1344). A full list of Russian commanders of the Brigade may be found in Amanallah Jahanbani, *Khatirati az Dawran-i Darakhshan-i Riza Shah-i Kabir* (Tehran, 1346), pp. 41–2.

40 Slaby, 'Austria'.

41 Lt-Col H. P. Picot, Report on the Organization of the Persian Army, Durand to Salisbury, 18 January 1900, FO881/7364, p. 86.

42 Picot, Report on the Organization of the Persian Army, p. 105.

43 For a discussion of attitudes towards office-holding prevailing in the Qajar period, see A. Reza Sheikholeslami, *The Structure of Central Authority in Qajar Iran, 1871–1896* (Atlanta, GA, 1997).

44 For a description of the results, see Picot, Report on the Organization of the Persian Army, p. 97.

45 See P. W. Avery and J. B. Simmons, 'Persia on a cross of silver, 1880–1890', in E. Kedourie and S. G. Haim (eds), *Towards A Modern Iran, Studies in Thought, Politics and Society* (London, 1980).

46 Vanessa Martin, *The Qajar Pact: Bargaining, Protest and the State in Nineteenth-Century Persia* (London, 2005), pp. 133–49.

47 A scathing view of the officers of the *nizam* regiments may be found in George N. Curzon, *Persia and the Persian Question* (London, 1892), p. 604. Picot offers a more balanced view: Picot, Report on the Organization of the Persian Army, pp. 87, 113.

48 Picot, Report on the Organization of the Persian Army, p. 118.

49 The Anglo–Russian Convention of 1907 divided Iran into spheres of interest, Russian in the north, British in the south-east, with a neutral zone in the south-west.

50 Ahmad Amirahmadi, *Khatirat-i Nakhustin Sipahbud-i Iran*, 2 vols (Tehran, 1373), Vol. 1, p. 47.

51 For a discussion of Sweden's motivation and role as a supplier of military advisors to foreign governments, including Iran, see Nils Palmstierna, 'Swedish army officers in Africa and Asia', *Revue International d'Histoire Militaire*, no. 26 (1967), pp. 45–73.

52 For the Swedish officers see Markus Ineichen, *Die Schwedischen Offiziere in Persien 1911–1916* (Bern, 2002). Two of the Swedish officers with the force have left memoirs: P. Nyström, *Fem år i Persien som Gendarmofficer* (Stockholm, 1925); Hjalmar Pravitz, *Frau Persien i Stiltje och Storm* (Stockholm, 1918).

53 For the Government Gendarmerie see Cronin, *The Army*; Lt-Col. Parviz Afsar, *Tarikh-i Zhandarmiri-yi Iran* (Qum, 1332); Jahangir Qa'im Maqami, *Tarikh-i Zhandarmiri-yi Iran* (Tehran, 1355).

54 In the early twentieth century oil joined Britain's older commercial and strategic interests in the area.

55 See Hassan Arfa, *Under Five Shahs* (London, 1964), pp. 51–2.

56 See Touraj Atabaki (ed.), *Iran and the First World War: Battleground of the Great Powers* (London and New York, 2006); Oliver Bast (ed.), *La Perse et la Grande Guerre* (Tehran, 2002).

57 See Cronin, *The Army*.

58 The Agreement was named after the prime minister, Muhammad Vali Khan Sipahsalar, with whom it was drawn up.

59 Marling to FO, 21 December 1917, FO371/2988/242011; Consul, Tabriz, to Marling, 20 February 1918, FO371/3264/33414.

60 Major-Gen. Sir Edmund Ironside, *High Road to Command: The Diaries of Major General Sir Edmund Ironside, 1920–22* (ed. Lord Ironside) (London, 1972).

61 British officers were already commanding various small-scale levy corps in different provincial areas. See W. E. R. Dickson, *East Persia: A Backwater of the Great War* (London, 1924); R. E. H. Dyer, *The Raiders of the Sarhad* (London, 1921).

62 For the SPR see Floreeda Safiri, *The South Persia Rifles*; W. J. Olson, *Anglo–Iranian Relations during World War I* (London, 1984), pp. 153–213.

63 Brig.-Gen. Sir Percy Sykes, *A History of Persia*, 2 vols (London, 1921), Vol. 2, p. 472.

64 Safiri, *The South Persia Rifles*, p. 151.

65 On the Anglo–Iranian Military Commission see Kavih Bayat, 'Qarardad-i 1919 va Tashkil-i Qushun-i Muttahid al-Shikl dar Iran', in *Tarikh-i Mu'asir-i Iran, Majmu'ah-i Maqalat* (Tehran, 1369), Vol. 2, pp. 125–40.

66 Report of the Anglo–Persian Military Commission, 1920, FO371/4911/ C197/197/34.

67 See Homa Katouzian, *State and Society in Iran: the Eclipse of the Qajars and the Emergence of the Pahlavis* (London and New York, 2000), Chapters 4, 5.

68 See, for example, the scheme outlined by the prime minister, Ala al-Saltanah, in July 1917. Memorandum from Ala-us-Saltaneh (sic) to Marling, 30 July, 1917, FO371/2981/200656.

69 For wider background on the British and the coup, see especially Stephanie Cronin, 'Britain, the Iranian military and the rise of Reza Khan', in V. Martin, *Anglo–Iranian Relations since 1900* (London, 2005), pp. 99–127.
70 Norman to Curzon, 6 June, 1921, FO371/6406/E9970/2/34.
71 See Tancoigne, *A Narrative of a Journey into Persia*, pp. 245–9.
72 This was with the exception of a small French mission to act as instructors at the cadet and staff colleges.
73 After 1941 US missions came fast and furious. They included: GENMISH/ Gendarmerie Military Mission, 1943; US Army Missions of Generals Wheeler, Greely and Ridley, 1943; Persian Gulf Service Command of General Donald H. Connolly, 1943; ARMISH/US Army Military Mission, 1947; MAAG/Military Assistance Advisory Group, 1950; ARMISH/MAAG consolidation 1958–62; extraterritorial legal status to US military advisors, 1962–4; TAFT/Technical Assistance Field Teams, 1973–8. For the missions see Thomas M. Ricks, 'US military missions to Iran, 1943–1978: the political economy of military assistance', *Iranian Studies* 12/3–4 (1979), pp. 163–93.

## Chapter 3: Building and Rebuilding Afghanistan's Army

1 The Taliban (literally 'religious students') were a new movement of largely Pashtun rural and refugee origin which, encouraged by Pakistan, emerged in 1994, capturing control first of Kandahar and then, in 1996, of Kabul. Their rule was based on a combination of a strict Hanafi interpretation of Islam, Pashtun nationalism, and the tribal code of conduct known as *Pashtunwali*. The Taliban regime, which remained in power until late 2001, gave sanctuary to Usama bin Laden and al-Qaida, Usama bin Laden and his followers from across the Muslim world having provided military and financial support for the war against the pro-Soviet People's Democratic Party of Afghanistan (PDPA) during the 1980s. It was from this sanctuary that bin Laden planned the attacks on targets in the US of 11 September 2001.
2 The new urgency of this task has recently produced a flurry of literature. See, for example, Anthony H. Cordesman, Adam Mausner and David Kasten (eds), *Afghan National Security Forces: Shaping the Path to Victory* (Washington D.C., 2009); Antonio Giustozzi, 'Auxiliary force or national army? Afghanistan's "ANA" and the counter-insurgency effort, 2002–2006', in *Small Wars and Insurgencies* 18/1 (2007), pp. 45–67; 'The Afghan National Army', *The RUSI Journal* 154/6 (2009), pp. 36–42; Obaid Younossi *et al.*, *The Long March: Building an Afghan Army* (Santa Monica, CA, 2009); Ali A. Jalali, 'Afghanistan: regaining momentum', *Parameters* (Winter 2007–8): pp. 5–19; 'The future of security institutions', in J. A. Thier (ed.), *The Future of Afghanistan* (Washington D.C., 2009), pp. 23–33; Robert Johnson, *The Afghan Way of War: How and Why They Fight* (London, 2011).
3 For a discussion of warlordism see Antonio Giustozzi, 'The debate on warlordism: the importance of military legitimacy', Crisis States Programme Discussion Paper, no. 13 (2005).

4 There is a considerable literature on the meaning of the designation 'tribal'. It is often incorrectly taken to imply a connection to pastoral nomadism. In Afghanistan, by the 1970s, only about 1 million, out of a population of around 12 million, were nomadic. Another 1 million were urban but the vast majority were settled peasants, tribal and non-tribal. At its simplest, tribes define themselves through descent from a common ancestor enshrined in an imaginary genealogy. This provides the members of a tribe with a strong sense of communal solidarity. This solidarity is reinforced by possession of common cultural mores, dress, customs and so on, most perfectly exemplified by the Pashtun code of conduct, *Pashtunwali*. Non-tribal rural communities, however, also owed their primary loyalty to their own kin or village, sometimes to their religious sect, and, recently and partially, sometimes to a notion of a broader ethnic group. In the context of state-building, the key features of both tribal and non-tribal rural communities are their group solidarity and their collective behaviour; their possession of their own leaderships; and their preference for political, social and cultural autonomy and a condition of equilibrium between different rural groups and between themselves and the state based on managed tension. Tribal and ethnic identity has proved divisive rather than unifying on a sub-national level. The potentially infinite proliferation of tribes and sub-tribes has historically turned each ethnic group into a bundle of warring sub-divisions. For some discussion of terminology see Richard Tapper (ed.), *The Conflict of Tribe and State in Iran and Afghanistan* (London, 1983), pp. 1–82. See also Antonio Giustozzi and Noor Ullah, '"Tribes" and Warlords in Southern Afghanistan, 1980–2005', Crisis States Programme Working Paper, no. 7 (2006).

5 Respectively, a low-ranking Muslim cleric, a religious figure claiming descent from the Prophet, and an elder in a Sufi brotherhood.

6 For a recent discussion of Afghan society see Thomas Barfield, *Afghanistan: A Cultural and Political History* (Princeton, NJ, 2010), pp. 17–65.

7 Antonio Giustozzi, *Empires of Mud* (London, 2009); Michael Bhatia and Mark Sedra, *Afghanistan, Arms and Conflict* (London, 2008).

8 For the case of Iran, see Stephanie Cronin, *Tribal Politics in Iran: Rural Conflict and the New State, 1921–1941* (London, 2006).

9 The Pashtuns are divided into lineages which are gathered into major descent groups. The two most important Pashtun descent groups are the Durrani and the Ghilzai. The Durrani are sub-divided into seven sub-tribes, including the two warring royal lineages of the Sadozai Popalzai and the Barakzai Muhammadzai. The Sadozai and Barakzai provided Afghanistan's rulers from Ahmad Shah to the first president, Muhammad Daud. Hamid Karzai of the Durrani Sadozai resumed this tradition after the interruption of the PDPA period.

10 For a biographical portrait, see Mohan Lal, *Life of the Amir Dost Mohammed Khan of Kabul* (facsimile of 1846 edition, Karachi, 1979).

11 B. D. Hopkins, *The Making of Modern Afghanistan* (New York, 2008), pp. 90–8.

12 The principle of royal primogeniture was only gradually accepted in the late nineteenth to early twentieth centuries. The absence of any recognized basis for succession tended to lead to violent conflict upon the death of a ruler.

13 Hopkins, *The Making of Modern Afghanistan*, p. 70; Jos J. L. Gommans, *The Rise of the Indo-Afghan Empire* (Leiden, 1995), pp. 135–43; 'Indian warfare and Afghan innovation during the eighteenth century', in Jos J. L. Gommans and Dirk. H. A. Kolff (eds), *Warfare and Weaponry in South Asia, 1000–1800* (New Delhi and Oxford, 2003), pp. 365–86.

14 M. E. Yapp, 'The modernization of Middle Eastern armies in the nineteenth century: a comparative view', in V. J. Parry and M. E. Yapp (eds), *War, Technology and Society in the Middle East* (London, 1975), pp. 330–66.

15 Vartan Gregorian, *The Emergence of Modern Afghanistan* (Stanford, 1969), pp. 75–6. For the phenomenon of European adventurers and renegades see Charles Grey, *European Adventurers of Northern India, 1785–1849* (printed by the Superintendent, Government Printing, Punjab, Lahore, 1929); Josiah Harlan, *A Memoir of India and Afghanistan* (Philadelphia, 1842).

16 Jean-Marie Lafont, *Fauj-i-Khas: Maharaja Ranjit Singh and his French Officers* (Amritsar, 2002); Seema Alavi, *The Sepoys and the Company: Tradition and Transition in North India, 1770–1830* (Delhi, 1995).

17 Geoffrey Parker, *The Military Revolution: Military Innovation and the Rise of the West* (Cambridge, 1988); Charles Tilly, *Coercion, Capital, and European States, AD 990–1992* (Cambridge, MA, 1992).

18 Hopkins, *The Making of Modern Afghanistan*, p. 71.

19 M. E. Yapp, *Strategies of British India: Britain, Iran and Afghanistan, 1798–1850* (Oxford, 1980), p. 307.

20 Yapp, *Strategies of British India*, pp. 309–50.

21 M. E. Yapp, 'Disturbances in Eastern Afghanistan, 1839–42', *Bulletin of the School of Oriental and African Studies* 25/1,3 (1962), pp. 499–523; 'Disturbances in Western Afghanistan, 1839–41', *Bulletin of the School of Oriental and African Studies* 26/2 (1963), pp. 288–313; 'The Revolutions of 1841–2 in Afghanistan', *Bulletin of the School of Oriental and African Studies* 27/2 (1964), pp. 333–81.

22 Christine Noelle-Karimi, *State and Tribe in Nineteenth-Century Afghanistan* (Richmond, 1997), pp. 258–67; Zalmay A. Gulzad, *External Influences and the Development of the Afghan State in the Nineteenth Century* (New York, 1994), pp. 69–73.

23 In 1879 Britain imposed the Treaty of Gandamak on Afghanistan, through which British India assumed control of Afghan fiscal, defence and foreign policies. From then until 1919 British India provided an annual subsidy in cash and weapons in order to enable the ruler to maintain domestic and therefore regional security.

24 Travelogues often provide descriptions of the regular troops of this period. See, for example, Peter S. Lumsden and George R. Elsmie, *Lumsden of the Guides* (London, 1899), pp. 162–8.

25 Noelle, *State and Tribe*, p. 262.

26 Martin Ewans, *Conflict in Afghanistan: Studies in Asymmetric Warfare* (London and New York, 2005), pp. 81–2. Ewans suggests that even here it was the irregulars who were decisive.

27 Lt. W. R. Robertson, Note on the Afghan Army, 1993, WO106/6298.

28 The British recognized Abd al-Rahman as amir as the lesser of many evils in an attempt to bring the second Anglo–Afghan war to a tolerable conclusion. British subsidies, amounting to as much as 28.5 million rupees during his reign, were intended to keep him both in power and under control.

29 For Abd al-Rahman's views on the army see Mir Munshi Sultan Mahomed Khan (ed.), *The Life of Abdur Rahman, Amir of Afghanistan* (Karachi, 1980), pp. 190–7.

30 Robertson, Note on the Afghan Army.

31 Hasan Kawun Kakar, *Government and Society in Afghanistan: The Reign of Amir 'Abd al-Rahman Khan* (Austin, TX, and London, 1979), p. 99.

32 Robertson, Note on the Afghan Army.

33 Ibid.

34 Kakar, *Government and Society in Afghanistan*, p. 98.

35 Ibid., p. 113. Nationalist historiography, seeking to burnish the pedigree of the Afghan state, has conferred on Abd al-Rahman the soubriquet of 'the Iron Amir'. His achievements in administrative and political unification appear considerable, perhaps best illustrated by the novelty of his son's uncontested succession. Yet their fragility is also shown by the failure of his successor, Habibullah, to build effectively on his father's legacy. In fact, under Abd al-Rahman little actual modernization took place and much of his success may be attributed to an increasing regional stabilization, including the drawing of definitive frontiers, under imperial domination, and British India's unwillingness to tolerate discord on its borders, rather than to an authentic indigenous state-building dynamic.

36 M. A. Babakhodjayev, 'Afghanistan's armed forces and Amir Abdur Rahman's military reform,' *Afghanistan* 3 (Fall 1970), pp. 8–20; Robertson, Note on the Afghan Army.

37 Robertson, Note on the Afghan Army; Gregorian, *The Emergence of Modern Afghanistan*, p. 141.

38 See, for example, the remarks of Amir Abd al-Rahman, in Mir Munshi Sultan Mahomed Khan (ed.) *The Life of Abdur Rahman*, p. 196.

39 Gregorian, *The Emergence of Modern Afghanistan*, p. 184.

40 The ideas of these intellectuals, and especially their pro-Ottoman views, may be traced in their newspaper, *Siraj al-Akhbar*. A run of this newspaper may be found in the International Institute of Social History, Amsterdam.

41 An Appreciation of the Royal Afghan Army at the end of 1950, Military Attaché, Kabul, 1 January 1951, FO371/92081.

42 Martin Ewans, *Conflict in Afghanistan*, pp. 89–95.

43 For Amanullah's reform programme see Gregorian, *The Emergence of Modern Afghanistan*, pp. 239–54; Leon B. Poullada, *Reform and Rebellion in Afghanistan, 1919–1929* (London and Ithaca, 1973); Roland Wild, *Amanullah: ex-King of Afghanistan* (London, 1932). See also Senzil K. Nawid, *Religious Response to Social Change in Afghanistan, 1919–29* (Costa Mesa, 1999).

44 Poullada, *Reform and Rebellion*, p. 112.

45 The British had already adopted this approach during the third Anglo–Afghan war. Amanullah followed their example in the 1920s, while aerial

bombardment was a notorious feature of Soviet tactics in the 1980s, and extensively used by NATO troops after 2001. In all cases, it has tended to be counterproductive.

46 Poullada, *Reform and Rebellion,* p. 116. For Nadir Khan and his rivalry with Amanullah see Amin Saikal, *Modern Afghanistan: A History of Struggle and Survival* (London, 2004), pp. 58–104.

47 Poullada, *Reform and Rebellion*, pp. 117–18.

48 Sirdar Ikbal Ali Shah, *The Tragedy of Amanullah* (London, 1933), pp. 182–4.

49 Poullada, *Reform and Rebellion,* pp. 144–5.

50 For the reaction in Iran to the introduction of a similar type of conscription by Riza Shah see Stephanie Cronin, 'Conscription and popular resistance in Iran, 1925–1941', *International Review of Social History* 43/3 (1998), pp. 451–71.

51 Sirdar Ikbal Ali Shah, *The Tragedy of Amanullah,* p. 184.

52 Poullada, *Reform and Rebellion*, pp. 160–95.

53 It was estimated that the tribes had looted around half a million rifles and light machine-guns from garrisons throughout the country during the 1929 rebellion. The Armed Forces of Afghanistan, Annual Appreciation, Military Attaché, Kabul, January 1953, FO371/106665.

54 Order of Battle of Royal Afghan Army, WO33/2392.

55 Half Yearly Report on the Afghan Army for the period ending 15th September 1943, Military Attaché, Kabul, FO371/39953/E212/212/97.

56 Ibid.

57 An Appreciation of the Royal Afghan Army at the end of 1950, Military Attaché, Kabul, 1 January 1951, FO371/92081; The Armed Forces of Afghanistan, Annual Appreciation, Military Attaché, Kabul, January 1953, FO371/106665.

58 An Appreciation of the Royal Afghan Army at the end of 1950, Military Attaché, Kabul, 1 January, 1951, FO371/92081.

59 Half Yearly Report on the Afghan Army for the period ending 15th September 1943, Military Attaché, Kabul, FO371/39953/E212/212/97.

60 Ibid. The similarities of these views with those of army officers in Iran is striking. See Stephanie Cronin, *The Army and the Creation of the Pahalavi State in Iran, 1910–1926* (London, 1997), pp. 210–11, 217–18.

61 Half Yearly Report on the Afghan Army for the period ending 15th September 1943, Military Attaché, Kabul, FO371/39953/E212/212/97.

62 An indication of the tribal backgrounds of senior officers may be found in the brief biographies compiled by the British Military Attaché. See, for example, Half Yearly Report on the Afghan Army, no. 3, for the period 16th September 1943 to 15th March 1944, Military Attaché, Kabul, FO371/39953/E3471/212/97; Half Yearly Report on the Afghan Army, no. 3, for the period 16th March to 15th September 1944, Military Attaché, Kabul, FO371/39953/E7311/212/97.

63 Half Yearly Report on the Afghan Army for the period ending 15th September 1943, Military Attaché, Kabul, FO371/39953/E212/212/97.

64 Half Yearly Report on the Afghan Army, no. 3, for the period 16th March to 15th September 1944, Military Attaché, Kabul, FO371/39953/E7311/212/97.

65 Turkish Military Mission and the Views of some Turkish Officers on the Military College, Kabul, and the Afghan Army, Military Attaché, Kabul, 26th March 1943, FO371/34937/E3369/3369/97.

66 Ibid.

67 Half Yearly Report on the Afghan Army, no. 8, for the period 16th September 1946 to 15th March 1947, Military Attaché, Kabul, FO371/61466/E3129/93/97.

68 Half Yearly Report on the Afghan Army, no. 3, for the period 16th September 1943 to 15th March 1944, Military Attaché, Kabul, FO371/39953/E3471/212/97.

69 Half Yearly Report on the Afghan Army for the period ending 15th September 1943, Military Attaché, Kabul, FO371/39953/E212/212/97.

70 Half Yearly Report on the Afghan Army, no. 3, for the period 16th March to 15th September 1944, Military Attaché, Kabul, FO371/39953/E7311/212/97; Half Yearly Report on the Afghan Army, no. 8, for the period 16th September 1946 to 15th March 1947, Military Attaché, Kabul, FO371/61466/E3129/93/97.

71 For such attitudes see, for example, Half Yearly Report on the Afghan Army, no. 3, for the period 16th March to 15th September 1944, Military Attaché, Kabul, FO371/39953/E7311/212/97.

72 In 1893 a British commission imposed on Afghanistan its new and fixed eastern and southern frontiers with British India (later Pakistan). The resulting line of demarcation became known as the Durand Line after the head of the commission, Sir Mortimer Durand. Since the Durand Line bisected the Pashtun areas, leaving the tribal populations split between two countries, it was never formally accepted by Afghanistan. After 1947 Afghanistan's rejection of these borders developed into its advocacy of the creation of a new entity, Pashtunistan, which would unite the Pashtun populations. This naturally brought it into direct conflict with Pakistan which was determined to resist any loss of territory. The existence of tribal kinship networks straddling the Afghanistan–Pakistan border has been a key factor in recent Afghan politics. It facilitated the training, supply and financing of the mujahidin in the 1980s and drew Pakistan deeply into the conflict. It enabled Pakistan to encourage the Taliban, and in recent years has caused the anti-Western insurgency to spread into the Pakistani Federally Administered Tribal Agencies (FATA) and further into Pakistan itself.

73 British Embassy, Kabul, to FO, 21 October, 1950, FO371/83077.

74 Half Yearly Report on the Afghan Army, no. 8, for the period 16th September 1946 to 15th March 1947, Military Attaché, Kabul, FO371/61466/E3129/93/97.

75 Ibid.

76 Half Yearly Report on the Afghan Army, no. 3, for the period 16th March to 15th September 1944, Military Attaché, Kabul, FO371/39953/E7311/212/97.

77 The Armed Forces of Afghanistan, Annual Appreciation, Military Attaché, Kabul, January 1953, FO371/106665.

78 Ibid.

79 See Saikal, *Modern Afghanistan,* pp. 117–32.

80 The Armed Forces of Afghanistan, Annual Review, Military Attaché, Kabul, February 1958, FO371/135719.

81 The Communist Threat in Afghanistan, FO371/170229/1032/63.

82 Ibid.

83 Ibid.

84 See Gilles Dorronsoro, *Revolution Unending, Afghanistan: 1979 to the Present* (London, 2000), pp. 65–76. The new educational institutions also incubated the embryonic Islamist movement. See Olivier Roy, *Islam and Resistance in Afghanistan* (Cambridge, 1986).

85 For the frustrations experienced by the products of the new educational system, see Barnett R. Rubin, *The Fragmentation of Afghanistan* (New Haven, CT, 1995), p. 77.

86 Anthony Arnold, *Afghanistan's Two-Party Communism: Parcham and Khalq* (Stanford, CA, 1983), pp. 30–1, 47–9.

87 For the Musahiban state's adoption of a policy of 'encapsulation' towards the tribal khans, see Rubin, *The Fragmentation of Afghanistan*, p. 62.

88 Dilip Mukerjee, 'Afghanistan under Daud: relations with neighboring states', *Asian Survey* 15/4 (1975), pp. 301–12.

89 Arnold, *Afghanistan's Two-Party Communism*, pp. 47–9.

90 Saikal, *Modern Afghanistan*, pp. 177–82.

91 The disparate array of tribal and militia opponents of the PDPA became known internationally as the mujahidin, literally 'holy warriors', a collective designation which implied a much greater degree of unity and coherence than they actually possessed.

92 Fred Halliday, 'War and revolution in Afghanistan', *New Left Review* I/119 (January–February 1980), pp. 20–41; Roy, *Islam and Resistance*, pp. 84–97.

93 For some discussion of the multi-faceted nature of these outbreaks, see M. N. Shahrani and R. Canfield, *Revolutions and Rebellions in Afghanistan* (Berkeley, CA, 1984).

94 Ewans, *Conflict in Afghanistan*, p. 134.

95 The military aspects of the conflict between the PDPA and its Soviet backers and the mujahidin have generated a substantial literature. The Afghan army itself, however, has received little attention. The most substantial account is that by Antonio Giustozzi, *War, Politics and Society in Afghanistan, 1978–1992* (Washington D.C., 1999). An indication of the Soviet/Russian view of the Afghan army may be found in The Russian General Staff, *The Soviet–Afghan War: How a Superpower Fought and Lost* (trans. and ed. Lester W. Grau and Michael A. Gress) (Lawrence, KS, 2002), pp. 48–52.

96 Giustozzi, *War, Politics and Society in Afghanistan*, p. 86.

97 Ibid., p. 157.

98 Grau and Gress, *The Soviet–Afghan War*, p. 51.

99 Giustozzi, *War, Politics and Society in Afghanistan*, pp. 84–5.

100 Grau and Gress, *The Soviet–Afghan War*, p. 50.

101 Giustozzi, *War, Politics and Society in Afghanistan*, pp. 117–18.

102 See Saikal, *Modern Afghanistan*, p. 113.

103 Anwar-ul-Haq Ahady, 'The decline of the Pashtuns in Afghanistan', *Asian Survey* 35/7 (1995), pp. 621–34; Ludwig W. Adamec, *Dictionary of Afghan Wars, Revolutions and Insurgencies* (Lanham, MD, 1996), p. 306.

104  Giustozzi, *War, Politics and Society in Afghanistan*, p. 111.
105  For the deterioration in the international climate see Halliday, 'War and revolution'.
106  Roy, *Islam and Resistance*, pp. 74–6.
107  See Giustozzi, *War, Politics and Society in Afghanistan*, for the best account of the rise of the militias.
108  See Astri Suhrke, 'Afghanistan: retribalization of the war', *Journal of Peace Research* 27/3 (1990), pp. 241–6.
109  Najibullah took sanctuary in the United Nations compound in Kabul. In 1996, when the Taliban captured Kabul, he was dragged from the compound and publicly executed.
110  For a discussion of the strategies adopted by army personnel after 1992 see Antonio Giustozzi, 'The demodernisation of an army: Northern Afghanistan, 1992–2001', *Small Wars and Insurgencies* 15/1 (2004), pp. 1–18.
111  See Giustozzi, *War, Politics and Society in Afghanistan; Empires of Mud*; Bhatia and Sedra, *Afghanistan, Arms and Conflict*.
112  Ahmed Rashid, *Taliban: The Story of the Afghan Warlords* (London, 2001), pp. 98–100. Although they did not adopt the model of a regular army, the Taliban possessed undoubted military capacity, often provided by ex-Khalqi Pashtun soldiers. See Anthony Davis, 'How the Taliban became a military force', in W. Maley (ed.) *Fundamentalism Reborn?* (London, 1998).
113  Ahmad Shah Masud had been assassinated two days before the 9/11 attacks by suspected al-Qaida agents.
114  Bhatia and Sedra, *Afghanistan, Arms and Conflict*.
115  For an early discussion of some of the likely difficulties, see Ali A. Jalali, 'Rebuilding Afghanistan's National Army', *Parameters* (Autumn 2002), pp. 72–86.
116  Cyrus Hodes and Mark Sedra, *The Search for Security in Post-Taliban Afghanistan* (Abingdon and London, 2007), p. 53; Antonio Giustozzi, 'The Afghan National Army', pp. 36–42.
117  'Progress toward Security and Stability in Afghanistan', January 2009, Report to Congress, p. 36. www.defense.gov/pubs/OCTOBER_1230_FINAL.pdf.
118  Hodes and Sedra, *The Search for Security*, p. 59; 'Progress toward Security and Stability in Afghanistan', January 2009, Report to Congress, p. 40.
119  Cordesman, Mausner, Kasten (eds), *Afghan National Security Forces: Shaping the Path to Victory*, p. 34.
120  Giustozzi, 'The Afghan National Army', p. 37; Younossi *et al.*, *The Long March*, p. 17.
121  Giustozzi, 'The Afghan National Army', p. 37.
122  Younossi *et al.*, *The Long March*, p. 18.
123  'Progress toward Security and Stability in Afghanistan', January 2009, Report to Congress, p. 39.
124  Younossi *et al.*, *The Long March*, p. 26.
125  Ibid., p. 21.
126  See, for example, Matthew Taylor and Richard Norton-Taylor, 'Renegade Afghan kills three British soldiers', *Guardian*, 14 July 2010; Christopher Bodeen, 'Afghan police recruit kills 2 Spanish officers', *Associated Press*, 25 August 2010.

127 Ben Bryant, 'The 24 British soldiers killed by rogue Afghan forces in "green on blue" attacks', *Daily Telegraph*, 8 January 2012. Available at www.telegraph.co.uk/news/worldnews/asia/afghanistan/9550916/The-24-British-soldiers-killed-by-rogue-Afghan-forces-in-green-on-blue-attacks.html (accessed 8 April 2013).

128 Giustozzi, 'The Afghan National Army', pp. 38–40.

129 For a description of the office corps see Jeff Haynes, 'Reforming the Afghan National Army', Foreign Policy Research Institute, 27 November 2009. Available at www.fpri.org/enotes/200911.haynes.reformingafghannationalarmy.html (accessed 8 April 2013).

130 Giustozzi, 'The Afghan National Army', p. 37.

131 Ibid., p. 39. For a discussion of the role of former officers of the regular army, see Mark Sedra (ed.) *Confronting Afghanistan's Security Dilemma* (Bonn, 2009), p. 30.

132 Younossi *et al.*, *The Long March*, p. 52.

133 Kenneth Katzman, 'Afghanistan: Post-Taliban Governance, Security and US Policy, Congressional Research Service Report for Congress', 20 July 2009, p. 43.

134 'Progress toward Security and Stability in Afghanistan', June 2009, Report to Congress, p. 28.

135 Kenneth Katzman, 'Afghanistan: Post-Taliban Governance, Security and US Policy, Congressional Research Service Report for Congress', 20 July 2009, p. 40.

136 Barnett R. Rubin, 'The transformation of the Afghan State', in J. Alexander Thier (ed.), *The Future of Afghanistan* (Washington, 2009), p. 18. The scale of the task which NATO has undertaken may be shown by a comparison with the military of previous Afghan governments. The army down to 1979 numbered less than 100,000 and even the PDPA army stabilized at around the same figure, approximately 90,000. Although comparisons of cost are difficult, there can be no doubt that the financial resources currently being absorbed by the ANA are unprecedented.

137 (US) Government Accountability Office, 'Afghanistan Security', 18 June 2008, p. 18. US concerns may be traced in detail in the reports of the (US) Government Accountability Office.

138 Jake Sherman and Victoria DiDomenico, *The Public Cost of Private Security in Afghanistan* (New York, 2009).

139 Julian Borger, 'Karzai poised to unveil "land, work and pensions" plan to woo Taliban', *Guardian*, 20 January 2010.

140 Jon Boone, 'Sash separates friend and foe in Afghanistan', *Guardian*, 9 March 2010; Jon Boone, 'US pours millions into anti-Taliban militias', *Guardian*, 23 November 2009.

141 For the debates surrounding this initiative see Cordesman, Mausner, Kasten (eds), *Afghan National Security Forces: Shaping the Path to Victory*, xxi–xxiv. See also Ali A. Jalali, 'Winning in Afghanistan', *Parameters* (Spring 2009), pp. 5–21.

142 Cronin, *Tribal Politics in Iran*.

143 The historiography of state-building in Iran and Afghanistan has been characterized by a marked teleological bias. See Conclusion, pp. 251–2.

144 The Qajar dynasty ruled Iran from the late eighteenth century to 1925.

145 Cronin, *Tribal Politics in Iran*.

146 See above, Chapter 2.

147 See above, Chapter 2. See also Cronin, *The Army*; Steven R. Ward, *Immortal: A Military History of Iran and its Armed Forces* (Washington D.C., 2009).

148 Fred Halliday, *Threat from the East? Soviet Policy from Afghanistan and Iran to the Horn of Africa* (London, 1982).

149 A curious symptom of the Karzai government's ambiguous stance towards its own society may be seen in the faux-traditional attire in which Karzai habitually presents himself to an international audience, attire which owes more to European Orientalism than to Afghan sartorial customs.

## Chapter 4: The Iranian Army under Monarchy and Republic

1 Biographical information about many of the senior officers who served the Pahlavi shahs may be found in Stephanie Cronin, *The Army and the Creation of the Pahlavi State in Iran, 1921–1926* (London, 1997); Abbas Milani, *Eminent Persians: the Men and Women who made Modern Iran*, 2 vols (New York, 2008), Vol. 1.

2 US Embassy, Tehran, A Political Analysis of the Iranian Army, 12 February, 1957, US National Archives (obtained by Mark Gasiorowski under the Freedom of Information Act).

3 Stephanie Cronin, 'Britain, the Iranian military and the rise of Reza Khan', in Vanessa Martin (ed.) *Anglo–Iranian Relations since 1800* (Abingdon, 2005), pp. 99–127.

4 For biographical details of Razmara, Zahidi and Bakhtiyar, see Milani, *Eminent Persians*, pp. 483–9, 430–7, 495–505.

5 Batatu, *The Old Social Classes and the Revolutionary Movements of Iraq.*

6 Only with the massive expansion of the officer corps in the 1970s did religious sentiment begin to appear in the officer corps.

7 *Sazman-i Ittila'at-i va Amniyat-i Kishvar* (National Intelligence and Security Organization). For a description of SAVAK's extensive network of activities see Fred Halliday, *Iran: Dictatorship and Development* (Harmondsworth, 1979), pp. 78–90.

8 Riza Khan became Shah in December 1925 when a constituent assembly voted in favour of a change of dynasty. The designation Riza Khan or Riza Shah has been employed in this text according to the chronological context.

9 The Cossack Brigade had been expanded to a Division under the Sipahsalar Agreement of 1916. See Olson, *Anglo–Iranian Relations*; Safiri, *The South Persia Rifles.*

10 Cronin, *The Army*, p. 110.

11 See above, Chapter 2.

12 A translation of the Bill as originally presented to the Majlis in April 1923 may be found in Loraine to Curzon, 28 April 1923, FO371/9021/E5823/71/34.

13 For a full account of these episodes see Stephanie Cronin, *Soldiers, Shahs and Subalterns in Iran: Opposition, Protest and Revolt, 1921–1941* (Basingstoke, 2010), Chaper 5; Baqir Aqalli, *Riza Shah va Qushun-i Muttahid al-Shakl, 1300–1320*

(Tehran, 1377), pp. 248–56; Husayn Makki, *Tarikh-i Bist Salah-i Iran*, 8 vols (Tehran, 1323), Vol. 4, pp. 415–39.

14 John Foran, *Fragile Resistance: Social Transformation in Iran from 1500 to the Revolution* (Boulder, CO, 1993), p. 221.

15 Annual Report, 1931, Hoare to Simon, 12 June 1932, FO371/16077/E3354/3354/34.

16 See, for example, Annual Report, 1936, Seymour to Eden, 30 January 1937, FO371/20836/E1435/1435/34.

17 A. C. Millspaugh, *The American Task in Persia* (New York, 1925), p. 196. See also: Imperial Persian Government, *The Financial and Economic Situation of Persia 1926* (New York, 1926). In 1922 Dr Arthur Chester Millspaugh (1883–1955), formerly an advisor at the US State Department's Office of Foreign Trade, was invited to Iran to reorganize the Finance Ministry. He remained until 1927 when obliged to leave following disagreements with Riza Shah over the army budget. He returned in 1942, at the head of another financial mission, but his mission was again terminated in 1945.

18 For a discussion of the complications of the War Office budget in the 1930s see Homa Katouzian, *The Political Economy of Modern Iran: Despotism and Pseudo-Modernism, 1926–1979* (London, 1981), p. 131. Breakdowns of military expenditure may be found in the annual reports prepared by the British minister in Tehran, see footnote following.

19 See, for example, Annual Report, 1933, Hoare to Simon, 24 February 1934, FO371/17909/E1620/1620/34; Annual Report, 1934, Knatchbull-Hugessen to Simon, 5 February 1935, FO371/18995/E1606/1606/34; Annual Report, 1935, Knatchbull-Hugessen to Eden, 28 January 1936, FO371/20052/E1147/1147/34; Annual Report, 1936, Seymour to Eden, 30 January 1937, FO371/20836/ E1435/1435/34; Annual Report, 1938, Seymour to Halifax, 3 March 1939, FO371/23264/E2586/2586/34; Intelligence Summary no. 5, 11 March 1939, FO371/23261/E2589/216/34.

20 For the air force see *Tarikh-i Nirui-yi Hava'i-yi Shahanshahi* (Tehran, 2535).

21 Annual Report, 1935, Knatchbull-Hugessen to Eden, 28 January 1936, FO371/ 20052/E1147/1147/34.

22 Cronin, *The Army*, pp. 122–4.

23 Loraine to FO, 4 September 1922, FO371/9024/E10179/457/34; Ahmad Amirahmadi, *Khatirat-i Nakhustin Sipahbud-i Iran*, 2 vols (Tehran, 1373), Vol. 1, p. 231.

24 Annual Report, 1928, Clive to Henderson, 14 July 1929, FO371/13799/E3676/34.

25 Annual Report, 1930, Clive to Henderson, 22 May 1931, FO371/15356/E3067/ 3067/34.

26 Bullard to Halifax, 6 February 1940, FO371/24582/E829/621/34.

27 Intelligence Summary nos. 18, 19, 20, 24 August–24 September 1941, FO371/ 27188/E6869/268/34.

28 Consul, Kermanshah, to Tehran, 1 September 1941, FO371/27153/E6300/42/34.

29 For a detailed account of this process see Cronin, *The Army*, pp. 89–107.

30 For a full account of the Pasyan episode see Cronin, *Soldiers, Shahs and Subalterns*, Chapter 2; Kavih Bayat, *Inqilab-i Khurasan, Majmu'ah-i Asnad va Madarik 1300 shamsi* (Tehran, 1370).

31  For the Lahuti episode, see Cronin, *Soldiers, Shahs and Subalterns*, pp. 101–27; Kavih Bayat, *Kudita-yi Lahuti, Tabriz, Bahman 1300* (Tehran, 1376).

32  Intelligence Summary no. 5, 4 February 1922, FO371/7826/E3815/285/34.

33  See Cronin, *The Army*, pp. 153–7.

34  For a description of this position among civilian liberals, see Muhammad Taqi Bahar, Malik al-Shu'ara', *Tarikh-i Mukhtasar-i Ahzab-i Siyasi-yi Iran*, 2 vols (Tehran 1323), Vol. 2, p. 41.

35  See Cronin, *The Army*, pp. 166–4; Aqalli, *Riza Shah va Qushun-i Muttahid al-Shakl*, pp. 272–84.

36  Cronin, *The Army*, pp. 174–5; Aqalli, *Riza Shah va Qushun-i Muttahid al-Shakl*, pp. 230–4. References to this episode may be found in the memoirs of Amirahmadi, *Khatirat*, Vol. 1, pp. 263, 267, and Sartip-i Haydar Quli Bayglari, *Khatirat-i Yak Sarbaz* (Tehran, 1350), pp. 40–7. See also Manshur Garakani, *Siyasat-i Dawlat-i Shuravi dar Iran* (Tehran, 1326), pp. 250–3. See also Amirahmadi, *Khatirat*, Vol. 1, p. 267, for an account of the field court-martial set up to deal with the mutineers.

37  Colonel Yusuf Khan was a cousin of Hasan Arfa, later one of Muhammad Riza Shah's senior generals.

38  Cronin, *The Army*, pp. 176–9; Kavih Bayat, *Qiyam-i Nafir-i Jam: Shurish-i Lahak Khan Salar-i Jang* (Tehran, 1375); Aqalli, *Riza Shah va Qushun-i Muttahid al-Shakl*, pp. 234–48. The British Military Attaché provided a full contemporary analysis of the military aspects of this rising and the mutiny at Salmas, see Fraser to Nicolson, 15 July, 1926, FO371/11488/E4553/195/34. There are also long reports concerning both mutinies in Intelligence Summary no. 14, 10 July 1926, FO371/11484/E4550/95/34. The British Consul-General in Mashhad provided his account in Meshed Diary no. 7, July 1926, FO371/1149/E6631/2142/34, and the Minister in Tehran in Annual Report, 1926, Clive to Chamberlain, 26 January 1927, FO371/12296/E870/870/34.

39  See Cronin, *Soldiers, Shahs and Subalterns*, Chapter 7; Najafquli Pasyan, *Vaqi'ah-i I'dam-i Jahansuz* (Tehran, 1370); Jalal Abduh, *Chihil Sal dar Sahnah-i Qazayi, Siyasi, Diplumasi-yi Iran va Jahan*, 2 vols (Tehran, 1368).

40  The British Military Attaché allowed himself the opinion that the army was 'pampered to a degree which should make its loyalty a matter of no doubt'. See Report on the Present Relations between the Shah and his Army and their Bearing on the Stability of the Pahlavi Regime, Percy C. R. Dodd, MA, 3 December 1930, Parr to Henderson, 3 December 1930, FO371/14542/E6707/469/34.

41  Pasyan, *Vaqi'ah-i I'dam-i Jahansuz*, p. 111–112.

42  Report on the Present Relations between the Shah and his Army and their Bearing on the Stability of the Pahlavi Regime, Percy C. R. Dodd.

43  Cronin, *The Army*, p. 155. Descriptions of the Shah's apparent paranoia may easily be found in the British sources. See, for example, Nicolson to FO, 2 October 1926, FO371/11490/E5612/284/34; Report on Personalities in Persia, Clive to FO, 18 December 1928, FO371/13783/E98/98/34.

44  Steven R. Ward, *Immortal: A Military History of Iran and its Armed Forces* (Washington D.C., 2009), p. 157.

45 See Kavih Bayat, *Farman-i Muqavamat, Khatirat-i Ibrahim Shushtari az Shurish-i Padigan-i Hava'i-yi Qal'ah-i Murghi, 8 Shahrivar 1320* (Tehran, 1376).

46 General Hassan Arfa, *Under Five Shahs* (London, 1964), p. 308.

47 Consul, Kermanshah to Tehran, 1 September 1941, FO371/27153/E6300/42/34.

48 For the emerging situation in the tribal territories see Cronin, *Tribal Politics in Iran*, p. 191–4.

49 Intelligence Summary no. 22, 8 October 1941, FO371/27188/E7213/268/34.

50 Ibid.

51 Major-General Kennedy, WO, to Sir H. Seymour, FO, 10 October 1941, FO371/27251/E6619/6619/34.

52 Annual Political Report for 1941, Bullard to Eden, 26 May 1941, FO371/31443/E3655/3655/34.

53 Ahmad Qavam (1876–1955), formerly Qavam al-Saltanah, a member of the old elite, had fallen into disfavour with Riza Khan in 1923 and gone into voluntary exile. Like many notables, he re-entered Iranian politics after the fall of Riza Shah in 1941. For the constantly changing governments of these years see Fakhreddin Azimi, *Iran: The Crisis of Democracy* (London and New York, 1989).

54 Bullard to Eden, 21 December 1942, FO371/35117/E239/239/34.

55 See Stephen L. McFarlane, 'Anatomy of an Iranian crowd: the Tehran bread riot of December 1942', *International Journal of Middle East Studies* 17/1 (1985), pp. 51–65.

56 Report on Political Events of 1942, Bullard to Eden, 26 March 1943, FO371/35117/E2450/239/34.

57 Bullard to Eden, 21 December 1942, FO371/35117/E239/239/34.

58 Ibid.

59 Major-General Kennedy, WO, to Sir H. Seymour, FO, 10 October 1941, FO371/27251/E6619/6619/34.

60 Pro-Axis sentiments were, in any case, not to survive the German defeats in the USSR and North Africa in 1943.

61 Bullard to Eden, 29 June 1942, FO371/35117/E3868/239/34.

62 I am grateful to Rowena Abdul Razak, a DPhil candidate at St Antony's College, Oxford, for sharing with me material related to this episode which she located in the National Archives. Information about the proposed coup may be found in FO248/1427.

63 Bullard to Eden, 23 November 1943, FO371/35117/E7569/239/34.

64 Ibid.

65 A. C. Millspaugh, *Americans in Persia* (Washington D.C., 1946).

66 British Military Attaché to Director of Military Intelligence, 13 December 1943, FO371/40165/E43/43/34.

67 Bullard to Eden, 29 June 1943, FO371/35117/E3868/239/34.

68 Report on Political Events of 1943, Bullard to Eden, 20 March 1944, FO371/40186/E2135/189/34.

69 Intelligence Summary no. 17, 30 April 1944, FO371/40205/E2850/422/34.

70 Review of Events of Persia for 1944, Bullard to Eden, 9 March 1945, FO371/45447/E2050/31/34.

71  Bullard to Eden, April 25 1945, FO371/45448/E3278/31/34.

72  Review of Events of Persia for 1944, Bullard to Eden, 9 March 1945, FO371/45447/ E2050/31/34.

73  Homa Katouzian, *The Persians: Ancient, Mediaeval and Modern Iran* (New Haven, CT, and London, 2009), p. 234.

74  Maziar Behrooz, *Rebels with a Cause: The Failure of the Left in Iran* (London and New York, 1999), p. 12–13.

75  Ward, *Immortal*, pp. 179–80.

76  Behrooz, *Rebels with a Cause*, pp. 20–1; Ahmad Shafaʻi, *Qiyam-i Afsaran-i Khurasan va Si va Haft Sal Zindagi dar Shuravi* (Tehran, 1365); Abuʼl Hasan Tafrishiyan, *Qiyam-i Afsaran-i Kurasan* (Tehran, 1367). A contemporary account of this episode is given in Bullard to Bevin, 7 November 1945, FO371/45452/ E9218/31/34. A very considerably different version is provided by General Hasan Arfa, *Under Five Shahs*, pp. 342–5.

77  Bullard to Bevin, 7 November 1945, FO371/45452/E9218/31/34.

78  Behrooz, *Rebels with a Cause*, p. 13.

79  Arfa, *Under Five Shahs*, pp. 346–8; Review of the Principal Events in Persia, 1945, Farquhar to Bevin, 6 April 1946, FO371/52673/E3499/5/34. On his return to Tehran Darakhshani was put on trial and sentenced to 15 years' imprisonment although he was released after three. In March 1978 he was arrested on a charge of spying for the USSR but died the same night. For Darakhshani's own account, see ʻAli Akbar Darakhshani, *Khatirat-i Sartip-i ʻAli Akbar Darakhshani* (Bethesda, 1994).

80  Gholamali Chegnizadeh, *Iranian Military Modernization, 1921–1979*. PhD thesis (University of Bradford, 1997), p. 181.

81  Army Military Mission. See Ricks, 'US military missions to Iran, 1943–1978', pp. 163–93.

82  Chegnizadeh, *Iranian Military Modernization*, p. 185.

83  Note on the Persian Army, Organisation, Deployment and Capabilities, July 1950, FO371/82356/EP1202/3.

84  Annual Report on the Persian Army for 1949, FO371/82356/EP1202/2.

85  Ibid.

86  Colonel G. Musavvar-Rahmani, *Khatirat-i Siyasi: Bist va Panj Sal dar Niru-yi Havaʼi-yi Iran* (Tehran, 1984), quoted in Homa Katouzian, *Musaddiq and the Struggle for Power in Iran* (London and New York, 1990), p. 130.

87  For Razmara see M. Reza Ghods, 'The rise and fall of General Razmara', *Middle Eastern Studies* 29/1 (1993), pp. 22–36.

88  Personalities in Persia – Military Supplement, 1947, p. 59, FO371/62035/E5964.

89  Annual Report on the Persian Army for 1949, FO371/82356/EP1202/2.

90  Annual Report on the Persian Army for 1951, FO371/98638/EP1201/1.

91  Wm. Roger Louis, 'Britain and the Overthrow of the Mosaddeq Government', in Mark J. Gasiorowski and Malcolm Byrne (eds), *Mohammad Mosaddeq and the 1953 Coup in Iran* (New York, 2004), p. 141.

92  Homa Katouzian, *Musaddiq and the Struggle for Power in Iran*, pp. 130–2. Most of the information about the Patriotic Officers comes from Musavvar-Rahmani, *Khatirat-i Siyasi*, cited by Katouzian.

93   Annual Report on the Persian Army for 1952, FO371/98638/EP1201/3.
94   Ibid.
95   Katouzian, *Musaddiq and the Struggle for Power in Iran*.
96   Ibid.
97   Annual Report on the Persian Army for 1952, FO371/98638/EP1201/3.
98   Ibid.
99   Wm. Roger Louis, 'Britain and the Overthrow of the Mosaddeq Government', p. 158.
100  Gasiorowski, 'The 1953 Coup d'État Against Mosaddeq', in Gasiorowski and Byrne (eds), *Mohammad Mosaddeq*, p. 232.
101  Gasiorowski, 'The 1953 Coup d'État Against Mosaddeq', p. 233.
102  For the Iranian government's official account of the murder of General Afshartus see FO371/104566/EP1015/137.
103  CIA Clandestine Service History: 'Overthrow of Premier Mossadeq of Iran, November 1952–August 1953' by Dr Donald Wilber, Appendix D, Report on Military Planning Aspect Operation of TP-AJAX, Electronic Briefing Book: The Secret CIA History of the Iran Coup. Available at www.gwu.edu/~nsarchiv/NSAEBB/NSAEBB28/ (accessed 8 April 2013).
104  Ibid.
105  Ibid.
106  Ibid.
107  Ibid.
108  Ibid.
109  Ibid.
110  Gasiorowski, 'The 1953 coup d'etat against Mosaddeq', p. 247.
111  Ibid., p. 249.
112  Ibid., p. 255.
113  Behrooz, *Rebels with a Cause*, p. 13. See also Maziar Behrooz, 'Tudeh factionalism and the 1953 coup in Iran', *International Journal of Middle East Studies* 33/3 (2001), pp. 363–82; Osamu Miyata, 'The Tudeh military network during the oil nationalization period', *Middle Eastern Studies* 23/3 (1987), pp. 313–28.
114  Behrooz, *Rebels with a Cause*, p. 14.
115  C. T. Gandy, 14 September 1953, FO371/104566/EP1015/137.
116  Ibid.
117  Ibid.
118  In 1950 ARMISH was reinforced when the Military Assistance Advisory Group (MAAG) was established to implement the Mutual Assistance Defence Program, designed to provide both training programmes and arms purchases. See Ricks, 'US military missions to Iran'.
119  Ward, *Immortal*, pp. 188–9.
120  Annual Report on the Iranian Armed Forces for 1954, FO371/110035/EP1202/1.
121  Annual Report on the Iranian Armed Forces for 1956, FO371/127111/EP1201/1.
122  US Embassy, Tehran, A Political Analysis of the Iranian Army.
123  Ibid.
124  Ibid.

125 Ibid.
126 US Embassy, Tehran, Role of the Military – Iran, 24 October 1959, US National Archives (courtesy Mark Gasiorowski).
127 Ibid.
128 Ibid.
129 Ibid.
130 This account of the Qarani episode is based on Mark J. Gasiorowski, 'The Qarani Affair and Iranian politics', *International Journal of Middle East Studies* 25/4 (1993), pp. 625–44.
131 For an example of these rivalries see US Embassy, Tehran, The Southern Tribes – A Pawn in Iranian Armed Forces Politics, 19 March 1957, US National Archives (courtesy Mark Gasiorowski).
132 Gasiorowski, 'The Qarani Affair', p. 633.
133 Ibid.
134 Annual Report on the Iranian Army for 1959, FO371/149792/EP1201/3.
135 Chegnizadeh, *Iranian Military Modernization*, p. 258.
136 Expressed in 1973 prices. Chegnizadeh, *Iranian Military Modernization*, p. 266.
137 The statistics in this paragraph are taken from Chegnizadeh, *Iranian Military Modernization*. See the very informative graphs on pp. 358–9, 365–6, 368.
138 Chegnizadeh, *Iranian Military Modernization*, p. 376. Of course, government spending in general increased enormously in this period.
139 Ward, *Immortal*, pp. 179–80, p. 197.
140 Chegnizadeh, *Iranian Military Modernization*. p. 359.
141 Ibid., p. 357.
142 Halliday, *Iran: Dictatorship and Development*, p. 97.
143 Annual Report on the Iranian Army for 1959, FO371/149792/EP1201/3.
144 Chegnizadeh, *Iranian Military Modernization*, p. 263.
145 A further source of frustration was the fact that, owing to the air force's manpower shortage, many of the *homafars* had been forced to stay in service even after their contracts had expired. Hooshmand Mirfakhraei, *The Imperial Iranian Armed Forces and the Revolution of 1978–1979*. PhD thesis (State University of New York, 1984), p. 330.
146 British Embassy, 26 July 1960, FO371/149792/EP1201/12.
147 Ibid.
148 Ward, *Immortal*, pp. 208–9.
149 Service Attachés Tehran – Annual Report, 1973, FCO8/2279.
150 Ibid.
151 William F. Hickman, *Ravaged and Reborn: The Iranian Army, 1982* (Washington D.C., 1982), p. 6.
152 Service Attachés Tehran – Annual Report, 1976, FCO8/2990.
153 For a brief survey of the pre-revolutionary army see Farhad Kazemi, 'The military and politics in Iran: the uneasy symbiosis', in E. Kedourie and S. G. Haim (eds) *Towards A Modern Iran: Studies in Thought, Politics and Society* (London, 1980).
154 Service Attachés Tehran – Annual Report, 1976, FCO8/2990.

155 Mark Roberts, 'Khomeini's Incorporation of the Iranian Military' (McNair Paper no. 48, January 1996), Chapter 3, p. 2.

156 For a vivid description of the disintegration of the army see Charles Kurzman, *The Unthinkable Revolution* (Cambridge, MA, 2004).

157 Ward, *Immortal*, p. 218.

158 Mirfakhraei, *The Imperial Iranian Armed Forces and the Revolution of 1978–1979*, p. 329–30.

159 For his own account see General Robert E. Huyser, *Mission to Tehran* (London, 1986).

160 Roberts, 'Khomeini's Incorporation of the Iranian Military', Chapter 3, p. 5.

161 Ward, *Immortal*, p. 222.

162 Hickman, *Ravaged and Reborn*, p. 11.

163 Ibid., p. 1.

164 See Kenneth Katzman, *The Warriors of Islam: Iran's Revolutionary Guards* (Boulder, CO, 1993).

165 Hickman, *Ravaged and Reborn*, p. 9. See also Gregory F. Rose, 'The post-revolutionary purge of Iran's armed forces: a revisionist assessment', *Iranian Studies* 17/2–3 (1984), pp. 154–94.

166 Rose, 'The post-revolutionary purge of Iran's armed forces', pp. 183–4.

167 Ibid., pp. 185–6; Hickman, *Ravaged and Reborn*, p. 16.

168 Hickman, *Ravaged and Reborn*, p. 18. See also Nikola B. Schahgaldian, with the assistance of Gina Barkhordarian, *The Iranian Military Under the Islamic Republic* (Santa Monica, CA, 1987) and Sepehr Zabih, *The Iranian Military in Revolution and War* (London, 1988).

169 The account of the Nuzhih plot given here is based on Mark J. Gasiorowski, 'The Nuzhih plot and Iranian politics', *International Journal of Middle East Studies* 34/4 (2002), pp. 645–66.

170 Ward, *Immortal*, p. 297; Hickman, *Ravaged and Reborn*, p. 30.

171 Ward, *Immortal*, p. 309. See also Daniel Byman, Shahram Chubin, Anoushirvan Ehteshami and Jerrold Green, *Iran's Security Policy in the Post-Revolutionary Era* (Santa Monica, CA, 2001); Anthony H. Cordesman, *Iran's Military Forces in Transition: Conventional Threats and Weapons of Mass Destruction* (Westport, CT, 1999); Anthony H. Cordesman and Martin Kleiber, *Iran's Military Forces and Warfighting Capabilities: The Threat in the Northern Gulf* (Westport, CT, 2007).

## Chapter 5: Tribes, Coups and Princes

1 The problem was not due to the size of the population. In fact the Saudi population base might easily produce a much larger army. The kingdom's pool of men of military age in 2001 was approximately 5.7 million. This compared with 5.6 million men in Iraq which was able to maintain a total military strength of perhaps double the size. See Anthony H. Cordesman, *Saudi Arabia Enters the Twenty-First Century: the Military and International Security Dimensions* (Westport, CT, 2003) p. 52.

2 For the forging of links between Ibn Saud and Britain see Jacob Goldberg, *The Foreign Policy of Saudi Arabia: The Formative Years, 1902–1918* (Cambridge, MA, 1986).

3 Mordechai Abir, *Saudi Arabia in the Oil Era: Regime and Elites; Conflict and Collaboration* (London, 1988), p. 3.

4 Alexei Vassiliev, *The History of Saudi Arabia* (London, 1998), p. 227.

5 For a discussion of the role of the *mutawwaʿa* see Madawi al-Rasheed, *A History of Saudi Arabia* (Cambridge, 2002).

6 Vassiliev describes these tribal groups as 'noble', in contrast to others whose role was confined to non-military and menial labour; see Vassiliev, *The History of Saudi Arabia*, p. 229.

7 Ibid., p. 229.

8 Ibid., pp. 228–9.

9 See Joseph Kostiner, 'Transforming dualities: tribe and state formation in Saudi Arabia', in P. S. Khoury and J. Kostiner (eds), *Tribes and State Formation in the Middle East* (London, 1991), p. 231.

10 Vassiliev, *The History of Saudi Arabia*, p. 272.

11 Joseph Kostiner, *The Making of Saudi Arabia 1916–1938: From Chieftaincy to Monarchical State* (New York, 1993), p. 122; Peter Sluglett and Marion Farouk-Sluglett, 'The precarious monarchy: Britain, Abd al-Aziz ibn Saud and the establishment of the kingdom of Hijaz, Najd and its dependencies, 1925–1932', in T. Niblock (ed.), *State, Society and Economy in Saudi Arabia* (London, 1982), p. 45; Clive Leatherdale, *Britain and Saudi Arabia 1925–1939* (London, 1983), p. 119.

12 Al-Rasheed, *A History of Saudi Arabia*, p. 87; J. C. Hurewitz, *Middle East Politics: the Military Dimension* (New York, 1969), p. 246.

13 This strategy is perhaps less extraordinary than al-Rasheed argues, see al-Rasheed, *A History of Saudi Arabia*, pp. 75–6. Fath Ali Shah of Iran, for example, pursued a similar strategy in nineteenth-century Iran and the practice may even be traced back to the Prophet himself.

14 Report on the Saudi Arabian Army, Quarter Ending 30 September 1948, WO202/958.

15 Ibn Saud's Armed Forces, Bullard to Halifax, 29 November 1939, FO371/24589/E1636/1636/25.

16 Ibid. The King frequently reiterated his hopes for the army. See Saudi Arabia Annual Review for 1948, 2 February 1949, FO371/75505/E1949/1011/25.

17 Report on the Saudi Arabian Army, 22 July 1947, FO371/62101/E6623.

18 Saudi Arabia Annual Review for 1948, 2 February 1949, FO371/75505/E1949/1011/25.

19 Vassiliev, *The History of Saudi Arabia*, p. 308.

20 Ibn Saud's Armed Forces, Bullard to Halifax, 29 November 1939, FO371/24589/E1636/1636/25.

21 Ibid.

22 Personalities in Saudi Arabia, 9 June 1943, FO371/35163/E3326/3326/25.

23 Leading Personalities in Saudi Arabia, Jedda, 14 September 1955, FO371/114873.

24 Ibn Saud's Armed Forces, Bullard to Halifax, 29 November 1939, FO371/24589/
E1636/1636/25.

25 Ibid.

26 It was in fact an Italian, General Giulio Douhet, who used the Italian experience in Libya to develop theories regarding the strategic value of mass aerial
bombardment. In his book *The Command of the Air* (1921) he argued that such
terror bombing would destroy enemy 'vital centres' of government and administration and shatter the population's morale and will to resist, causing them to rise
up and insist on their country's capitulation. Douhet later became a supporter of
Italian fascism. The Germans experimented with his theories in their bombing of
Guernica during the Spanish Civil War, and both Germany and Britain deployed
the strategy during World War II. It has continued to be a Western technique of
warfare in the twenty-first century.

27 Italian interest in providing military assistance to Saudi Arabia was an extension of
its ambition to build an African empire based on those states bordering the Red Sea,
especially Ethiopia but also Somalia and Eritrea. As part of this strategy, Italy had
been fostering support on the Arab Red Sea coast, notably in Yemen, from at least
1911, and projecting its power towards Saudi Arabia was a corollary of this geopo-
litical strategy. See Joseph Kostiner, 'Britain and the challenge of the Axis powers
in Arabia: the decline of British–Saudi cooperation in the 1930s', in M. J. Cohen
and M. Kolinsky (eds), *Britain and the Middle East in the 1930s: Security Problems
1935-39* (London, 1992); J. Baldry, 'Anglo–Italian rivalry in Yemen and Asir 1900–
1934', *Die Welt des Islams* 17/1–4 (1976–7), pp. 155–93; 'The struggle for the Red Sea:
Mussolini's policy in Yemen 1934–43', *Asian and African Studies* 16 (1980), pp. 53–89.

28 For an example of Ibn Saud's enthusiasm for an air force, see Annual Report, 1937,
Bullard to Halifax, 26 March 1938, FO371/21908/E2338/2338/25.

29 Bullard to Halifax, 11 March 1939, FO371/23274/E1810/1810/25.

30 Ibn Saud's Armed Forces, Bullard to Halifax, 29 November 1939, FO371/24589/
E1636/1636/25.

31 Political Review of Saudi Arabia, 1939, Stonehewer-Bird to Halifax, 18 July 1940,
FO371/82639/E2720/1194/25.

32 Anthony H. Cordesman, *The Gulf and the Search for Strategic Stability* (Boulder,
CO, 1984), p. 93.

33 Ibid., p. 95.

34 Ibid., p. 95

35 Report on the Saudi Arabian Army, 22 July 1947, FO371/62101/E6623.

36 Ibid.

37 Report on the Saudi Arabian Army, Quarter Ending 30 September 1948,
WO202/958.

38 Report on the Saudi Arabian Army, 31 March 1949, WO/202/959.

39 Report on the Saudi Arabian Army, 22 July 1947, FO371/62101/E6623.

40 Report on the Saudi Arabian Army, Quarter Ending 30 June 1949, WO/202/997.

41 Ibid.

42 Saudi Arabia Annual Review for 1948, 2 February 1949, FO371/75505/
E1949/1011/25.

43 Report on the Saudi Arabian Army, Quarter Ending 30 June 1948, WO202/958.

44 Ibid.

45 Report on the Saudi Arabian Army, 22 July 1947, FO371/62101/E6623.

46 Cordesman, *The Gulf and the Search for Strategic Stability*, p. 97.

47 Annual Review of Events for 1951, 5 February 1952, FO371/98821/E51011/1.

48 Copy of a memorandum (Reference SM-1604-52) dated 7 July 1952 from the US Joint Chiefs of Staff to the Secretary Chiefs of Staff Committee, FO371/98838/E51993.

49 Annual Report for Saudi Arabia for 1955, 22 January 1956, FO371/120753; Nadav Safran, *Saudi Arabia: The Ceaseless Quest for Security* (New York, 1985), p. 81; Vasiliev, *The History of Saudi Arabia*, p. 339–40.

50 For example, in mid-1957 reports again surfaced of unrest in the Saudi army and the arrest of 21 officers. British Embassy, Washington, 12 June 1957, FO371/127167/E51201/1.

51 Cordesman, *The Gulf and the Search for Strategic Stability*, p. 178.

52 Annual Review for 1952, 1 January 1953, FO371/104852/E51011/1.

53 King Faysal was himself assassinated in 1975. He was succeeded by King Khalid (1975–82), King Fahd (1982–2005) and King Abdullah (2005–present).

54 Cordesman, *The Gulf and the Search for Strategic Stability*, p. 110.

55 Defence Attaché's Report for 1969, FCO8/1501.

56 Ibid.

57 Pollack, *Arabs at War*, p. 427.

58 Defence Attaché's Annual Report, 1 January 1972 to 31 May 1973, FCO8/2118.

59 Ibid.

60 Notes on Conditions in Saudi Arabia, 1967, FCO8/783.

61 Cordesman, *The Gulf and the Search for Strategic Stability*, p. 183.

62 Simon Henderson, 'After King Abdullah: Succession in Saudi Arabia', Policy Focus no. 96, Washington Institute for Near East Policy (2009), pp. 6–7. Available at www.washingtoninstitute.org/uploads/Documents/pubs/PolicyFocus 96.pdf (accessed 8 April 2013).

63 Plan for the Modernisation of the National Guard, British Ministry of Defence Proposals, DEFE68/238.

64 Defence Attaché's Annual Report for 1979, 18 April 1980, FCO8/3755.

65 Ibid.

66 See James Buchan, 'Secular and religious opposition in Saudi Arabia', in T. Niblock (ed.), *State, Society and Economy in Saudi Arabia*, pp. 106–24.

67 Defence Attaché's Annual Report for 1979, 18 April 1980, FCO8/3755.

68 Ibid.

69 Ibid.

70 Pollack, *Arabs at War*, p. 428.

71 A typical example of the procrastination and uncertainty on this issue which permeated the senior ranks may be found in the following conversation. In August 1979 it was announced that all fit men between 18 and 35 would be called up. In the following January the British Defence Attaché asked Brigadier Bahayri, commander of the air base at al-Taif, what plans had been made for conscription.

The Brigadier replied 'evasively that it was still under consideration but was a very difficult subject; it would be unpopular; what ages should be taken; who would be exempt, a very tricky one; how long would they serve and could the Regular Forces train and absorb them?' Defence Attaché's Annual Report for 1979, 18 April 1980, FCO8/3755.

72 Pollack, *Arabs at War*, p. 432.

73 Ibid., p. 428.

74 Ibid., p. 434.

75 Ibid., p. 443.

76 Ibid., pp. 443–6.

77 'Defence and security issues in the GCC states', *Gulf Yearbook 2008–2009* (Dubai, 2009), p. 204.

78 For the expansion of the US military and security 'shield' in the Gulf region see, for example, Jeffrey R. Marcus, *The Politics and Security of the Gulf: Anglo-American Hegemony and the Shaping of a Region* (Abingdon, 2010).

79 The British press confirmed that the Saudi National Guard was still being trained by a British military mission, present with the force since 1963, and now consisting of 11 army personnel under the command of a brigadier. Jamie Doward and Philippa Stewart, 'UK training Saudi forces used to crush Arab spring', *Guardian*, 28 May 2011. Available at www.guardian.co.uk/world/2011/may/28/uk-training-saudi-troops (accessed 8 April 2013).

## Conclusion

1 Nazih N. Ayubi, *Over-Stating the Arab State: Politics and Society in the Middle East* (London and New York, 1995).

2 Kuwait has a form of conscription but it is easily avoided by most Kuwaiti citizens.

3 See, *inter alia*, J. M. Black, *A Military Revolution? Military Change and European Society 1550–1800* (Basingstoke, 1991); C. J. Rogers (ed.) *The Military Revolution Debate: Readings on the Military Transformation of Early Modern Europe* (Boulder, CO, 1995); G. Parker, *The Military Revolution, Military Innovation and the Rise of the West, 1500–1800* (Cambridge, 1996).

4 This summary of the military revolution thesis is drawn from Ralston, *Importing the European Army*, pp. 1–12.

5 Ralston, *Importing the European Army*, p. 11.

6 See, for example, Yezid Sayigh, *Armed Struggle and the Search for State: The Palestinian National Movement, 1949–1993* (Oxford, 1997).

7 See, for example, the discussion of Iraq by Mohammad A. Tarbush, *The Role of the Military in Politics: A Case-Study of Iraq to 1941* (London, 1982).

8 That conscription is still perceived as an unwelcome imposition was dramatically demonstrated in Egypt in 1986 when some 17,000 poorly paid conscripts to the Central Security Force (CSF), reacting to rumours that their term of service was to be extended by one year, staged violent protests in and around Cairo. The disturbances lasted three days until suppressed by the army, apparently leaving

107 people dead and 1,324 members of the CSF under arrest. See *Europa Regional Surveys of the World: The Middle East and North Africa, 2006* (London and New York, 2006) p. 333.

9  Elizabeth Picard, 'Arab military in politics: from revolutionary plot to authoritarian state', in A. Hourani, P. S. Khoury and M. C. Wilson (eds), *The Modern Middle East* (London and New York, 1993), p. 564.

10  James T. Quinlivan, 'Coup-proofing: its practice and consequences in the Middle East', *International Security* 24/2 (1999), pp. 131–65.

11  Pollack, *Arabs at War*, p. 428.

12  See, for example, the group of young journalists and intellectuals who provided the main base of support for Riza Khan in the early 1920s. Homa Katouzian, *The Persians: Ancient, Mediaeval and Modern Iran* (New Haven, CT, and London, 2009), p. 204.

13  William L. Cleveland, *A History of the Modern Middle East* (Boulder, CO, 1994).

# Select Bibliography

Abduh, Jalal, *Chihil Sal dar Sahnah-i Qazayi, Siyasi, Diplumasi-yi Iran va Jahan*, 2 vols (Tehran, 1368).

Abir, Mordechai, *Saudi Arabia in the Oil Era: Regime and Elites; Conflict and Collaboration* (London, 1988).

Adamec, Ludwig W., *Dictionary of Afghan Wars, Revolutions and Insurgencies* (Lanham, MD, 1996).

Afsar, Lt-Col. Parviz, *Tarikh-i Zhandarmiri-yi Iran* (Qum, 1332).

Ahady, Anwar-ul-Haq, 'The decline of the Pashtuns in Afghanistan', *Asian Survey* 35/7 (1995), pp. 621–34.

Aksan, Virginia H., 'Ottoman military recruitment strategies in the late eighteenth century', in E. J. Zürcher (ed.), *Arming the State: Military Conscription in the Middle East and Central Asia* (London and New York, 1999).

Alavi, Seema, *Sepoys and the Company: Tradition and Transition in North India, 1770–1830* (Delhi, 1995).

Amanat, Abbas, *Pivot of the Universe: Nasir al-Din Shah and the Iranian Monarchy, 1851–1896* (London and New York, 1997).

Amini, Iradj, *Napoleon and Persia* (Richmond, 1999).

Amirahmadi, Ahmad, *Khatirat-i Nakhustin Sipahbud-i Iran*, 2 vols (Tehran, 1373).

Anderson, Lisa, *The State and Social Transformation in Tunisia and Libya, 1830–1980* (Princeton, NJ, 1986).

Aqalli, Baqir, *Riza Shah va Qushun-i Muttahid al-Shakl, 1300–1320* (Tehran, 1377).

Arfa, Hassan, *Under Five Shahs* (London, 1964).

Arnold, Anthony, *Afghanistan's Two-Party Communism: Parcham and Khalq* (Stanford, CA, 1983).

Atabaki, Touraj (ed.), *Iran and the First World War: Battleground of the Great Powers* (London and New York, 2006).

Atkin, Muriel, *Russia and Iran, 1780–1828* (Minnesota, 1980).

Avery, P. W. and Simmons, J. B., 'Persia on a cross of silver, 1880–1890', in E. Kedourie and S. G. Haim (eds), *Towards A Modern Iran, Studies in Thought, Politics and Society* (London, 1980).

Ayubi, Nazih N., *Over-Stating the Arab State: Politics and Society in the Middle East* (London and New York, 1995).

Azimi, Fakhreddin, *Iran: The Crisis of Democracy* (London and New York, 1989).

Azzam, Maha, 'Egypt's military council and the transition to democracy', Chatham House Briefing Paper, May 2012, p. 3. Available at www.chathamhouse.org/publications/papers/view/183547 (accessed 8 April 2013).

Babakhodjayev, M. A., 'Afghanistan's armed forces and Amir Abdur Rahman's military reform', *Afghanistan* 3 (Fall 1970), pp. 8–20.

Bahar, Muhammad Taqi, Malik al-Shu'ara', *Tarikh-i Mukhtasar-i Ahzab-i Siyasi-yi Iran*, 2 vols (Tehran, 1323).

Bakhash, Shaul, *Iran: Monarchy, Bureaucracy and Reform under the Qajars: 1858–1896* (London, 1978).

Baldry, J., 'Anglo–Italian rivalry in Yemen and Asir 1900–1934', *Die Welt des Islams* 17/1–4 (1976-7), pp. 155–93.

———, 'The struggle for the Red Sea: Mussolini's policy in Yemen 1934–43', *Asian and African Studies* 16 (1980), pp. 53–89.

Barfield, Thomas, *Afghanistan: A Cultural and Political History* (Princeton, NJ, 2010).

Bast, Oliver (ed.), *La Perse et la Grande Guerre* (Tehran, 2002).

Batatu, Hanna, *The Old Social Classes and the Revolutionary Movements of Iraq: A Study of Iraq's Old Landed and Commercial Classes and its Communists, Baathists and Free Officers* (Princeton, NJ, 1979).

Bayat, Kavih, *Kudita-yi Lahuti, Tabriz, Bahman 1300* (Tehran, 1376).

———, *Farman-i Muqavamat, Khatirat-i Ibrahim Shushtari az Shurish-i Padigan-i Hava'i-yi Qal'ah-i Murghi, 8 Shahrivar 1320* (Tehran, 1376).

———, *Qiyam-i Nafir-i Jam: Shurish-i Lahak Khan Salar-i Jang* (Tehran, 1375).

———, *Inqilab-i Khurasan, Majmu'ah-i Asnad va Madarik 1300 shamsi* (Tehran, 1370).

———, 'Qarardad-i 1919 va Tashkil-i Qushun-i Muttahid al-Shikl dar Iran', in *Tarikh-i Mu'asir-i Iran, Majmu'ah-i Maqalat* (Tehran, 1369), Vol. 2, pp. 125–40.

Bayglari, Sartip-i Haydar Quli, *Khatirat-i Yak Sarbaz* (Tehran, 1350).

Be'eri, Eliezer, *Army Officers in Arab Politics and Society* (New York and London, 1970).

Behrooz, Maziar, *Rebels with a Cause: The Failure of the Left in Iran* (London and New York, 1999).

———, 'Tudeh factionalism and the 1953 coup in Iran', *International Journal of Middle East Studies* 33/3 (2001), pp. 363–82.

Bennison, Amira K., 'The "New Order" and Islamic Order: The Introduction of the *Nizami* Army in the Western Maghrib and its Legitimation, 1830–73', *International Journal of Middle Eastern Studies* 36/4 (2004), pp. 591–612.

Bhatia, Michael and Sedra, Mark, *Afghanistan, Arms and Conflict* (Abingdon, 2008).

Bill, James A., 'The military and modernization in the Middle East', *Comparative Politics* 2/1 (1969), pp. 41–62.

Black, Jeremy, *A Military Revolution? Military Change and European Society 1550–1800* (Basingstoke, 1991).

———, *War and the World: Military Power and the Fate of Continents, 1450–2000* (New Haven, CT, 1998).

Bosworth, C. E., 'Army ii: Islamic, to the Mongol Period', in *Encyclopaedia Iranica*. Available at www.iranicaonline.org/articles/army-ii (accessed 8 April 2013).

Brown, L. Carl, *The Tunisia of Ahmed Bey* (Princeton, NJ, 1974).

Buchan, J., 'Secular and religious opposition in Saudi Arabia', in T. Niblock (ed.), *State, Society and Economy in Saudi Arabia* (London, 1982).

Byman, Daniel, Chubin, Shahram, Ehteshami, Anoushirvan and Green, Jerrold, *Iran's Security Policy in the Post-Revolutionary Era* (Santa Monica, CA, 2001).

Calmard, J., 'Les réformes militaires sous les Qajars (1795–1925)', in Y. Richard (ed.), *Entre l'Iran et l'Occident* (Paris, 1989).

Calmard-Compas, Jaqueline, 'Ferrier, Joseph Phillipe', in *Encyclopaedia Iranica*. Available at www.iranicaonline.org/articles/ferrier-joseph-philippe (accessed 8 April 2013).

Chegnizadeh, Gholamali, *Iranian Military Modernization, 1921–1979*. PhD thesis (University of Bradford, 1997).

Cleveland, William L., *A History of the Modern Middle East* (Boulder, CO, 1994).

Cook, Steven A., *Ruling but not Governing: the Military and Political Development in Egypt, Algeria and Turkey* (Baltimore, MD, 2007).

Cordesman, Anthony H., *The Gulf and the Search for Strategic Security* (Boulder, CO, 1984).

———, *Iran's Military Forces in Transition: Conventional Threats and Weapons of Mass Destruction* (Westport, CT, 1999).

———, *A Tragedy of Arms* (Westport, CT, 2002).

———, *Saudi Arabia Enters the Twenty-First Century: The Military and International Security Dimensions* (Westport, CT, 2003).

Cordesman, Anthony H. and Kleiber, Martin, *Iran's Military Forces and Warfighting Capabilities: The Threat in the Northern Gulf* (Westport, CT, 2007).

Cordesman, Anthony H., Mausner, Adam and Kasten, David (eds), *Afghan National Security Forces: Shaping the Path to Victory* (Washington D.C., 2009).

Cronin, Stephanie, *The Army and the Creation of the Pahlavi State in Iran, 1910–1926* (London, 1997).

———, 'Conscription and popular resistance in Iran, 1925–1941', *International Review of Social History* 43/3 (1998), pp. 451–71.

———, 'Britain, the Iranian military and the rise of Reza Khan', in V. Martin (ed.) *Anglo–Iranian Relations since 1800* (Abingdon, 2005), pp. 99–127.

———, *Tribal Politics in Iran: Rural Conflict and the New State, 1921–1941* (London, 2007).

———, *Soldiers, Shahs and Subalterns in Iran: Opposition, Protest and Revolt, 1921–1941* (Basingstoke, 2010).

———, 'Deserters, converts, Cossacks and revolutionaries: Russians in Iranian military service, 1800–1921', in S. Cronin (ed.), *Iranian–Russian Encounters: Empires and Revolutions since 1800* (Abingdon, 2012).

Curzon, George N., *Persia and the Persian Question* (London, 1892).

Darakhshani, 'Ali Akbar, *Khatirat-i Sartip-i 'Ali Akbar Darakhshani* (Bethesda, 1994).

David, Anthony, 'How the Taliban became a military force', in W. Maley (ed.), *Fundamentalism Reborn?* (London, 1988).

Dickson, W. E. R., *East Persia: A Backwater of the Great War* (London, 1924).

Domantovich, A. I., 'Vospominanie o prebivanii pervoi russkoi voennoi missii v Persii', *Russkaia Starina* (1908), no. 2, pp. 331–40, no. 3, pp. 575–83, no. 4, pp. 211–216.

Dorronsoro, Gilles, *Revolution Unending, Afghanistan: 1979 to the Present* (London, 2000).

Dunn, John P., *Khedive Ismail's Army* (Abingdon, 2005).

Dyer, R. E. H., *The Raiders of the Sarhad* (London, 1921).

Eskandari-Qajar, M. M., 'Mohammad Shah Qajar's Nezam-e Jadid and Colonel Colombari's Zambourakchis', *Qajar Studies* 5 (2005), pp. 52–79.

*Europa Regional Surveys of the World: The Middle East and North Africa, 2006* (London and New York, 2006).

Ewans, Martin, *Conflict in Afghanistan: Studies in Asymmetric Warfare* (London, 2005).

Fahmy, Khaled, *All the Pasha's Men: Mehmed Ali, his Army and the Making of Modern Egypt* (Cambridge, 1997).

Fèrrieres-Sauveboeuf, Comte de, *Mémoires Historiques, Politiques et Géographiques des Voyages du Comte de Ferrières-Sauveboeuf Faits en Turquie, en Perse at en Arabie, depuis 1782 jusqu'en 1789* (Paris, 1790).

Fisher, Sydney, *The Military in the Middle East: Problems in Society and Government* (Columbus, OH, 1963).

Flandin, Eugene, *Voyage en Perse* (Paris, 1851).

Foran, John, *Fragile Resistance: Social Transformation in Iran from 1500 to the Revolution* (Boulder, CO, 1993).

Forster, George, *A Journey from Bengal to England* (London, 1798).

Garakani, Manshur, *Siyasat-i Dawlat-i Shuravi dar Iran* (Tehran, 1326).

Gardane, Alfred de, *Mission du Général Gardane en Perse sous le Premier Empire* (Paris, 1865).

Gardane, P. A. L., *Journal d'un Voyage en la Turquie d'Asie et la Perse fait en 1807 and 1808* (Paris, 1809).

Gasiorowski, Mark J., 'The Qarani Affair and Iranian politics', *International Journal of Middle East Studies* 25/4 (1993), pp. 625–44.

——, 'The Nuzhih Plot and Iranian politics', *International Journal of Middle East Studies* 34/4 (2002), pp. 645–66.

——, 'The 1953 coup d'etat against Mosaddeq', in M. J. Gasiorowski and M. Byrne (eds), *Mohammad Mosaddeq and the 1953 Coup in Iran* (New York, 2004).

Gasiorowski, Mark J. and Byrne, Malcolm (eds), *Mohammad Mosaddeq and the 1953 Coup in Iran* (New York, 2004).

Gawgani, Borhan Khoschnewis, *Die Österreichische Militärmissionen in Persien 1852 bis 1881*. PhD dissertation (Universität Wien, 1978).

Ghods, M. Reza, 'The rise and fall of General Razmara', *Middle Eastern Studies* 29/1 (1993), pp. 22–36.

Giustozzi, Antonio, *War, Politics and Society in Afghanistan, 1978–1992* (Washington D.C., 1999).

——, 'The demodernisation of an army: Northern Afghanistan, 1992–2001', *Small Wars and Insurgencies* 15/1 (2004), pp. 1–18.

——, 'The debate on warlordism: the importance of military legitimacy', Crisis States Programme Discussion Paper, no. 13 (2005).

——, 'Auxiliary force or national army? Afghanistan's 'ANA' and the counter-insurgency effort, 2002–2006', Small Wars and Insurgencies 18/1 (2007), pp. 45–67.

——, Empires of Mud (London, 2009).

——, 'The Afghan National Army', The RUSI Journal 154/6 (2009), pp. 36–42.

Giustozzi, Antonio and Ullah, Noor, '"Tribes" and Warlords in Southern Afghanistan, 1980–2005', Crisis States Programme Working Paper, no. 7 (2006).

Goldberg, Jacob, The Foreign Policy of Saudi Arabia: The Formative Years, 1902–1918 (Cambridge, MA, 1986).

Gommans, J. L., The Rise of the Indo–Afghan Empire (Leiden, 1995).

——, 'Indian warfare and Afghan innovation during the eighteenth century', in J. L. Gommans and D. H. A. Kolff (eds) Warfare and Weaponry in South Asia, 1000–1800 (New Delhi and Oxford, 2003).

Gordon, Joel S., Nasser's Blessed Movement: Egypt's Free Officers and the July Revolution (New York, 1992).

Gotowicki, Stephen H., 'The role of the Egyptian military in domestic society', FMSO Publications, 1997. Available at http://fmso.leavenworth.army.mil/documents/egypt/egypt.htm (accessed 8 April 2013).

Gregorian, Vartan, The Emergence of Modern Afghanistan (Stanford, CA, 1969).

Grey, Charles, European Adventurers of Northern India, 1785–1849 (Lahore, 1929).

Gulf Yearbook 2008–2009 (Dubai, 2009).

Gulzad, Zalmay A., External Influences and the Development of the Afghan State in the Nineteenth Century (New York, 1994).

Halliday, Fred, Iran: Dictatorship and Development (Harmondsworth, 1979).

——, 'War and revolution in Afghanistan', New Left Review 119 (1980), pp. 20–41.

——, Threat from the East? Soviet Policy from Afghanistan and Iran to the Horn of Africa (London, 1982).

Halpern, Manfred, Middle Eastern Armies and the New Middle Class (Princeton, 1962).

Haneda, M., 'Army iii: Safavid Period', in Encyclopaedia Iranica. Available at www.iranicaonline.org/articles/army-iii (accessed 8 April 2013).

Harb, Imad, 'The Egyptian military in politics: disengagement or accommodation?', Middle East Journal 57/2 (2003), pp. 269–90.

Harlan, Josiah, A Memoir of India and Afghanistan (Philadelphia, 1842).

Hashim, Ahmed S., 'The Egyptian military, Part One: from the Ottomans through Sadat', Middle East Policy Council, September 2011. Available at www.mepc.org/journal/middle-east-policy-archives/egyptian-military-part-one-ottomans-through-sadat (accessed 8 April 2013).

Haynes, Jeff, 'Reforming the Afghan National Army', Foreign Policy Research Institute, 27 November 2009. Available at www.fpri.org/enotes/200911.haynes.reformingafghannationalarmy.html (accessed 8 April 2013).

Heller, Mark, 'Politics and the military in Iraq and Jordan', Armed Forces and Society 4/1 (1977), pp. 75–99.

Henderson, Simon, 'After King Abdullah: Succession in Saudi Arabia', Policy Focus no. 96, Washington Institute for Near East Policy (2009), pp. 6–7. Available at www.

washingtoninstitute.org/uploads/Documents/pubs/PolicyFocus96.pdf (accessed 8 April 2013).

Hickman, William F., *Ravaged and Reborn: The Iranian Army, 1982* (Washington D.C., 1982).

Hinnebusch, Raymond A., *Authoritarian Power and State Formation in Ba'thist Syria: Army, Party and Peasant* (Boulder, CO, 1990).

Hodes, Cyrus and Sedra, Mark, *The Search for Security in Post-Taliban Afghanistan* (Abingdon, 2007).

Hopkins, B. D., *The Making of Modern Afghanistan* (Basingstoke, 2008).

Hughes, Matthew, 'British private armies in the Middle East: The Arab Legion and the Trans-Jordan frontier force, 1920–1956', *The RUSI Journal* 153/2 (2008), pp. 70–5.

Hurewitz, J. C., *Middle East Politics: The Military Dimension* (London, 1969).

——, 'Soldiers and social change in plural societies: the contemporary Middle East', in M. E. Yapp and V. J. Parry (eds) *War, Technology and Society in the Middle East* (London, 1975).

Huyser, General Robert E., *Mission to Tehran* (London, 1986).

Ineichen, Markus, *Die Schwedischen Offiziere in Persien 1911–1916* (Bern, 2002).

Ironside, Major-Gen. Sir Edmund, *High Road to Command: The Diaries of Major General Sir Edmund Ironside, 1920–22* (ed. Lord Ironside) (London, 1972).

Ittihadiyyah, Mansurah and Sadigh, S. Mir Muhammad (eds), with an introduction by Jean Calmard, *Zhinral Saminu dar Khidmat-i Iran-i Qajar va Jang-i Hirat, 1236–1266* (Tehran, 1375).

Jalali, Ali A., 'Rebuilding Afghanistan's National Army', *Parameters* (Autumn 2002), pp. 72–86.

——, 'Afghanistan: regaining momentum', *Parameters* (Winter 2007–8), pp. 5–19.

——, 'Winning in Afghanistan', *Parameters* (Spring 2009), pp. 5–21.

——, 'The future of security institutions', in J. Alexander Thier (ed.) *The Future of Afghanistan* (Washington D.C., 2009).

Jali, Abbas Quli (trans.) *Khatirat-i Kulunil Kasakufski* (Tehran, 1344).

Jaubert, Pierre Amédée, *Voyage en Armenie et en Perse* (Paris, 1821).

Johnson, Robert, *The Afghan Way of War: How and Why They Fight* (London, 2011).

Kakar, Hasan Kawun, *Government and Society in Afghanistan: The Reign of Amir 'Abd al-Rahman Khan* (Austin, TX, 1979).

Katouzian, Homa, *The Political Economy of Modern Iran: Despotism and Pseudo-Modernism, 1926–1979* (London, 1981).

——, *Musaddiq and the Struggle for Power in Iran* (London and New York, 1990).

——, *State and Society in Iran: The Eclipse of the Qajars and the Emergence of the Pahlavis* (London and New York, 2000).

——, *The Persians: Ancient, Mediaeval and Modern Iran* (New Haven, CT and London, 2009).

Katzman, Kenneth, *The Warriors of Islam: Iran's Revolutionary Guards* (Boulder, CO, 1993).

Kazemi, Farhad, 'The military and politics in Iran: the uneasy symbiosis', in E. Kedourie, and S. G. Haim (eds), *Towards A Modern Iran: Studies in Thought, Politics and Society* (London, 1980).

Kazemzadeh, F., 'The origin and early development of the Persian Cossack Brigade', *The American Slavic and East European Review* 15/3 (1956), pp. 351–63.

Kerner, Robert J., 'The mission of Liman von Sanders: 1, its origin', *The Slavonic Review* 6/16 (1927), pp. 12–27.

——, 'The mission of Liman von Sanders: 2, the crisis', *The Slavonic Review* 6/17 (1927), pp. 343–63.

——, 'The mission of Liman von Sanders: 3', *The Slavonic and East European Review* 6/18 (1928), pp. 543–60.

——, 'The mission of Liman von Sanders: 4, the aftermath', *The Slavonic and East European Review* 7/19 (1928), pp. 90–112.

Khan, Mir Munshi Sultan Mahomed (ed.), with an introduction by M. E. Yapp, *The Life of Abdur Rahman, Amir of Afghanistan* (Oxford, 1980).

Kibovskii, Aleksandr, '"Bagaderan" – Russian deserters in the Persian army, 1802–1839', *Tseikhgauz* 5 (1996), translated by Mark Conrad. Available at http://marksrussianmilitaryhistory.info/Persdes2.html (accessed 8 April 2013).

Kibovskii, Aleksandr and Yegorov, Vadim, 'The Persian regular army of the first half of the nineteenth century', *Tseikhgauz* 5 (1996), translated by Mark Conrad, pp. 20–5. Available at http://marksrussianmilitaryhistory.info/PERSIA.html (accessed 8 April 2013).

Kosogovski, V. A., 'Persia v kontse xix veka', *Novii Vostok* no. 3 (1923), pp. 446–69.

——, 'Ocherk razvitia persidskoi kazachei brigady', *Novii Vostok* no. 4 (1923), pp. 390–420.

Kostiner, Joseph, *The Making of Saudi Arabia 1916–1938: From Chieftaincy to Monarchical State* (New York, 1993).

——, 'Britain and the challenge of the Axis Powers in Arabia: the decline of British–Saudi cooperation in the 1930s', in M. J. Cohen and M. Kolinsky (eds), *Britain and the Middle East in the 1930s: Security Problems 1935–39* (London, 1992).

——, 'Transforming dualities: tribe and state formation in Saudi Arabia', in P. S. Khoury and J. Kostiner (eds), *Tribes and State Formation in the Middle East* (London, 1991).

Kotzebue, Moritz von, *Narrative of a Journey into Persia* (London, 1819).

Kurzman, Charles, *The Unthinkable Revolution* (Cambridge, MA, 2004).

Lafont, Jean-Marie, *Fauj-i-Khas: Maharaja Ranjit Singh and his French Officers* (Amritsar, 2002).

Lal, Mohan, *Life of the Amir Dost Mohammed Khan of Kabul* (facsimile of 1846 edition, Karachi, 1979).

Leatherdale, Clive, *Britain and Saudi Arabia 1925–1939* (London, 1983).

Levy, Avigdor, 'The officer corps in Sultan Mahmud's new Ottoman army, 1826–1839', *International Journal of Middle East Studies* 2/1 (1971), pp. 21–39.

Lewis, Bernard, *The Emergence of Modern Turkey* (London, 1961).

Louis, Wm. Roger, 'Britain and the Overthrow of the Mosaddeq Government', in M. J. Gasiorowski and M. Byrne (eds), *Mohammad Mosaddeq and the 1953 Coup in Iran* (New York, 2004).

Lumsden, Peter S. and Elsmie, George R., *Lumsden of the Guides* (London, 1899).

Maghraoui, Driss, 'From "tribal anarchy" to "military order": the Moroccan troops in the context of colonial Morocco', in O. Moreau and A. el Moudden (eds), *Réforme par le haut*, pp. 227–46.

Makki, Husayn, *Tarikh-i Bist Salah-i Iran*, 8 vols (Tehran, 1323).

Malcolm, John, *The History of Persia* (London, 1829).

al-Marashi, Ibrahim and Salama, Sammy, *Iraq's Armed Forces: An Analytical History* (Abingdon, 2008).

Marcus, Jeffrey R., *The Politics and Security of the Gulf: Anglo–American Hegemony and the Shaping of a Region* (Abingdon, 2010).

Martin, Vanessa, *The Qajar Pact: Bargaining, Protest and the State in Nineteenth-Century Persia* (London, 2005).

Matthee, Rudi, 'Between sympathy and enmity: nineteenth-century Iranian views of the British and the Russians', in B. Eschment and H. Harder (eds), *Looking at the Coloniser: Cross-Cultural Perceptions in Central Asia and the Caucasus, Bengal and Related Areas* (Wurzburg, 2004).

——, 'Facing a rude and barbarous neighbour: Iranian perceptions of Russia and the Russians from the Safavids to the Qajars', in A. Amanat and F. Vejdani (eds), *Iran Facing Others: Identity Boundaries in a Historical Perspective* (New York, 2012).

McFarlane, Stephen L., 'Anatomy of an Iranian crowd: the Tehran bread riot of December 1942', *International Journal of Middle East Studies* 17/1 (1985), pp. 51–65.

McGregor, Andrew James, *A Military History of Modern Egypt: From the Ottoman Conquest to the Ramadan War* (Westport, CT, 2006).

Milani, Abbas, *Eminent Persians: The Men and Women who Made Modern Iran*, 2 vols (New York, 2008).

Millspaugh, A. C., *The American Task in Persia* (New York, 1925).

——, *Americans in Persia* (Washington D.C., 1946).

Mirfakhraei, Hooshmand, *The Imperial Iranian Armed Forces and the Revolution of 1978–1979*. PhD thesis (State University of New York, 1984).

Mitchell, Timothy, *Colonising Egypt* (Cambridge, 1988).

Miyata, Osamu, 'The Tudeh military network during the oil nationalization period', *Middle Eastern Studies* 23/3 (1987), pp. 313–28.

Moreau, Odile, 'Une "mission militaire" ottomane au Maroc au début du 20ᵉ siècle', *The Maghreb Review* 30/2–4 (2005), pp. 209–24.

——, *L'Empire ottoman à l'âge des réformes. Les hommes et le idées du 'Nouvel Ordre' militaire (1826–1914)*, Maisonneuve et Larose (Paris), collection *Passé ottoman, présent turc* (Paris, 2007).

——, 'L'occidentalisation des forces armées turques', *Cahiers d'histoire socioculturelle des armées* 30 (2007), pp. 90–102. Published by le Centre d'Etudes d'Histoire de la Défense.

Moreau, Odile and el Moudden, Abderrahmane (eds), 'Réforme par le haut, réforme par le bas: la modernisation de l'armée aux 19e et 20e siècles', *Quaderni di Oriente Moderno* (special issue) (2004).

Morier, James, *A Journey through Persia, Armenia, and Asia Minor, to Constantinople, in the years 1808 and 1809* (London, 1812).

——, *A Second Journey through Persia, Armenia, and Asia Minor, to Constantinople, between the years 1810 and 1816* (London, 1818).

el Moudden, Abderrahmane, 'Looking Eastward: some Moroccan tentative military reforms with Turkish assistance (18th to early 20th centuries)', *The Maghreb Review* 19/3–4, pp. 237–45.

Mukerjee, Dilip, 'Afghanistan under Daud: relations with neighboring States', *Asian Survey* 15/4 (1975), pp. 301–12.

Musavvar-Rahmani, Colonel G., *Khatirat-i Siyasi: Bist va Panj Sal dar Niru-yi Hava'i-yi Iran* (Tehran, 1984).

Nashat, Guity, *The Origins of Modern Reform in Iran, 1870–1880* (Urbana, IL, 1882).

Nawid, Senzil K., *Religious Response to Social Change in Afghanistan, 1919–29* (Costa Mesa, CA, 1999).

Noelle, Christine, *State and Tribe in Nineteenth-Century Afghanistan* (London, 1997).

Nyström, P., *Fem år i Persien som Gendarmofficer* (Stockholm, 1925).

Olivier, Dr G. A., *Voyage dans l'Empire Othoman, l'Égypte et la Perse* (Paris, 1800–7).

Olson, W. J., *Anglo–Iranian Relations during World War I* (London, 1984).

Pakravan, Emineh, *Abbas Mirza* (Paris, 1973).

Parker, Geoffrey, *The Military Revolution: Military Innovation and the Rise of the West* (Cambridge, 1988).

Pasyan, Najafquli, *Vaqi'ah-i I'dam-i Jahansuz* (Tehran, 1370).

Perry, J. R., 'Army iv: Afšar and Zand Periods', in *Encyclopaedia Iranica*. Available at www.iranicaonline.org/articles/army-iv (accessed 8 April 2013).

Picard, Elizabeth, 'Arab military in politics: from revolutionary plot to authoritarian state', in A. Hourani, P. S. Khoury and M. C. Wilson (eds), *The Modern Middle East* (London and New York, 1993).

Pichon, J. *Journal d'une Mission Militaire en Perse (1839–1840)* (Paris, 1900).

Piemontese, A., 'An Italian source for the history of Qāğār Persia: the reports of the General Enrico Andreini (1871–1886)', *East and West* 19 (1969), pp. 147–75.

——, 'L' esercito persiano nel 1874–75: organizzazione e riforma secondo E. Andreini', *Rivista degli Studi Orientali* 49 (1975), pp. 71–117.

Polak, Jakob, *Persien, das Land und seiner Bewohner* (Leipzig, 1865).

Pollack, Kenneth M., *Arabs at War: Military Effectiveness, 1948–1991* (Lincoln, NE, 2004).

Porter, Patrick, *Military Orientalism: Eastern War through Western Eyes* (London, 2009.)

Posnett, Edward, 'Treating His Imperial Majesty's warts: British policy towards Iran 1977–79', *Iranian Studies* 45/1 (2012), pp. 119–37.

Poullada, Leon B., *Reform and Rebellion in Afghanistan, 1919–1929* (New York, 1973).

Pravitz, Hjalmar, *Frau Persien i Stiltje och Storm* (Stockholm, 1918).

Qa'im-Maqami, Jahangir, *Tahavvulat-i Siyasi-yi Nizam-i Iran* (Tehran, 1326).

——, *Tarikh-i Zhandarmiri-yi Iran* (Tehran, 1355).

Quinlivan, James T., 'Coup-proofing: its practice and consequences in the Middle East', *International Security* 24/2 (1999), pp. 131–65.

Quzanlu, Jamil, *Tarikh-i Nizam-i Iran*, 2 vols (Tehran, 1315).

Rabi, Uzi and Ter-Oganov, Nugzar, 'The Russian military mission and the birth of the Persian Cossack Brigade: 1879–1894', *Iranian Studies* 42/3 (2009), pp. 445–63.

Ralston, David B., *Importing the European Army: The Introduction of European Military Techniques and Institutions into the extra-European World, 1600–1814* (Chicago, IL, 1990).

al-Rasheed, Madawi, *A History of Saudi Arabia* (Cambridge, 2002).

Rashid, Ahmed, *Taliban: The Story of the Afghan Warlords* (London, 2001).

Ricks, Thomas M., 'US military missions to Iran, 1943–1978: the political economy of military assistance', *Iranian Studies* 12/3–4 (1979), pp. 163–93.

Roberts, Mark, 'Khomeini's Incorporation of the Iranian Military', McNair Paper no. 48, January 1996.

Rogers, C. J. (ed.) *The Military Revolution Debate: Readings on the Military Transformation of Early Modern Europe* (Boulder, CO, 1995).

Rollman, Wilfrid J., *The 'New Order' in a pre-Colonial Muslim Society: Military Reform in Morocco, 1844–1904.* PhD dissertation (University of Michigan, 1983).

———, 'Military officers and the "Niẓām al-Ğadīd" in Morocco, 1844–1912: social and political transformation', in O. Moreau and A. el Moudden (eds) *Réforme par le haut* (2004), pp. 205–25.

Rose, Gregory F., 'The post-revolutionary purge of Iran's armed forces: a revisionist assessment', *Iranian Studies* 17/2–3 (1984), pp. 154–94.

Roy, Olivier, *Islam and Resistance in Afghanistan* (Cambridge, 1986).

Rubin, Barnett R., *The Fragmentation of Afghanistan* (New Haven, CT, 1995).

———, 'The transformation of the Afghan State,' in J. A. Thier (ed.) *The Future of Afghanistan* (Washington D.C., 2009).

Russian General Staff, *The Soviet–Afghan War: How a Superpower Fought and Lost* (trans. and ed. Lester W. Grau and Michael A. Gress) (Lawrence, KS, 2002).

Safiri, Floreeda, *The South Persia Rifles*. PhD thesis (University of Edinburgh, 1976).

Safran, Nadav, *Saudi Arabia: The Ceaseless Quest for Security* (New York, 1985).

Saikal, Amin, *Modern Afghanistan: A History of Struggle and Survival* (London, 2004).

Sampson, Anthony, *The Arms Bazaar: From Lebanon to Lockheed* (New York, 1977).

Sayigh, Yezid, *Armed Struggle and the Search for State: The Palestinian National Movement, 1949–1993* (Oxford, 1997).

Schahgaldian, Nikola B., with the assistance of Barkhordarian, Gina, *The Iranian Military Under the Islamic Republic* (Santa Monica, CA, 1987).

Schölch, Alexander, *Egypt for the Egyptians! The Socio-Political Crisis in Egypt, 1878–1882* (London, 1981).

Sedra, Mark (ed.), *Confronting Afghanistan's Security Dilemma* (Bonn, 2009).

Sercey, Count F. E de, *Une Ambassade Extraordinaire. La Perse en 1839–1840* (Paris, 1928).

Shafa'i, Ahmad, *Qiyam-i Afsaran-i Khurasan va Si va Haft Sal Zindagi dar Shuravi* (Tehran, 1365).

Shah, Sirdar Ikbal Ali, *The Tragedy of Amanullah* (London, 1933).

Shahrani, M. N. and Canfield, R., *Revolutions and Rebellions in Afghanistan* (Berkeley, CA, 1984).

Shaw, Stanford J., 'The origins of Ottoman military reform: the nizam-i cedid army of Sultan Selim III', *The Journal of Modern History* 37/3 (1965), pp. 291–305.

Sheikholeslami, A. Reza, *The Structure of Central Authority in Qajar Iran, 1871–1896* (Atlanta, GA, 1997).

Sherman, Jake and DiDomenico, Victoria, *The Public Cost of Private Security in Afghanistan* (New York, 2009).

Slaby, Helmut, *Bindenschild und Sonnenlöwe: Die Geschichte der Österreichisch-Iranischen Beziehungen bis zur Gegenwart* (Graz, 1982).

———, 'Austria, diplomatic and commercial relations with Persia', in *Encyclopaedia Iranica*. Available at www.iranicaonline.org/articles/austria-1 (accessed 8 April 2013).

Sluglett, Peter and Sluglett, Marion F., 'The precarious monarchy: Britain, Abd al-Aziz ibn Saud and the establishment of the kingdom of Hijaz, Najd and its dependencies, 1925–1932', in T. Niblock (ed.), *State, Society and Economy in Saudi Arabia* (London, 1982).

Springborg, Robert, 'Roundtable: rethinking the study of Middle Eastern militaries', *International Journal of Middle Eastern Studies* 43/3 (2011), pp. 397–9.

Stoker, Donald (ed.) *Military Advising and Assistance: From Mercenaries to Privatization, 1815–2007* (London, 2008).

Stuart, Lt-Col, *Journal of a Residence in Northern Persia and the Adjacent Provinces of Turkey* (London, 1854).

Suhrke, Astri 'Afghanistan: retribalization of the war', *Journal of Peace Research* 27/3 (1990), pp. 241–6.

Swanson, Glen W., 'War, technology and society in the Ottoman Empire from the reign of Abdulhamid II to 1913: Mahmud Şevket and the German military mission', in M. E. Yapp and V. J. Parry (eds), *War, Technology and Society* (London, 1975).

Sykes, Brig.-Gen. Sir Percy, *A History of Persia*, 2 vols (London, 1921).

Tafrishiyan, Abu'l Hasan, *Qiyam-i Afsaran-i Khurasan* (Tehran, 1367).

Tancoigne, J. M., *A Narrative of a Journey into Persia and Residence in Tehran* (London, 1820).

Tapper, Richard (ed.), The Conflict of Tribe and State in Iran and Afghanistan (London, 1983).

Tarbush, Mohammad A., *The Role of the Military in Politics: A Case-Study of Iraq to 1941* (London, 1982).

*Tarikh-i Nirui-yi, Hava'i-yi Shahanshahi* (Tehran, 2535).

Ter-Oganov, N. K., *Persidskaya Kazachya Brigada, 1878–1921* (Moscow, 2012).

Tilly, Charles, *Coercion, Capital, and European States, AD990–1992* (Cambridge, MA and Oxford, 1992).

Tousi, Reza Ra'iss, 'The Persian Army, 1880–1907', *Middle Eastern Studies* 24/2 (1988), pp. 206–29.

Tripp, Charles, 'Ali Maher and the politics of the Egyptian army', in C. Tripp (ed.), *Contemporary Egypt: through Egyptian Eyes: Essays in Honour of Professor P. J. Vatkiotis* (Abingdon, 1993), pp. 45–71.

Trumpener, Ulrich, 'Liman von Sanders and the German–Ottoman Alliance', *Journal of Contemporary History* 1/4 (1966), pp. 179–92.

Turfan, M. Naim, *Rise of the Young Turks: Politics, the Military and Ottoman Collapse* London, 2000).

Utas, Bo, 'Borowsky, Isidore', in *Encyclopaedia Iranica*. Available at www.iranicaonline. org/articles/borowsky-isidore (accessed 8 April 2013).

Vaikiotis, P. J., *The Egyptian Army in Politics: Pattern for New Nations?* (Bloomington, 1961).

Vassiliev, Alexei, *The History of Saudi Arabia* (London, 1998).

Ward, Steven R., *Immortal: A Military History of Iran and its Armed Forces* (Washington D.C., 2008).

Wasti, S. Tanvir, 'The 1877 Ottoman Mission to Afghanistan', *Middle Eastern Studies* 30/4 (1994), pp. 956–62.

Wild, Roland, *Amanullah: ex-King of Afghanistan* (London, 1932).

Willis, Michael, *Politics and Power in the Maghreb: Algeria, Tunisia and Morocco from Independence to the Arab Spring* (London, 2012).

Wright, Dennis, *The English Amongst the Persians* (London, 1977).

Yapp, M. E., 'Disturbances in Eastern Afghanistan, 1839–42', *Bulletin of the School of Oriental and African Studies* 25/1,3 (1962), pp. 499–523.

——, 'Disturbances in Western Afghanistan, 1839–41', *Bulletin of the School of Oriental and African Studies* 26/2 (1963), pp. 288–313.

——, 'The revolutions of 1841–2 in Afghanistan', *Bulletin of the School of Oriental and African Studies* 27/2 (1964), pp. 333–81.

——, 'The modernization of Middle Eastern armies in the nineteenth century: a comparative view', in M. E. Yapp and V. J. Parry (eds), *War, Technology and Society in the Middle East* (London, 1975).

——, *Strategies of British India: Britain, Iran and Afghanistan, 1798–1850* (Oxford, 1980).

Younossi, Obaid *et al.*, *The Long March: Building an Afghan Army* (Santa Monica, CA, 2009).

Zabih, Sepehr, *The Iranian Military in Revolution and War* (London, 1988).

Zürcher, Erik Jan, 'The Ottoman conscription system, 1844–1917', *International Review of Social History* 43, art. 3 (1998), pp. 437–49.

Zürcher, Erik Jan (ed.) *Arming the State: Military Conscription in the Middle East and Central Asia* (London and New York, 1999).

# Index